PRAISE FOR *A DEATH IN WHITE BEAR LAKE*

"Telling detail . . . and crack research . . . [fill] Barry Siegel's book. But those are not the only authorial virtues displayed. There's the book's very structure, which keeps the revelations coming, one right after the next. Then too there's the restraint. Siegel lets the players damn themselves as they reminisce about the case . . . And Siegel manages, despite the widespread national publicity the case received, to keep suspense high." —*The Washington Post*

"Fascinating reading." —*Detroit Free Press*

"One of the most startling nonfiction books of the year." —*Playboy*

"Chilling in its exactness and precise in its details."
—*Star News* (Pasadena)

"To read it is to stare steadily through the windowpane at the vicious underside of middle-class respectability." —*Omaha Metro Update*

"[Siegel] tells a great deal about ordinary people dealing with extraordinary circumstances." —*The Boston Herald*

"Siegel doesn't spare the reader . . . emphatically indicting a society that looks the other way." —*Kirkus Reviews*

"This is a haunting story about ordinary people caught in a web that allows a terrible act to go unpunished for two decades. Barry Siegel is one of the finest reporters we have. He does not stop where others do; he keeps probing deeper and deeper until he strikes gold—that place where we come face-to-face with ourselves." —Sara Davidson,
New York Times–bestselling author of *Cowboy*

A DEATH IN
WHITE BEAR LAKE

A DEATH IN WHITE BEAR LAKE

The True Chronicle of an All-American Town

BARRY SIEGEL

OPEN ROAD

INTEGRATED MEDIA

NEW YORK

Copyright © 1990 by Barry Siegel

Cover design by Amanda Shaffer

ISBN: 978-1-5040-4757-9

This edition published in 2017 by Open Road Integrated Media, Inc.
180 Maiden Lane
New York, NY 10038
www.openroadmedia.com

To Marti
for Everything

CONTENTS

A DEATH IN
WHITE BEAR LAKE

PART ONE

VOICES FROM THE PAST

CHAPTER 1

Memories

Months later, in the airless cubicles of the solitary police station where White Bear Lake detectives do their business, there was confusion among some of them about just what they truly recalled of the Jurgens case on that damp September day in 1986 when Jerry Sherwood first appeared, demanding their attention.

"I didn't remember anything about the case, I just remembered White Bear was flooded that spring," Detective Ron Meehan, the department's chief investigator, initially told those who asked. "I listened to her story and it didn't ring a bell," Lieutenant Clarence "Buzz" Harvey agreed. For a while, Harvey even went so far as to suggest he'd been a "rookie cop" in 1965, although the records would show that claim to be something of a stretch, since by then Buzz had been on the force a good six years. Chief Philip Major, only a high school senior that year, remembered volunteers frantically sandbagging the rampaging Mississippi and hymn-singing civil rights demonstrators marching up Cedar Street in downtown St. Paul, but of course he recalled nothing of the Jurgens case.

Then, as time went by, the stories evolved. Buzz Harvey acknowledged, a little sheepishly, that yes, he'd been aware of the case from the start. Ron Meehan allowed that "everyone knew, but it was none of our business." Gerry Sarracco, the dispatcher on the critical Palm Sunday morning in 1965, said, "We all knew something was wrong, but we didn't know what."

Just as these mutating versions of distant memories were understandable considering the passage of time, so too were the hazy recollections about more recent days. The prosecutors and police and doctors, after all, could hardly be expected to know they'd later be asked to account for every move, moment by moment, during those pivotal hours following Jerry Sherwood's first appearance. All the same, studying the faces of those involved, watching them aimlessly shuffle papers across their desks, it did sometimes seem their murkiness had as much to do with a certain nervous reluctance as with simple forgetfulness.

That too was understandable.

This much can be said—it was midmorning on Thursday, September 11, 1986, when Buzz Harvey looked up from his desk to find the station's office clerk standing in the doorway of his small office.

"Someone called while you were out, wanting to talk to you," Heidi Riemenschneider reported. "Something about his brother being murdered. Said he would call back later. His name was Dennis Craig McIntyre."

Buzz Harvey's eyes traveled to a dog-eared manila file cradled in her right arm. He raised his eyebrows in inquiry.

"Oh yeah," she said, placing the file on Harvey's desk. "The guy mentioned something about a Jurgens case. Happened twenty-one years ago. I pulled our file. Thought you'd want to see."

Alone again, Harvey considered the closed file before him, shutting his eyes as an unwelcome feeling took hold. Yes, he remembered the Jurgens case. A little boy had died.

Harvey had never seen the file that sat before him. Two other officers had handled the Jurgens case in 1965, Pete Korolchuk and Bob VanderWyst, both now retired. What Harvey recalled came from them. Korolchuk, he remembered, had talked back then of certain pressures and problems connected with his investigation, but what exactly had happened Harvey could not say. He'd been busy with his own work and it had not been his case.

Harvey labored to concentrate. He'd recently given up a lifetime of smoking, and now longed for a cigarette. The sausage pies across Highway 61 at the Pizza Hut that he'd turned to as a substitute filled his considerable gut without at all soothing his nerves. Slowly, Harvey opened the Jurgens file and began to leaf through the pages.

As he did so, the unwelcome feeling sharpened and tightened.

There was something strange here. *Mr. and Mrs. Ivan Demars have given us a signed statement. Mr. and Mrs. Lloyd Zerwas have given us signed statements also*, Pete Korolchuk had written. But Buzz could find no such statements in the file. He continued turning the pages, his concern mounting. The police logs seemed riddled with discrepancies. Harold Jurgens told VanderWyst that his little boy had fallen and struck his head on the floor, but the autopsy report mentioned head-to-toe bruises. So many bruises from a fall on the floor? The doctor at the death scene told VanderWyst he noticed bruises just on the forehead, since he only checked the boy's chest and face. Why wouldn't the doctor look at the body under the blankets? When Buzz reached the file's last sheet he stared at it, then shuffled back through the pages, searching in vain. Where was the ending? There'd been no prosecution, no disposition at all of this case. What had happened?

And who now was asking about the case? The call had come from a Dennis Craig McIntyre. What did he have to do with this?

Buzz called Ron Meehan into his office.

"Remember the Jurgens case?" the lieutenant asked.

Meehan, a former Marine M.P., college football player, and amateur boxer, was a brawny man with a barrel chest and muscular arms. Then fifty-one, he'd been a White Bear Lake cop for twenty-five years and the department's chief investigator since 1973.

Meehan merely nodded. Yes, he remembered the Jurgens case. He'd never forgotten the Jurgens case.

"Somebody called about it," Harvey said. "Told Heidi he was a brother to the dead boy. Said he'd call back. I'll keep you posted."

The call came four days later, late in the afternoon on Monday, September 15. The voice was young, unpolished and hostile. Dennis Craig McIntyre told Harvey he was calling for his mother. Her name was Jerry Sherwood.

"We want to talk to you about my brother who was murdered twenty-one years ago," McIntyre said. "Can we come in now?"

Harvey glanced at the clock on his wall. He worked an eight to four shift, and it was nearly four o'clock.

"I'm only here until four," Harvey said.

"Oh shit," McIntyre said.

Harvey was taken aback, but in the coming days, he would hear that expression more than once from McIntyre.

"I'll call back tomorrow," the young man said.

Tuesday passed, though, without a call. Harvey's phone finally rang late on Wednesday afternoon. "Can we come in tomorrow morning?" McIntyre asked.

Harvey looked at his calendar. That would be Thursday, September 18. "Yes, fine," he said. "Make it at ten in the morning."

It is possible to drive through White Bear Lake without noticing either its charm or its lake. Due in good part to the arrival of interstate highways, the town of twenty-two thousand qualifies as what the urban planners call a second-ring suburb of St. Paul, the Minnesota capital, which rises ten miles to the south. I-35E carries commuters north from downtown St. Paul to westbound I-694. State Highway 61, an exit off 694, carries commuters north again through White Bear Lake.

Highway 61 is a four-lane divided thoroughfare that offers little to please the eye. Approaching the town from the south, the road passes three gas stations, a Wendy's, a McDonald's, a Dairy Queen, the Polar Chevrolet and Tousley Ford car dealerships, a Jiffy Print, a Two Guys from Italy restaurant, the Johnson-Peterson Funeral Home, a liquor store, and dozens of small shops offering wares ranging from live bait to video rentals. Only by looking alertly to the right while negotiating Highway 61 can you catch a passing, fragmented glimpse between buildings of the sparkling-clear twenty-five-hundred-acre lake that forms the city's core. To discover the relatively bucolic villagelike town center hugging the lake's southwestern shore, you would need to turn right off Highway 61 at Fourth Street. There, a quiet retail quarter offers a tableau less jarring to the eye, at least to those who do not mind the sort of stores that go by names such as Country Goose or The Sheepy Shop or Timberdoodle. Just beyond the business district, on winding Lake Avenue, a row of gracefully weathered frame houses faces the water, one-time summer cottages expanded over time into stately, picturesque homes. An arched bridge off Lake Avenue connects the mainland with the even more affluent Manitou Island, a green and richly wooded enclave of baronial mansions. Most days in the summer, sailboats and fishermen move languidly about the lake—not vacationers but neighbors, stealing an hour or two of pleasure before or after work.

The White Bear Lake police station is not located in this quarter of town. Instead of turning right at Fourth Street and heading toward the lake, a visitor to the police station must turn left, away from the water, cross over the railroad tracks that divide Highway 61, and then bear left again on Miller. A block down the road on the southwest corner, the police station occupies a one-story structure that resembles a local library but for the patrol cars parked diagonally along the building's east side. Compact frame homes with small porches face the station from across the street, like an audience at a play or ball game. When Buzz Harvey and Ron Meehan joined the force around 1960, it numbered nine men, and by late 1986 it had grown to twenty-eight.

Fall in White Bear Lake was taking hold the morning of September 18, 1986. The temperature reached only sixty degrees, a full ten degrees below the norm for mid-September. A trace of rain dampened the sidewalk outside the police station.

Buzz Harvey's visitors arrived precisely at ten o'clock. There were three of them. Dennis Craig McIntyre, nineteen, had a sullen manner and long brown hair with bangs that obscured much of his forehead. His sister, Misty McIntyre, twenty-three, a quietly composed young woman with layered shoulder-length brown hair, gave off no attitude at all. Their mother, Jerry Sherwood, forty-two, was a tall woman with an elaborately coiffed mane of blond hair. Those in the station familiar with the downtown strip joints in nearby St. Paul might have recognized her from an earlier tenure at Alary's Club Bar. Her features were still attractive, although the years had added a certain hardness to her face and thickness to her arms and legs. She looked like a cocktail waitress with mileage.

Buzz asked investigator Ron Meehan to join them, and five people in Harvey's nine-by-twelve office made for some cramping. The lieutenant sat at his desk facing the door, his back to a small window. Sherwood and her son Dennis sat in straightback chairs facing him across the desk. Misty sat in a chair to the left of Harvey. Meehan leaned awkwardly against a credenza along one wall.

Jerry Sherwood had a story to tell. She spoke with feeling, her voice harsh and forceful.

When she was seventeen and living in a juvenile home, she said, she gave birth to a boy, Dennis, who was quickly taken from her and adopted by a family named Jurgens—Lois and Harold Jurgens— who lived in White Bear Lake. Two husbands and four children later, Sherwood had gone searching for her firstborn, only to learn that

he'd died years before, in 1965, at age three. From a yellowing newspaper notice of his death that she'd found during her search, she'd
learned that the boy's body bore multiple injuries and bruises. From
the death certificate, she'd learned that the coroner had never ruled
whether the death was an accident, a homicide or the result of natural causes. They'd just buried the body, and that was all.

"They beat my baby," Jerry said. "They beat my baby to death."

Sherwood sobbed as she spoke, but she was not just grieving. She
was angry. She wanted justice and she clearly doubted she'd get that
from the police or anyone else in authority. It did not, in fact, seem to
her she'd seen much justice in any part of her life. Her story was both
hard and familiar: a mother who took off when she was three, years
of shuttling among relatives and foster homes, the four children
besides Dennis all coming by the time she was twenty-three, all by
the same man who fathered Dennis, a man Jerry eventually married.
Misty had arrived eighteen months after Dennis and had also been
taken to a foster home, but that one Jerry managed to get back. In
time, she'd divorced the children's father and married again, but this
second union also ended in divorce. After that, she'd supported the
four children as best she could, sometimes managing an apartment
building, sometimes drawing welfare assistance, sometimes dancing
at Alary's.

"They wouldn't let me keep Dennis," she told Buzz, her bitterness
undisguised. "They told me they would take my baby to people who
could give him all that I couldn't. Well, they were right. I could never
have given him death. My four other children have had it rough, but
they're still alive."

Harvey was impressed. He thought Jerry a tough, emotional lady,
but he also sensed it would be best to calm her down, so he tried to
speak both gently and firmly. "Something should have been done
twenty years ago," he told her. "We will investigate this, we will look
into this."

His words, though, had no effect. In fact, no one in the room
seemed to hear him, and now the meeting was slipping from his control moment by moment. Everyone was talking and Jerry's voice kept
growing louder and more tearful.

"I brought him into the world, someone else took him out. No
child should have to die like Dennis died . . ."

Leaning against the credenza at the side of the wall, Ron Meehan felt confused. He remembered the dead boy had a brother, but wasn't his name Robert? Yes, Robert was the Jurgenses' other son. Buzz had told him the brother was coming in, so Meehan thought it would be Robert. Now Meehan was laboring to place all these people. Sherwood was saying, "Dennis." Was she talking about her son Dennis Craig, sitting here in the room with them, or the dead Dennis? And this Dennis Craig kept calling the other Dennis his brother. How could that be?

"I'm not going to drop this," Jerry Sherwood was saying. "I'm not going to forget this."

When she stopped talking, her son Dennis Craig started. He sprawled in his chair, sneering, looking not unlike the sort of punk the White Bear cops sometimes threw in jail on Saturday nights. "What are you going to do?" he demanded. "What are you going to do?"

Buzz Harvey began to feel under siege. He and Ron were being treated as if they were the enemy, as if they had something to do with Dennis's death.

"We share your desire for justice." He forced the words through gritted teeth. "We are on the same side."

Jerry asked to read the 1965 police reports in the file sitting on Harvey's desk. Buzz, knowing what they contained, hesitated. He would have preferred to do some editing first.

"You can if you want," he said, "but I'd recommend that you not. I'd rather read it to you."

Fearful of what was coming, but now unable to control events in his own office, Buzz began to read aloud from the report written by Officer Bob VanderWyst on the day of Dennis's death in 1965. Within moments he reached the description of the small boy's body:

> Dennis was laying on his back in the crib with his head facing west and his feet pointing east. His arms were towards the east or alongside of his body with his hands about 8 inches off the bed. There were covers partly on Dennis, they were up to about the middle of his body. Dennis had many black and blue spots or bruises on his face, head and arms. The rest of his body was covered up. On his face and forehead there were at least a dozen black and blue places, some were very large and others small. His nose was almost blood red and peeling.

Jerry Sherwood's sobs interrupted him. She was unraveling, breaking down, her angry resolve crumpling for the moment. This was just what Harvey had expected. "You don't want to hear any more," he said, but she insisted he continue, so he did, although he skipped over other descriptions of Dennis's body, his editing guided by the rise and fall of Jerry's sobs.

The meeting lasted an hour and a half. Sherwood left Harvey's office much as she had arrived—overwrought and hostile and full of distrust. At the door, she turned and delivered her parting words.

"I will be calling in regularly," she promised.

Harvey thrust the Jurgens file into Ron Meehan's hands. Ron, after all, was the chief investigator.

Although Meehan remembered the Jurgens case from 1965, this was the first time he'd ever seen the file. He retreated to his office, about half the size of Harvey's, and began reading. The phone rang. A visitor dropped by. The phone rang again. Meehan grabbed the file and bolted for his car. He drove south on Highway 61 toward the interstates and his home, turned left on County Road E, and followed it east one mile to a McDonald's. In the drive-through lane, he bought a cup of coffee with milk, then pulled his car to the rear of the parking lot and started to read.

Meehan, his pals on the force liked to say, was one of those guys who could have ended up in jail if he hadn't become a cop. In his younger days, the story went, he'd once been stopped over in Roseville driving recklessly at ninety miles per hour. He'd seen his fair share of brawls and bar fights, and word was, if you were going against him, you wanted to make sure you didn't run down on energy, for Ron just kept coming like an enraged bull. Once in a gym, just playing around, he and another cop, Roger Belanger, had put the gloves on together. Belanger thought they'd dance around a little, but Meehan barged in, full bore, slugging. Belanger, falling back, quickly yanked off his gloves. "Hey Ron," he gasped. "Okay," Meehan said, simply and quickly.

His voice was a distinctively deep bass that sounded as if it welled up from the bottom of his chest and then passed through a smashed nose. He seemed slow and thick, like a punch-drunk fighter, but his manner was misleading. He chain-smoked Winstons and had a taste for Jack Daniel's.

Ron knew VanderWyst and Korolchuk well. They were his friends, and looking at their words in the 1965 reports took him back to a time he remembered fondly. The cops were all in their thirties then, their houses full of young children. They fished and camped together, they drank together, they patched and wired one another's homes. Most evenings after work, they'd gather at Bob VanderWyst's house, those on late shifts showing up all times of the night. They'd drink rum and Coke and eat whatever hot dishes people brought over. They'd laugh so hard it hurt, then get silly and sing songs—"Across Galway Bay," "Near You," "Tennessee Waltz." Sometimes an exuberant officer would wave his firearm in the air and VanderWyst's eight kids would stare wide-eyed from the top of the stairs. No matter how late they stayed or how much they drank, the cops would show up for work the next morning full of energy.

VanderWyst had written some of the early pages in the Jurgens file, Korolchuk most of what followed. This was long before the White Bear police department budget allowed for secretaries and typewriters, and neither VanderWyst nor Korolchuk had particularly polished handwriting. Their words sprawled across the pages, slanting, dipping into margins, hard to decipher.

As he turned the twenty-six pages of the 1965 reports, Meehan stiffened behind the steering wheel of his car, the glow of nostalgia slowly turning to a chill. We're going to need direction on this, he thought. What with Jerry Sherwood raising hell and all, better get this to the county attorney.

White Bear Lake is part of Ramsey County, and the county seat is St. Paul. Sitting shoulder to shoulder with St. Paul is Minneapolis, in Hennepin County. The two are called the Twin Cities, but they are more like distant cousins, each with a distinct personality. Minneapolis, cosmopolitan and sophisticated, casts much the longer shadow, with its towering glassy skyline and image as a Manhattan of the upper Midwest. St. Paul is a full-sized city of 261,000, but it has remained much more provincial, doggedly midwestern and down-to-earth, and this appears to be by choice. "You can walk the streets here all day and not meet one guy with pink hair," boasts a local newspaper columnist, Dennis Anderson. The region's roots are largely Scandinavian. People born in Ramsey County tend to stay there, displaying little desire to turn outward, and everyone seems to know one another.

White Bear Lake police officers regularly consult with the Ramsey County attorney's office in downtown St. Paul, for the county attorney prosecutes all of the small town's felonies and major misdemeanors. After White Bear police investigate, the county prosecutors decide whether to file charges or call for more legwork or tell the cops they've got a dead horse.

On the morning after the meeting with Jerry Sherwood, Meehan drove the ten miles south to downtown St. Paul. The Ramsey County attorney occupies quarters on the fourth floor of a medical building around the corner from the county courthouse. Ron knew the offices well, for he'd carried a fair number of files to prosecutors in his thirteen years as White Bear Lake's chief investigator. This morning, he had an appointment with Jim Konen, chief of the Criminal Division.

Konen was smirking when Ron entered his office. There was no way to miss it—Konen was enjoying the moment and seemed in no hurry to have it end too quickly. He was a veteran office strategist, a survivor who walked the fine line between management and staff by favoring accommodation over confrontation. Konen was not a yes-man, but he knew when to say yes. Both Buzz Harvey and Jerry Sherwood's son had already called him, so he knew what Ron's visit was all about, and the subject apparently stimulated him. He bummed a cigarette and Meehan handed him a Winston. Konen lit it and slowly inhaled.

"Yeah, Buzz called me," Konen said with a grin.

Meehan pretended not to notice, refusing the bait, his face placid as a cow's. Konen was wasting his effort. Ron seemed inscrutable in moments like this, uncomplicated but powerfully contained. He saw no reason to get worked up about anything unless necessary, and right now, he didn't even know if he had a case. It's up to the prosecutors, he reasoned. Let them tell us whether or not this is a dead horse.

Ron handed over a photocopy of the twenty-six-page file and backed out of Konen's office, eager to be on the road back to White Bear Lake.

Alone in his office, Konen quickly read through the reports, then immediately walked down the hall to his boss, the Ramsey County attorney, Tom Foley.

"This one is dynamite," Konen told Foley. "Wait till you read this."

◆   ◆   ◆

Days passed. September turned to October, and still the county attorney did not reveal his intentions. On October 2, two weeks after she had confronted Buzz Harvey at the White Bear Lake police station, an impatient Jerry Sherwood appeared in downtown St. Paul at the office of the Ramsey County medical examiner, Michael McGee. Just as the county attorney prosecutes cases for small towns such as White Bear Lake, the medical examiner handles their autopsies and rules on causes of death. The medical examiner occupies his own one-story building hard by the Mississippi River, just down sloping Hill Street from the county courthouse. The frame structure looks more like a home displaced from its residential neighborhood than it does a county office. Inside, a long front counter, a bank of secretaries' desks, and a row of offices and meeting rooms do nothing to suggest the purpose of the building—the autopsies are conducted downstairs in the basement.

Standing at the front counter, speaking to the receptionist, Jerry Sherwood explained who she was and asked if she might see the coroner's file on Dennis Jurgens. This request was passed to McGee and his chief assistant, Jim Essling, who conferred by phone with the county attorney's office. No, the county attorney's office told him, they couldn't show Jerry Sherwood that file. She would first need to get a court order, since she didn't have legal custody of Dennis when he died.

When Essling explained this judgment to Sherwood, she glared at him.

"I plan to pursue this," she said. "I want to know what happened to my child. I can't find out. I want some help."

After Jerry departed, Essling considered. A knowing veteran of the county government, he was on intimate terms with the system's nooks and crannies, and something about Sherwood's tale intrigued him. Five minutes passed, then ten. Finally, Essling reached for his phone and dialed the county records management office. He wanted to look at the Dennis Jurgens file himself.

Such aging files are kept in a secured warehouse in the basement of the county Human Services Department building on the corner of Kellogg and Robert in downtown St. Paul. Essling gave the records clerk there a file number, 30001.

The next morning, a records department messenger delivered a large worn manila envelope to his office. Essling pulled a single thin file from the envelope. When he opened it, a small card fell out onto his desk. It was a clothing list, itemizing what had been taken off the dead boy's body prior to the autopsy. *Two diapers, one pair of rubber pants, one shirt, pajamas . . .* Essling stared at the signature on the bottom of the card. It was his own.

Now Essling remembered the case, even though it was more than twenty-one years old. As a young aide in the old coroner's office, he'd been on duty that afternoon when the body arrived. His mind raced. So this was what Jerry Sherwood was talking about. Hard to believe this one wasn't prosecuted as a homicide back then.

Essling leafed through the rest of the file. There was a one-page report by the coroner's investigator, brief notes by the coroner's aide who received the body, and a three-page report by the pathologist who conducted the autopsy.

The documents spelled out only a sketchy story. A three-and-a-half-year-old Caucasian male was found dead at a private residence located at 2148 South Gardenette Drive in White Bear Lake. The physician on the scene was a Dr. Roy Peterson. The body and face were covered with bruises, radiating in all directions, and there was a laceration around the base of the penis. The immediate cause of death was peritonitis, due to perforation of the bowel.

There was no other information in the file as to the manner of death—that is, whether the perforated bowel had been the result of an accident, or natural causes, or an act of homicide. Where the coroner was supposed to indicate mode of death, he had instead written the word *deferred*. The question, in other words, had never been decided.

Essling walked the file down the hall to his boss.

"Doc, you've got to look at this file," he told Michael McGee. "I remember it. And it's bad."

McGee leafed through the pages, then turned to Essling. "Are you telling me this case is out of our office?" he asked.

"Not only that, but a woman came in here asking about it," Essling said.

McGee turned back to the file. He was a tall, thin man, thirty-nine years old, with close-cropped hair just turning to gray. By instinct and commitment he was fiercely religious, by training a forensic pathologist, and his intensity was palpable. He tended to stare at anyone he was talking to with penetrating eyes, and his words were direct and unadorned.

"Get the police reports," McGee said. "Talk to the pathologist. We have to do the whole nine yards on this. I can't believe it."

Essling started to leave.

"Jim," McGee called after him. "Did this happen often back then?"

Essling shrugged. "Oh, yeah," he said. "Often."

McGee placed a call to Buzz Harvey at the White Bear Lake police. The medical examiner started to explain the details of the case, but Harvey interrupted.

"Yes, she's been out here too," Harvey said.

"I need your reports, old and new." McGee was biting off his words. "I'm sitting here thinking I have a homicide. I need documentation. I need whatever you've got."

Three days later, on October 5, the police reports in hand, McGee phoned Dr. Thomas Votel, the Ramsey County coroner back in 1965, now a doctor in private practice at a St. Paul clinic.

"I'm getting ready to change one of your old death certificates," McGee said. "I'm sorry to cause you trouble. There will be news media attention and all that. But I have to—I think it's homicide. Do you remember this little boy, Dennis Jurgens?"

Votel remembered the case well. "Yes," he said softly. He hesitated, then continued. "I always thought it was a homicide too. There may be three or four other cases like this in the old files. You'd better look."

McGee could not resist a question. "Why didn't you sign off at the time?"

Votel was a pleasant, mild-mannered physician who long ago had built a comfortable practice, largely in the field of industrial medicine. He measured his reply.

"I was waiting for the county attorney and police to do further investigation. The coroner's job was just part-time then. I was a private general practitioner."

McGee offered his regards and hung up, for he didn't have time to consider Votel's role just now. He needed one more piece of documentation. He had noticed a cryptic note scribbled on the bottom of one page in the coroner's file. "Nick Burkowski called and asked to take pictures." That was all the note said.

McGee showed the note to Essling. "Who was Burkowski?"

"He was the old private photographer we used to hire to take photos of corpses," Essling said.

McGee stared at the note. That meant photos of Dennis Jurgens's body had been taken. But they weren't in the coroner or police files. Where were they?

Needing help, McGee called the prosecutor's office the next day, not then knowing the county attorney was also looking into the Jurgens case. His call was forwarded to a young lawyer named Ann Hyland, head of the juvenile division. County Attorney Tom Foley had handed her the Jurgens file.

The case involved a small boy, after all, and his death had never been called a homicide. Let Ann sort this out, Foley had reasoned. She was a crack administrator, sharp and full of energy, and that's what was needed here. She lacked trial experience, but this wasn't going to involve a trial. We can't correct the mistake, we're not going to go back now and prosecute anyone for something that happened twenty-two years ago, Foley figured. That would be too complicated, just about impossible. But at least we can ventilate the deal, examine what happened, see why the system failed.

The Jurgens matter had drawn Hyland's attention only for a while. Dressed in her blue jeans, she'd spent hours one day in a dusty basement storage room, searching vainly for the county attorney's file. Then other matters had demanded consideration and eventually she'd become distracted.

"I have this twenty-two-year-old case. Somewhere, somewhere, there are photographs," McGee began.

Hyland had a surprise for the medical examiner. She'd never found the county attorney's file, she told McGee, but she had found another one. Soon after Dennis's death there'd been a hearing in juvenile court concerning the welfare of the Jurgenses' surviving son, a boy named Robert. She'd uncovered a court file on that proceeding, and in it were the photos McGee wanted. Since it had been a juvenile proceeding, however, the file was sealed and she would need a court order to give the photos to the medical examiner.

"You talk to the judge and get the file unsealed," McGee snapped. "I need to see those photos."

He got what he wanted that same afternoon. The medical examiner was accustomed to disquieting images of death, but what he saw still disturbed him. The six eight-by-ten-inch glossies in his hands were of a small, scrawny boy's body. Raw, angry wounds spread across the center of the forehead and the base of the penis. Ugly bruises covered most of the rest of the body. It looked as if the kid was tortured, McGee thought. It looked as if he was worked over with a baseball bat.

What struck McGee most, though, was the body's odd position and extreme rigor mortis. The rigid arms, flexed at the elbows and raised in the air, told him the boy had died at least ten hours before the photos were taken, and not while lying on his back in his crib. He must have died while in a posture that kept his arms lifted and outstretched. Then, long after rigor set in, he must have been moved to his crib.

McGee also saw something else in the photos. Dennis's clenched fists and twisted facial expression told him the boy had died writhing in pain.

The next day, October 7, the medical examiner called Foley. Be warned, he told the prosecutor. I'm sending you a letter. I'm changing this to a homicide.

The letter, addressed to Ann Hyland, consisted of six paragraphs. The first four summarized his experiences since Jerry Sherwood first arrived at the medical examiner's office. The fifth paragraph offered his conclusions:

> As a result of the review of the above noted records including the coroner's file #30001, autopsy photographs and reports from the White Bear Lake police department, it is my impression that this case represents a homicide. As a result, I have filed an affidavit to amend the cause and manner of death in the case of Dennis Jurgens. The amended immediate cause of death will be listed as peritonitis due to perforation of small bowel due to multiple traumatic injuries consistent with battered child syndrome. Under other significant conditions will be listed multiple soft tissue contusions, abrasions and injuries. The manner of death will be listed as homicide.

Even as McGee was acting, Jerry Sherwood, distrustful and impatient, was continuing her own campaign. For advice, she turned to the medical examiner's chief investigator. The county attorney is dragging his feet, she complained to Jim Essling. What can I do?

Essling considered. He had a good contact at the local newspaper, the *St. Paul Pioneer Press Dispatch*—a young reporter named Brian Bonner. Talking to him might light a fire. Essling not infrequently worked certain back channels like this. He gave Bonner's name and number to Sherwood, and suggested she call him. This she did, and in the following two days, Bonner visited Sherwood's home three times for extended interviews. He began preparing a story for his newspaper.

Harold and Lois Jurgens no longer lived in White Bear Lake, but Bonner managed to track them to a house in a rural area near Lake Elmo and the historic town of Stillwater, some twenty minutes to the northeast of downtown St. Paul. Midmorning on Thursday, October 9, the reporter set out for the Jurgens house.

From Interstate 694, which girdles the Twin Cities, he headed east toward Lake Elmo. St. Paul's urban core quickly gave way to an open plain. At intervals, half-finished housing developments sprouted at the side of the road—clumps of modern two-story wood and glass homes sitting amid the farmland, waiting expectantly for the city to catch up. Soon the terrain turned more resolutely rural. For two miles the road curved through flat prairie farmland, most of it plowed, some left as green pasture, all bordered by stands of tall elm, pine and maple. Then the road grew hilly and twice changed names at curves before becoming Nolan Avenue. The homes here were no longer simple farmhouses but aspiring manors, set well off the road up sloping rises on large lots, obscured by dense stands of elm and oak. The last half mile grew narrower and even more densely wooded with aspen, birch and evergreens.

Bonner had to gun his car up a steep curving dirt driveway overgrown with a thick tangle of oak and maple branches, pebbles flying off his tires as they bit into the gully-pitted road, before he could see Harold and Lois Jurgens's frame rambler home. It sat on a large wooded rise, painted an odd orange-brown, surrounded and hidden by towering elms. Bonner knocked and rang the doorbell, but no one answered. He sensed someone inside watching him. Okay, he thought, let's try to do it by phone.

He drove back to his office in downtown St. Paul, settled at his desk, and dialed the Jurgenses' number. That worked—Lois Jurgens answered on the second ring. She sounded to Bonner like a sweet, elderly grandmother.

"Is this the Lois Jurgens whose adopted son died in 1965?" Bonner asked.

"Yes," Lois Jurgens said.

"The cause of death was not determined back then, but it has been now," Bonner said. "It's been classified a homicide."

"Well, who is doing this?" Lois Jurgens asked.

"The Ramsey County medical examiner," Bonner said.

"I am very much surprised," Lois Jurgens said. "Let me put it this way: I'm very puzzled. I can't understand what's going on. This seems really farfetched to me."

She was beginning to sound rattled. She had a question. "How did this come up?" she asked.

"Jerry Sherwood, the birth mother, started looking into what happened," Bonner said. Here he saw his opening. "She found a newspaper clipping that talked of peritonitis and a fall down some steps. Is that what happened? How did Dennis die?"

Lois Jurgens was not that rattled.

"I would have to talk to my lawyer," she said. "I'm not saying anything to you until I talk to my lawyer."

Three days later, Sunday, October 12, 1986, Brian Bonner's article appeared on the front page of the *St. Paul Pioneer Press Dispatch*, illustrated with a large photo of Jerry Sherwood and her son, Dennis Craig McIntyre, standing over the other Dennis's grave at St. Mary's Cemetery in White Bear Lake. Following the newspaper's policy, the article identified Sherwood by name but not the Jurgenses or their dead child, for no charges had been filed against them.

"The 1965 death of a three-year-old adopted White Bear Lake boy was ruled a homicide last week after the child's mother urged authorities to reexamine the case," the article began.

There were quotes from McGee. "It took me about a minute and a half to rule on the case. It isn't some medical mystery."

There were quotes from Buzz Harvey. "I went to the files and began to wonder why there wasn't a prosecution."

There were quotes from the former coroner, Tom Votel. "It troubled me greatly at the time. Clearly in our minds all of our suspicions were there."

There were quotes from the prosecutor, Tom Foley. There were quotes from the unidentified dead boy's adoptive mother. Finally, there were quotes from Jerry Sherwood.

"The killer is going to pay," she said in the article's closing paragraph. "Somebody's going to pay for my son's death."

By Sunday evening, Bonner's article had fueled a host of local television and radio newscasts. It was difficult to walk by a television screen that night and not see Jerry Sherwood's face. The story and broadcasts stirred interest in countless homes, but in a few, they did more than that. In a few, they rekindled long-buried memories. Although the Jurgens family had not been identified by name, there were those who felt sure they knew whom this report involved.

In her North St. Paul home Sunday morning, Lois Jurgens's niece, Pam Docken, read Bonner's article and promptly walked to the phone to dial her sister Karlene's number in Arizona. Pam had been six years old in 1965, Karlene twelve. When her sister answered, Pam spoke just one sentence: "I think they got her."

Shortly after ten o'clock that Sunday evening, Barbara Venne happened to walk into the bedroom of her North St. Paul home, where her husband Gary was watching the television news. She caught a glimpse of Jerry Sherwood's face at the tail end of a story. A birth mother was trying to find out about a baby adopted in White Bear Lake, a three-year-old who'd died years ago. Barbara felt faint. As a teenager in the mid-1960s, she'd been close friends with one of Lois Jurgens's nieces, so had spent much time at the home of Lois's parents. Barbara's childhood for a time had been a fairy tale. Then her mother died and her father went off the deep end. Her memories of those years were hard, but they had always stayed with her.

"Gary," she said. "They're talking about Dennis."

"Girl, will you leave this drop?" Gary said.

Barbara stared at the TV screen. An adopted boy, three years old, White Bear Lake.

"It's Dennis," she said.

At half past seven the next morning, Marion Dinah Nord and her husband David were driving from their farm to their jobs in Caledonia, a town in the southeastern corner of Minnesota. As they headed up Fishes Hill (or Zenner's Hill, Marion always told visitors, depending on how long you've lived in these parts) they heard a radio newscast. *A mother . . . adoption twenty years ago . . . child found dead . . . a question about the manner of death.* Marion broke out in a cold sweat and felt her heart racing. Not more than two weeks before she'd been telling a fellow social worker at the Caledonia Health Care Center about her memories of a horrible case she'd handled so long ago. The intervening years had been a roller coaster for her—a traumatic divorce and years of drinking before finding God and abstinence. Through it all, she'd always dreamed authorities would one day reopen that case. Now, she was convinced, they were doing just that.

"David," she said as their car descended Fishes Hill, "that's got to be the Jurgens case. I know that's the Jurgens case."

In other homes in White Bear Lake, clean and well-lit homes filled with people satisfied and comfortable in their middle or later years, similar moments unfolded that weekend. These were people who had never forgotten what happened on Gardenette Drive in White Bear Lake in 1965. These were people who had never stopped wondering what they could have done or should have done.

CHAPTER 2

White Bear Lake

White Bear Lake has long beckoned to those seeking restoration or sustenance or a new beginning. Indians hunted and fished in the region for thirty-six hundred years before white men appeared midway through the nineteenth century, pushing aside the Chippewa, Sioux and Dakota. French-Canadian farmers and fur traders began settling in 1844, followed soon after by veterans of the Mexican War, farmers from the East, immigrants from Great Britain and enterprising speculators. They were seeking fertile, inexpensive land, and this they found.

In 1848, a lumberman could buy land at $1.25 an acre in White Bear Township, war veterans could present warrants for free plots, and anyone planning to build a cabin and try some farming could claim public land by preemption. By 1850, speculators were snapping up entire government lots of forty to eighty acres, and settlers enticed by glowing newspaper accounts were traveling up the Mississippi by steamboat to see for themselves this "region back of St. Paul" full of rich prairies, heavy forests and beautiful lakes.

The abundance they found dazzled them. Here were mixed forests of elm, alder, ash, linden, black, burr and white oak, tamarack and sugar maple. The forests were full of bear and deer; the marshes rich with cranberries, blueberries, wild rice, ducks, wild geese, grouse, pigeons, quail, foxes and pheasants; the waters thick with pike, pickerel, salmon bass, crappies, sunfish and perch.

White Bear Lake itself was a vision, carved eons ago by retreating glaciers—a twenty-five-hundred-acre sheet of crystal-clear water, six miles long by two to three miles wide, surrounded by gently swelling wooded hills. From its surface, fish could be seen swimming to depths of twelve feet. Its shore was lined with sparkling pebbles—white, red, black—mixed with lustrous carnelians. In the middle of the lake sat an island of some one hundred acres, crowded with hard maple, oak, ash and elm.

Such beauty beckoned to pleasure-seekers as much as to speculators and pioneers. In the summer of 1851, after the county built a new road between White Bear Lake and St. Paul, replacing the old Indian and fur trade trails, parties of ladies and gentlemen from St. Paul began packing picnic lunches and riding horses and carriages the three hours to White Bear Lake for a day of fishing and hunting. In the summer of 1853, Villeroy B. Barnum opened the region's first resort hotel by enlarging his log cabin, built four years earlier on the 175 lakefront acres he'd selected after arriving by steamboat from St. Louis. Other hotels soon sprang up, many facing the water along Lake Avenue, curving around the lake's western and southern banks. Some were converted private homes, others elegant Colonial structures with stately columns, and most bore the name of their proprietors—the Murray House, the Williams House, the Benson House, the Hotel Liep. Word began to spread about the splendid resort north of St. Paul. Travelers in ill health came seeking cures or to escape summer epidemics in the lower states, while others came simply for the cool, undisturbed beauty. By 1860, White Bear Lake had churches, schools, a postmaster and a township government. It was a resort town with a national reputation.

The railroad arrived in September of 1868. With the connection to St. Paul no longer a three-hour horse-and-buggy journey, the population doubled from 267 in 1860 to 431 in 1868. Tradesmen and professionals arrived—an attorney, an architect, realtors, insurance agents, blacksmiths, boat builders, contractors, masons, shoemakers, dressmakers, barbers, painters. Newly opened stores sold groceries, building materials, pharmaceuticals, meat, dry goods, hardware, flour and feed, clothing, shoes. There were two saloons, three bakeries, a restaurant and a lunchroom. For those who could not find or afford a hotel room, there were tent villages, some luxuriously furnished. By 1893, up to twenty-five trains ran daily in the summer to White Bear Lake. The new White Bear Yacht Club organized frequent regattas and three steamships plied the lake, carrying large pleasure, picnic and excursion parties. Midsummer night concerts, lawn tennis, dances and musicals multiplied.

A Dakota Indian legend explaining the origin of the lake's name soon was being retold by enthralled visitors. One such traveler recounted the legend in a letter to his relatives:

Every spring, for perhaps a century, an island in the middle of White-bear Lake has been visited by a band of Indians for the purpose of making maple-sugar. Tradition says that many springs ago, while upon this island, a young warrior loved and wooed the daughter of his chief, and it is said, also the maiden loved the warrior. He had again and again been refused her hand by her parents, the old chief alleging that he was no brave, and his old consort called him a woman! One evening, the young warrior took down his flute and went out alone, once more to sing the story of his love. As he mounted on the trunk of a leaning tree and raised his flute to his lips, his blanket slipped from his well-formed shoulders, and lay partly on the snow beneath. He began his weird, wild love song, but soon felt that he was cold, and as he reached back for his blanket, some unseen hand laid it gently on his shoulders. It was the hand of his love. She took her place beside him, and for the present they were happy; for the Indian has a heart to love. As the legend runs, a large white bear took up his journey southward and came to the lake which now bears his name the spring the lovers met. They had left their first retreat, and were now seated among the branches of a large elm which hung far over the lake. For fear of being detected they talked almost in a whisper, and now, that they might get back to camp in good time and thereby avoid suspicion, they were just rising to return, when the maiden uttered a shriek which was heard at the camp, and bounding toward the young brave, she caught his blanket, but missed the direction of her foot and fell, bearing the blanket with her into the great arms of the ferocious monster. Instantly every man, woman and child of the band were upon the bank, but all unarmed. Cries and wailings

went up from every mouth. What was to be done? One deaf-
ening yell from the lover warrior is heard above the cries of
hundreds of his tribe, and dashing away to his wigwam he
grasps his faithful knife, returns almost at a single bound
and springing with the fury of a mad panther, pounced upon
his prey. The animal turned, and with one stroke of his huge
paw brought the lovers heart to heart, but the next moment
the warrior, with one plunge of the blade of his knife, opened
the crimson sluices of death, and the dying bear relaxed his
hold. That night there was no more sleep for the band or the
lovers, and as the young and the old danced about the car-
cass of the dead monster, the gallant warrior was presented
with another plume, and ere another moon had set he had
a living treasure added to his heart. Their children for many
years played upon the skin of the white bear—from which
the lake derives its name—and the maiden and the brave
remembered long the fearless scenes which made them one.

Mark Twain heard of this legend when he passed through White
Bear Lake in 1882, while visiting the Twin Cities. "It is a lovely sheet
of water," he wrote later in *Life on the Mississippi*, "and is being uti-
lized as a summer resort by the wealth and fashion of the state. It has
its clubhouse, and its hotel, with the modern improvements and con-
veniences; its fine summer residences; and plenty of fishing, hunting and pleasant drives. There are a dozen minor summer resorts
around about St. Paul and Minneapolis, but the White-bear Lake is
the resort."

Twain, however, was not as enamored with the legend behind the
lake's name as he was with the region itself.

"Connected with White-bear Lake is a most idiotic Indian legend . . ." he wrote.

It is a perplexing business. First, she fell down out of the tree—
she and the blanket; and the bear caught her and fondled
her—her and the blanket; then she fell up into the tree again—
leaving the blanket; meantime the lover goes war-whooping
home and comes back "heeled," climbs the tree, jumps down
on the bear, the girl jumps down after him—apparently, for she
was up the tree—resumes her place in the bear's arms along

with the blanket, the lover rams his knife into the bear, and saves—whom? The blanket? No—nothing of the sort. You get yourself all worked up and excited about that blanket, and then all of a sudden, just when a happy climax seems imminent, you are let down flat—nothing saved but the girl! Whereas, one is not interested in the girl; she is not the prominent feature of the legend. Nevertheless, there you are left, and there you must remain; for if you live a thousand years you will never know who got the blanket. A dead man could get up a better legend than this one. I don't mean a fresh dead man either; I mean a man that's been dead weeks and weeks.

In 1899, the Twin City Rail Transit Company began regular streetcar service from St. Paul to White Bear. In order to attract business to the line, the company that year also built the Wildwood Amusement Park on the southeast shore of the lake, in Mahtomedi. Steamships carried visitors back and forth between the town and the park, and in 1904, the railroad company added a branch electric line that ran around the southern and western shores from Wildwood to White Bear. Visitors paid no admission to enter the park—only the streetcar fare of ten to fifteen cents.

Open from Memorial Day to Labor Day, 11:00 A.M. to 11:00 P.M., Wildwood became a popular attraction. Visitors from the Twin Cities, some five hundred on weekdays, more than a thousand on weekends, would arrive after a curving, hour-long, sixty-mile-per-hour ride from North St. Paul in forty-eight-passenger streetcars that featured half benches, wicker seats, a motorman and a conductor. The giant five-hundred-foot Pippin Roller Coaster dominated Wildwood's profile, along with the glittering Parker Ferris Wheel and a colossal water slide. Wildwood had shaded picnic grounds, a spacious bathing beach, locker rooms and bathing houses, a restaurant, bumper cars, a merry-go-round with hand-carved animals, water-toboggan rides, skeeball alleys, bowling alleys, shooting galleries, a penny arcade, rental boats and speedboat rides. Steamboats—the *Saint Paul*, the *Wildwood*, the *Dispatch*, the *Manitoba*, the *White Bear*, some with dance floors and orchestras—provided lake tours for twenty-five cents.

For many, though, Wildwood's highlight was a lakeside brick dance pavilion with a shiny hardwood floor maintained with powdered wax. Guests dressed up and dined elegantly in the pavilion's restaurant, consuming fish and chicken dinners while listening to music provided in later years by such as Guy Lombardo, Red Nichols and His Five Pennies, Dave Dahl and Fats Waller. Late at night after the show, the musicians sometimes took speedboat tours, serenading the lakeside residents, who often reciprocated with a most welcome bottle.

Dances were held on the pavilion afternoons and evenings four days a week, and the ten-cent admission included checkroom privileges. On Sunday afternoons and evenings the bands and orchestras played on the dance pavilion veranda. A white-haired floorwalker named Archie Newcomb, dapper and charming in his tuxedo, would tap couples on the shoulder if they were dancing too close.

Apart from Wildwood, White Bear Lake's golden resort era did not last far into the twentieth century. Henry Ford started assembly line production of automobiles in 1903, and gradually, the car changed patterns of transportation and vacations. People could turn elsewhere for entertainment. By 1912, most of the resort hotels had burned down and, with shrinking traffic, the steamships serving Wildwood were dismantled and sunk.

White Bear Lake became more of a private resort than a public one. Cottages spread through the woods, serving as summer homes for city folk from throughout the upper Midwest. F. Scott Fitzgerald spent the summer of 1921 in a cottage at Dellwood, near White Bear Lake, where he wrote his novel, *The Beautiful and the Damned*, and received as guests Sinclair Lewis and Charles Flandrau. The next summer he spent August at the White Bear Yacht Club, where he wrote and located his short story "Winter's Dream." Between 1925 and 1935, gangsters also sojourned in the region, hiding in Willernie, Bald Eagle Lake and White Bear Beach. Among them were Ma Barker and her sons, George (Machine Gun) Kelly, Harvey Bailey, Volney Davis, Harry Campbell, Bill Weaver, Verne Miller, Jess Doyle and—some stories have it—Baby-Face Nelson, John Dillinger and Al Capone. White Bear Lake at this time included movie houses, saloons, dance halls, pool halls, a bowling alley, a roller skating rink and a bandstand.

Wildwood Park lingered on until the Depression, closing in 1932 but for the dance pavilion, which folded in 1937. The St. Paul and Duluth Railroad leveled the complex the following year, selling the land to private parties for lakeside residential development. The Roaring Twenties were long gone, the Depression Thirties drawing to a close. In 1940, the outside world demanded White Bear Lake's attention. World War II loomed.

The outside world was something new and strange to most of the White Bear Lake boys who marched off to war. Most had been born and raised around the lake and knew nothing else. Their parents were largely Scandinavian—the earlier French-Canadian settlers had long ago been edged aside—so they grew up largely in quiet, stoic, work-oriented homes where people rarely talked of private matters or wallowed in their troubles or aired dirty laundry. Instead they got on with the business of living, presenting a stolid front. They were good people, always willing to help others—in fact they existed to help others—but they were not the sort to probe their psyches or anyone else's. They were Catholic or Lutheran and attended church every Sunday. They had seen very few black men and had heard almost no swearing. Guns and bullets they knew, but only for hunting wild game. The people they met and the war they fought shocked them. When the fighting ended, they wanted nothing but a rapid return to White Bear Lake, preferring to turn their backs on the strange and difficult things they'd seen, for they had sensed enough of what the world offered. They wanted to get on with building the good and decent lives they had always imagined. They wanted to buy homes and raise children and make a living for their families.

Everything seemed possible then. White Bear Lake in 1950 was a two-mile-by-two-mile square on the water's southwest shore, with a population of 3,700 and a network of dirt roads. Farmland surrounded and threaded through the town—Henry Hoffman's vegetable stand on County Road E and Highway 61 backed onto a cornfield. The land was cheap enough that those with a strong back but an empty pocket could get started.

Sandy McCabe, arriving from Rapid City, South Dakota, felt like an outsider when she wandered into a hardware store on County Road E. The owner knew every customer, so they got waited on before she did. One man came in wanting copper tubing, but didn't know how much he needed. The clerk handed him the full roll. Here, she said, take it home, cut off what you need, bring it back. What a town, Sandy thought.

Hugo Drew, a loan officer at First State Bank, made bank loans based on a man's word and character, since he usually knew his borrowers. Flashing stock certificates as collateral didn't impress him— "It's gonna cost me to collect if it came to that," he'd say. The daughter of the mortician, Jim Honsa, drove a new car over to the bank lot one day, parked it, walked in, and asked Hugo Drew for a loan. "Why not?" he said.

With virtually no industry and little commerce in town, the local White Bear Lake Bank in 1956 had deposits totaling just $3.8 million. Reluctant to get tied up in thirty-year mortgages, faced with very few business loan applications, the bank mainly made retail loans for cars and home improvements. As time went by, the bank couldn't keep up with the demand—it didn't have enough money to finance all the Tousley Ford and Polar Chevy sales, so some folks had to try the Ford Credit Corporation.

The hangout was Dave's Courtyard, right next to city hall. Dave Olson's place offered pizza, a bar, a piano player, singing and Roger, the bartender. Customers were a mixed lot—mainly middle-class commuters to St. Paul and blue-collar workers, sprinkled with some wealthy summer residents from Lake Avenue and Manitou Island. Conversations there, frequently punctuated by phrases such as "you bet" and "okay," often yielded plans for a Sunday pancake breakfast fund-raiser. If townsfolk weren't open, they certainly were friendly.

The police force totaled three men. Its chief was a crusty old gent named Louis Kieffer, who'd been working as the town's water meter reader back in the 1940s when a desperate city manager turned to him after the town's solitary policeman quit. Kieffer officially became police chief in 1958, when a civil service ruling required the city manager to give up that title. At first, Kieffer had only a single panel truck for use as patrol car, ambulance and street sander. When the department did get squad cars, off-duty cops would ride with the working officers just to keep them company, since there usually was only a single policeman scheduled for any one shift. They had no car radios. Instead, two red lights hung in town—one at Fourth and Washington just off Highway 61, the other at Second and Broadway—and when an officer walking his beat saw those lights blink on, he'd run to a phone and call the station.

Bicycle thieves and drunk drivers were their main worry, although there were a few tough families full of construction and ironworkers who populated the saloons and welcomed a good brawl. From time to time young people regarded by the law as hoodlums gathered in large numbers at the local beach or downtown, outside Dean's ice cream shop. On one such night, the town's municipal judge, Bill Fleming, ordered a whole crowd arrested on disorderly conduct charges, calling their behavior "disgraceful" and promising that "this conduct is not going to be tolerated." On another night, when a rumble seemed imminent at a park near Second and Highway 61, someone thought to summon a National Guard force that happened to be meeting two blocks away—an act that resulted in Judge Fleming's getting a heated phone call the next day from Minnesota's governor, Orville Freeman.

The schools did have their rowdies, some from families outside White Bear Lake's town limits. When Roy Wahlberg arrived in White Bear Lake in 1957 to start as vice principal at the high school, his boss, O. V. Johanson, told him, "Your job is to maintain discipline in the cafeteria." Wahlberg, from Sandstone, Minnesota, and Gustavus Adolphus College, had flown B-29s for the air force and in time would become a lieutenant colonel in the air force reserve. Discipline was not something he minded.

His first day at work, White Bear Lake High School seemed to him a jungle—paper plates and food flying, cutting in line, fighting and disrespect, vandalism. He tried to break up a fight. The kid wouldn't stop, and instead turned and swung at him. By the end of the lunch hour, Wahlberg, his shirt torn and tie askew, had the boy on the floor with a knee on his chest. "He's expelled. If you don't, I'm not staying," Wahlberg told the principal. That worked—the kid was sent away without a hearing. Six weeks later, school superintendent R. J. Hansen came to Wahlberg and asked, in his deep, rolling voice, "Well, Roy, how many kids have you expelled so far?" Fourteen, Wahlberg said. "Not enough. Got to show who's boss," Hansen growled, turning on his heel.

By the end of that first year, Wahlberg had expelled sixty-five. He sometimes endured vandals at his home and hammers flying through his front picture window. Once someone drove a car over his newly sodded lawn, leaving a threatening typed note, but with a plaster cast of the tire marks and test samples from every typewriter in three typing classes, plus the classes' seating charts, Wahlberg tracked the culprit down. For a while after that he never went anywhere without a billy club in hand, but eventually things calmed down. At White Bear Lake High School, there were no low-slung pants like Elvis's, no long hair, no cleats on shoes.

The fire department was a thirty-man volunteer crew, financed in part by exuberant Lions Club fund-raisers. When the alarm went out, Fred Lenhart, who lived in an apartment above his Lenhart's Bar, just off Highway 61, would sometimes get so excited he'd run barefoot along the railroad tracks to the fire barn. Lenhart was a burly former professional fighter nicknamed Tarzan by his friends, in honor of the time he fell from a tree while hunting deer near Danbury. If he had enough liquor in him he would do the Charleston.

Fishing dominated conversation and activity like a religion, and brought a good deal more bliss to some than did church. Everyone owned a boat, and it seemed most also owned a weekend cabin on "the lake"—which could mean any one of the ten thousand or so in Minnesota. Debates waged about boat motors, trolling techniques, secret spots, walleye moods. When White Bear Lake froze over in late fall, dozens of ice-fishing houses would sprout, occupied by hearty fishermen undeterred by winter, dropping lines through holes cut in the ice.

Without much fanfare, White Bear Lake after the war had become the quiet, uncomplicated upper Midwest town that its residents wanted, no longer exotic or particularly breathtaking in appearance. Memories of its storied past lingered mainly in an annual chamber of commerce concoction called "Manitou Days," a week-long summer festival full of parades, dances and shows that seemed to please the populace almost as much as it promoted the interests of the local merchants. George Rivers, who was thirty when he first drove into town along Highway 61 one day in 1954 seeking a teaching job, didn't feel nearly as impressed as did the first French-Canadian fur trappers. Here was a wide, plain road with unused rusting railroad tracks running down its middle. Where was the town? Rivers wondered.

Three years later, when White Bear Lake in 1957 proudly entered the "All-America Cities" competition then sponsored each year by the National Municipal League and *Look* magazine, its defeat was a surprise only to the most ardent of civic boosters. In truth, conditions were no longer all that idyllic or tranquil in White Bear Lake.

As the 1950s unfolded, the town had increasingly assumed the nature and problems of suburbia.

The population grew by a thousand people each year in that decade, quadrupling from three thousand to twelve thousand. The number of new homes expanded by three hundred each year, the growth coming mainly in the flat open farmland to the south of the lake and the original town. Most newcomers were young couples just starting families, and the postwar baby boom was self-evident—half the town's families had children under six and almost half the population was under the age of eighteen.

White Bear Lake, inundated, struggled to accommodate this growth, wrestling with the typical suburban problems of inadequate zoning, water lines, sewers, flood control, roads, sidewalks, recreational facilities and schools. The school population tripled between 1953 and 1963—from 2,812 to 7,054—so the citizens of the White Bear Lake school district found it necessary to pass bond issues in 1951, 1953, 1955, 1956, 1957, 1960, 1962, 1963, 1964 and 1965. Five schools were built in five years between 1959 and 1964. White Bear Lake citizens were proud of their schools, but their support came with a price. The town had little industry, so by 1960, the entire burden of school and city taxes rested on the shoulders of homeowners.

For all the problems growth brought, though, White Bear Lake embraced expansion. The city leaders were young men in their thirties, merchants and businessmen, largely Republican. Looking back years later, they would proudly claim they were the Yuppies of their era. They were go-getters and civic promoters, active in the chamber of commerce and Lions Club, upwardly mobile, involved, thinking always of such matters as budgets and a broadened industrial tax base. They drew up intoxicating projections, showing White Bear Lake's population mushrooming at a steady pace, upward to seventy thousand by the turn of the century.

They had campaigned for and promoted the newfangled notion of suburban housing developments ever since the close of World War II, and they had finally started realizing their wish in 1950 when developer Kenneth W. Bacchus of St. Paul bought acres of land south of the lake. The town's first housing development, Lakeridge Development—large contemporary homes priced from $20,000 to $40,000—rose on South Shore Boulevard, drawing a mix of white- and blue-collar buyers.

Soon after, another development rose one-third of a mile farther south of the water, anchored by a pair of roads that formed an oval— Gardenette Drive North and South. By nature and appearance these two- and three-bedroom stucco and wood homes were disconnected from the lake, more conventionally suburban than elegant or playful. Selling for $12,000 to $14,000 each, they were roomy and comfortable but by no means palatial, on lots averaging 80 feet by 155 feet. Gardenette Park was meant mostly for young families who had little money but still desired to own a home with a big yard in a quiet neighborhood.

All sorts moved in the 1950s to Gardenette Park: Tom Axelrod, a telephone company lineman; Jim Neely, a laborer at the Hamm's Brewing Company; Ivan DeMars, a precision grinder at the Paper Calmenson & Company steel mill; Bob Brass, proprietor of the Ben Franklin five-and-dime in downtown White Bear Lake; Howard Engfer, a pharmaceutical salesman. Axelrod had toured Europe with the Seventieth Division's K Company, Neely had spent the tail end of the war in Japan as an M.P., DeMars had seen just about the whole world with the navy and merchant marine. They were ready to settle down.

Gardenette Park soon acquired the nickname "Bassinet Park," for dozens of children filled the streets day and night, playing tag and kicking balls. It was by all accounts an open, friendly neighborhood. Friday nights meant penny poker games and soda pop, at least when they could afford that indulgence. Fifteen families would roll north for a weekend of camping at Detroit Lakes, gathering around giant bonfires. They laid sod and painted and did repairs for neighbors. We didn't have a window or a pot, they would say much later, but we all helped one another.

In the fall of 1957, a new couple joined the neighborhood, moving into the corner house next door to the DeMarses at 2148 South Gardenette, where that street met Hazel. The husband was a tall, mild-mannered electrician, thirty-five years old, the wife a short, attractive, voluptuous housewife of thirty-one. They had no children, and they tended to keep to themselves. Their names were Harold and Lois Jurgens.

CHAPTER 3

Lois and Harold

There are of course no biographies of Lois Jurgens, no hardbound memoirs, no volumes of collected letters. There are only uncertain scattered memories—her own, her family's, her friends'—and the more distant impressions of doctors and social workers, often filtered through the cloudy language of their official reports. From such glimpses, a life can be imagined more than known. This much seems clear—Lois Jurgens as a teenager fancied mirrors, and for good reason. She was strikingly pretty, delicate and fragile, petite at five feet three inches, with wide lively eyes, dark hair and finely chiseled features. Her siblings and chums remember her then as being outgoing and happy-go-lucky. Above all, she loved to dance, although it is hard to say just how much dancing informed her life.

Lois was one of sixteen surviving children born to John and Lois Zerwas, and the family was abysmally poor, partly due to the Depression and partly to John Zerwas's legendary aversion to sustained work. The mother's roots were an English-French-Spanish mix; the father's reached back to a clan of German factory workers who had migrated to the United States two generations before. Lois, their fourth child, was born on August 12, 1925, in St. Paul, and soon thereafter, the family moved to a farm near the small town of Richwood, Minnesota. By the start of the Depression they were in Fargo, North Dakota, with John Zerwas painting, hanging wallpaper, and working milk cows, but that didn't last either. Throughout the 1930s, the rapidly growing family moved ever more frequently in search of work, living on farms or in worn houses without water or electricity, for most meals filling their stomachs with piles of pancakes and potatoes. From North Dakota they moved to North St. Paul, then Maplewood, then down to a farm in Hastings, back up to Rice Street in North St. Paul, English Street in Maplewood, Mahtomedi, North St. Paul again, up north 210 miles to Park Rapids, back down to Larpenteur Avenue in Maplewood, and finally, in 1949, to a modest, weathered yellow frame house at the end of Park Street in White Bear Lake. They were at the edge of a swamp, across the railroad tracks, far from the water.

No one who knew the family in those days on Park can remember John Zerwas working. One son does claim his father labored briefly for a company laying pipe, but it didn't last. "He never was much for having a boss," Lloyd Zerwas explained. "Dad disdained working for someone else. He always said they'll just use you up and throw you out." Old John Zerwas was not one to get himself used up. Most remember him sitting in a chair on his porch, leaning back, amusing himself by burning the hair off his arm with a lit cigarette.

It is said that some of his sons followed his ways, sleeping until noon, then scavenging for junk in the countryside—old parts, copper wire, iron, whatever would sell. Those children with jobs had to give most of their paychecks and their income tax refunds to their father. The eldest, Eloise, remembers working at the local Montgomery Ward one day when her parents, in need of groceries, showed up at the store's door to collect her paycheck. The net amount of the check would be twelve or fourteen dollars, but with that they could fill the whole backseat of the car and return three dollars to Eloise for her own use.

As the Zerwas children married and bore their own children, the mushrooming clan in time acquired a certain reputation in White Bear Lake. "Carefree and fun-loving" was the generous way some people put it, while those less charitable considered them simply wild and no good. Bud Korfhage, director of White Bear Lake's recreation department, found he had to call the Zerwas family often about their kids' disruptions at parks, skating rinks, tennis courts, recreational events. Once when he phoned the Zerwas home, they told him, "Don't call us, call the cops," and next thing Bud knew, a constable was at his door, accusing him of abusing a kid. That was his experience with the Zerwas clan. Bill LeVasseur knew the family because they shopped at his grocery store. Most were on welfare, so the wives would come in without money, asking for credit, and Bill would agree, $5 worth at least, but only if he could pick the groceries—no junk, no cigarettes.

The scribbled summaries and typed memos that later came to comprise the Lois Jurgens file offer only blurred, conflicting suggestions of how she fared as a young girl in this milieu. One classmate in elementary school recalls her as being not vibrant but shy and withdrawn and half-starved, waiting eagerly for recess so she could get her free graham cracker and milk from the lunchroom. A neighbor walking past the Zerwas home often could hear Lois's father shouting inside, violent and noisy.

It seems clear Lois longed for escape. Whether by choice or need, she quit school in the eighth grade, when she was fourteen, and after that, when she wasn't working or doing chores, she went dancing and bowling and roller-skating. At a dance at the Gladstone School one night in the early spring of 1941, when she was fifteen, Lois caught the eye of the bandleader, a quiet, unassuming nineteen-year-old boy who played the saxophone and clarinet. Everyone called him Hetz and his nine-piece band was the Hetz Jurgens Orchestra, but his true name was Harold Jurgens. With his tenor saxophone and his gentle manner, he must have offered promise of passage to a new world.

Harold's file is much thinner than Lois's, and simpler and less filled with memories, for years later many found they just couldn't recall his presence—not at his own high school graduation, not at family gatherings, not at any of the other critical events they felt certain Harold must have attended. It is known he grew up an only child in North St. Paul, and that both his parents always worked—his mother in an office, his father as a radio repairman for the Bill Hoest Electric Company—so even during the Depression he never lacked for money. He went camping with his father at times, and his mother was protective and domineering, but neither was around that much, and he was largely raised by a grandmother. He loved music even as a young boy, and took piano lessons from the ages of seven to twelve before turning to the sax and clarinet.

The Hetz Jurgens Orchestra played many high school and college dances, and even some gigs in local nightclubs, and for a time Harold dreamed of making a living with his own dance band. After graduating from high school in 1940 he drifted, working at Armour's, then Montgomery Ward, playing band dates at night when he could.

The Gladstone School dance in the spring of 1941 was just such an engagement. He thought Lois pretty and nice, full of life and spunk, far more so than he. They dated for several months, from early spring until July, but then Harold, still full of plans, eager for adventure and better pay, headed for Panama and a job working on the canal.

Those who only knew Harold later would have trouble imagining him at this time of his life—a young man with muscle and hope, during the day laboring under the hot Central American sun, at night playing in Panamanian dance bands, all the while writing Lois letters and wondering about his future. Then, in time, for reasons uncertain or never clearly understood, Harold gave up his dream, or perhaps fashioned a new one. There came a moment, he explained later, when he realized a dance band was not the type of life for a married man, and by then he understood that what he wanted, above all, was to settle down with a family. The bond with Lois, whatever its glue, had held. In December of 1943, when Harold decided to return home and enlist in the service, he also decided to get married.

Lois and Harold's wedding took place in Mason City, Iowa, on January 31, 1944, when Lois was eighteen years and five months old. They'd "run off," Lois would say later, because their parents did not approve. Her mother had already gone through weddings for three of her children, and his parents, Lutherans, were not pleased that their son was marrying a poor, uneducated Catholic.

That spring, Harold enlisted in the naval air corps and Lois traveled with him to North Carolina, but when he was transferred to Indiana, she came home, moving in with Harold's parents. Back in Minnesota after his discharge in October of 1945, Harold drifted uncertainly for a time, from a pulpwood business to a $40-a-week factory job, until he eventually fixed on work as an electrician. He took the required training and qualified as a union journeyman in December of 1952.

The couple by then was settled in a house at 654 Second Avenue SW in North St. Paul, one Harold had largely built himself at Lois's urging. From a distance, they seemed happy enough, financially steady and launched on their way in life. There was a problem, though. After eight years of marriage, they had been unable to conceive a baby. It seemed that Harold was sterile.

Lois was suffering in other ways as well. Her complaints included fatigue, insomnia, lower-abdomen pains and chronic constipation. Her sleep, when it did come, often was tortured by fearful nightmares. She felt irritable and cranky and, above all, overwhelmingly tired. Harold took her to several doctors, to no avail.

On July 5, 1951, Harold sat down in their Second Avenue home with a pen and a piece of lined six-by-nine-inch notepaper. He had decided to write to the famed Mayo Clinic in Rochester, Minnesota.

"Dear Sirs," he began. "I believe that if it would be possible to send my wife through your clinic, much could be accomplished. She is 25 years of age and hasn't been well for quite some time. I have sent her to several doctors repeatedly, but no good has come of it and money was spent foolishly. I am awaiting your reply. Very truly yours, Harold R. Jurgens."

The Mayo Clinic wrote back on July 13, saying they were sorry Harold's wife was having difficulty and offering their assistance. The Jurgenses had two options. They could make an advance appointment for sometime in early September, or they could come to the clinic immediately, without an appointment, and wait their turn. The Jurgenses left soon after for Rochester—September seemed too far in the future.

Lois was admitted to the Mayo Clinic on July 17 and stayed there until August 3. After a general medical examination yielded no results out of the ordinary, on July 30 she was seen by a psychiatrist, Dr. Norman P. Goldstein. He found her friendly and willing to answer all questions, although at times a little repetitive. They talked at length, and in a written narrative, the psychiatrist later summarized what she had told him.

The patient came from a large, impoverished family, Dr. Goldstein reported. The father was "alcoholic and brutal toward mother and children." Lois left home at age fifteen "because father was drunk and beating mother—patient tried to intervene and call police but father beat her with the telephone . . ." Because of the home's crowded conditions, "she can remember at night hearing mother and father having intercourse . . ." Then and now, she resented being taken out of school at the eighth grade to help out at home. Despite everything, though, she was relatively well until she got married and began to

battle with her mother-in-law. Harold's parents had wanted the marriage annulled because Lois was not educated. "At first mother-in-
law did not want them to have children but now she does and she
blames [Lois] for [infertility] . . ."

Harold was an only child too closely attached to and dominated
by his mother, Lois told Dr. Goldstein. She "broke him of that," but
he wouldn't convert to Catholicism, as she wished. She fought with
her mother-in-law partly over religion, partly over control of Harold. She felt certain her mother-in-law once tried to gas her to death
when she was asleep in their house. She didn't enjoy intercourse
with her husband, since they couldn't have children. She wanted to
be more religious. She had lots of fears and compulsions—fears of
death, of cancer, of going crazy, of the dark, of automobiles. She was a
perfectionist, with a compulsion to keep things tidy and in place. She
was easily disgusted with life, upset by every little thing.

"I'm just exhausted all the time, even if I rest," Lois said. "I used
to be a bundle of energy, I used to love going out dancing, now I care
for nothing. I want children. I want them so badly. I just want to stay
home and raise children. I want to give them the clothes and education and home I never had."

At the end of their session, Dr. Goldstein prepared a decidedly
cautionary diagnosis and prognosis:

> A 26-year-old married woman with a long-standing psy-
> choneurosis of the mixed type, starting back to childhood
> as evidenced by enuresis [bedwetting] until age 13, fears,
> nightmares, etc . . . It is fortunate that this woman has not
> been able to carry through pregnancy at this time as a child
> will only compound and complicate her emotional distur-
> bance—she would be a poor candidate for adopting a child at
> this time . . . They cannot afford psychiatric care, which she
> desperately needs—she may without it go on to a paranoid
> schizophrenia.

Because of their financial limitations, Goldstein referred the Jurgenses to a therapist at the University of Minnesota's department of
psychiatry. It is unclear whether the Jurgenses ever contacted that
university doctor, but Lois did continue to seek help. Her paper trail
offers convincing evidence of unceasing efforts: She visited at least

one private psychiatrist, a Dr. J. Allen Wilson, in 1952 and 1953. She stayed at the Hamm Memorial Psychiatric Clinic in St. Paul from December 13, 1954, through January 24, 1955. She underwent electroshock treatment in early 1955 while at Crestview Hospital in the Twin Cities area.

Three months after Lois left Crestview, in June of 1955, the Jurgenses sought solace of a different sort. They filed an application with the Bureau of Catholic Charities in St. Paul. They wanted to adopt a child.

The records do not show whether the Jurgenses revealed all of Lois's psychiatric history to Catholic Charities, but the couple clearly didn't hide Lois's visits to the Mayo Clinic. The Jurgenses said she went there to determine, among other things, whether or not she had cancer, and they willingly signed a consent for release of medical information form. The Mayo Clinic's report to Catholic Charities, however, was not encouraging, for it included Dr. Goldstein's judgment that Lois would be a poor candidate for bearing or adopting a child. With this advice in hand, Catholic Charities in mid-1955 turned down the Jurgenses' request to adopt a child.

Harold and Lois now apparently felt the need to shake up their lives. Disenchanted with North St. Paul, attracted to the seeming promise of Florida, they sold their house on an impulse and moved to Tallahassee. That didn't work either. Within months, restless and searching, they returned to Minnesota, where Harold quickly found a job with the Tony Muska Electric Company in St. Paul.

Still hoping for children, they began looking for a home with extra bedrooms and a large backyard, in a quiet and comfortable neighborhood. Because Lois's parents lived on Park Street in White Bear Lake, the Jurgenses looked in that region, although their taste and budget allowed for something more comfortable than the Zerwas milieu. Across the railroad tracks from Lois's parents' house, one-third of a mile south of the lake, they found a pleasing neighborhood, built just six years before, arranged around an oval-shaped street lined with rows of staked saplings—spruce, fir, cherry, elm, birch, maple. A corner house was on the market just then for $14,000, a beige gabled stucco structure with a big backyard, three bedrooms and a basement.

The home at 2148 South Gardenette Drive beckoned, offering promise of just what the Jurgenses had been longing for.

Lois's days now unfolded amid a sea of children. Gardenette Park well merited its nickname of Bassinet Park, for the streets filled with kids day and night, dozens at a time playing whiffle ball, kick ball, hide-and-seek, laughing and shouting wildly from early morning to nightfall. The weekly Zerwas family gatherings on Sunday afternoons at Lois's parents' house were no less populated by youngsters. Many of her fifteen siblings now had their own children—some by then had half a dozen or more—so armies of barefoot, dirty kids darted in and out of the rooms.

By all accounts, those Sunday parties were lively, colorful affairs. Everyone was welcome to drop by, for old man Zerwas would never throw anybody out. Lois's mother made pancakes, and those who wished brought potluck dishes to pass—casseroles, salads, pies. The Zerwas men played guitars and harmonicas and sang country-western, one son sounding just like Hank Williams, another yodeling, old man Zerwas laughing and full of fun, always loving music around him. The women gathered in the kitchen, smoking cigarettes, holding babies, gossiping. Checkers and cards were played in the living room, horseshoes and baseball in the backyard.

The fun, though, could quickly turn sour and angry. Stories abound about simmering grudges and resentments erupting at the turn of a word. Then the Zerwas siblings would throw right jabs and whatever else was handy. Once, one sister hauled off and punched another, then ripped her blouse. Despite the ferocity, the battling could stop as quickly as it started, for the Zerwases were close and tightly knit. After a fight, the one who threw the punch might show up with a beefsteak for his victim's black eye. They took pride in their family, and regularly gathered the sprawling clan together in rented halls for their parents' wedding anniversaries and in park gazebos for posed family portraits. They shot thousands of feet of home movies and pasted photographs into bulging albums. They baby-sat and brought presents to each other's children.

Lois was a force to reckon with at these family gatherings. When in good humor she was full of wisecracks, but her presence often tended to tone down the spontaneity. People were careful what they said and did around her, seeming almost afraid, for she could be cold, even censorious. Everyone always knew when she was about to appear, the word passing through the rooms like a warning. Some felt that she put on airs, as if she were special. In truth, she was, in a way. The family had to admire and respect Lois, for in their eyes she had married money, someone with a fine steady income, and they lived in tony Gardenette Park.

Like most of the Zerwases, both the men and the women, Lois dominated her mate in public. When Harold talked, she often cut him off, correcting his story. She told him when it was time to leave. Harold seemed afraid of Lois—when she addressed him, he came to attention, and when she told him to shut up, he closed his mouth. Most of the time he sat in the background, his legs crossed, as if trying to avoid aggravating her. Those who had visited the Jurgens home swore Harold was not allowed to use the front door or the upstairs bathroom. If Harold wanted to go to a ball game after work, it was said he couldn't go home first, for he'd never be allowed back out.

All the same, Lois seemed more refined than anyone else in her family. When one distant cousin came to family gatherings, she always sought out Lois right away, finding her the most interesting and pleasant of the bunch. Sometimes, Lois would cry her eyes out to a relative about a story she'd read in the newspaper—tragic stories about a child getting abused or hurt in an accident, or a mother losing her whole family in a car accident. Knowing that her siblings were poor, she brought their children presents on all sorts of occasions. When babies were born she was right there, bringing a gift and holding the newborn, loving them with hugs. When her brother Jerome's wife Rose had to reenter the hospital just days after giving birth to their second child, Lois came straight over and cared for the baby for a full week.

All things considered, Lois did not seem unusual, either in the colorful, rough-edged Zerwas clan or on Gardenette Drive. There were far weirder neighbors on that street. The block's crazy lady, in the eyes of the neighborhood children, lived in a white frame house in the middle of the street. She'd throw pancake breakfasts for the neighborhood, her husband yelling at her all the while about her cooking. Once she went out to the mailbox naked but for a mink coat, which blew open, leaving her bare for all the world to see. She'd dress her kids in snowsuits in the middle of summer, then holler when they'd peel them off and run around naked. When older children in the neighborhood baby-sat for her, she paid them with unpainted plaques of the Last Supper instead of money. After her husband cut out, she left her four children in the house alone one winter day and went to Alaska, searching for another mate.

The Jurgenses, by contrast, seemed simply quiet and private, keeping to themselves far more than did their neighbors. They were not invisible, though. Lois regularly gardened out in her well-tended front yard, and there, in her shorts, she was a vision that gave more than one man pause. At thirty-one she still had delicately attractive features, slim legs, a full rounded body and thick dark hair. One neighbor across the street, a researcher for 3M, couldn't take his eyes off her.

The Jurgenses, though, still were childless.

"I was in this big house all alone," Lois said some years later, "and when I would be around children and come home to this empty house, it bothered me."

CHAPTER 4

All That a Child Could Desire

The Jurgenses had been living on South Gardenette Drive for three years when word reached them, in early 1960, of a pregnant waitress working at a coffee shop on County Road F who intended to give up her newborn for adoption. Just how that information got to them would later be a matter for considerable speculation, but whatever the source, the news offered great promise—a newborn, and no need for formal approvals. Although frowned upon by government agencies, private placements in Minnesota were not illegal then.

The prospect of adopting a baby outside official channels was particularly appealing to the Jurgenses because of troubles they'd been having recently with the Ramsey County welfare department. In 1959, four years after the Bureau of Catholic Charities rejection, Lois and Harold had applied to the county to adopt a child, only to encounter resistance there as well, from caseworkers who found Lois rigid. Then, when the county finally offered them a two-year-old boy—the available records don't reveal how this happened, or whether caseworkers at this point knew of Lois's psychiatric problems—the Jurgenses turned him down, saying he was too old and seemed handicapped.

So Harold, seeing the chance to bypass the authorities, did not hesitate. Once armed with the name of the waitress, he quickly contacted an attorney. Just that suddenly and easily, the Jurgenses became parents.

The baby boy was born on June 22, 1960, and four days later, on the afternoon of June 26, he was delivered to the Jurgens home on South Gardenette Drive. Harold and Lois gave him the name Robert, in honor of Harold's father, and outfitted one of their two extra bedrooms with a crib. Despite resistance from welfare department officials, who disliked such arrangements and recalled their negative experiences with Lois, the Ramsey County juvenile court approved the placement after the fact. Harold and Lois finally had a child.

Those visiting the Jurgenses at this time found their life resolutely domestic. Robert was a somewhat sickly baby, quiet and relatively inactive, so he did not greatly disrupt the household routine. As the months unfolded, Harold took delight in playing with him on the living room floor while Lois watched television in the dining area, particularly "I Love Lucy."

Looking closer, of course, some might have found it odd that the Jurgens home, despite the addition of a child, remained immaculately clean and precisely ordered. Others might have thought it unusual that the Jurgenses taught their baby prayers—Harold by now had converted to Catholicism, so from the time Robert was nine months old, the Jurgenses made a point of reciting their morning, evening and before-meal invocations in front of him. It is difficult to say just how many people would have felt as proud as the Jurgenses did when Robert, at age one and a half, began making the sign of the cross.

In truth, although delighted with Robert, Harold and Lois still felt incomplete. In the year 1961, Harold Jurgens earned $9,150— $168 a week plus overtime—and found that easily sufficient to support his family. They had an empty bedroom, and Harold was forty, Lois almost thirty-seven, both nearing the point where they'd be considered too old to adopt. It was unlikely that private channels would so easily provide another baby like Robert, at least not without a long wait. So on the day after Christmas in 1961, the Jurgenses again applied to the Ramsey County welfare department, seeking to adopt a second child.

This time around, Harold and Lois would need official approval.

March 1, 1962, a Thursday, was bitterly cold in White Bear Lake, the morning temperatures plummeting to minus twenty-five degrees, easily shattering the record for the day. Gerane Rekdahl, a Ramsey County welfare department caseworker, was shivering when the

Jurgenses greeted her at their front door and ushered her inside. Shedding her mittens and scarves, the caseworker looked about.

The furnishings, she noted approvingly, were of good quality but comfortable. The floors were hardwood, the kitchen tiled. Harold had converted a breezeway off the kitchen into a room, making for a large open family, dining and cooking area, and Robert's toys were confined to a corner of this space. A large bass fiddle occupied one corner of the living room, a piano another corner. Gerane thought the Jurgens home quite lovely.

Next she turned her attention to the couple before her. Harold was tall and rather swarthy, with dark brown hair and eyes; Lois was fairly attractive, although quite short and now a trifle on the chubby side. As they began to talk, the difference in their personalities became clear—Harold seemed friendly and in his rambling conversation almost too talkative, obviously eager to please, while Lois was not as openly amiable. In fact, Gerane sensed that Lois considered her presence to be an imposition.

Robert, twenty months old then, was brought forward to meet the stranger, and to Gerane he seemed happy and outgoing, not at all afraid. She also thought him quite well disciplined, for when Harold and Lois sent him off to play with his toys, he did so without protest.

Standing in Lois and Harold's living room that March 1, Gerane was an eager, open-faced young woman of twenty-seven who possessed considerably more idealism than experience. She had a bachelor's degree in social work and sixteen months of casework under her belt, and she was a good dozen years younger than the Jurgenses. Having seen too many babies without homes, she very much wanted children to be with parents. She'd grown up in southwest Minnesota, part of the hard-core Scandinavian farm belt, and this circumstance had shaped her. People living around her hometown of Clarkfield were friendly and caring, but private, not inclined to reveal themselves or intrude on other folks' affairs. Stoicism was a virtue, not a limitation to one's character. In those days, Gerane thought well of people, and tended to blame herself whenever she entertained contrary thoughts. She'd become a social worker to help people, not expose them.

All the same, Gerane would later recall that she had arrived at the Jurgens home not with naive enthusiasm, but with a negative bias because of the Jurgenses' poor record in the welfare department files. There was, to begin with, Lois's psychiatric history—a catalog of depression and hospitalizations and shock treatments that department officials by now were well aware of, although it remains uncertain whether they had Dr. Goldstein's bleak diagnosis from the Mayo Clinic. There were also three different discouraging reports from the welfare department intake workers who'd interviewed Lois each time the Jurgenses had tried to adopt a child. Gerane had drawn this couple not because she was a novice, but precisely because she was known as good with difficult cases. She had arrived on South Gardenette Drive prepared for trouble.

As the three settled in the living room, Lois brought out coffee and cake on a tray. The Jurgenses' conversation began with talk of Robert and how happy they all were together. When Gerane raised the issue of Robert's unsanctioned placement, Lois became defensive.

"We may not have anything else, but we have love," Lois said.

"We turned to a private placement as a last resort," Harold offered, trying to dilute his wife's argumentative tone.

Gerane chose her words carefully, for she knew it would be difficult to establish a rapport and hear the Jurgenses' true feelings if they felt she or the department was condemning them.

"Independent placements do not necessarily turn out bad every time," she said cautiously, "but it is much safer and happier to adopt through an agency."

Gradually, the Jurgenses seemed to relax.

"We're anxious to go through a home study in the right way now," Lois said. "We're looking forward to having a brother or sister for Robert. I think only children tend to become spoiled, and big families are much more fun. I was one of many brothers and sisters, and we always had a good time."

As the visit continued, certain themes began to repeat themselves in Lois's conversation—*Robert is so good . . . We love Robert so much . . . We're such great parents.* In time the claims sounded too insistent to Gerane—excessive, as if Lois had a need to see herself in a perfect light. When the tone intensified, expanding from insistence to righteousness and downright bragging, Gerane started to feel irritated. Despite the caseworker's natural goodwill, this lady turned her off.

All the same, Gerane labored to see the positive. The Jurgenses' home was quite attractive. They were churchgoers of the same faith. They had money and job security. Albeit with lukewarm reviews, they'd passed the intake screening, which usually weeds out the unacceptable cases. The department supervisor had told her to be objective and professional.

She would move slowly, Gerane decided, for this was a family with its share of defenses, but all in all, the Jurgenses had been acceptable for a first visit. They deserved a chance, after the anguish of not being able to have their own kids.

"I did feel that they related very well to me today," Gerane wrote in her log, "and the things we did discuss seemed to be done quite freely and openly."

When Gerane next called on the Jurgenses on April 19, she found Lois much more relaxed, dressed casually in a pair of pedal pushers and a blouse, and the house didn't seem so resolutely neat. Robert had just risen from a nap and Lois was dressing him. When they settled in the living room, he sat quietly on his mother's lap.

Gerane asked Lois to speak of her early life, and she did so readily. Her account now differed considerably from what she'd told Dr. Goldstein at the Mayo Clinic.

There were always lots of babies, Lois said. The siblings near her age were all boys, so she hung around with them and became something of a tomboy. She remembered living on a farm with lots of animals, playing in the woods and creating their own games, for they were too poor to buy anything. They always ate, for her mother gardened, canned and baked, and the boys loved to hunt and fish. There were hayrides, sleigh rides and picnics, the whole family together and happy. She didn't always have enough to wear, though, and she was teased at school for her "welfare clothes." Teachers tended to be a little harder on welfare children, Lois thought—at least, that was her personal opinion, and even if it weren't so, it certainly seemed that way to her at the time. She liked school well enough until the fourth grade, Lois said. Then she wore nail polish to class one day and the teacher got angry, and that year Lois flunked, even though most of her grades were Cs, but for the F in arithmetic. She didn't like school after that, and quit in the eighth grade.

Everyone in the family had duties. Lois's job from the time she was five had been to take the chairs out each week and scrub them, and by the time she was nine, she said, she was doing the whole family's ironing by herself. Her mother could not always make the children behave, but her father was strict. Yes, her dad definitely did have a leather strap that he used on them, but not very often. He was strict but quite fair, she said, although he did not like his daughters going out with boys. The children were taught to say their prayers, to say please, and to be seen but not heard.

"Give me an example of how he disciplined you," Gerane asked.

Lois didn't need to search her memory for very long.

"One summer day when I was fourteen, I quit ironing because it was so hot and started walking down the road. When my father called after me, I talked back, telling him it was too hot. He got quite angry, spanked me and told me to get back to the ironing."

"How did you feel?" Gerane asked.

"I felt angry with him then, but later realized that he had been right," Lois said firmly. "The ironing was my job to do."

Gerane pressed the issue, but Lois remained adamant.

"Dad had lots of kids and they got what they deserved," she insisted. "They were brought up with right values. Dad did use a strap but it was no big deal. I don't hold anything against him. He has been very fair with me."

Gerane was good at making people feel comfortable precisely because she basically liked them, and now she found within herself a part that could like Lois. Over the course of the hour-and-a-half session, she'd seen Lois relax and laugh when talking of the activities she shared with Harold and Robert, and she'd felt in Lois a soft sadness when speaking about her life without children. Gerane believed Lois had come a long way toward making an adequate adjustment in her life. Her psychiatric problems probably stemmed from her childhood deprivation, but this was no drawback—she was trying to rise above all that, she was trying to make it in the world. Gerane was rooting for her.

"In today's interview I felt that a great deal was accomplished in the way of getting Mrs. J to open up and talk," she wrote in her log. "By the end of the interview she was quite relaxed, was laughing readily and easily, and was relating to me in quite a positive manner."

When Gerane arrived to interview Lois again on June 14, she found her outside in the yard working on her flower garden under a warm sun. Down the street, a dozen neighborhood kids were playing kick ball in the road, and Gardenette Park, a dozen years old and now abundant with maturing trees, seemed to Gerane comfortable and beckoning. The caseworker and the Jurgenses had passed through two seasons together.

Lois seemed even more relaxed today, not at all defensive. The two women settled in the living room with cups of coffee, Lois in a straight-back chair, Gerane on the sofa. Their conversation meandered for a while, touching on matters of discipline and toilet training and feeding.

Sipping her coffee, Gerane steeled herself. Today she had to raise the still-unspoken matter of Lois's psychiatric treatment. This kind of questioning upset her, for she didn't enjoy hurting people or prying in that way.

"We have information that you've been treated for depression," Gerane said, as casually as she could manage. "We were wondering about that."

Lois smiled.

"I was under stress because my husband's sterile. Life was the same old thing before Robert. I worked myself to death before and that's why I was in the hospital. Getting Robert helped so much. Life is real full now and I'm happy."

Gerane wasn't that well-tutored in psychological matters, but still, she couldn't entirely buy Lois's explanation.

"Tell me a little bit more about your early family life," Gerane said. "Didn't your mother have a hard time keeping the home clean all the time with so many children?"

"We didn't have much to eat or wear," Lois answered quickly, "but I remember that our house was always clean when I was little."

"Was it?" Gerane pushed. The caseworker had a report in her file suggesting otherwise.

Lois's smile vanished now—in fact, all expression drained from her face. She sat stiffly.

"Yes, the home was always quite clean," Lois insisted. "The family was very close . . . Two of my brothers now drink too much, but my father and mother do not drink . . . Oh sure, there were quite a few arguments with that many children in the family, but never any delinquency . . ."

Lois was talking without emotion, her tone flat, almost a monotone.

". . . of course, the children were left pretty much on their own, and I had to care for the younger ones and not continue my own education . . . I did resent that a bit, and how I was teased in school. . . . But my parents love me and I love them and my brothers and sisters. My parents were good to us . . . They did what they could . . ."

It would not be accurate to say that the message of Lois's words entirely escaped Gerane. She heard the repressed anger beneath the glowing family portrait, but in the end, she chose to see Lois's response in a positive light. Lois wants to create a different life for herself, Gerane reasoned. She wants to deny her past. Why not?

"I felt that in today's interview Mrs. J opened up a great deal and tried to be as truthful as possible with me," the caseworker wrote in her log. "She seemed able to discuss some of her weaknesses and certainly did not become too nervous or upset when speaking of her mental depression of several years ago."

On August 27, Gerane collected recommendations from two of the Jurgenses' neighbors. Gladys DeMars, one door to the east, saw Lois almost every day, if only casually out in the yard, and she thought the Jurgenses friendly, acceptable people who'd be very good parents to another child. Dorothy Engfer, two doors to the east, provided Gerane a three-page letter that offered even higher praise—"Harold is friendly, helpful, hardworking, loving to his family and devoted to the child they now have, a good provider and dependable . . . Mrs. J has a delightful sense of humor, is devoted to her husband, church, home, has always been quite busy with her yard and house, is a good listener and very understanding of others. They are both fond of music, gardening, home and family . . ."

On the morning of August 30, Gerane visited the Jurgenses' priest, Father Bernard Reiser, at the St. Mary's of the Lake Catholic church.

St. Mary's light gray limestone belfry on Fourth and Bald Eagle, two blocks from the police station, soars above the surrounding neighborhood, the building's rough-hewn stone and symmetrical lines casting an image both rustic and contemporary. The church started in 1880 in a thirty-by-sixty-foot wooden building at Second and Bald Eagle—built for $1,000, the altar made of packing boxes and decorated with evergreens—then moved to its present location in 1897. Father Reiser had arrived in June of 1949 to become assistant pastor to Father Nicholas Finn.

The priest greeted Gerane in his small office with a firm, direct handshake. It was, in fact, a powerful handshake—Reiser's thick forearms looked more like a laborer's than a priest's. He had a warm, open Irish face, but his eyes were more knowing than beatific. He seemed sure of himself.

Reiser had married most of the Zerwases and buried a few, and he figured he knew the family as well as he did any in White Bear Lake. To him, Lois was the one child in the clan who stood out with more class and culture and polish than the others, always well-dressed, well-groomed, gracious, good-spirited and cheerful when she approached, always a smile, never a long face. Reiser had first written a letter of recommendation for the Jurgenses in April of 1959, when they initially applied to Ramsey County, and had served as a reference when they adopted Robert. In response to Gerane's questions, he spoke casually and directly.

The Zerwas family, he said, were all "lazy and carefree, with the exception of a couple of them." The parents' home was a "shambles," and "old John Zerwas is just plain lazy." None of them were active in church.

Lois and Harold Jurgens were the exceptions, he said. They were one of his better church families, very sincere in their faith and active in the parish. Harold was a hardworking man with lots of ambition. Lois was to be commended for raising herself a little higher than the standards the rest of her family set for themselves. Lois received a lot of criticism from her family because she had done so much better in life than they had, but she had worked hard for what she had in life and had a right to feel proud.

"But Lois tends to defend her family and paints a glowing picture of her childhood," Gerane pointed out.

"Of course," Reiser said. "She feels a loyalty to her family and likes to make them appear as good as she can. This is the reason she probably tends to build them up."

Reiser very strongly favored the Jurgenses having another child. He knew of Lois's mental problems but thought them not serious, something she had recovered from. She loved Robert.

"They would give the child a happy, religious, secure home," the priest said, "which is all that any child could desire."

Much later, Gerane would say Father Reiser was the conclusive element in her study.

"I really did believe in Father Reiser . . . In my estimates he was the strongest reference. He knew them so well. I gave lots of credence to him as a religious person who knows people . . ."

On the same day she met Father Reiser, Gerane again visited Harold and Lois at their home. The day had turned sticky, typical for August in Minnesota, with brief, recurrent thunderstorms and a temperature near eighty. As usual, the Jurgens house was spotless, but for some of Robert's toys strewn about. Lois was anxious to show Gerane her living room, for she recently had recovered all the furniture.

"Doesn't it make the room look much better?" Lois asked. "And it was much cheaper than having to buy all new furniture."

Gerane labored to suppress her vague unease. She surely wouldn't want Lois as her mother, but she felt that thought was unfair, and no basis for a judgment.

"You are going to be approved for a child," Gerane told the Jurgenses.

Lois and Harold both smiled broadly and offered their thanks. Talk turned to what they hoped for in a child. They wanted a healthy Caucasian of at least average intelligence, they said. They did not care about the sex, but they definitely wanted the child to be as young as possible, preferably under the age of one.

There was one other thing. They wanted a Catholic.

CHAPTER 5

Dennis

Sauk Centre, a village of thirty-seven hundred that stands ninety-five miles to the northwest of the Twin Cities in central Minnesota, is best known as the model for the fictional Gopher Prairie in Sinclair Lewis's *Main Street*. This is a dubious distinction at best, considering that Lewis's heroine, Carol Kennicott, upon arriving in Gopher Prairie, found "no dignity in it nor any hope of greatness," but the town at least can claim a famous author for its own—Sinclair Lewis was born in Sauk Centre in 1885. Seventy-six years later, as it happened, Sauk Centre provided the setting for another birth of some import.

There, at St. Michael's Hospital on December 6, 1961, twenty days before the Jurgenses first filed their adoption application with the Ramsey County welfare department, an eight-and-a-half-pound, twenty-one-inch baby boy entered the world without complications. The father, Dennis McIntyre, was an unmarried nineteen-year-old sometime construction worker from St. Cloud, an Irish-Swedish Catholic, six feet tall and 185 pounds, with light brown hair and hazel eyes. The mother was an unmarried seventeen-year-old named Jerry Ann Puckett, an attractive if troubled girl of Danish-German background. At five feet five inches and 160 pounds, with long blond hair and blue eyes, she was an overweight but well-built young woman with striking facial features. Jerry named her baby Dennis Craig Puckett. The young mother was Protestant by background, a member of the Free Church in Bloomington, Minnesota, but just then she was planning to take instruction in the Roman Catholic faith, so nine days after his birth, Dennis was baptized a Catholic.

Jerry came from Maryville, Missouri, and had a father and stepmother living nearby in Savage, Minnesota, where her father operated a fleet of three trucks. Jerry, though, was confined at the Home School for Girls in Sauk Centre, having run into trouble with juvenile authorities in the rootless, disjointed years that followed her mother's departure when she was three. Jerry was of average intelligence and had completed the tenth grade. Those who dealt with her considered her somewhat hostile and sullen, although they noticed her attitude changed whenever she was met with any degree of warmth or acceptance. She was erratic and moody, at one moment comfortable and pleased with herself, at the next giving unrestrained voice to her considerable anger. Caseworkers thought her reluctant to undertake emotional commitments because of her traumatic and short-lived past relationships. They regarded her as unhappy and emotionally immature, full of desire for a dependent relationship with a mother figure.

Jerry's legal residence when not confined at the Sauk Centre reform school was in Scott County, to the southwest of the Twin Cities, so her fate and Dennis's fell to authorities in that region's welfare department. Jerry wanted to keep her baby, but the Scott County caseworkers thought her unlikely to be an adequate caretaker. After some debate, but with Jerry's reluctant consent, Dennis that December 15 was discharged from the hospital and taken to the foster home of Mr. and Mrs. William Martens, an elderly couple in rural New Prague. Termination of Jerry's parental rights took place in the Scott County Juvenile Court four months later, on April 18, 1962.

There is in the Scott County records a description of Dennis in his foster home written in late May of that year. He is solidly built, with blue eyes and blond hair. His foster mother, Mrs. Martens, beams when she talks about him, calling him "a real nice baby" and a "clown," for he always laughs at himself or at other people when they are around. He is extremely strong, already able to turn himself over. He has no teeth yet, but they are coming—he's drooling. He naps in both the forenoon and afternoon and eats well.

In Dennis's brief life there were several fateful moments when his destiny could have been changed. The first came now. Soon after authorities took her baby from her, Jerry dropped her plans to convert to Catholicism, but by then Dennis was already registered as Catholic on the state adoption rolls, and Catholic he remained. This made him somewhat unusual—at that time there were very few Catholic babies in the state registry, since private agencies such as the Bureau of Catholic Charities handled most of those placements.

So the official notice sent on November 2, 1962, from Elizabeth Tillotson, a Minnesota state adoption unit social worker, to Dwight V. Dixon, director of the Scott County welfare department, was not an entirely random event. The state department of public welfare, in its effort to facilitate cross-county adoptions, had made a match between Scott County DPW file number 96962 and Ramsey County DPW file number 72407. The agency had a prospective adoptive home for a Catholic child who had then been residing in a Scott County foster home for almost one year. The child was Dennis Puckett. The adoptive parents were Harold and Lois Jurgens.

"Although we have some reservations as to the suitability of this home for Dennis," wrote the state social worker, "we are referring it to you for your consideration as it is the only Catholic home available at this time. If you do not wish to proceed in this matter, feel assured that we will continue to search for new homes for this little boy."

On the morning of November 28, Gerane Rekdahl drove twenty minutes southwest from St. Paul to the Scott County welfare department office in the town of Shakopee. The purpose of her journey was a conference called to discuss the possible placement of one Dennis Puckett in the Jurgens adoptive home.

Present at the meeting when she arrived were Dwight Dixon, the Scott County welfare department director; Laura Chamberlain, a Scott County field representative; and an older woman, a Scott County caseworker introduced to Gerane as Miss Donnelly. The Scott County people began by describing Dennis: He was an ideal little baby who should move into placement very easily, as he was afraid of no one. He was very active, quite alert and curious. He needed to be watched all the time.

Gerane, listening and looking at the documents, felt concerned. Dennis was within days of being one year old, and the Jurgenses had wanted a younger child—Lois had been quite rigid about that. Gerane pointed out the problem, but the Scott County officials thought it unimportant, and Gerane finally agreed. It did seem a good placement, and besides, it was improbable that the Jurgenses would be offered another Catholic baby in the near future. Gerane saw nothing in Dennis's background that indicated the Jurgenses couldn't accept him. He was healthy and normal.

Then something else aroused her concern. Leafing through the Scott County summary sheets, she noticed a paragraph about religion:

> Jerry Puckett at the present time . . . has no intention of join-
> ing the Catholic Church. She is Protestant by background . . .
> It would be our understanding that the child is Protestant
> and that if Jerry had retained custody of Dennis she would
> have brought him up in the Protestant faith.

"What is this?" Gerane asked. "We don't place across religious lines, unless at the request of the birth parent. I thought Dennis was being matched to the Jurgenses because he was Catholic."

No, no, don't worry, that was a mistake in the report, the Scott County officials said. It's been cleared up.

That afternoon, Miss Donnelly drove Gerane to the Martenses' foster home in New Prague to meet Dennis. He was sleeping when they arrived, and Mrs. Martens went to wake him up. Gerane, seated in the living room, looked up a moment later to see a husky, smiling, blond-haired toddler scoot out from a bedroom. She held back, remaining seated, for she was accustomed to young kids being crabby after awakening and fearful of strangers. To her surprise, though, Dennis came straight to her without hesitation and scrambled onto her lap, friendly and outgoing, babbling and showing her his toys. Gerane thought him extremely appealing—such beautiful blue eyes, so spontaneous and sparkly, so exuberant.

Mrs. Martens, her arms crossed over her ample midsection, laughed with appreciation. "He'll go to anyone and has never been shy a day in his life," she said. "He's a little wild one. He never stops from morning to night. He's a good child, not deliberately bad, but he does get into things easily. He keeps us on the go."

Gerane looked about her in the living room. There was a gate blocking access to the kitchen. Most everything that Dennis might harm had been put up beyond reach—the room was filled with toys, a crib and playpen.

Gerane and Miss Donnelly tried to take some photos of Dennis with a Polaroid camera, but neither was adept at its operation, so the pictures kept turning out poorly. Dennis grinned throughout this process, trying to talk to the visitors, coming to them over and over to show them a book or take back a toy. When Gerane picked him up, Dennis laughed all the more. He seemed to her downright jolly.

Gerane decided she would call Lois and Harold, and then inform Scott County of when the Jurgenses wanted to see the child—that is, if they wanted to see him at all.

When Gerane reached Harold late that day, he seemed quite excited over the description of Dennis and not the least concerned that the boy was a bit older than they'd wanted. So the next morning, November 29, the Jurgenses met Gerane at the Ramsey County welfare office in St. Paul for a preplacement interview. As they settled in their chairs, Lois spoke.

"We're rather disappointed in the child's age," she said, "but wanted to hear more about him."

Gerane looked at Harold. He glanced away, saying nothing.

Gerane related what she knew of Dennis from the Scott County referral summary and from her own observations in the foster home. When she mentioned that Dennis was quite active, Lois leaned forward.

"He doesn't sound very well-behaved. Robert was leaving things alone at the age of one . . . Does he look like Robert? Could they be brothers?"

They had the same coloring, Gerane said, but Dennis was larger-boned and huskier. That could happen with natural siblings.

"No," Lois said, after studying Gerane's photos of Dennis. "He doesn't look very much at all like Robert."

"I don't think you are ever going to get a child that will look exactly like Robert," Gerane said. "If this is what you expected, we probably could never find a child for you."

"I didn't mean the child should look exactly like Robert," Lois responded. "I just hoped he'd look like Robert's brother." She pulled from her purse photos of Robert and held them next to the pictures of Dennis, but still appeared disappointed.

Gerane again looked at Harold. He remained silent.

What about the background of Dennis's parents? Lois wondered. What was their size? What did they look like? Did they have musical talents? Education?

Gerane related what she could, then asked if the Jurgenses wanted to see the boy.

Yes, definitely, they wanted to see the boy and give it a try. Lois, though, looked worried, even frightened.

"What would happen if we decide to reject the child? Would we get another chance? Do we have to accept Dennis or get no child at all?"

"That's not how it works," Gerane answered. "If you continue to have negative feelings, we and the state would feel it best for you not to take the child."

"Yes," Lois said, "I know it wouldn't be good for us to take the child if we continue to have negative feelings after seeing him. But is it sure we'd get another child? Is that sure?"

Gerane couldn't provide such flat assurance. Their name would be returned to the state register and they would be considered for other children, Gerane said. But they were Catholic, and there were very few Catholic babies on the register, so it was a high possibility they'd wait for quite a long time. She didn't want this to influence their decision, Gerane said, but in all truthfulness, the reality of this situation had to be told to them.

The caseworker by now had a queasy feeling in her stomach. She wished Lois would just say no to this placement. That was how her agency saw its role—it highlighted issues, talked out the angles, counseled, then let the parents make the decisions.

With Lois and Harold sitting before her, Gerane picked up the phone and called Miss Donnelly in Scott County. The Jurgenses, the two social workers decided, could visit Dennis that same afternoon.

When the Jurgenses arrived in New Prague hours later, Dennis rushed to them with the same enthusiasm he offered all strangers. Soon Harold was playing with him on Mrs. Martens's living room floor, and later, the couple took Dennis for a drive. The visit seemed successful, but something about it nonetheless troubled Miss Donnelly after the Jurgenses had left. Lois just had never seemed to respond to Dennis at all. In fact, upon further reflection, Miss Donnelly realized Lois had never once even touched him.

When Gerane called the Jurgenses the next morning, Lois didn't sound enthusiastic.

They were still undecided, she said, but frankly weren't hopeful. They planned to decide over the weekend. She wasn't impressed with his looks.

"He's sloppy fat," Lois said. She had other complaints. His navel stuck way out, "purple and awful looking." He didn't look at all like them. He was so large. His eyes weren't the same color as Robert's. His "nationality" was wrong. He really needed to lose weight. There might be something wrong with his feet—his shoe size was so wide.

"If you decide against Dennis," Gerane said, "and another child is picked for you, that child may not look like Robert either. It may be very hard to match the two exactly."

She didn't really want to appear too fussy, Lois replied, since she knew they might never get a child that way. But she just didn't feel as though Robert and Dennis fit together well at all. Dennis's aggressiveness and "wild behavior" were extremely unlike Robert. He would "manhandle Robert." How had Dennis been raised so far?

It wasn't so much his upbringing as his inherent personality, Gerane suggested. He was just a more active child, and no matter how much anyone tried to discipline him he would probably always be more active than Robert.

"Children can be trained to behave themselves," Lois said.

"Dennis is still fairly young to be so disciplined," Gerane countered. She hesitated, considering her next words. "If there are so many negative feelings, it might be wise to turn the child down and go back on the state register," she said finally.

Lois wavered.

"We'll let you know on Monday."

On December 3, the phone rang on Gerane's desk. It was Harold Jurgens. "When can we get our boy?" he asked.

Gerane was amazed, for she'd been certain they were going to reject the child.

"Does this mean you want to take Dennis?"

"Yes . . . Definitely, yes."

Gerane tried to discuss his wife's objections but Harold ignored her questions. Dennis was a real nice boy and could fit into their home just fine, he said. They'd talked to various people and had now decided they could take him.

Two days later, determined to force the issues that worried her, Gerane visited the Jurgenses at their home. "Our agency and Scott County are both a little concerned as to the negative feelings you've expressed toward this child," she said. "Perhaps this really is not the child for you."

The Jurgenses seemed to her hesitant and defensive now.

Yes, Dennis had a few problems, but he was a child who needed a home, Harold said. And they definitely wanted to have another child. Dennis could fit into their home.

Lois appeared even more conflicted. We're not getting any younger, she said. We know the agency doesn't place babies with people over forty, so if we don't take Dennis we'll probably never get another one.

Gerane searched for the right response. She felt angry at the state for making this referral, then leaving the ball in the county's court. She wished the Jurgenses would just turn the boy down. Should she lie now about the prospects of getting offered another child? Should she be nebulous? No, she reasoned, she couldn't lie, that just wasn't right, that was not her nature. She had to answer directly.

"It is our general rule not to place babies with those over forty," Gerane said, "but children could be placed."

Age was the main problem with Dennis, Lois said. If he were just younger.

"Perhaps it's best for you not to take the child." Gerane was almost pleading now. "It's possible that another child will come along that would fit much better into your home."

Just then, Robert woke from a nap. Lois left the living room to get him, but did not soon return. The minutes ticked by. Gerane could hear Robert and Lois in the back bedroom, then in the bathroom. They were taking a great deal of time, much more than Gerane thought necessary. It seemed apparent to her that Lois, feeling uncertain what to say, did not want to rejoin their conversation.

When Lois did return at last, talk was difficult, for Robert was crabby and whining, insisting that he sit on Lois's lap, hugging her and refusing to get off. Harold tried to make the boy laugh by teasing him, but Robert just grew mad and told him to stop. Gerane finally interjected.

"Do you want Dennis or not?" she asked, point-blank.

Lois gathered herself for a reply.

"Even with all the negatives, I really don't feel as though we want to turn the baby down. We'd at least like to give it a try."

Gerane, searching for an escape hatch, proposed a week-long trial visit. When Harold and Lois readily agreed, the caseworker left the house feeling somewhat relieved. At least there will be a pre-placement period, Gerane told herself. Maybe they'll decide against taking the kid.

On December 7, 1962, President John Kennedy triumphantly announced the removal of the last of the Soviet missiles and the nation heaved a collective sigh of relief as the Cuban missile crisis waned. In St. Paul that day, Jay North, the pint-sized blond whirlwind star of television's popular "Dennis the Menace" show, played visiting host at the city's annual children's Christmas party. That afternoon, winter took a strong hold in the Twin Cities region, as light snow flurries dusted the streets while temperatures dipped into the teens. Because Harold had already taken off so much time from work, Lois traveled by herself to Scott County to pick up their visitor. In the early afternoon, Dennis arrived for the first time at the Jurgens home on South Gardenette Drive. He weighed twenty pounds, and he was exactly one year and one day old.

Lois sounded happy and positive when Gerane called her five days later. She was having a rough time because of Dennis's energy and Robert's jealousy, but they were also having fun, she reported. Dennis seemed quite happy and had already adjusted. He did wake up now and then at night and cry out, but this, she felt, was because he was used to getting a bottle in the middle of the night. She wasn't going to give this to him. Dennis really never had any training, or a chance to prove that he could be a good boy, she said, but they would try to give him this training and restrict him from getting into things in the house. Dennis did still have "a lot of sloppy fat on him," but she was going to change that with more vegetables and meat and less milk.

"Does this mean you're going to keep Dennis?"

Lois couldn't say. She and Harold needed more than a week's visit—they wanted more like two weeks to a month.

"Between washing diapers and feeding babies," Lois replied, laughing, "I don't know."

The next day, Lois took Dennis to the family's pediatrician, Dr. E. Dale Cummings, who for some time had been caring for Robert. Cummings was a round butterball of a man, with a jowly bulldog face, triple-thick eyeglasses, hunched shoulders and a belt that rode high over his round belly. Cummings thought the Jurgenses were terribly nice and concerned parents, for they asked questions and cared.

Examining Dennis, what struck Cummings most was the stark contrast between this boy and the Jurgenses' other son, Robert. Here was a robust, healthy kid, nothing abnormal at all, while Robert was a puny, sickly child, constantly ill. You put Robert somewhere, he stayed. Dennis, by contrast, was a normal, active kid. In the examining room, he kept running around and jabbering away. Friendly is the word that occurred to Cummings. Some kids smile at you, play with your tie and stethoscope, laugh. Other little kids scream, cry, want their mommy. Dennis was definitely the first type. A little joy, Cummings thought. The kind of patient who makes the day go by better.

"What about that protruding belly button?" Lois asked.

Cummings looked and shrugged. "A mild navel hernia . . . No big deal."

When Harold called Gerane five days later to say they had decided to keep Dennis, she felt both surprised and scared. She conferred with her supervisor, Betty Hunt, and for a time, sitting together, the two women hung on the edge of a decision that could go either way. In the end, as Gerane saw it, they chose yes and hopefulness over no and denial.

"It sounds cold," she would say later, "but it was the luck of the draw."

On December 27, Harold came to Gerane's office to sign the adoptive placement agreement, since Lois was home sick with the flu. They were now quite happy with Dennis and couldn't imagine ever giving him up, he said. They'd really grown quite attached to him.

On January 3, Gerane visited the Jurgens home to finalize the placement with Lois's signature and to conduct her first postplacement interview. The house, perfectly clean and neat, was still decorated for Christmas, and Lois looked happy—for the first time in a long time, Gerane saw her smiling and laughing, which made for a pleasant sight. In fact, Gerane was amazed at the change in her.

Dennis and Robert were standing in the kitchen, both dressed in little overalls and sweaters and looking terribly cute. Dennis smiled and immediately came to her, starting to jabber, trying so hard to talk. Robert hung back, watching, keeping his eye on his eager, noisy brother.

Dennis was sleeping through the night without a bottle now, Lois reported. In fact, she had taken him off the bottle entirely, and had also cut back his carbohydrates, for he loved to eat.

Dennis did look slimmer, Gerane thought.

By the end of the interview, she was feeling much better about the placement. There would be a one-year probationary period in the Jurgens home before the formal adoption, after all, during which the county retained official custody of Dennis.

"I certainly had the feeling that the J's had made a very great adjustment . . ." the caseworker wrote in her log. "There were great doubts as to whether or not they could accept this child, but after today's visit I really felt quite comfortable . . ."

After Lois signed the adoptive placement agreement, Gerane back-dated it by one day, so officially, Dennis was placed in the Jurgens home on January 2, 1963.

In all, Gerane made five postplacement visits to the Jurgens home over the course of 1963, and what she saw each time left her increasingly encouraged. Dennis would come running to the door to greet her, babbling and showing her his toys, never subdued or crabby, and he'd run just as readily to Lois. When he started talking real words, he would sing nursery rhymes and tell Gerane all about his toys. At each visit Lois seemed to grow increasingly casual and relaxed, both in her manner and the appearance of her house. She no longer prepared for Gerane's visit or complained of Dennis.

Gerane felt relieved. This placement, she thought, seems to be working.

She felt that way even after her phone rang on August 28. Lois Jurgens was calling, sounding a little upset. Dennis had burned himself with some very hot water, she said, and the doctor felt he might need some sort of skin graft. The burning had happened seven days before, on August 21, and since that time Dennis had been at Mounds Park Hospital.

Gerane expressed some concern that Lois hadn't called before. Lois explained that she'd been trying to call but had been unable to reach her. Since nothing had been done to Dennis yet they felt it wasn't that urgent.

What happened? Gerane asked.

Dennis had wet his diapers, Lois explained, and she'd taken them off and set him in the sink to wash him. She'd run into the other room for a clean diaper and just in that minute or so that she was gone, Dennis had turned on the hot water tap, and had severely burned himself. The burn was on and around his penis. At first, Lois hadn't noticed anything wrong because Dennis didn't cry or complain until later, when he began holding himself and saying that he had an "owie." It was then Lois looked, found the genital area growing red, and called the doctor.

Lois wondered whether Gerane should phone the physician, a Dr. Roy Peterson, to give the county's consent for skin grafting if it proved necessary. Lois sounded nervous, and Gerane felt she was probably upset for fear of what the agency would think of such a thing happening to Dennis.

"I tried to assure her that these things happen in any family," Gerane wrote in her log, "that this is something that cannot be helped."

When Nancy Dahl, a physical therapist at Mounds Park Hospital, first saw her new young patient, he seemed so small—a tiny toddler standing in an oversized crib. Dennis then weighed twenty-three pounds, just three pounds more than when he had first arrived at the Jurgens home nine months before. He stood whimpering, his legs spread apart, without a diaper, for his scrotum, red and angry, was swollen to the size of a tennis ball. Nancy Dahl had never seen such a grotesque or unusual injury—just the penis and scrotum so badly burned. She had to ease him slowly into a whirlpool for treatment twice a day. Dennis would cry out in pain, but once in, the waters seemed to soothe him.

Other nurses caring for Dennis in the hospital couldn't help but notice a number of bruises tattooing the small boy's body. Some were bothered enough about the markings to mention them to Dennis's attending physician, Dr. Peterson. Years later, the doctor would unhesitatingly recall the nurses' concerned comments, but the line of communication could not be traced further, past Peterson. Gerane Rekdahl had no recollection of the doctor talking about bruises, nor a written record. The phone conversation with Peterson that she did summarize in her log had a decidedly more benign tone:

> I called Dr. Peterson about Dennis Puckett and . . . the doctor indicated that Dennis does have a fairly severe burn and that he probably will need some skin grafting . . . Dennis would probably be in the hospital at least another two weeks before they would even be able to know if he needed grafting . . . I asked him about Dennis's condition and emotional behavior at the present time . . . He said that Dennis is in no pain and is receiving whirlpool baths each day to keep the area clean. He seems to be a well-adjusted and happy child . . . He has not been crying or frightened . . . Dennis receives much attention because of his outgoing personality. . . .

Gerane, under the burden of a heavy caseload, did not find the time to visit Dennis in the hospital. By the third week of September, it seemed not to matter—the doctors had decided skin grafts weren't needed and Dennis, home from the hospital, was soon dashing about as usual.

In early November, Gerane paid her first visit to the Jurgenses since the August burn incident. This was the only time she ever saw Lois not neatly dressed—she had been painting a bedroom and was wearing an old pair of pants and a sweatshirt splattered with paint. The two boys were running around playing, in good moods. Dennis's continued rapid development amazed Gerane. Now he was talking clearly in full sentences, still as friendly and sparkly as ever. The long hospital stay hadn't affected him at all.

He's so fearless and adventuresome, Lois reported, he'd just as soon climb the backyard fence and run through the streets and neighbors' yards if he had half a chance. He sometimes climbs to the top of the swing set and from there tries climbing to the trees and over the fence. This had thrown her because Robert never tried anything like that.

"Dennis is a wonderful little boy," Lois said, "but for the next child we hope to get one a little younger. Then perhaps we'll be able to teach a few things early enough."

Gerane paid her final postplacement visit to the Jurgenses a month later, on December 3. The nation was still reeling in shock from President Kennedy's assassination days before, and the initials L.B.J. were now topping the news pages. Lois and Harold were both home for the interview, and they opened the door together. They were anxious to complete the adoption, for they wanted to apply for a third child, a little girl this time.

Gerane pressed them a final time about the earlier negative feelings. They had absolutely no doubt, they said. They wanted Dennis and loved him deeply. They couldn't conceive of giving him up.

Gerane had known this family now for almost two years and several turns of season. She had felt more uncomfortable about the Jurgenses than about any other couple she'd visited in her brief career. Throughout the postplacement year, though, Dennis had continued to appear happy and healthy, and Lois had seemed increasingly relaxed. Harold now was earning $10,700 a year. Their house was worth nearly $19,000. They owned a 1963 Chevrolet pickup and a 1960 Ford Falcon station wagon. They carried assorted life insurance policies worth $10,000. Their investments and savings totaled $2,200. They owed $6,000 on the house and $930 on the truck. Gerane saw no basis to say they could not have this child.

The Jurgenses completed the necessary paperwork, and then Gerane left. Later that day, she wrote the final entry in her Jurgens case file: "Presently it appears as though the Jurgenses are providing very adequately for Dennis's physical, spiritual and emotional growth. The adoption should be approved at this time."

Two months later, in response to a petition filed by the Jurgenses, the Minnesota commissioner of public welfare prepared a one-page document. It read:

Dennis Craig Puckett, a minor child, the subject of the above entitled petition, was committed to the Commissioner of Public Welfare as a dependent child on April 18, 1962, from Scott County, and was placed for adoption in the home of the petitioners on January 2, 1963.

After investigation of the facts of the above entitled petition and of all the files and proceedings herein, the Commissioner of Public Welfare is satisfied that this petition should
be granted.

Now, therefore, as guardian of the subject of this petition,
the Commissioner of Public Welfare hereby consents to the
adoption of Dennis Craig Jurgens by Harold and Lois Jurgens, his wife.

Ove Wangensteen, an assistant commissioner in the DPW's division of child welfare, signed the document before two witnesses and
a notary public, then filed it with the Ramsey County juvenile court.
It was February 11, 1964. Dennis was two years and two months old.

CHAPTER 6

Halcyon Days

In December of 1963, just as Dennis's adoption was receiving final approval, Harold and Lois's neighbor Bob Brass was elected White Bear Lake chamber of commerce president for the coming year. The Brasses lived across the street from the Jurgenses and five houses up from the corner. Some one hundred yards separated their lives.

Bob Brass was thirty-eight then, but his appearance still suggested a schoolboy. He was tall and lean and earnest—almost anxious—with plain black frame glasses and a smooth, clean-shaven face that at times seemed to settle into a natural frown. He'd been proprietor of the local Ben Franklin five-and-dime store for eighteen years, and had resisted the temptation to modernize or update the shop on Fourth Street that he'd inherited from his father after the war. The Ben Franklin still looked like a traditional five-and-dime, with cluttered dusty rows of odd objects watched over by elderly lady clerks. Brass's office was a desk on a raised wooden platform at the rear of the store.

Brass knew just about everybody in town—he drank coffee next door at the bakery with the White Bear Lake police lieutenants, Dr. Roy Peterson's office abutted his store on the other side, and Father Reiser had presided at his marriage to Camille back in 1951. He'd lived in White Bear Lake since 1937, when his family moved from a Minneapolis suburb while he was in the sixth grade, and he'd left only once, at eighteen, to fight in World War II.

Air force training down South had provided a considerable education. Brass saw blacks living in shacks that he wouldn't trust with his garden tools, and once in Biloxi, on a bus, he felt painfully embarrassed as he watched young blacks being ushered to the back. Everyone in his troop swore—long, continual strings of oaths throughout the day, tossed off without thought or import. With a shock of recognition, Brass realized how isolated his life had been in White Bear Lake. All the same, when the war ended, he came directly home, and he had never afterward considered leaving.

As he prepared to assume the chamber of commerce's presidency at the start of 1964, Brass's thoughts turned to how much the town had changed in the eighteen years since he'd returned.

The early 1960s alone had been quite an exciting time, for as the decade began, city leaders looked about them and decided the town needed to get moving. The downtown White Bear Lake business district had been built in the late 1800s for horses and buggies. Buildings now were crumbling, there was no parking, retail stores were giving way to service outlets or vacant windows, and the doomsayers were talking of downtown becoming a nest of pawnshops and secondhand stores. Every month, another shopping center seemed to rise on the town's outskirts, until by 1960, four different ones were soaking up the market—Hoffman's Corners, Sunrise Park, Alla-Bar and the White Bear Shopping Center. The retail blight threatened to spread to the adjacent residential neighborhood facing the lake, where those fine, graceful, historic homes marked White Bear Lake's origins.

In a small town such as White Bear Lake, the chamber of commerce wielded as much if not more influence as the city government, so the campaign for urban renewal fell largely to the merchants. Absentee landlords and a cautious city council balked at first, but in May of 1963, the councilmen approved the chamber's plans, and by that summer, the project had shifted into high gear. Six dilapidated buildings were demolished to make way for a bank, a sprawling supermarket, a service station and new parking lots. Three retail outlets were rehabilitated with an old-style "Klondike" architectural motif, using rough timber and stylized signs and totem poles designed and developed by the high school art class. By the end of the year, seven substandard buildings had been removed, five new ones completed, six more planned, nine remodeled. In June of 1964, almost an entire city block was razed between Third and Fourth, Washington and Banning, including the historic Brings Feed and Seed Company. By the time Bob Brass took over at the chamber of commerce, White Bear Lake was well on the way to transforming its downtown.

The town's population then totaled some eighteen thousand, and the citizens were mostly middle class and white collar, with only a handful of blacks and foreign-born. In the newer region to the south the young couples raising children were brimming with energy and demanding services. They flooded the recreation department's park programs and they joined everything—the Jaycees, the Lions Club, the American Legion, the Knights of Columbus, the Masons, the Toastmasters. They attended church—White Bear Lake supported some eighteen places of worship, a third of them Lutheran. They also voted, and in 1964 one from their ranks, Milt Knoll, an unknown in the entrenched political world to the north, ran successfully for the office of White Bear Lake mayor.

Once in control, they acted. They built the much-needed sewers and storm drainage systems and sidewalks. Employing a choir, a band and a priest in a gala dedication, they opened an innovative, award-winning $2.5 million, 220,000-square-foot circular high school in October of 1964, complete with folding movable partitions, private study areas, eighty teacher stations, a four-hundred-seat theater, a two-thousand-seat varsity gym, a carpeted library and assorted laboratories. They built a new municipal building and post office. They organized a youth commission, a human relations committee, a senior citizens' club. Under Bud Korfhage's leadership they developed a multipart city recreation department offering swimming, gardening, slow-pitch softball, girls' softball, Little League baseball, peanut baseball, junior baseball, trampoline, physical fitness exercise, family archery, teenage dances, soccer, Ping-Pong, pool, horseshoes, track, figure skating, skiing, tennis, drawing, golf, roller-skating, horsemanship. They remodeled a church building into a community theater and breathed life into a repertory group called the Lakeshore Players, which in the 1964–5 season offered six plays—*Sunday in New York, All the Way Home, The Philadelphia Story, Come Back, Little Sheba, Present Laughter*, and a special show for children. They sold out the Lions Club's annual fund-raising vaudeville show four nights running.

Desperate to expand the tax base beyond the beleaguered home-owners, they annexed land, reaching for adjoining unincorporated areas—at one point the town's original two square miles swelled to fourteen, before settling at nine square miles after certain unincorporated areas fought back in court, asserting their rights to independence. They wooed industry, and exulted in December of 1962 when the Reynolds Metals Company called to say it had decided to build a large plant on Ninth Street that would employ seventy-five workers to make aluminum cans for the Hamm's Brewing Company in St. Paul.

White Bear Lake was emerging from its bucolic shell. Two interstate highways were on the drawing boards, promising high-speed links to the Twin Cities and beyond by the middle of the decade. The backward if picturesque police department was taking steps to modernize. In February of 1963 an outside consulting firm had deplored Chief Louis Kieffer's management style—asked by an FBI agent once where he could find a certain case file, the crusty old former meter reader reportedly had pointed to his own head. By July of 1964, some thirty applicants were taking the civil service test, and in October, city manager Ed Bayuk announced that the new police chief starting November 2 would be Wayne Armstrong, forty-five, then the chief of the fifty-man force in Rapid City, South Dakota.

Proud and eager for promotion, chamber of commerce officials in mid-1963 once more considered entering White Bear Lake in the annual All-America Cities competition conducted by the National Municipal League and *Look* magazine, but they finally decided to wait one year, until the downtown renewal had been largely completed. In this fashion, the task of running the All-America Cities campaign fell, in mid-1964, to the chamber of commerce headed by Bob Brass.

On August 8, 1964, that group's secretary-treasurer, Georgia Hillman, wrote away for the application forms, and a package of documents arrived three days later from the National Municipal League. Hillman leafed through the pages.

"A city need not be a model community," one booklet advised. "Citizen leadership, not perfection, is the criterion."

At this juncture in the town's history, only an impolite curmudgeon would have pointed out that the All-America Cities contest was hardly an exclusive honor, and not a measure of much. The competition had started in 1949, and by 1964 there had been some 175 winners.

"The All-America Cities contest is as pertinent to the future of American cities as the Miss America contest is to the future of womanhood," a National Urban Coalition official told one reporter who had a mind to write about the competition.

"About half of the entries look like chamber of commerce packages," allowed one judge.

All the same, cities clamored for the award—some two hundred tried to win every year—for it meant national recognition and the chance to ballyhoo the victory indefinitely with signs, emblems and parades. Most important of all, winning cities got to make up brochures and trot out the title to woo new industries. Chambers of commerce claimed the award could be worth hundreds of thousands of dollars, even millions, in new business.

So on September 24, 1964, Brass signed the application papers and Georgia Hillman mailed the town's package to the National Municipal League. Less than a month later, in a letter dated October 12, William J. D. Boyd, senior associate at the League, wrote back to Hillman:

> It is a pleasure to notify you, on a confidential basis, that White Bear Lake has been selected as one of the 22 finalist cities to appear before the All-America Cities Awards Jury during the 70th Annual National Conference on Government to be held at the Sheraton-Palace Hotel, San Francisco, Nov. 19–20.

At 6:00 P.M. on October 20, when a press announcement from the League made the news public, White Bear Lake filled with excitement. Brass and other chamber of commerce officials began scrambling to prepare the required audiovisual presentation and raise money for the trip to San Francisco. They sent out a call for color slides of city scenes, commandeered a local resident who worked in public relations for 3M to write a script, compiled a promotional pamphlet, formed an organizing committee, sold one-dollar buttons ("White Bear Lake—All-America City") and induced the Lions Club, Women's Club, Jaycees, American Legion and local newspaper to promote the "Buy a Button" campaign. The St. Paul chamber of commerce sent $150, the League of Women Voters $25, and soon the town had collected more than $1,800.

Compliments, congratulations and credit flew through the air.

"White Bear Lake deserves to be in the race," editorialized the *St. Paul Pioneer*. "It is a community which has blended its talents, energies and ideas to attack problems . . . White Bear Lake is a vibrant, progressive city whose social, cultural and economic growth has been impressive and should be an inspiration for communities throughout the nation who are willing to study its history, its achievement and, what may be most important of all, the spirit of its people."

Civic leaders took a brief respite from the All-America preparations on October 31, gathering at noon for the grand opening of the new municipal parking lot, built as part of the downtown renewal. Cheered on by the White Bear Lake High School band and pom-pom girls, assisted by Miss White Bear Lake, Sally Eckman, Mayor Milt Knoll cut the opening ribbon while Bob Brass spoke about what the parking lot meant to the town's fortunes. A twist contest, All-America City button sales and merchant drawings continued throughout the afternoon.

On Wednesday morning, November 18, the seven-person delegation boarding Western Airlines flight 701, bound for San Francisco from the Twin Cities airport, included Bob Brass, Georgia Hillman, Mayor Milt Knoll, Bud Korfhage, School District Officer Bill Knaak, White Bear High School Counselor Bob Eddy and David Farkell, the 3M public relations man. Georgia Hillman, an Arkansas native who'd taken over her husband's insurance business in 1947 when he fell ill, claimed a window seat, 21A, and stared with wonder as the plane lifted from the runway. Bob Brass's naturally worried expression deepened, for he disliked flying.

"Bob, the rivets are popping off the wings," one of the others called out, and Brass nearly jumped from his seat.

"Milt, we should have worn our rust-stained T-shirts," someone shouted at the mayor. The town's lingering problem with dirty water was a chronic city hall topic.

Later, after the fasten-seat-belt lights dimmed, the travelers took to the aisles, pinning White Bear Lake All-America buttons on stewardesses and other passengers. By the time they crossed the Rockies, they'd made a number of new friends. When they landed in San Francisco, Georgia Hillman yanked the small plaque denoting her seat number from the surface of the plane's overhead storage bin and stuffed it in her purse for a souvenir.

They attended a one-hour briefing session for all candidates at ten o'clock the next morning in the Sheraton-Palace's Ralston Room. They would have ten minutes total, they were told, with a warning gong at the nine-minute mark. Going alphabetically, White Bear Lake would present second to last, not until the next day at 11:25 A.M. The jury listening to them would include the pollster George Gallup, the *Look* magazine publisher, the president of the National Education Association, the executive vice president of Keep America Beautiful, the assistant to the president of the Greater Cleveland Associated Foundation, the president of the National Federation of Business and Professional Women's Clubs, the president of the American Chamber of Commerce Executives, the president of the League of Women Voters of the United States, the former president of the Chamber of Commerce of the United States and the secretary of the San Francisco Labor Council AFLCIO.

The White Bear group felt abashed by such an imposing group.

The program began at 2:15 P.M. that afternoon in the Ralston Room with opening remarks by the jury's chairman, George Gallup. The scene most closely resembled a cavernous courtroom—two rows of jurors sat on the dais at tables covered with sheets, facing the audience, while speakers addressed them from microphones and a lectern at the front of the room. Brass listened to the first seven towns—Atchison, Kansas; Bluefield, West Virginia; Charlotte, North Carolina; Columbia, South Carolina; Fort Worth, Texas; Gainesville, Georgia; Green Bay, Wisconsin—and took heart. One town ran out of time and was gonged into silence, and another, using all ten minutes for talking, couldn't show its slides. A third seemed to have trouble with the jury's follow-up questions.

The White Bear delegation, retreating to a hotel room for more rehearsal, fired possible questions at one another: What about race relations? The annexation battles? The dirty water? They fixed on honest answers. Progress, not perfection—that was the key.

They broke for dinner, eating at the Old Spaghetti Factory on Green Street, marveling at the restaurant's setting, a warren of rooms with Victorian bric-a-brac. Bob Eddy, their chief speaker, then retired early to rest his voice, while the others attended a play and walked the streets of San Francisco, turning in at midnight. In the morning they set up their display table with brochures, buttons and photos, then settled in to wait.

At 11:25 A.M., following the presentation by South Portland, Maine, George Gallup rapped his gavel and announced: "The next city we will hear from will be White Bear Lake."

Dave Farkell and Bob Eddy stood and walked to the podium while Bud Korfhage took his position behind the slide projector. They'd brought their own projector from home and a backup set of slides, just in case. Swallowing hard as they surveyed the august gathering before them, the White Bear Lake visitors began, while a sea of flashbulbs popped in their faces.

"Four years before Minnesota became a state," said Farkell, "a settlement was started on the shores of a large lake located about ten miles north of St. Paul. This lake carried the name of White Bear, a name given to it by the Indians who had populated the area for many years . . ."

Korfhage caught his cue, and a pastoral view of the lake flashed on the white screen to the side of the dais.

"In the one hundred ten years since its nearest real protection came from the federal troops stationed at Fort Snelling, White Bear has grown through a period in which it was primarily a resort and amusement center, to take its place as one of the most progressive communities in a succession of fine cities spread across the northern plains . . ."

Korfhage punched a lever and a shot of White Bear Lake's downtown in pioneer days filled the screen.

They were off, outlining the story of the town's expansion and renewal in modern times without federal aid, the slides flashing across the screen offering growth charts and shots of the city before and after rehabilitation.

"In nineteen hundred and sixty-two, a small group of men who were determined to breathe life into the renewal program met with success . . ."

Click, click, click—shots of the new supermarket, the bank, the public parking lot filled the screen. Then views of a softball game, the new post office, the municipal building, a group of senior citizens, and finally, an aerial view of White Bear Lake.

". . . These are some of the reasons why we submit that White Bear Lake is not the 'average' suburban community," Eddy was saying.

"Through the efforts of many people we have had to run to catch up with our rapid growth . . . We are determined to stay ahead. Win or lose here in San Francisco, we know that we have already won on the home front, and that to our citizens, all 17,950 of them, White Bear Lake is an All-America City."

Brass looked at a stopwatch—nine minutes and forty seconds. They had made it with twenty seconds to spare.

A juror asked a question about the school district. Bill Knaak answered. Another juror asked about the number and types of activities covered by the recreation program. Bud Korfhage jumped up. "You name it lady, we got it," he roared.

When it was over, the White Bear delegation accepted compliments and distributed souvenirs to the jurors and audience—White Bear Lake key chains and pencils and small banks donated by the Reynolds Metals Company that bore the inscription "White Bear Lake, November 1964." Then they joined everyone at lunch in the Rose Room and listened to the governor of Michigan, George Romney, speak on "modern constitutions for modern states."

They flew home that afternoon, greeted by an icy Minnesota night. As they drove north on Highway 61 toward White Bear Lake, it seemed to them that San Francisco and the All-America Cities competition were a long distance away.

Bob Brass reached his home on South Gardenette Drive late that evening. His wife Camille and four children greeted him at the front door, hurling questions his way. He told them of the airplane flights and San Francisco and White Bear's moment in the spotlight. He had a present for his six-year-old boy Mike, a small brass skeleton hung on a necklace—brass for a Brass.

Bob Brass had reason to feel good about his family. Camille, thirty-six then, was a warm, chatty woman, interested in books and the neighborhood and other people. If her curiosity sometimes bordered on the gossipy, Camille balanced that tendency with a caring, empathetic nature. In those stretches when her own four children didn't demand all her attention, she worked as a substitute teacher in the nearby public and Catholic school systems.

Her father had come to White Bear Lake from St. Paul in 1925 to be the Ford dealer, and she was born there three years later. She'd known Bob since the seventh grade, when she was a student at the

St. Joseph's Academy private Catholic school. When all the veterans came home from the war, there were for a time three guys to every gal, most of them older, and loads of dances and parties. After her twenty-first formal dance, though, Cam decided enough was enough and fixed on Bob as her steady. They started dating in 1949, when she was twenty-one, and they married on June 9, 1951.

Asking the new young assistant pastor at St. Mary's to handle the wedding had kicked up some trouble, for old Father Finn took offense at the Brasses' preference for Reiser. Later, to settle the matter, Father Finn had visited them at home on Gardenette Drive, where he sat in their living room downing whiskey until amends were made.

The Brasses enjoyed their neighborhood. Camille talked to everyone—Dorothy Engfer and Gladys DeMars across the street, Donna Neely, Alice and Tom Axelrod up at the corner. They knew the Jurgenses, but not as well. Bob Brass drove by their house five or six times a day and sometimes saw their two boys playing in the yard while their parents gardened, but he talked to them only once, when Lois came collecting for the Red Cross. Camille was on speaking acquaintance with Lois—"Now don't you work so hard in your yard," she'd call out, waving, as she passed by—but that was all. The Brasses' son Mike was the true social animal—he knew absolutely every kid in the neighborhood, and there were tons of them. Block tag was real big—thirty kids would split into two groups for mass hide-and-seek games, running through the oval formed by north and south Gardenette Drives, cutting across neighbors' unfenced backyards. The kids, going back and forth into each other's homes, in a sense brought their parents together. No one could afford baby-sitters, so they would call the city and get the block barricaded for summer night street parties, everyone bringing out record players and kegs of beer and potluck dishes. They would literally dance in the streets. No one locked his door, and people, taking after their kids, just walked into one another's homes—you had to be careful not to sit around in your underwear, Tom Axelrod liked to observe.

When the Gardenette Park Civic Association wanted to build a beach where Hazel Street ran six blocks straight to the lakeside, they raised enough money with dinners and dances, then dumped forty truckloads of sand and made their beach. After that, families would take their kids down to swim at the end of hot days and the Red Cross provided lessons. In winter, they would ice skate and ice fish—there'd be five or six hundred shacks out on the frozen lake. They'd golf on the ice over at Mahtomedi. They'd also iceboat—sailboats with one beam down the middle and two blade runners could careen from bank to bank at seventy or eighty miles an hour. The wind in your face then was something to remember.

In early December of 1964, just days after Bob Brass's return from San Francisco, the Jurgenses held a birthday party for Dennis when he turned three. Mike Brass, then seven, was one of ten neighborhood kids who attended. They ate cake and played games, including pin the tail on the donkey, in the living room and out in the big fenced backyard. Mike was wearing the brass necklace his father had brought back from San Francisco, and sometime during the party, a leg to the skeleton broke off and got lost. Mike had a good time, but felt puzzled. He couldn't understand why he'd been invited, why he was there, for he didn't know the Jurgens boys, Dennis and Robert. In fact, he had never seen them before. Their mother never allowed them to leave their fenced backyard to play in the Gardenette Park street games.

CHAPTER 7

Wintertime

The first time the Jurgenses took Dennis to the Zerwas clan's weekly Sunday gathering at the parents' house on Park Street, Lois sat in a wooden chair off from the kitchen table, holding her little boy while a crowd gathered excitedly, leaning over and making baby noises at the ebullient newcomer. Some, expecting a newborn, were surprised to find instead an active one-year-old. Everyone held him and talked to him and played with him, and Dennis greeted all comers with a big bubbly smile. In fact, he made faces at the strangers, offering goofy expressions, as if he were trying to start a game or pass on a joke. He reached eagerly for whatever caught his eye and even managed to speak a few words. Karlene, the ten-year-old daughter of Lois's sister Donna, buried her nose in Dennis's neck and thought he smelled so good. She loved the way his mouth opened in a wide circle of astonishment at everything he saw, so unguarded and eager and trusting. Lois acted happy, Robert appeared pleased to have a little brother, and Harold in his pride was like a father just after birth. Harold, in fact, was the most thrilled person in the house, walking around constantly with Dennis in his arms. Karlene would never forget that afternoon in January of 1963, for a simple reason—everyone in the Zerwas family was happy for a day.

As the weeks and months went by, the Jurgenses came to more and more Zerwas clan Sunday gatherings with their children, and Dennis soon embraced the wild gang of kids running and screaming in the backyard. They played all sorts of games—ring-around-a-rosy, duck-duck-gray duck, tag, jump rope—and Dennis always tried to participate in everything. Being the youngest, he couldn't get the rules right and couldn't run fast enough, but he was happy.

His brother Robert, by contrast, was quiet and shy. The older teenage nieces would try to give him candy and cookies, but he'd absolutely refuse. Robert was the best-behaved child they'd ever seen—if his mother said sit, he sat. Dennis would readily take the cookies and candies they offered, then get in trouble. One niece played games with Lois over that, purposefully trying to get her mad, which was not hard—Lois would come in and snatch the candy from Dennis's hands, cussing and yelling.

"Damn you, I told you not to give that to Dennis," she'd shout. Others felt quite frightened of Lois, but not this niece. She'd flip her aunt the finger or stick her tongue out, and then run off.

One Sunday, down Park Street at the home of Lois's brother Gerhard, all the family's teenagers were in the living room, dancing to rock and roll music. Dennis toddled in and started copying them, doing his version of the twist and the pony. Everyone thought it so neat—he really could dance, he really had rhythm, this was not just a baby goofing around. The teenagers all applauded and cheered and called him Dennis the Menace because he had such a devilish look in his eye. Then Lois came into the room, furious, and yanked Dennis away by his arm. Everyone froze, worrying that they were in trouble, and moments later the Jurgens family left.

Although the Jurgenses seemed happy enough during these visits, in truth they were not entirely satisfied. A by-now-familiar yearning tugged at them, spurring them on. Harold and Lois once more were feeling the urge to expand their family.

In early March of 1964, one year after first getting Dennis and nineteen days after formally adopting him, Lois called the Ramsey County welfare department to inquire about applying for a third child. Intake worker Alice Cone explained that, by agency policy, they had to wait three months after an adoption before reapplying. Lois knew this, for Gerane Rekdahl had informed her of the rules, but now on the phone, she raised a question.

Given their ages, so close to the agency's upper limit for adoptive parents, should they be required to wait the three months?

Alice conferred with Gerane and their supervisor, who, after considering the Jurgens file, decided that in this case the agency would adhere to the rule.

In mid-May of 1964, when the waiting period expired, the Jurgenses and Alice Cone exchanged phone calls, but missed each other. Then an appointment had to be canceled when an emergency call summoned Harold to the Spring Lake Park area to repair a grocer's broken freezing unit. The Jurgenses finally met the intake interviewer at the Ramsey County welfare department's office in downtown St. Paul on the morning of June 2.

By then Alice Cone had decided she was going to try to talk this couple out of the idea of taking a third child, largely because of Lois's initial reaction to Dennis. She did not succeed in this effort. The Jurgenses were quite insistent—they wanted a girl, definitely under the age of one this time.

They had arrived for their appointment precisely on time, Harold in his work clothes but clean. As they sat before her in a small partitioned cubicle, Alice thought Lois, now almost thirty-nine, was very pretty and nicely dressed. The couple, describing their family life, made a great point of how much they enjoyed their children.

"We have a ball," Lois said, more than once.

Apparently, Alice noted, this is an expression she uses frequently.

After the Jurgenses left, she felt less than enthusiastic, but she didn't believe she had any clear basis for blocking their application at this point. Their file, Alice Cone decided, should go to a caseworker for another home study.

This time, the Ramsey County welfare department sent a veteran. Norma Potter, forty-two, had worked for the county for twenty years, dealing with foster homes and placements and retarded people, everywhere from the inner city to suburbs. She'd seen all that happened in homes, from incest to child beatings, and she felt skillful at the business of evaluating families. Having read their case file, Norma harbored reservations about the Jurgenses. Like the others before her, she hoped the couple might decide not to pursue their request.

The Jurgenses' gabled stucco house looked pleasant and well-tended to Norma when she first visited there on October 6, 1964. A black wrought-iron railing ringed the front yard, where the orange-rust leaves of an elm tree were just starting to drop. Lois, opening the

door, at first surprised Norma with her appearance and manner—
she looked relaxed and quite slender and feminine, in a dress and
earrings that brought out the blue of her eyes.

Norma thought Lois must have lost a lot of weight since her previous application. Gerane Rekdahl had described her as somewhat
chubby.

Gerane had occupied the desk right behind Norma in the office,
but she was gone now, off the previous May to California, where
her husband had won a scholarship. Gerane was always so nice and
gentle, Norma thought, never hard or judgmental, so forgiving that
maybe she hadn't been equipped for this type of work. Then again,
maybe no one is. It was funny, though—Gerane had never said anything to her about this case.

Harold, coming home minutes after Norma's arrival, brought
in the two boys, who'd been playing out back. With appreciation,
Norma noticed the large fenced backyard and the recreation room
in the basement, both full of toys.

Robert held back, quiet, listening, while Dennis rushed to the
strange visitor, reciting nursery rhymes, telling Norma all about
what he'd been doing outside. Dennis now spoke very well, in a high,
piping little voice that she easily understood. Norma thought his
face had a pixie quality. Funny again—Gerane had described him as
husky, but in truth, he struck her as small and slight.

As they all settled in the living room, Dennis climbed onto Lois's
lap and sang "Take Me Out to the Ball Game" from start to finish,
without help or prompting, carrying the tune quite well. Then Harold sent the children to play in the basement, and Norma, sitting in a
chair facing the Jurgenses on the couch, began the interview.

Why did they think they were ready to adopt another child? she
asked. Why was another child so important?

"I wish I could tell you exactly what it was like to not have any
children," Lois replied. "The living from day to day was quite empty,
even though we loved each other. After work or supper, we'd wonder
where to go. Now we just love to stay home and care for our little
boys. They've made life worthwhile."

When Norma asked about the family's sleeping arrangements if a
third child arrived, Lois rose, inviting her on a tour of the bedrooms.

The nursery, still Dennis's room, was spotless, full of what
Norma considered very expensive baby furniture. Robert's adjoining

room—the boys' shared room if they got a new baby—had two chests of drawers and two twin beds. Harold and Lois's bedroom was across the hall, adjacent to the bathroom. Norma felt vaguely uneasy when she looked into this room. Everything was extremely neat and immaculately clean. Nothing was out of place, and everything matched. There were pastel colors on the walls, lacy curtains on the windows, fluffy gay-colored pillows on the bed. Harold and Lois's room was so feminine, Norma thought—so much like a woman's bedroom.

Looking about her as they returned from the bedrooms, Norma realized the living room and kitchen also were thoroughly ordered, with nothing out of place.

"How do you maintain such order in your house?" Norma asked.

Everybody has responsibility to pick up after himself, Lois explained. The downstairs basement was the playroom and where Harold read the paper. He used the bathroom down there when he was dirty.

Norma listened, trying to absorb without making a judgment. It was hard to make a decision based on what somebody was going to do two years or ten years from now. She had a bad feeling, but why? There appeared to be nothing tangible or too negative in the information she was gleaning during this first visit.

Go slow on this one, Norma told herself as she walked toward her car. Her mentor from years before, a wily child welfare director, had advised them many times in staff meetings what to do in these situations: when you're not sure, drag your heels.

Winter and the Christmas season now arrived in White Bear Lake.

A Shoreview couple died at the start of December when a train slammed into their car at an unmarked crossing on Otter Lake Road, and the week after, twenty mothers braved below-zero weather to picket the site, demanding that the Soo Line Railroad install a crossing signal. They waved placards that said "Murder Crossing" and "Money for orphans, no money for signals." By the end of the day the women had collected signatures from 350 passing cars for a petition that declared the neighborhood lived in fear, not knowing which one of them would be killed next.

On Tuesday, December 15, a *Look* writer-and-photographer team—David Maxey and James Karales—arrived in town to shoot pictures and prepare material in case White Bear Lake should win the All-America City award. They'd called Georgia Hillman at the chamber of commerce the week before to say they were coming, but almost didn't get their message across. On the phone, the *Look* secretary kept asking Hillman for "Mr. Brace." There's no Mr. Brace here, Hillman kept responding. She was about to hang up when she realized they meant "Mr. Brass"—Bob Brass.

Once in town, Maxey and Karales checked into Jantzen's Motel on Highway 61 and stayed four full days, taking shots of everything from the circular high school to old-timers sipping coffee at the Little Bear Café. They wanted a photo of an ice fisherman in his shack on the lake, so Bud Korfhage found old Chet Sickler and got him out early on a bone-chilling morning. Conducting a tour of the school, the principal, Roy Wahlberg, couldn't pass up the chance for one of his patented puns.

"Now we'll see what develops," he said as the photographer snapped his shots.

The *Look* writer, David Maxey, responded in kind days later when he penned a thank-you letter. "Just let me say we appreciate the candid way you dealt with us," he wrote. "We Leica your attitude. Any other would make us shutter."

In late December, the grocer Bill LeVasseur was elected chamber of commerce president for 1965, replacing Bob Brass. At a banquet one Saturday night at the Holiday House emceed by Roy Wahlberg, Brass received a plaque and a gavel, and heard much praise for his labors, particularly in guiding the town's All-America Cities entry. Then LeVasseur rose to speak.

"Be alive in sixty-five," he shouted. "That's our slogan for the year!"

The grocer, a garrulous man with a ready smile, by then had been operating his downtown food store for more than twenty years, taking over after the war from his father, the legendary Prosper J. LeVasseur, who'd founded the shop in 1912 at the corner of Bald Eagle and Birch Lake Avenues. Bill was third-generation—his grandfather had settled in White Bear Lake in 1880, opening one of the first resort hotels, the White Bear House on Fourth and Washington Square.

"We here in the White Bear Lake area are sitting on top of a gold mine," LeVasseur continued. "Are we ready for this gold rush? Are we ready to mine our share? Are we going to be satisfied with just a pocketful, a wheelbarrow full or a truckload? It is predicted that the average American family will reach a standard of living never before achieved by any country at any time . . . In 1963 the Dow Jones hit an all-time high of 767.21. On November 18, 1964, that all-time-high record was broken when the Dow Jones hit 891.61. Up 15 percent . . . and 1965 will be even bigger and better for business. Are we in a position to reap this harvest? Set your sights high! Think positive, forget negative attitudes . . ."

The audience, which was full of distinguished guests, including mayors of adjoining towns, rose to applaud. The band struck up, and dancing began.

Near-blizzard conditions belted the White Bear Lake area two days before Christmas. Snow mixed with freezing rain and forty-mile-per-hour winds created hazardous driving conditions and so many traffic accidents that the police and sheriff's departments couldn't keep up with them. All the same, the Jurgens family set out early that evening to pay a holiday visit to Father Bernard Reiser.

Harold and Lois were not alone in their high regard for Father Reiser. In truth, he was worshiped by the White Bear Lake community. People felt they could always stop and confide in him at any time, for he seemed a real person—compassionate and comforting and common as an old shoe—who'd just as soon be talking to you as doing anything else. He saw the positive in everything, and felt people could just do no wrong. "Isn't it wonderful . . . what a great day," he always said in greeting. People ended up feeling good around him, no matter how down they'd been before.

The White Bear city manager, Ed Bayuk, probably had one of the best stories about the much-loved priest. It seemed a fellow getting a haircut was complaining that a kid had broken his picture window with a baseball. Reiser, in another chair, asked the size and age of the boy. When told, the priest sighed with appreciation. "Isn't it wonderful," he said, "that a boy of ten could hit a ball so straight and hard it could break a window?"

Sometimes Reiser came into Bill LeVasseur's grocery store and bought a couple of beef roasts, paying cash instead of using the church account. LeVasseur would be puzzled.

"Father," he'd say, "your housekeeper just bought a roast."

"Well, Bill . . ." Father Reiser would reply, looking away.

Then LeVasseur would realize Reiser was buying the roast for someone else, for a poor parishioner he was on the way to visit. LeVasseur would try to give him a discount, but Reiser would always refuse.

For the Jurgenses, visiting Father Reiser on December 23, 1964, was not a short trip, for the priest had left St. Mary's the previous June to become pastor of the new Church of the Epiphany just getting started in Coon Rapids, some sixteen miles to the northwest. In their Falcon station wagon, Harold and Lois had to negotiate a web of treacherous, ice-filled roads. There wasn't an actual church in Coon Rapids yet—mass was held in the Coon Rapids High School—so they parked their station wagon in front of the building where Reiser was living, a salmon-colored house abutting a farm silo and the open plain where the church would soon rise. Harold and the two boys stayed in the car while Lois darted through the blizzard to Father Reiser's front door.

She came into his living room bearing a gift, a leafy pure-white poinsettia. This was special—at Christmas season, the priest received plenty of red poinsettias, but rarely a white one. An attached card said, "All our love, Harold and Lois and the children." Father Reiser was touched.

After visiting for a few minutes, he walked Lois back to the station wagon to greet Harold and the boys. A floodlight by the garage pointed directly on the car, so Reiser could see Robert and Dennis sitting quietly in the backseat. They were always like that, he thought, so well-groomed and well-trained.

The whole family would sometimes drop in after services on a Sunday, and he found Harold and Lois easy to visit with. They'd all sit in the living room of the rectory, Lois so proud of her two adopted kids, both letter-perfect and turned out. They'd sit still and never tear around or get into things like other kids would.

Father Reiser stood at his doorstep, waving, as the Jurgenses' station wagon pulled back into the blowing storm. Returning to his living room, he placed the white poinsettia in a corner spot and stepped back to study the arrangement. How lovely, he thought. Only the Jurgenses brought him white poinsettias.

During the holidays, Norma Potter discussed the Jurgens case twice with her supervisor. Lois Jurgens, she explained, was a lady who wanted children badly and could present herself to them as anything she wanted to be. How could they say no without something definite? They had to see what Lois was really like—how she responded when her guard was down and the stress level high.

The two social workers fixed on a plan. Norma would use herself as a trigger. She would try to push Lois, to challenge her with independent and even nasty behavior, so they could observe her response.

Norma had to steel herself for this meeting. Most people shrink from confrontations, and she was no exception. It was hard to stand up to an insistent, forceful woman so determined to have children, she told herself, but she had to do her job.

The children were napping when Norma arrived after lunch on Friday, January 8, 1965. Lois was wearing slacks, and the house, as usual, was exactingly ordered. The artificial Christmas tree still up, with the boys' gifts—musical instruments—artfully arranged underneath. Norma took the chair in the living room, facing Lois on the couch, and waited for her opening.

They started talking about the Jurgenses' general interest in adoption, and Lois, as she had on previous occasions, said that Robert was "nothing short of a miracle."

Norma immediately interrupted.

"Can you explain that further?" she demanded, her tone insistent. "I find this hard to understand. Do you really think it was a miracle, that you did nothing which helped arrange for Robert to come to live in your house? Just what do you mean by this?"

Lois froze, unsure how to proceed.

No caseworker has done this before to her, Norma thought. Gerry Rekdahl didn't, and Robert they got privately.

Lois held her ground, though.

Yes, she said stiffly, she believed it really was God's will that Robert had come to live with them. She of course knew they had done something to get him, but it was God's will they were singled out as the people who could do the things that would make it possible for Robert to come to them.

"I think it must be easy for you to relieve yourself of responsibility for whatever happens," Norma responded, "if you consider everything God's will."

Lois still held herself together. When she got married she had wanted to have children so much, she said, and being childless had been a big blow. That's why they had tried so hard to adopt children.

"Mrs. Jurgens, you must know I have great doubts about this application," Norma said. "You are a very directive person, and I have doubts about your response to the children's independence."

Lois answered calmly, offering explanations about how nicely their family lived together.

It wasn't working—Norma wasn't getting the response she'd expected. She pushed Lois into all the corners she could find, but Lois's tone and attitude remained unaggressive. She must be cross with me, Norma thought, but she's keeping her focus on what she wants—another child.

"Can I show you our kitchen?" Lois asking suddenly, standing. "You've seen the rest of the house, but not the kitchen."

Having seized control of the exchange, Lois began a story. Harold started remodeling this kitchen himself, she said, but he kept delaying and never finished it, so one day she called a carpenter to come and take down the wall and complete the addition.

Norma tried one more time.

"What did your husband say when he came home?" she demanded. "What did he think?"

Lois stood stark still in her kitchen. She was catching on. "Well," she said finally, looking at Norma, "I guess you would have said I shouldn't have done that, shouldn't have taken over."

"What did your husband say?" Norma insisted.

Lois looked Norma in the eye.

"He said, 'Well, okay, Lois, you asked me and I didn't finish it, I understand.'"

For a moment, the two women stood silently in the kitchen, staring at each other.

Norma felt unstrung when she left the Jurgens home in late afternoon. She didn't like creating discomfort with people in this way. Within hours, the temperature had plummeted from the mid-thirties to below zero, with blowing winds and a trace of snow on the ground, and forecasters were promising a mighty storm by the morning. Norma shivered and pulled her cloth overcoat tightly about her.

At the end of January, Lois's thirty-six-year-old sister Barbara died of a brain tumor. Services were held on Monday, February 1, at the

Lake Mortuary, with a requiem mass across the street at St. Mary's of the Lake and interment in the church's cemetery. Mourners braved a ferocious near-blizzard and temperatures of minus twelve degrees—more than half of Minnesota's January days had been below zero. Father Finn conducted the ceremony, with Father Reiser also in attendance, along with the vast Zerwas clan—more than a hundred of them, dressed in their finest clothes. The casket sat open, strewn with flowers, in a twenty-five-by-fifteen-foot viewing room furnished with chairs and sectional sofas. Family members approached in pairs to view the body while Barbara's six children stood nearby, crying. Then Father Finn started the service.

Midway through, as the recital of the rosary began, Dennis and Robert Jurgens approached the front of the room and knelt before the casket, dressed in neatly pressed white suits with short pants. With straight backs and clear, unwavering voices, working one bead at a time through the circular rosary necklace, they led the repeating cycle of prayers—Apostles' Creeds, Our Fathers, Hail Marys, over and over. "I believe in God, the Father, Almighty Creator of Heaven and Earth . . ." "Our Father Who art in Heaven, hallowed be Thy Name . . ." "Hail Mary, full of grace, the Lord is with Thee . . ." On and on they recited for twenty minutes, never once hesitating or forgetting.

Relatives and priests watched with growing astonishment and, in some cases, appreciation. Father Finn paused to say he wanted to congratulate the parents of these children, for he hardly ever saw young people who knew their rosary and it was truly wonderful. Robert and Dennis's cousin Karlene, then twelve, was flabbergasted—she knew only bits and pieces of the rosary herself, and these two small boys sounded like little priests.

A few in the room, though, were as puzzled as they were amazed. Dennis, after all, was just three years old. Lois's cousin, June Bol, had taught school for seven years and raised four children. This isn't what such little children do, she thought to herself. I wonder how Lois got them to say the rosary like that.

Lois's sister Eloise and niece Karlene had another question. They wondered why Dennis was wearing sunglasses inside the mortuary. All through the ceremony, even while reciting the rosary, a pair of red plastic sunglasses had covered Dennis's eyes.

CHAPTER 8

All-America City

One week before Barbara's funeral, on Sunday, January 24, 1965, some thirty thousand visitors mobbed White Bear Lake for the annual ice-fishing contest, part of the St. Paul Winter Carnival Days. Joe O'Doherty beat out six thousand other fishermen by bringing in a four-pound seven-ounce northern pike just fifteen minutes before the contest's close, good enough to win a boat, an outboard motor and a fishing trophy. Six weeks later, on March 4, the angry picketing and petitioning by the band of mothers the previous December bore fruit—the Minnesota Railroad and Warehouse Commission ordered the Soo Line Railroad to install a $10,850 signal at the treacherous Otter Lake Road crossing, site of six accidents and four deaths over the past fifteen years. That same month the White Bear Lake Mrs. Jaycees began preparing for their annual style show, a cocktails and luncheon affair at McGuire's Restaurant featuring fashion entertainment by Miss White Bear Lake. The local planning commission just then released an annual report outlining what it considered the town's most urgent needs—purified public water, park and recreation land and an upgraded sewer system.

Other events from well beyond White Bear Lake's borders were also starting to make themselves felt, at least in some quarters of the town. Day after day in the early weeks of 1965, the newspaper headlines filled with increasingly familiar names: Selma, Pleiku, Viet Cong, LBJ, George Wallace, U Thant, Sheriff Jim Clark, Nguyen

Khanh, Malcolm X, Da Nang. The war in Vietnam was escalating and Martin Luther King, Jr., was marching in Selma. During the second week in March, the Minnesota state legislature sitting in St. Paul passed a resolution urging Governor Wallace and Alabama to "recognize the rights of all citizens." In St. Paul on Saturday, March 13, more than a thousand people marched with placards up Cedar Street to the state capitol, where they sang "We Shall Overcome" and listened to the state's new young senator—Walter Mondale, elected just the previous November—predict the passing by Congress of a historic voting rights act. If most folks in White Bear Lake did not zealously involve themselves in such distant events, a few did recognize them. That month, a small ad hoc civil rights group formed the summer before coalesced into a more permanent organization—the White Bear Lake Area Human Relations Council—while the White Bear Lake Unitarian Church sent its minister, the Rev. Richard E. Sykes, to Mississippi for a week of observation and support.

Civil rights and Vietnam, however, were not the town's chief concerns just then. This moment in White Bear Lake's history was most indelibly marked by a letter that arrived on the desk of chamber of commerce secretary Georgia Hillman on March 7. It was dated March 4, typed on the letterhead of the National Municipal League, and signed by the chairman of the league's council, George H. Gallup.

"Congratulations!" Gallup began. "It gives me great pleasure to notify you, *on a confidential basis*, that White Bear Lake has been named an All-America City for 1964 by the National Municipal League and *Look* magazine. This decision was reached by the All-America Cities Award Jury, of which I was foreman, at San Francisco, California, last November following the presentations. Subsequent investigations confirmed our judgment. I salute the citizens of White Bear Lake whose effective actions have won this award and sincerely hope they will view this honor as a further incentive to play a positive role in the affairs of their community. Once again may I extend my most sincere congratulations."

The official public announcement would not come until 7:00 A.M., Eastern Standard Time, on April 8. Civic leaders congratulated themselves privately, but not with overt exuberance. The All-America organizers, after all, were a relatively conservative group of young Republicans, not given to excessive or uninhibited partying. The National Municipal League on March 8 and *Look* magazine on March 10 wrote follow-up letters, asking that White Bear Lake schedule a presentation ceremony sometime during the two-week period that *Look* would be on magazine stands with its All-America edition. Chamber of commerce officials soon plunged into planning that project. On March 12, *Look* shipped to White Bear by insured parcel post the three-by-five-foot flag of honor that proclaimed, in white lettering on a red background, "White Bear Lake—All-America City." Two weeks later, *Look* shipped, by Railway Express, the framed award certificate.

By then, White Bear Lake was preparing for another event of almost equal import—the Lions Club annual fund-raising show.

The Lions Club had always played a central role in the life of White Bear Lake—it was the town's primary service organization, as well as one of its most important forums for socializing. The Lions Club successfully brought together the newcomers from the south end of town with the more entrenched residents to the north—the club was a north-end tradition fueled by the south end's unbounded energy and resources. Once a year, at the Lions Club show's three-night run over a spring weekend, almost everyone in town convened in the Central Junior High auditorium, easily making it among White Bear Lake's top social events.

It was also the most fun. Everyone got silly, painting their faces and dressing up as clowns, speakeasy dancers, riverboat gamblers and circus ringmasters, then singing and dancing and acting out unabashedly corny skits. As late as 1963, there were still some of the blackface minstrel numbers that had pervaded the shows in earlier years, but this custom was soon to vanish. In 1964, the theme of the three-night production had been "She Ain't What She Used to Be," comparing White Bear's colorful past with its more modern suburban present. With 112 actors, forty speaking parts, two choruses and twenty-three skits, the show had raised more than $3,000 for the ambulance and rescue squad, college scholarships, a Braille encyclopedia set and eyeglasses for needy children.

Now, for 1965, the Lions Club searched for a new theme. The club's officers—including George Rivers, Bud Korfhage, Bill LeVasseur, Bob Brass and Roy Wahlberg—finally fixed on "Vaudeville! What's That?" featuring re-created top name vaudeville acts such as Fred Allen, Sophie Tucker, Olson & Johnson and Jack Benny. As it had before, the club recruited a former actor and producer, Bob Bruce, to write and direct the show, but also as usual, assorted Lions Club members ended up gathering in Bruce's basement to add their own contributions. On March 11, 1965, the Lions Club staged a preview performance to test sample scenes for the show's opening night on April 8. The preview drew appreciative laughter, according to those present, and excited talk.

After a short stretch of unseasonably warm weather in late January, winter had returned to the White Bear Lake area with a vengeance in February and March, producing first bitter, below-zero temperatures and gusting snow, then warming temperatures, torrential rains and the biggest problem of all—ever-rising floodwater. Highways and schools closed because of high water and streets turned into lagoons when storm sewers became clogged with ice. Flooded basements were common, especially in suburban houses without sewer connections.

The Jurgens home on South Gardenette Drive was one that suffered this fate. Down in their basement, Lois began pushing the water out with a garage broom, struggling for hours to save their furnace from rusting while she nursed a growing anger toward Harold. The basement water was the result of poor drainage in the yard, she complained to others. The flooding could have been prevented by proper banking of the basement by her husband.

On the streets of White Bear Lake, police officer Ron Meehan was also griping, for frozen culverts had forced the closing of the central intersection at White Bear Lake Avenue and County Road E, where three feet of water covered the road, overwhelming two straining sump pumps. Meehan, then still a patrolman, spent hours of overtime directing traffic away from that lagoon, and the experience did not increase his appreciation for local citizens. Some of those knuckleheads, he told friends later, would drive right into the swamp without even slowing down.

In late March a new storm hit with three inches of snow, followed by more rain and warming temperatures, then another storm with almost a foot of snow, and yet another with half a foot, until the roads were a sloppy mix of water, slush and frost. Hotels filled, buses stopped and the temperature dropped to five below zero amid high winds. Early April brought rising temperatures, but they weren't at all welcome, for they and the coming spring rains promised even more monstrous floods. That promise was soon fulfilled.

To the southeast of the Twin Cities on April 8, the rampaging Vermillion River battered the town of Hastings with its worst flood in history, while the swollen Blue Earth River smashed through a dike near the confluence of the Minnesota River and the town of Mankato. As 7,500 people quit their homes, hundreds of volunteers, bracing for the crest, rushed to hold back the still-rising Minnesota River with a hastily constructed dike of sticky gray mud topped with thousands of sandbags. It was no use, though—water was everywhere, with more snow melting hourly in the highlands above the river valley.

"The entire world seems to be made of water, sand and gooey mud," cried out one volunteer.

Despite these assaults of nature, Thursday to Sunday, April 8 to April 11, 1965, were heady days in White Bear Lake. Amid flag-raising ceremonies and waves of congratulations, news of the town's All-America City award became public just as the annual Lions Club show began its three-day run in the Central Junior High auditorium.

When White Bear Lake's All-America City award was announced on Thursday morning, April 8, the town—at least, a certain portion of it—swelled with pride. Merchants and businessmen talked endlessly of flags, buttons, posters, street signs and industrial brochures. Bud Korfhage, Bill LeVasseur and the banker Dick Long visited the local businesses, selling a $45 package that included a flag, banner and storefront bunting, and soon the renewed downtown was fully decorated. Long had proudly designed the town's All-America shield—a V-shaped patch with red stripes and white stars and the words "All-America City White Bear Lake"—and within hours this began appearing on everything from bumper stickers and shoulder patches (for the police and Boy Scouts) to highway signs and doors. Telegrams arrived from everyone important—Senators Eugene McCarthy and Walter Mondale, Vice President Hubert Humphrey, President Lyndon Johnson.

Two probable benefits were mentioned over and over—the award would make national industry more aware of White Bear Lake, and it would spark pride among the citizens.

"This is one of the biggest things that has ever happened to this city," said Bill LeVasseur.

"This will give everyone in town more drive," said Bob Brass.

That same night, the Lions Club show opened to a full house of eleven hundred, the first of three successive sellouts. By showtime, the auditorium was bursting with people, with not a single empty seat—three sections, ten seats across, eighteen rows in the main floor, plus a balcony and extra folding chairs in the aisles. At precisely eight o'clock, the curtain pulled back to reveal scenes for the various skits painted on towering sixteen-by-twenty-foot boards propped up on stage. From the orchestra pit, the high school band struck up an overture. Out of sight, in a room below the stage, performers readied themselves. Officially, no alcohol was allowed on school premises, but the players needed fortification, so Fred "Tarzan" Lenhart, proprietor of Lenhart's Bar, carried a gym bag into the understage room that broadcast the suspicious noise of clanking bottles.

Bob Brass, his natural frown deeper even than normal, sat nervously with his wife Camille, watching their daughter Mary Kay folk dance. Bill LeVasseur eyed his wife Betty high-kicking in the chorus line in her black net stockings. George Rivers played Costello to someone else's Abbott and goofed his lines. City attorney Don Kelly played a bunny rabbit—at least, he paraded about in a bunny costume. Between scenes, the Tartanaires mixed-couples chorus sang and danced at the edge of the stage. Bob Shield was so nervous trying to play his ukulele, dance, and sing "Good-bye, My Coney Island Baby" all at once that pianist Jim Koelling midway through finally looked up and bellowed, "Smile, Shield." By the time he reached the skit where he played a judge with a white powdered wig and long red winter underwear with a trapdoor, Shield had loosened up.

There were dance choruses and comedy teams and magic shows and banjo pickers. The men dressed as hula dancers and the women, showing their legs, played ladies of the night. Dave Olson did a Sophie Tucker routine, Ralph Colaizy did Eva Tanquay, Cliff Japs did Fanny Brice. The Reverend Tom Herbranson led Pastor Tom & His Heavenly Harmony Four in a rousing set. Planned for two hours, the show stretched to three, the crowd munching popcorn and downing soft drinks. Below the stage, Lenhart's gym bag grew lighter with each half hour.

The official All-America flag-raising took place the next morning, Friday, April 9, at 11:30 A.M., before a scattered gathering of some three hundred in front of the post office at Third and Washington. The trees were bare, and those attending stood wrapped in heavy overcoats, proud but subdued. This moment was more ceremony than celebration. The White Bear High School band played and Roy Wahlberg served as master of ceremonies, introducing some fifteen on the podium, including all the members of the chamber's steering committee. Sally Eckman, Miss White Bear Lake, and Kathy Swenson, Snoball Queen at White Bear High, passed the All-America City official flag to a two-man American Legion color guard. Mayor Milt Knoll raised the flag atop the pole, where it would fly throughout the year. Just then a military B-52 happened to fly by overhead and Roy Wahlberg, being a lieutenant colonel in the air force reserve, couldn't resist.

"My friends are giving us a salute," he proclaimed, leaning into the microphone, which was borrowed from the high school's audio department.

Citizens in the crowd, asked later by a local reporter how they felt, used words such as "flabbergasted" and "thrilled," and talked of how much they enjoyed living where they did.

Following their usual habits when it came to civic affairs, the Jurgenses took no part in the Lions Club or All-America City festivities. In fact, Harold departed early that Friday morning for Hawthorne, Wisconsin, where he planned to spend the weekend helping a friend wire his home. Lois, left alone to care for Robert and Dennis, also found it necessary just then to wash and iron piles of clothes for two nieces, the children of her recently deceased sister Barbara. When the floodwaters again began seeping into their basement that Friday, Lois, once more pushing the garage broom, could barely contain her anger.

"She griped about the water in the basement and the kids and stuff, the basement being flooded . . ." Harold recalled later. "[She was] angry at me . . . for leaving her with the mess with the water in the basement and stuff, more than she could handle . . . [She was] vocal, largely vocal . . . You would swear to God you were talking to five people."

Lois was not the only one who found it necessary to focus on matters other than White Bear Lake's celebration, for the storms and rampaging waterways had not abated. In fact, late that Friday, watching the skies and the swollen Mississippi River that threads through the city's downtown district, St. Paul braced for the worst. Floodwaters were rising at the rate of a foot every nine hours, and engineers predicted if the increase continued, water would reach the twenty-foot mark by late Sunday afternoon—six feet over flood stage. Appeals went out for carpenters and laborers as city workers rushed with plywood boards to heighten the floodwall that ran on the river's east side from Market Street to Randolph Avenue. A private barge company offered four diesel-powered tugboats to the St. Paul police and fire departments, the Ramsey County sheriff's office readied six patrol boats, and two Minnesota National Guard amphibious carry-all vehicles were en route from Camp Ripley. The small downtown St. Paul airport was abandoned to the rising river, and volunteers spent Saturday night filling sandbags.

At half past six that Saturday evening, April 10, another eleven hundred White Bear Lake citizens made their way to Central Junior High, clutching overcoats and umbrellas. After three days of festivities, this night would culminate in the Lions Club show's closing performance.

This time George Rivers managed not to flub his Lou Costello lines, and Bob Shield, no longer nervous, was downright hammy with his ukulele. Shield was so relaxed, in fact, that while chugging from a gallon jug of beer, dressed as the judge in long red underwear, he bobbled the glass jug and it crashed to the floor, spreading glass shards across the stage. No one minded, though, for the last night of the Lions Club show was always loose and irregular. Soon after, the cast began dropping baby chicks from the ceiling at the end of strings just as one star actor or another was in the middle of delivering his lines. Ducks flew across the stage at other odd moments.

After the final curtain fell, the cast and their families and friends drove east on Highway 96 to the Rod and Gun Club, which stood on the outskirts of town. This "afterglow" party was a traditional celebration staged each year following the last performance. Cars slid in the mud of the club's unpaved parking lot as they arrived, for it was raining steadily. Inside, mud from everyone's shoes dried into dust as they danced and reenacted scenes from the show, parodying their own already outlandish acts, falling to the floor with belly laughs.

Bill LeVasseur brought food for a buffet table and others brought their own liquor to spike the setups. Shirley Arkin let the high school dancers attend, but kept an eagle eye on them. All told, one hundred people filled the dance floor—the cast, spouses, boyfriends, girl-friends—laughing and light-headed with relief and accomplishment.

Late that Saturday night, near midnight, the light rain outside deepened into a thunderstorm. Bright lightning filled the roaring skies, and within minutes, a half-inch of rain pummeled the soggy earth, dumped suddenly as if from a giant bucket. The Mississippi River was reaching its flood stage at fourteen feet, and ten miles from White Bear, thousands of volunteers grabbed at sandbags as St. Paul Mayor George Vavoulis declared a state of emergency, calling for aid from "all persons, agencies, companies or groups."

The churchgoers among those at the afterglow party departed by three in the morning, while the rest stayed until dawn. As they finally left the Rod and Gun Club, these stragglers could see the sun rising and reaching through the clearing thunderclouds. It was Palm Sunday, April 11, 1965.

CHAPTER 9

Palm Sunday

White Bear Lake police officer Robert VanderWyst reported for duty at eight o'clock Sunday morning, April 11, 1965, and soon after began cruising through town in his patrol car. Palm Sunday was his wife Kay's thirty-eighth birthday, so VanderWyst's mind drifted to their plans for that evening, after his shift ended at four.

VanderWyst was thirty-six, and had eight children. His sprawling family inhabited a two-story frame house on Hinckley Street, just across from Ramaley Park, where they had ample space but little elegance. They lived just blocks from Lois Jurgens's parents' house on Park, in that midsection of town that comprised White Bear's one distressed pocket. VanderWyst had joined the police department in the fall of 1957, and now made $500 a month—$6,000 a year plus overtime. He had a soft, round face and mild manner, and he chain-smoked cigarettes, lighting one off the end of another.

Born in St. Paul of Dutch-German parents, he'd worked for a time after high school at his father's dry-cleaning business before drifting into police work, attracted by the job security and steady paycheck. Do your job as a cop, he figured, you don't have anything to worry about. In a way, though, VanderWyst seemed miscast as a policeman, for he was uncomplicated and lacking in guile—the other cops thought him terribly square, and such a Christian. Once on night patrol when he discovered two undressed teenagers feverishly copulating in the backseat of a car, he took them to their homes wrapped in police blankets rather than let them get dressed. "Tell your parents what you were doing," he instructed them as he dropped them at their front doors.

Even if miscast, VanderWyst liked police work. He could almost smell driving violations. A car would pass and he'd say to his partner, that guy doesn't have a license. They'd pull the car over and sure enough, no license. One night, VanderWyst's decision to pull over a car led to the discovery inside of fourteen stolen firearms. VanderWyst wrote many close tickets, and clocked everyone with his radar—he loved to run the radar. Those even five miles over the limit got pulled over, as did those who rolled through stop signs. Some days, he'd have several cars lined up in a row, waiting for their citations. Other cops who rode with VanderWyst knew they were in for smoke-filled cars and busy evenings. Judge Bill Fleming grew irritated hearing what he called Bob's "crappy borderline cases," but the cops believed VanderWyst never gave a ticket that wasn't at least technically merited, and for that reason, they found no fault.

VanderWyst was not the least malevolent—he simply was a book cop who thought that his was the way to do police work. He'd give tickets to City Attorney Don Kelly's lawyer friends, who would yell at Kelly, who would appeal to VanderWyst, all to no avail. One Christmas season, the downtown businessmen asked City Manager Ed Bayuk to go easy on the parking meters, and Police Chief Louis Kieffer agreed, but VanderWyst all the same kept slapping tickets on shoppers' cars parked at expired meters. A furious Herb Tousley, then a councilman as well as owner of Tousley Ford, finally called Bayuk, threatening to fire the unfortunate city manager.

"I tried," Bayuk told Tousley. "But it is an ordinance, and Vander-Wyst won't ignore it. He says, 'Tell Tousley to change the ordinance.'"

VanderWyst never had to deal much with violence during his years as a cop. Once, he was summoned to a bar where a fight was underway, but by the time he got there, it was over, one guy floored by a haymaker, the other by a cue stick. VanderWyst told one fellow to go out and wait in the squad car while he tended to the other, and that's just what happened. There'd been no murders, not even a shoot-out, on his beat in eight years, and for this he felt lucky.

Ten miles to the south on Palm Sunday morning, sightseers jammed downtown St. Paul to watch as the Mississippi River rose to historic

levels, while thousands of volunteers scrambled to build dikes and
floodwalls, but during his first two hours of cruising, Bob Vander-
Wyst had found nothing to do. He was alone, the only cop on duty
just then. The sky was thick with clouds and the wet streets were full
of pooled water, but last night's thunderous storm had passed. Temperatures reached toward the upper forties.

Then, at 10:09 A.M., VanderWyst's car radio crackled to life. Officer Gerry Sarracco, sitting that morning as dispatcher in the police
station, was talking to him. Proceed to 2148 South Gardenette Drive,
Sarracco told him. We've had a call from Dr. Peterson. It's a DOA—a
small child. Dr. Peterson is waiting there.

VanderWyst at that moment was near the center of town, about
a mile from Gardenette. He drove down Highway 61, then wound
around the lake's southern shore on White Bear Avenue. To his left,
the water, smooth as a sheet, shimmered in the early sun, and two
sailboats glided in the distance, guided by bold, guiltless men willing
openly to eschew church. VanderWyst turned left on South Shore,
then right on Hazel, which ran into Gardenette Drive. The trip took
only three minutes, but that was plenty of time for VanderWyst to
figure out whose home he was heading for. He did not socialize with
Harold and Lois Jurgens, but he knew them well enough to greet
them on the street, for Lois was sister to the White Bear Lake police
department's number-two man, Lieutenant Jerome Zerwas. Jerry's
sister, VanderWyst thought as he pulled up at 2148 South Gardenette
Drive. This is Jerry's sister's house.

Dr. Roy Peterson opened the front door. VanderWyst knew
Peterson even better than he knew the Jurgenses—Peterson was the
VanderWyst family physician, as he was for most of the White Bear
Lake police force. The cops thought highly of him, for his policy,
ever since hanging out a shingle in 1951, was to charge policemen
and ministers nothing for his services, and give their families a fifty
percent discount. Peterson, a kinetic man with a friendly but edgy
and intense manner, explained this policy by saying he just thought
ministers and cops were deserving and underpaid.

At the front door, Peterson briefed VanderWyst. Harold Jurgens
had called him at about quarter past nine that morning at home, saying he feared his son was dying. By the time he reached their house, the
boy was dead. A DOA, dead on arrival. It was Dennis, their younger
boy. He died around 9:35 A.M., Peterson said. The doctor had called

the White Bear police and the Ramsey County coroner's office—he was, as it happened, the coroner's deputy for the White Bear Lake area.

VanderWyst stepped into the living room and greeted the Jurgenses. Harold and Lois both seemed agitated and distraught to him, but he saw no tears. Harold paced about, unwilling to sit down. Lois moved from the front room to the hallway to the bedroom and back, sitting for a moment on the living room couch, then rising again to restart her journey.

VanderWyst glanced into the back bedroom and saw Dennis. Arms, shoulders and a small head poked above a blanket. He quickly pulled back from the doorway and returned to the living room. Bob figured he'd wait for the coroner's investigator before looking further at the body.

VanderWyst spoke first with Harold, then Lois, and they told much the same story. Dennis had been suffering from a bad cold. The morning before—Saturday—he had slipped on the basement floor near the bathroom, damp from flooding caused by the thaw, and struck his forehead on the tile. Harold had been away, out of town—he'd left Friday morning to help a friend with electrical work in northern Wisconsin. Lois had called Harold on Saturday to say Dennis was sick, and Harold had returned home that night. He checked Dennis several times during the night. At eight o'clock Sunday morning he took Dennis to the bathroom and placed him on the toilet. Dennis was fine then, talking normally, even noticing that his dad's watch was broken. When Lois went into Dennis's bedroom to check him again, though, he was gasping for breath, gurgling. They had immediately called Dr. Peterson.

VanderWyst, asking questions and taking notes, tried to get Harold and Lois to fill in their story and clarify the sequence of events, but the Jurgenses resisted. In time, he realized they were emphasizing a handful of themes, and wanted to dwell only on them: *Slipping on the floor . . . bad cold . . . well taken care of . . . Harold out of town.* The Jurgenses kept going back to the same points over and over. Only on one issue did the story ever vary. Dennis had also fallen down the basement stairs during the past week and struck the back of his head, Lois said at one point. He slipped near the bathroom and he also fell down the stairs.

VanderWyst, still waiting for the coroner's investigator to arrive, searched his mind for what to do next. The Jurgenses' other boy,

Robert, had been sitting with them in the living room earlier, but now was up and running about.

"Is there anything I can do for you?" VanderWyst asked Lois. "Do you want me to take Robert over to my house for a while? Kay could take care of him."

That would be a good idea, Lois said.

VanderWyst left the Jurgens home with Robert shortly before eleven o'clock. They drove the one mile in silence. It never occurred to VanderWyst to question his young companion. What, after all, could a five-year-old tell him?

VanderWyst's wife Kay could not remember ever seeing Robert before. He was such a slight child—thirty-three pounds, three feet two inches tall, average measurements for a three-year-old. He would not talk much, and stood off to the side, watching as Kay's eight kids scrambled about their front yard. She figured he was bashful. Then again, he was pretty much outnumbered, eight to one, by these older kids. It probably was quite overwhelming. Like her husband, Kay did not try to question Robert.

As he was driving back to the Jurgens home, VanderWyst's car radio crackled again at 11:04 A.M. A car was blocking a driveway at 823 Fifth Street, the dispatcher said. Reported by a Mr. Charles. VanderWyst was the only officer on duty, and this address was just six blocks away, so he turned north on Highway 61. By the time he reached the house on Fifth, the guilty car had already pulled away, so he turned and drove back to the Jurgenses.

He reached South Gardenette Drive at 11:25 A.M. A moment later, the coroner's investigator, Saveiro C. Pitera, and the ambulance driver, John Stone, arrived. Together, the three entered Dennis's bedroom and approached the crib by the north wall.

Dennis was lying on his back in the crib with his arms tautly stretched alongside his body, the hands and forearms reaching upwards, lifted, stiff, eight inches off the mattress. Bed covers pulled up to below his armpits obscured the lower part of Dennis's body, but VanderWyst could see a good number of black-and-blue spots on his face, head and arms. An awful lot, VanderWyst thought, and different shades—some dark and fresh, some faded and healing. On Dennis's face alone, VanderWyst counted at least a dozen bruises, large and small. A big harsh abrasion covered the center of his forehead. Dennis's nose was blood red and peeling—so red, VanderWyst thought, it looked like if you just wiped it once the skin would pull away.

"Let's prepare the body for removal," Pitera said.

The three men backed out of the bedroom, Stone walking to the ambulance for a plastic sheet, Pitera and VanderWyst joining the Jurgenses and Dr. Peterson in the living room. When the ambulance driver returned moments later, he, Pitera and Harold Jurgens reentered the bedroom. Stone had trouble wrapping the plastic sheet around Dennis's body, so Harold assisted him. The body, Pitera thought when they finished, was wrapped much as a mother would bundle a baby. Coroner's work was a part-time occupation for him—he taught during the week at St. Gregory's, the parochial school over on Montreal.

Stone carried the body in a cradle position through the kitchen and out the house's back door, held open by VanderWyst. They all passed through the backyard and the garage, then down the driveway to the hearse.

"Did you ever see rigor mortis set in like this?" Pitera asked VanderWyst as they walked toward the hearse.

While Stone put Dennis's body on a cart pulled from the rear of the hearse, VanderWyst reached out and pushed down on Dennis's arms, which were protruding from the plastic wrapping. The arms barely moved they were so stiff, so VanderWyst quickly stopped pushing, fearful they would break.

Odd, VanderWyst thought. From 9:35 A.M. to 11:30 A.M., somebody doesn't get that stiff.

"Do you have a camera in your patrol car?" Pitera asked VanderWyst. "We should take pictures."

No, VanderWyst said, he did not.

Stone closed the hearse's rear door as Pitera gave VanderWyst a copy of the coroner's report for him to witness. A moment later, with Stone at the wheel and Pitera beside him on the front seat, the hearse backed out of the driveway and headed for the Ramsey County morgue.

VanderWyst, alone in the driveway, turned and walked back into the house. Sitting together in the living room, the Jurgenses again repeated their points—Dennis had been ill, he'd slipped on the basement floor, Harold had checked him all through the night until eight in the morning, he'd been okay in the bathroom, Lois had found him gurgling shortly after nine o'clock.

VanderWyst hesitated. Dennis's stiff arms had stirred in him a vague caution. Better shut my mouth for a while, he told himself. Better not ask too many pointed questions. Instead, VanderWyst looked at Dr. Peterson for direction. Bob knew and trusted him. Peterson was his own family's doctor, and a deputy coroner as well.

Peterson glanced away, saying nothing.

The doctor did not want to be there. Two hours before, sitting in his waterside home on the southeast shore of White Bear Lake, Sunday morning had seemed so promising. From the patio off his living room and the balcony off his bedroom, he could look across the lake to Manitou Island, and beyond, to the town of White Bear. He had lived in this home since 1953, and it gave him much pleasure. It was full of redwood and log railings, and the lawn and trees ran almost to the water's edge, a good hundred feet of lake frontage in all. Mornings there were wonderful, but the dusk was the doctor's favorite time, for the sun set each evening over the water and trees, falling behind Manitou Island, leaving behind a fiery orange sky.

Peterson's house sat precisely on the site of the old Wildwood Amusement Park. The roller coaster had been just to the west of his lot, the water slide just to the east, and the dance pavilion exactly where his house now stood, the old foundation still there below his lawn and patio. The electric streetcar with overhead power lines, running as a spur off the main railroad tracks along Highway 61, would stop just three doors down. When they cleared land for his basement, they'd found old rolls of amusement park tickets—three rides for a nickel.

In winter, they got the north wind, so the lake froze too rough for ice skating. Instead, Peterson would build an ice rink on his front lawn—he'd raise a circular wood wall, lay in six inches of leaves gathered from all the neighbors for mulch, then cover that with sheet plastic, one hundred feet long, fifty feet wide, and fill it with water from the hose. When it froze, he'd hang lights on the seven surrounding elm trees, put out snow sculptures of bears and seals tinted with food coloring, and invite all the neighborhood kids to join his own two children in skating and hockey games.

In summer, Peterson caught little sunfish off his dock or from his motorboat—they had the loveliest taste, the fillet just the size of a half dollar, two good bites each. They also caught crappies and smallmouth bass and northern pike, but the sunfish were the best. From their patio, they could see huge bass jumping in the water. When the wind was up, Peterson would take out his sixteen-foot sailboat and glide toward Manitou Island and the town of White Bear.

"I think my son is dying," Harold Jurgens had told the doctor on the phone that morning. As Peterson followed Wildwood Avenue west along the lake's shore toward Gardenette Park, he'd rehearsed in his mind the resuscitation techniques he knew from the rescue squad. When he arrived at the Jurgens home, though, he'd realized all that was pointless. The boy was obviously dead. There's nothing worse, Peterson had thought, than seeing a dead child. The situation had made him uncomfortable, so uncomfortable that he hadn't pulled down the blankets or examined the body further.

Now VanderWyst was looking at him, asking a question: "What was the cause of death?"

The doctor's eyes slid to a corner of the room. He couldn't comprehend anyone torturing a kid, Peterson would explain many years later. But this death didn't look as though it was from natural causes. There was obviously going to be trouble, and he didn't want to get involved. It was not his job to do anything other than pronounce the boy dead.

"I can't say at this time."

VanderWyst didn't push the matter. He knew Peterson as a man always willing to help others, as a doctor very much for his patients. He never wanted to say a bad word about anyone. They just weren't going to get any damaging information from him.

Peterson departed soon after. Moments later, VanderWyst, rising to leave, asked Lois if there was anything else he could do, such as call her brother Jerome. Strange, he thought, that she hadn't called her brother, the police lieutenant.

No, Lois said, sounding definite. If he's notified there would be fifty people at her house, and she didn't want that many people around.

VanderWyst climbed into his patrol car and backed down the Jurgens driveway at 11:48 A.M.

VanderWyst's departure did not go unnoticed. Nor had his arrival two hours before. From behind their curtains and blinds, the Jurgenses' neighbors on Gardenette Drive had been watching the comings and goings all morning with mounting interest. They saw the hearse sitting in the Jurgenses' driveway, and a big blue convertible, and the police car parked awkwardly, askew, as if the officer had been in a hurry. At first Bob Brass thought the squad car was Lois's brother's, but then they saw VanderWyst in the driveway. Camille Brass knew the blue convertible belonged to Dr. Peterson. Soon the word spread from house to house—there'd been a death, the younger Jurgens boy had died. They said it was from a fall down the basement stairs.

The neighbors talked among themselves that afternoon. They felt sad, and also naggingly disturbed. After all, Dorothy Engfer more than once had seen Lois smack Dennis so hard the blood flowed from his nose, and Gladys DeMars had watched Dennis over two summers wither from a husky, jolly baby to a wan little boy covered with bruises and black eyes and split lips. Gladys and Dorothy talked frequently to each other about what they had seen, not unaware that they'd recommended the Jurgenses to the welfare department caseworker. They wanted to do something, but felt it was none of their business. Who'd listen? they figured. It would be no use. Instead, Dorothy Engfer began telling others in the neighborhood what she'd seen. She talked about it all the time, in fact. Lois was mean to Dennis—Cam Brass and Donna Neely and the others understood that much.

A dead boy, though, was something else. How could a kid fall down the steps and die? Donna Neely wondered, as she studied the Jurgenses' now-silent house from her front window. Our kids have fallen down steps and not died.

CHAPTER 10

The Size of a Nickel

There was no question what Bob VanderWyst had to do when he left the Jurgens home shortly before noon on Palm Sunday. Even if he hadn't received an order over the car radio, he would, on his own, have ended up where the dispatcher directed him.

From Gardenette Park, he crossed Highway 61 and plunged into a neighborhood of small modest ramblers, which at a turn onto Park Avenue gave way suddenly to something less tamed and manicured— a country lane, narrow and curb-less, densely treed and tangled with weeping willows. One block down, where Park dead-ended into a wooded marshland, stood Lois Jurgens's parents' home, a pale yellow one-story frame and brick-gabled structure. VanderWyst glanced at it, noticing a torn cast-off sofa in their side yard, but then turned his wheel and pulled into the driveway of the house across the street, at 1952 Park. This was an even smaller home—a gray-blue bungalow with a wood rail fence, a basement window rising off the driveway, and the dark, dense swamp lapping at the back side. As VanderWyst climbed from his squad car, a figure appeared at the front door to greet him.

Standing next to VanderWyst in his driveway, Lieutenant Jerome Zerwas provided a striking study in contrast. Where VanderWyst slouched, Jerome stood erect, almost at attention, six feet and 180 pounds of hard muscle, his stomach flat as a washboard. Born two years after his sister Lois, he was then thirty-eight and the father of five children.

VanderWyst couldn't help but like Jerome, for he was an open, outgoing man, full of spirit and masculine charm and a flirtatious way with women—all the things Bob was not. Still, VanderWyst usually felt wary in his presence, for Jerome had a way about him that VanderWyst thought almost too charming. "Wheeler-dealer" was the description that usually popped into his mind when he thought of his boss.

Jerome was one of those people who seemed to stomp through life, getting his way sometimes by the exercise of power, other times by sheer force of personality. In downtown St. Paul on a busy Friday afternoon, VanderWyst once saw a bulky lady march imperiously across a major boulevard at midblock, stopping traffic with a commanding glare and an outstretched palm, and that was precisely the attitude he saw every day in Jerome.

The encounter between Jerome Zerwas and Bob VanderWyst that Palm Sunday afternoon would later be described by the two men in quite different fashions. Jerome sent his children to play in the basement recreation room—that much seems certain—but what followed would forever after remain under dispute.

"VanderWyst said that the child fell down the stairs and there was a small bruise like a scrape mark approximately the size of a nickel on his forehead and he had a red mark on his nose . . . He didn't mention any other injuries . . ." Jerome said one month later, and then again, over and over, in later years.

Just why VanderWyst would feel motivated to downplay Dennis's condition to Jerome is a question left unanswered. "I don't know," Jerome would always say, "but that's what Bob told me."

Maybe so. It is not hard to imagine VanderWyst overwhelmed in Jerome's presence, struggling to hold his own, offering accommodations, wanting to be friends and equals. All the same, VanderWyst's own version of this meeting does not match Jerome's in the least, although the two accounts share a common theme.

"I told Jerome there were so many bruises on the body you couldn't fit a nickel in between them," is the way VanderWyst put it years later.

As it happens, such puzzling disparities between Jerome Zerwas's version of events and other people's would become a common theme in the Jurgens saga. Time after time, various figures in the story would recall episodes one way, while Jerome would either describe them quite differently, or—even more frequently—insist they'd never happened at all.

If Jerome was a puzzlement, he was an interesting one. He was an almost legendary figure in White Bear Lake, sinister to some, admirable to others, but always worth talking about. Even those who knew they were being manipulated had to admit Jerome was a personable, fun-loving guy. He knew everyone in town and was a good time in a bar or at a party, ogling women in miniskirts, offering jokes and crazy comments, sending his friends home laughing. He also helped his pals—if you needed your house wired or a hole dug in the backyard, he showed up.

Whatever else his colleagues on the force thought, they didn't consider Jerome a coward. He'd back them up whenever needed, always ready to help out with a 2:00 A.M. search warrant and interrogation. He had a way of interviewing suspects that might not entirely embrace the finer points of the law, but the method all the same proved effective in reaching the truth quickly. *Don't give me any bullshit, I want to hear the truth, mister,* he'd say, towering over his unfortunate subjects. *Mister, you tell me the truth. I know all about you. You better tell the truth.* Jerome's exploits had appeared more than once in the pages of the local *White Bear Press.* When Al Kochen's two-year-old daughter fell down the steps while they were visiting a friend's home in White Bear Lake, Jerome rushed little Kimberly Rose to St. John's Hospital in his squad car with speed and calm, where her head was sutured by Dr. Roy Peterson. After four emotionally disturbed juveniles assaulted a child care worker and escaped from the Lino Lakes Treatment Center in a stolen car, Jerome single-handedly captured them at gunpoint following a high-speed chase.

Jerome built and nurtured relationships in all sorts of ways.

For example, he endeared himself to the downtown merchants by collecting on their bad checks. He'd drop by Bill LeVasseur's grocery for Twinkies and a Coke and learn that LaVasseur was holding two bad checks, for, say, $33 and $45. He'd take the checks, go visit whoever wrote them, then come to LaVasseur a couple days later with the money. Jerome's fellow cops were sure he was making a good commission, but the grocer later insisted Jerome would never take anything from him.

Jerome's attitude toward traffic violations did not always match VanderWyst's.

A White Bear Lake insurance agent was driving home from a Minnesota Twins baseball game late one school night with his children, speeding past Jantzen's Motel on Highway 61 in his effort to get the kids home to bed, when red lights started flashing behind him. The man reached for, but couldn't find, his driver's license.

"Where are you going?" Jerome said. "Why the rush?"

"I'm trying to get the kids home."

"I gotta give you a ticket."

"No, you don't."

"I already called it in."

"Come on."

Jerome grinned then. "Okay, get out of here. Get those kids home."

Another night, a local bank loan officer was a passenger with half a dozen other guys, some drinking, in a car going down Highway 61 after a party over on Bald Eagle. The banker playfully grabbed the wheel just as the driver was turning left onto Fourth Street, and the car overshot its turn, ending up against the old railroad depot. Jerome was sitting right there at the intersection in his squad car.

"What the hell you doing?" he demanded.

"Something's wrong with the cam on the car," the banker said.

Jerome looked from fellow to fellow. He knew them all.

"Get out of here," he said. "Go on home."

A nephew recalls that a week before the spring police auctions, Jerome would phone the Zerwas clan kids and let them come down early for their choice of bikes. On the Fourth of July, a niece remembers, he'd confiscate the neighborhood kids' illegal fireworks, then bring them home for the Zerwas children.

Unlike some of the siblings in the Zerwas clan's large, impoverished Depression-era family, Jerome always scrambled. By fifteen he was on his own in California working at a shipyard, sending half his paycheck home to his parents, and by eighteen he was in the army. After his discharge in July of 1947, he worked at assorted jobs—construction, spray-painting cars, hauling scrap iron and vegetables—before answering White Bear's newspaper ad in 1954 seeking a patrolman. Even after becoming a police officer, Jerome was always pulling off one deal or another.

One story had him starting with a cow, swapping it for a wooden-wheel bike, and eventually ending up with a 1958 Chevy

that yielded him a $2,000 profit. When the freeways started com-
ing in, he bought the homes that had to be cleared for the right of
way and moved them to seven open acres of land he'd purchased
in White Bear's northwest corner, laying block and digging founda-
tions and working himself ragged. He ended up selling five houses in
two years—"Zerwas Acres" the other cops called it—and word had
it he cleared $75,000. Jerome also dabbled in automobiles. The city
was not particular how it got rid of old squad cars, for example, and
somehow many of them ended up needing tune-ups just before they
were junked. Then Jerome would buy and sell them. When Roger
Belanger was new to the White Bear police force, he happened to
mention to Jerome that his brother was looking for a used car. Two
nights later, Jerome pulled up at the station with a rusting clunker
he wanted to sell to Roger. The kids in the Zerwas family called him
"Uncle Buck."

His colleagues inside the White Bear police force and the mayor
back then, Milt Knoll, say there was no question that Jerome, officially the lieutenant and number-two man, dominated the department in the mid-1960s.

This was so partly because of who occupied the chief's office.
Even those who thought well of Wayne Armstrong allowed that he
probably was too mild a man to run a police force. Then forty-five,
he'd arrived in White Bear Lake just six months before Dennis Jurgens's death. White Bear's thirteen-man force was a good deal smaller
than the force Armstrong had headed in Rapid City, South Dakota,
but the $8,200 civil service annual salary was higher. Armstrong's
debut in town had been marked by a photo, atop page one of the
local *White Bear Press*, which portrayed the new chief shaking hands
with Lieutenant Jerome Zerwas, both men smiling, Armstrong in a
business suit, Jerome looming some three inches above him in his
freshly pressed uniform.

The new chief's most daunting task upon arriving was to find a
house big enough for his wife and ten children, and this mission was
not helped by his seemingly chronic shortage of funds. When one
of his uninsured sons got involved in an auto accident, Armstrong's
license was revoked because he was the car's registered owner, and
for want of money needed to remedy matters, the town's police chief
drove around without a license until a city official loaned him $400.
One winter, the Armstrongs spent two weeks in Jerome Zerwas's

basement, after the lieutenant found his chief's whole family living out by Dellwood in cabins on stilts that lacked water or heat.

However, neither his unfamiliarity with the job and town, nor his apparent discomfort with making hard decisions, represented Armstrong's chief problem. It was his constant tendency to fall asleep—at his desk, in meetings, while talking to his officers—that seemed the most trying complication. Only years later, after he'd left the force, did doctors figure out he'd been suffering all that time from narcolepsy.

For whatever the combination of reasons, Armstrong by all accounts relied increasingly on Jerome for guidance, and the extent of this dependency eventually alarmed other officers. Once, driving together to a conference in Arden Hills, Roger Belanger tried to warn the chief, but Armstrong just nodded and said nothing.

"When Louis Kieffer was chief, Jerome ran the outside operation," said Belanger, who in time became a lieutenant himself. "But when Armstrong came in 1964, Jerome really came to power. He got on the inside track with Wayne, who fell asleep a lot and was not aggressive. Jerome could manipulate him. Jerome basically ran the department then. He'd tell you to do this, don't do that. If you had a foot patrol, Jerome would tell you to go do something else. Anything he said, Wayne would go along with."

It is fair to say that by 1965, Jerome Zerwas had pulled himself far above his beginnings. He drank liquor with cops, shared coffee with merchants such as Bob Brass, lunched over at Jantzen's Motel with Judge Bill Fleming and the city hall crowd, and had connections throughout Ramsey County. If there was one thread in Jerome's character that everyone agreed upon just then, it was his great pride—in himself and in the Zerwas name and in what he had accomplished in life. Aspersions about his roots did not sit well with the lieutenant.

"You pushed his button if you said stuff against his family," said White Bear Police Officer Gerry Sarracco, "like if you said his dad drank or was abusive. To Jerome, he was a saint."

In all, Bob VanderWyst and Jerome Zerwas spent some twenty minutes together that Palm Sunday afternoon. Jerome describes the conversation as being rather sparse after Bob reported Dennis's nickel-sized bruise and fall down the steps.

"We sat and had coffee and that was it. There was no more said about it . . . I thought the kid had broke his neck and that was the last I heard of it . . ."

VanderWyst headed for the police station when he left the lieutenant's house. Jerome does not recollect going anywhere. In fact, when the question arose much later, he was quite adamant.

"I stayed home on Sunday," he insisted. "I never left the house on Sunday."

CHAPTER 11

Suspicions

While Jerome Zerwas and Bob VanderWyst talked, Dennis's body was being carried through a garage into the basement autopsy room of the coroner's office in downtown St. Paul, a twenty-by-forty-foot cavern with a dirty white tile floor and twelve gleaming stainless steel crypts set in one wall. In the middle of the room, two banks of fluorescent lights hung low over a stainless steel table, and that is where Foster Brown, the morgue attendant, placed Dennis.

Minutes later, Saveiro Pitera, troubled by what he'd seen in the Jurgens home, asked Brown to undress the dead child. As the attendant removed a pair of pajamas, an undershirt, rubber pants and two diapers, Pitera could see that the arm and facial bruises he had viewed at the Jurgens home continued across virtually all of Dennis's body, radiating in every direction, varying from the size of a dime to a half dollar. Brown and Pitera counted five bruises on the left leg, eleven on the right leg, eight on the right arm, two on the left arm. There was a deep laceration at the base of the penis.

Pitera walked to a phone in the small office just off the autopsy room and called Nick Burkowski, a photographer who regularly took photos for the coroner's office. Then he went looking for Thomas Flaherty, the coroner's chief investigator.

"All those bruises can't be natural," Pitera told Flaherty. "And I've never seen rigor set in so quickly. Look at those raised arms."

After Flaherty saw the body for himself, he called the Ramsey County coroner, Dr. Thomas Votel.

"This looks like one you ought to see," Flaherty told Votel.

Another dead kid, the coroner thought when he showed up soon after. Fourth one like this in the past year. Just in recent weeks, there'd been a ten-month-old with a ruptured liver and a three-month-old with a skull fracture. Votel was a general practitioner, with no expertise in forensics or pathology, but he couldn't help feeling uneasy.

Votel and Flaherty wanted Dennis's body X-rayed, so after Nick Burkowski photographed it at 12:30 P.M., Pitera again bundled the corpse and carried it in a cradle position to the ambulance. Lost in his own thoughts, he stayed with Dennis for the ride to Ancker Hospital's radiology department and back.

At 2:00 P.M., Dr. Robert Woodburn, a pathologist from Charles T. Miller Hospital who handled coroner's assignments on the side, began his autopsy. He counted from fifty to one hundred bruises running the length of the body, the exact number hard to judge because so many overlapped. They varied in color, some fresh, some old—black and blue, yellowish green, reddish. They covered the legs, the arms, the hands, the front and back of the head, the shoulders, the buttocks, the small of the back, the middle of the back, the back of the left leg. There was a large, swollen abrasion on the forehead. There was a bluish mark on the right side of the head that started at the temple and extended to behind the right ear. There was a deep, ulcerous lesion at the base of the penis and dark bruises on the tip.

Something else besides the bruises seemed odd to Woodburn. The body was severely undernourished, nearly emaciated—he could find no subcutaneous fat at all. How could that be? Everyone normally has some fat in varying degrees, and young children quite a lot.

None of this, however, was what had killed Dennis. During the internal autopsy, Woodburn found a quarter-inch perforation in the boy's small bowel. The hole had allowed a fifth of a quart of infectious, purulent fecal material to flow into the abdominal cavity. The perforation, Woodburn judged, had occurred one to two days before the child's death. During that time, the abdominal cavity's surface tissue, normally shiny, had turned dull, and the pus-filled matter had solidified, forming adhesions, matting together pieces of the bowel—classic signs of peritonitis. Dennis most likely had died after an extended period of agonizing pain, Woodburn realized, and he'd died needlessly. Peritonitis was usually treatable with antibiotics, and a rent bowel could be repaired, but only if you chose to summon a doctor.

In his one-page written autopsy report, Woodburn offered a diagnosis of peritonitis due to traumatic perforation of the small bowel, but he did not speculate on the nature of the trauma. Nor did he comment on the body's extreme rigor or oddly raised arms. His job as pathologist was to determine the immediate cause of death—it was up to the coroner to rule on the mode by which that cause of death was reached.

When the young coroner's assistant Jim Essling reported for work early that Sunday afternoon, the morgue attendant pulled him aside.

"Boy, there's a bad one in there," Foster Brown said.

Sergeant Pete Korolchuk arrived at 4:00 P.M. that Sunday for his evening shift at the White Bear police station, and Bob VanderWyst immediately began briefing him about the Jurgens death.

Korolchuk, then thirty-eight, was a cop with no funny corners. Quiet and always self-contained, methodical and soft-spoken, he was respected in the station, but he was not the sort of man others got to know too well.

VanderWyst's story quickly drew Korolchuk's attention, for he had a connection to the Zerwas clan. As a boy, back in 1941 and 1942, coming from a troubled home and left at loose ends, he'd lived in the Zerwas home for two years. Lois was about his age. He hadn't seen much of Harold and Lois for the past twenty-odd years, although one Sunday just the year before, he and his wife had bumped into the Jurgenses walking back from St. Mary's Church with their two boys. The Jurgenses had stopped by Korolchuk's house, just blocks from the church, and stayed for half an hour. Their two boys, so well behaved, had sat on little stools in the living room the whole time.

As VanderWyst and Korolchuk were talking, the police dispatcher interrupted. The Ramsey County coroner had just called, she said, asking if the policeman who handled the Jurgens call could come to the coroner's office right away. Korolchuk, in charge at the police station that afternoon, decided to accompany VanderWyst.

Tom Flaherty met them at the door and led them downstairs to the autopsy room. He wanted the officers to look at Dennis's body. It was now 5:00 P.M.

"Did you see it this morning?" Flaherty asked VanderWyst.

"I just looked to see there was a body there," VanderWyst answered. "The doctor was there, and I knew him. Peterson said the boy was dead and hadn't been moved. I didn't question further. I looked to see if there was a body there and that's it. Just saw the head, little bit of the arms. People from the coroner's office were coming."

"Well, you better take a look, it's in mighty bad condition," Flaherty said.

Korolchuk, leaning over, saw the bruises and abrasions. So many different colors, he thought. Looking behind Dennis's ears, he noticed small marks and scars. These were unique, quite different from the other markings—little slits, several behind each ear, each about three-eighths of an inch long, narrow and slightly curved, like half-moons. Korolchuk's eyes, running down the length of the three-foot-long body, stopped again at the penis. The injury at its base seemed like a raw open wound. It looked to Korolchuk as if it had been there for quite some time, as if it had healed and broken open again repeatedly. The bluish mark at the tip of the penis was of a different sort—it seemed as though something with force, some sort of pressure, had caused this one. It looked to Korolchuk like a bite mark.

VanderWyst felt sick. I really goofed, he told himself. I should have called a photographer, professional or not, to take pictures in the home. I have nothing to show what he looked like in the house. Shaken, searching for a reason to explain this failure, VanderWyst finally fixed on Peterson. The doctor had appeared so calm and collected. He'd given no indication there was something wrong.

"At the house, I touched the boy's arm, pushed it down hard to where I thought it might break, and it didn't move," VanderWyst told Flaherty. "Could anybody get as stiff as he was within two, two-and-a-half hours?"

Flaherty shook his head. "Absolutely not."

Returning to the White Bear police station, Sergeant Korolchuk called Chief Armstrong, asking that he come down for a briefing. He also decided to summon Harold Jurgens.

At 6:30 P.M. Sunday evening, Harold settled into a chair in the police department's squad room, located just behind the dispatcher's station. To VanderWyst, Harold seemed fidgety, very nervous. Korolchuk did most of the questioning.

The sergeant told Harold what they'd seen at the coroner's office, and asked whether Harold could explain why the boy had so many bruises all over his body.

Dennis usually did have bruises on him, Harold said, because he frequently fell and bruised easily.

Korolchuk asked about the fresh bruises.

Harold could think of no cause other than the fall in the basement the day before.

How could so many bruises be present in various parts of the body unrelated to the area injured in the fall?

Dennis was the sort of individual who was insensitive to pain, Harold explained, and therefore didn't complain or tell them when he was hurt.

As the questioning continued, Harold's answers tended to ramble. He was tacking on all sorts of comments, straying to unrelated matters, responding to anticipated questions that had not yet been asked. Dennis always had constipation problems, he said. As far as he was concerned, the boy didn't seem to know how to force a stool from his rectum.

Korolchuk asked about the open wound at the base of the penis.

One time last summer, Harold said, Dennis had been standing in the bathtub and had turned on the hot water faucet, which scalded his genital area. Dennis was treated then, but the penis kept healing slowly and cracking open again.

The pathologist thought Dennis's condition bordered on malnutrition, Korolchuk said.

Dennis ate good, Harold said, the same things Robert ate. He didn't seem to know how to eat properly, though, didn't know how to chew. Sometimes he swallowed chunks of food without chewing.

Harold again explained that he hadn't been home for a couple of days, he'd been gone in Wisconsin from Friday morning to Saturday night, and didn't know about the fall in the basement until he returned home.

Korolchuk studied Harold. The boy was dead, somebody had to have caused this death. They needed proof, though. He would try to force the issue.

"Has Dennis been hit or kicked in any way?" Korolchuk asked.

"Not to my knowledge," Harold said.

Now, as the questions grew more pointed, Harold became more cautious, less inclined to talk at all. He wanted only to repeat his themes—Dennis was uncoordinated, Dennis fell a lot, Dennis bruised easily, Dennis did not feel pain.

Has Dennis been hit or kicked? Korolchuk asked again.

"Not to my knowledge," Harold repeated.

After half an hour, the meeting broke up. Harold left the police station shortly after seven o'clock.

An hour later, Korolchuk and VanderWyst met Dr. Peterson at his office on Fourth Street. Peterson had outfitted his single-story storefront with wood veneer paneling and an inexpensive shag carpet. Beyond the waiting area, five examination rooms branched off the right side of a corridor. Peterson's cramped office was at the end of the hallway, off to the left. The doctor sat there behind a small desk, his diplomas on the wall behind him, with the two policemen before him in straightback chairs.

The two officers felt ill at ease in this setting. Peterson, after all, was their own family doctor, and he was well liked in White Bear Lake. Most days, he kept the five examining rooms full, never stopping for lunch. He made his rounds in the morning at two hospitals, Mounds Park and St. John's, doing some general surgery—gall bladder, hysterectomy, ovarian cysts, vein stripping—then had office hours in the afternoon, two evenings and Saturday. Somehow, he also fit in house calls and emergency work for the town's rescue squad. If he got a call at three in the morning from the rescue squad or police, heart attack or something, he'd be on his way. Your son was sick or needed a football physical, you could bring him right over. If someone didn't have the money, he'd put it on the bill. If you couldn't pay the bill, he'd say someday you'll have it. Without charging anything, he regularly cared for an old welfare couple who lived near him on the lake.

For all the good feeling Peterson inspired, though, not everyone respected him as a doctor. He worked very fast, always on the go, never stopping or standing still, moving through his five examination rooms in the time other doctors might handle one room, and even those who liked him thought he was not terribly thorough. Office visits did not last long because Peterson usually prescribed something within a couple of minutes.

In truth, Peterson was considered loose with the prescription pad. "Penicillin Pete" was his widely known nickname around town. Penicillin, it seemed to some of his patients, was his cure for everything. Diet pills were also popular solutions, and sometimes available by phone.

All in all, Peterson was rather flashy for a doctor in White Bear Lake. He drove sports cars and convertibles, for one thing. And he was quite sociable—a woman, having a baby at St. John's and sharing a room with a patient of Peterson's, was startled one night when the doctor visited them with a cocktail for his patient and the suggestion that they all lunch together. Then there was the doctor's wife Laurie, a vivacious, flirtatious blonde and accomplished professional actress, and Peterson's own blackface Al Jolson solos at Lions Club shows—his towering, commanding "Suwannee," "Lucky Old Sun," "Old Man River" renditions could silence a jam-packed auditorium.

"You're not going to contemplate the nature of disease and medical philosophy in Roy Peterson's office," the doctor's good friend, Judge Fleming, once observed. "If I were going to ask someone the cause of death, I wouldn't turn to Peterson."

That was just what Korolchuk and VanderWyst needed to do, though. Sitting in the doctor's office, the officers described the body as they'd seen it at the morgue. Because Peterson was a deputy coroner, Korolchuk also told him that the pathologist had diagnosed the cause of death to be peritonitis, due to a ruptured bowel.

This news transformed Peterson. VanderWyst always knew him to be talkative, friendly, happy-go-lucky, but now, as if a switch had been thrown, Peterson became guarded and uncomfortable. He no longer wanted to talk. Questions drew vague or clipped answers.

When Peterson indicated that he'd last seen Dennis just two and a half months ago, the officers asked about the open wound on the penis, but the doctor couldn't remember seeing anything like that. When Korolchuk asked if it were possible for Dennis, with peritonitis, to be conscious and easily talking at 8:00 A.M., just an hour and a half before he died, Peterson did not answer. When Korolchuk asked about the bruised, wounded condition of Dennis's body, Peterson said he couldn't recall any but the forehead and facial bruises because he hadn't viewed the rest of the body.

Looking down at his nearly empty notepad, VanderWyst realized that the doctor just was not giving conclusive answers to any of their questions. The policeman could think of nothing more to say, though. The fact was, despite the empty notepad, VanderWyst liked Peterson, liked him very much. He did so much for people. The cop thought the doctor was a classy guy.

"What pathologist performed the autopsy?" Peterson asked.

"Woodburn," Korolchuk replied.

"Okay, I'll call Dr. Woodburn and discuss with him the cause of death," Peterson said. "I'll also send in a report to the coroner's office."

The three men chatted for a few more moments, then the two officers rose and departed.

At 8:30 P.M., Korolchuk and VanderWyst stopped by the Jurgens home and asked to see the basement where Dennis had fallen. Harold opened a door off the kitchen and led them down a steep wood stairwell, painted gray. The basement was damp and only partly finished, with a green-beige linoleum-tile floor. An exercise bicycle and a spring rocking horse occupied the middle of the room. Harold led the officers some fifteen feet from the bottom of the stairs to an area in the basement's southeast corner, just outside a small bathroom.

Dennis, he said, fell as he was coming out of the bathroom. Right outside the door, he slipped on the damp tile and fell, face forward, spread-eagled, striking his forehead.

Korolchuk frowned. At the police station, didn't Harold say something about Dennis falling down the stairs? The sergeant asked again how Dennis could have sustained so many bruises from such a fall.

Dennis was always bumping into things, falling down, Harold replied.

Passing through the living room, heading toward the front door, Korolchuk studied Lois. They had lived as children in the same house, but now he hardly knew her.

Back at the station, Korolchuk received a phone call from Tom Flaherty at the coroner's office. A John Norton had called Ramsey County Sheriff's Deputy Vern Phillips earlier that evening, Flaherty reported, and Phillips in turn had called him. This Norton had information about the Jurgenses.

Korolchuk and VanderWyst reached John Norton's home at 11:00 P.M. He lived in Willernie, a small pocket of a town to the southeast of White Bear, just off the far corner of the lake where the Wildwood Amusement Park once stood. Norton was a talkative man, given to punctuating his conversation with meaningful nods and winks. He escorted the policemen into a small, plainly furnished living room.

He'd already heard of Dennis's death through the family grapevine, he explained. He did not himself know the Jurgenses personally, but he had relatives who'd married into the Zerwas family. He'd heard that Dennis had been abused for a long time. He was sure most of the Zerwases were aware of Dennis's mistreatment, as well as persons outside the family.

He gave the policemen a list of several names, relatives who might talk. Above all, he said, you should visit Lois's brother Lloyd Zerwas and his wife Donna, who was a Norton. They lived right in White Bear. He had their address—1584 Lorane Avenue.

As John Norton spoke, Korolchuk balanced the man's advice against its context. He knew the Nortons had created a rift in the Zerwas clan, a "Norton wing" to the family, by marrying two of their siblings—Donna Norton had married Lois's brother Lloyd and Richard Norton had married Lois's sister Donna. The Nortons weren't Catholic and the Nortons were outspoken, and for both reasons they clashed with the Zerwases. What either wing of the family said about the other was not likely to be admiring.

Still, John Norton sounded so insistent. In fact, his face in the dim living room appeared overly animated, exaggerated, the eyebrows raised, the mouth open, like a gargoyle. Norton was leaning toward the officers, his voice a near-whisper. Talk to Lloyd and Donna Zerwas, he kept urging. Talk to Lloyd and Donna.

It was nearing midnight when the two White Bear policemen returned to their station. VanderWyst had been working for sixteen straight hours. Kay's birthday is almost over, he thought. They weren't quite finished, though.

Within minutes, the two officers returned to their squad car and headed north, leaving White Bear's city limits as they crossed the Soo Line Railroad tracks and plunged into a dark open marshland. Up ahead in the black horizon, a solitary street, a patch of reclaimed land alone amid the swamp, branched to the right. Lorane Avenue was just one block long. Korolchuk and VanderWyst directed their headlights from house to house until they found the one marked 1584.

Lloyd Zerwas opened his front door at the officers' first knock. He looked a good deal like his brother Jerome—tall, hard, lean and good-looking in a cowboy sort of way—although at thirty-three he was five years younger. He also had Jerome's cocky, charming manner—fun-loving, full of humor and flirtatious—but for some reason he didn't make VanderWyst wary, the way his brother did. Lloyd was the only other Zerwas son with a steady job; he'd worked for years at the Strauss Skate Company.

Donna, who was two years younger than Lloyd, dark-haired and pretty, joined them in the living room. Being a Norton, she talked nonstop and had definite opinions, which she delivered in a loud, powerful voice.

"We adore kids," Donna explained. "Have six foster kids from Ramsey County besides our own Nancy. Something should be done about Dennis. Yes, we'll give you a statement."

Pete glanced at Bob, then pulled a pen from his shirt pocket and opened a notebook.

It was past 1:00 A.M. when Korolchuk and VanderWyst finally pulled away from Lloyd and Donna Zerwas's home after more than an hour's visit, but they couldn't let go of their day just yet. They drove silently, headed for Gardenette Park. They were simply curious. They parked their unmarked squad car, an aging green-blue Chevy, two houses down from the Jurgens house, shutting off the engine and headlights. Facing west, some 125 feet from the Jurgens's corner lot, they settled in for a stakeout.

Sometime in the next half hour, headlights poured into their window as a car turned the corner heading east and pulled up before the Jurgens house. As Korolchuk and VanderWyst ducked below the line of vision, VanderWyst's arm caught the horn button. The blast was brief but distinct in the black stillness. "Shhhh," Korolchuk hissed. Both officers, crunched under the dashboard, punch-drunk now with knowledge and the late hour, couldn't suppress a fit of laughing.

The mishap did not matter. Perhaps the late-night visitor had not yet turned off his engine when VanderWyst hit the horn, and perhaps he simply was lost in his own thoughts. For whatever the reason, Jerome Zerwas, climbing out of his car, did not turn his head as he walked toward the Jurgenses' front door.

◆　　◆　　◆

Of course, maybe it wasn't the lieutenant at all—later, Jerome would adamantly deny the moment, and in truth, it was late on a dark, wearying night. Maybe the two exhausted officers imagined they saw Jerome, maybe they confused this with another night, maybe they were lying, maybe they were just mistaken. All the same, Vander-Wyst and Korolchuk many years later still stood by their story. We staked out the Jurgens home, they insisted. We saw Jerome.

CHAPTER 12

The Investigation

Rising at the rate of one-tenth of a foot per hour, the Mississippi River swept past its record high of twenty-two and two-tenths feet by late afternoon on Monday, April 12. As the water inched toward the downtown St. Paul area, thousands of workers battled to hold back the force of nature. The Red Cross prepared 7,500 sandwiches and ninety gallons of coffee at Humboldt High and distributed the supplies to weary dike workers via five mobile canteens. Central routes to the city closed, downtown traffic came to a jammed standstill, and the Ramsey County commissioners declared a state of emergency.

Despite these troubles, St. Paul Postal Worker Stanley Wiatros managed to work his way to the Ramsey County courthouse on Kellogg that morning, for this was his first day of jury duty. Once in the courthouse, he sat and waited, part of the overflow group that did not get called for a trial. Sometime in midmorning, a man appeared before them who said he was from the coroner's office. He wanted six from their group to view a body. Because it was going to be an unpleasant sight, he wanted all men and all volunteers. Wiatros raised his hand.

They rode in a limousine down sloping Hill Street from the courthouse to the coroner's office, which stood on a rise set back from the tumultuous Mississippi, but not by much. Wiatros could see the spreading waters covering the parking lots below where they stood. The coroner's man ushered them downstairs into the autopsy room, then wheeled out a gurney.

We're going to show you this body, he said, and just tell you a name for future reference. We want you to observe and remember what you see. The name is Jurgens, Jurgens from White Bear Lake.

That interested Wiatros, for he knew White Bear Lake well. From 1952 to 1956, he'd owned a liquor store there, on Third and Washington, and thought it a real decent community, a place he might have moved to if he weren't already settled, married with a family. He once even dressed up in a hula skirt for a Lions Club show out there, looking idiotic, a two-hundred-pounder in a skirt, but what the heck, he'd figured. Wiatros remembered with fondness the old police chief, Louis Kieffer, and that nice Dr. Peterson, a man not afraid to answer any call, once even going out to clean up an old messy hermit. Wiatros had sold out in 1956, then bought and later sold another liquor store in St. Paul, then looked in vain for a Dairy Queen or Ben Franklin operation before ending up with a post office job. The work there was hard—people tapping you on the shoulder, saying go here, go there, take a break—but they took care of you. At forty-three, Wiatros valued security.

Slowly, the coroner's man pulled back the sheet covering the body. As he looked, Wiatros felt bad, very bad. He was the father of six, and this one—so small—looked just the age of his own son. Oh my God in heaven, he thought, how could this ever happen? The forehead so red, the front, the back, the sides, the arms . . . Everywhere you looked, something was wrong with this kid. Wiatros couldn't imagine how a kid could get that black and blue without being beaten all over.

The coroner's man lifted the body's penis, so Wiatros had to look. That's not a cut, he thought. That's a rip.

Wiatros felt light-headed and close to tears, but he couldn't speak—they'd told the jurors not to converse with each other. He'd never imagined that things like this happened in this world, in this community.

Sure, growing up in St. Paul, he got spankings sometimes, but his parents always treated him right. There was food on the table. His old man worked on the railroad and was so mild he never gave them a licking. If their mother was going to lick them, they'd run to their dad. That was all Stan knew.

Then again, Wiatros thought, that wasn't altogether true. When he was a teenager, maybe eighteen, there was that one guy down the street, a block and a half away, who did beat up his kid and throw him down the stairs. The kid, fifteen or sixteen, Johnny was his name, had finally swung back and decked his father. The police came, said the kid was wrong, you don't deck your parent. They took the boy to Red Wing, the young man's prison. The father, an old Polish drunk, later died a horrible death, a suicide, the poison just burning him inside. His sons played happily at his funeral, but Stan Wiatros's mother, a religious woman, made him go talk to Johnny. In truth, they'd known that family quite well, and they'd known about Johnny getting beaten for a long time. In those days, though, around 1940, you just didn't report stuff like that.

You see these things and you wonder, Wiatros thought as they drove back to the courthouse.

That night, he told his wife about what he'd seen. For a while after that, whenever he looked at his own kids, he would think of the boy in the morgue. In fact, he thought of the boy many times over the years. No one at the coroner's or the courthouse, though, ever called him back about that case. He never heard another word.

Soon after Wiatros and the other jurors left the coroner's office, a mortician arrived from the Lake Mortuary in White Bear Lake. He had bemused eyes and a long, narrow, expressive face, full of lines and angles. Jim Honsa had worked at Lake for five years and knew the Zerwas clan well, for he'd handled a couple of the family's funerals. Half of those Zerwases were in trouble half the time, penny ante stuff, imbibing and breaking windows—that was the way Honsa knew the clan.

Jerome Zerwas had called him on Sunday about Dennis, so Honsa was coming for the body now. He carried it out on a stretcher, wrapped in a sheet, and placed it in the back of his station wagon for the ten-mile drive to Third and Bald Eagle, across from St. Mary's.

Back at the mortuary, the first job was to give the body a bath. Unwrapping the sheet, Honsa's eyes widened. He'd never seen the body of a little child beat up like that. Being in the funeral business, he knew people assumed he was hardened, but that wasn't so. Old people, sure—a ninety-six-year-old dies, you don't get disturbed—but car accidents or a little kid, Honsa felt those. He had two little girls of his own. They'd told him this baby fell down the basement steps, but that didn't make sense—there were no broken bones, no skull fracture that he could see. How could this happen? Honsa wondered. What could this be the result of? Why would a little boy have to go through something like this?

Honsa then had another thought: How am I going to cover up this crap?

That Monday morning, Bob VanderWyst and Pete Korolchuk began a week-long series of interviews with the Jurgenses' relatives and neighbors. Most of the neighbors were not particularly helpful. The officers' reports recorded a string of fruitless interviews:

> Robert A. Hatch told me that he is not closely associated with Jurgens and really never observed any bruises . . . Mrs. Dahlberg stated she didn't see the Jurgenses very much because from her house she could not see the backyard of the Jurgens' and that is where the boys stayed . . . Mrs. Latcham stated that the Jurgenses were good neighbors because they never bothered anyone. She'd seldom seen the Jurgenses except in the summertime when they were working in the yard . . . Mrs. George Lundgren said both her and her husband work days. She stated she has seen Robert and Dennis playing in the backyard when they drive by . . . She does not see the Jurgenses very often.

Even the usually talkative Dorothy Engfer did not prove terribly helpful.

"In talking to Dorothy Engfer," Korolchuk wrote, "she said she observed Dennis Jurgens with a black eye and bruised cheek about two years ago, and said that Mrs. Jurgens told her Dennis had fallen partway down some steps. Other than that the Engfers have not associated much with the Jurgenses since Dennis and Robert were adopted. The Engfers had given character references for the Jurgens when they adopted the children."

In time, though, the officers apparently found a few willing to talk. In their reports, they made tantalizing references to these successful contacts, without filling in the details of what precisely they'd learned. Korolchuk wrote:

"Mr. and Mrs. Ivan DeMars have given us a signed statement.

"Mr. and Mrs. Lloyd Zerwas have given us signed statements also.

"The following persons have given us verbal statements that in part corroborate the statements of the above mentioned four persons, and the following persons have told us they will sign written statements . . .

"Mr. and Mrs. Richard Norton.

"Mr. and Mrs. Clarence Bartholmy . . ."

(Clarence Bartholmy was married to Lois's eldest sister Eloise.)

"At this time," Korolchuk concluded, "there are a number of persons yet to be contacted who supposedly have information and are relatives of the family."

That Monday evening, the day after Dennis's death, Norma Potter settled into her favorite living room chair to read the afternoon *St. Paul Dispatch*. The veteran Ramsey County caseworker hadn't seen the Jurgenses since her uncomfortable confrontation with Lois on January 8. Dragging her heels still seemed the best approach to that case, and besides, the Jurgenses hadn't yet supplied the family medical reports she needed.

"St. Croix Joins Flood Parade" announced the two-line lead headline. "Order Sought to Speed up Evacuation" proclaimed a second headline. A deep vertical photo claimed most of the page's top left quarter, portraying a surging Mississippi River threatening the Swift and Armour meat packing plants as company workers scrambled with bulldozers and dump trucks, patrolling a dirt-and-sandbag dike.

A much smaller headline at midpage caught Norma's eye just as she was about to turn the page.

"White Bear Boy's Death Studied," the headline read.

Below it ran a brief, three-paragraph story.

"White Bear police and the Ramsey County coroner's office are investigating the death Sunday of a White Bear Lake boy," it began. "Reported dead about 9 A.M. Sunday was Dennis Jurgens, 3½, son of Mr. and Mrs. Harold R. Jurgens, 2148 Gardenette Dr. Police said the parents told them the child had fallen. Thomas W. Votel, county coroner, said an autopsy is being performed to determine the cause of death."

Norma grew agitated as she examined the news item.

How can this be? she thought. Newspapers do get things wrong. Maybe this isn't true. It can't be true.

Dawn the next morning, Tuesday, April 13, offered a clear blue sky, the first in a week. From her window, Norma watched the sun rise, waiting until 8:00 A.M. before phoning the White Bear police. Her call was referred to a lieutenant, and she explained to him who she was.

Dennis Jurgens's family had an adoptive application pending with our agency, Norma said. We want to know if the police are investigating his death, and if so, have any results been found.

The lieutenant told Norma she should contact Sergeant Korolchuk.

"Whom am I talking to now?" Norma asked.

Jerome Zerwas identified himself, and explained that he was Lois Jurgens's brother. Dr. Roy Peterson should also be contacted, Jerome told Norma. Dennis had never been well and had very sensitive skin that bruised easily. When Norma pressed for more details, asserting her need and right to know, Jerome resisted.

Many years later, Jerome would deny having this conversation, but the caseworker would insist she could still recall his words: *Don't tell me what to do, I'll tell you. I'm not sure it's any of your business. You're a caseworker, and this is a matter for the police.*

Norma thought Jerome loud and noisy more than directly threatening, but all the same, she felt incapable of challenging him further. It had all happened already and she was just fact-finding. What could she say? There was always a rift between police and social workers anyway. Don't get the police angry at Ramsey County, Norma's superiors always counseled. That's not a smart thing to do. If you don't have any reason, don't provoke.

Norma had been aggressive with Lois back in January, but she saw this moment with Jerome differently. She had the facts with Lois, but not now. And Lois was subtle in her aggression, where Jerome was blunt.

"My interest is only in finding the result of the investigation since the family might adopt another child . . ." Norma said quietly, seeking a conciliatory tone. "I know the Jurgens family will already be under stress because of the other recent death in the family since the first of the year."

Given Jerome's adamant denials, perhaps the caseworker was mistaken about this exchange. All the same, later that day, writing in her Ramsey County welfare department log, Norma made note of the conversation:

> I called the White Bear Police Department and was referred to a Lt. . . . I then learned I was talking to Lt. Sweras [sic], Mrs. J's brother. Lt. Sweras said that Dr. Peterson should be contacted regarding Dennis, that he had never been well and that he had a very sensitive skin which bruised easily. . . .

Midmorning that Tuesday at the Lake Mortuary, Jim Honsa labored with extra care over Dennis's body, preparing for the visitation period that would begin at 6:00 P.M. Dennis was in his casket, in the chapel where he would be viewed—the mortician wanted to work on him under the same lights that the visitors would be experiencing.

Someone from the family had brought in a crown of roses to place on Dennis's head, and this presented to Honsa another challenge, one beyond that of obscuring bruises. He'd never seen such a crown—it was like a round halo. With the pillow up behind the head, how could he put that on properly, so it wouldn't stick out? Honsa finally decided to cut out the back of the halo and then place the crown on Dennis's forehead, like a decathlon runner's headband. He studied the result with satisfaction. Yes, that worked.

As he was leaning over the body, Honsa realized someone was standing at the door to the chapel. Jerome Zerwas greeted Honsa easily, for they knew each other fairly well, what with death calls and police escorts for funerals.

Jim, I want to look behind the ears, Jerome said.

Honsa watched the lieutenant's inspection with curiosity and interest. Honsa had never noticed the marks behind the ears until now. Jerome seemed serious and businesslike as he looked at the body.

Of course, perhaps it wasn't the lieutenant at all, for afterward Jerome would flatly deny this moment, too. Perhaps the mortician was another who imagined or lied or was mistaken. Many years later, though, Honsa, like the others, would claim he recalled Jerome's

words that day. They were words, after all, that had made the mortician feel proud: *Jim, you did a good job of cleaning that up.*

The swollen Mississippi River continued to rise at St. Paul on
Tuesday, reaching past twenty-four feet, as temperatures in the fifties
hastened the snow melt and loosened upriver ice. To the east, the
ice-filled St. Croix River on Minnesota's border with Wisconsin also
rose, climbing a foot an hour until it was pressing against and threatening the interstate highway bridge to Stillwater. That night, White
Bear High School principal Roy Wahlberg settled in his living room
with the evening *St. Paul Dispatch*. "Flood Here Tops Records" proclaimed the banner headline across the front page. Wahlberg read
the articles and eyed the photo of the downtown St. Paul airport,
its high fences barely visible, its administration building's top floor
isolated in a vast sea. He turned the page once, then again a moment
later. Another picture of the swollen Mississippi occupied the top left
quarter of page four, a Sears ad the right top. Wahlberg's eye stopped
at a small, one-column-wide headline sandwiched between the two.

"Tot's Death Due to Peritonitis," it read.

Wahlberg read the brief three-paragraph article.

"An autopsy on the body of 3½-year-old Dennis Jurgens, son of
Mr. and Mrs. Harold R. Jurgens, 2148 S. Gardenette Dr., White Bear
Lake, showed he died of peritonitis caused by a ruptured bowel, Dr.
Thomas W. Votel, Ramsey County coroner, said today. The body also
bore multiple injuries and bruises, Dr. Votel said. White Bear Lake
police and the coroner's office were investigating the death. The boy
was reported dead in his home about 9:00 A.M. Sunday. Police said
the parents told them the child had fallen."

Wahlberg dropped the newspaper in his lap as his mind drifted.
The headline had caught his attention because he once had suffered
from peritonitis, back in 1941. He'd played in a high school football
game even though he had appendicitis, and the deadly infection had
followed. They didn't have penicillin in those days, so after surgery,
he'd sat in the hospital for four weeks with tubes draining out of him.
He'd prayed a lot, he recalled. These days, of course, what with penicillin and operations, you can save someone with peritonitis fairly
easily, but not then.

I could have been dead, too, Wahlberg thought. Then he roused
himself and turned the page.

CHAPTER 13

The Funeral

Jim Honsa always believed the most important part of his job as a mortician was to help people with their grief. Yes, he embalmed and provided a casket and all that, but the core of his work was the comforting. He knew almost everyone in the White Bear community—he'd been active in the chamber of commerce and the Lions Club for years—so when they came to him with a death, he could help them grieve and deal with their pain and loss.

That was why, preparing for Dennis Jurgens's funeral on Wednesday morning, April 14, he felt so troubled. Harold and Lois Jurgens had never let him comfort them. When they came in the day before for the viewing, they showed no emotion, absolutely none. It was as if they were drugged. Honsa had tried in vain to talk to them.

Can I take your hat and coat? he said when they first appeared. They hadn't even answered—there was no response, not even a no.

Would you like to go in and wait? he asked. Again, no response.

Okay, why don't you come with me? he said then, deciding to take more active control.

They followed as he led them to the casket. The Jurgenses stood for a few moments looking at the body, then walked away.

Honsa was lost. Normally, people acted just the opposite. His job usually was to keep the family away from the body, to keep them under control, to prevent emotional breakdowns. Doing something day in, day out, Honsa had come to expect certain behavior.

In the end, the mortician gave up. He handled all the funeral arrangements—pallbearers, timing, car lineup—through Lois's brother Jerome. By early Wednesday morning, everything was in order. The funeral would start at 10:00 A.M.

Ten miles to the south that morning, elaborate preparations of another sort were underway. President Lyndon Johnson was due to land at 10:30 A.M. at Wold-Chamberlain Field in St. Paul to inspect what had become the worst flooding in Minnesota's history. The waters now had spread havoc from the south all the way to the Canadian border, threatening scores of communities, including the Twin Cities, and virtually sealing off the lower half of the Minnesota-Wisconsin border. Weather forecasters were warning that the worst was yet to come. The battle against the rampaging Mississippi centered in St. Paul and the adjoining downstream river communities, the struggle with the St. Croix in Hudson and Stillwater.

At St. Paul, the swollen Mississippi, rising relentlessly toward its predicted Good Friday crest of twenty-seven feet, forced its way through the emergency dikes and pushed against the plywood restraining walls, reaching twenty-five feet. Mayor George Vavoulis ordered evacuation of a low two-mile stretch of road along the east bank as the river surged there faster than workers could pump it out. A ten-foot-high sandbag dike was protecting the Northern States Power plant, which stood surrounded by water.

President Johnson's plane landed in St. Paul one hour late. A light drizzle fell as he walked down from Air Force One and stood on the runway in a dark suit, talking to a crowd of hundreds.

"None of us are immune to disasters of nature," LBJ said. "One of seven Americans were touched by such disasters during the last year . . . I will pledge to you today that we will do everything we can as promptly as we can and will render the maximum amount of federal aid . . . I regret that I must come here under these circumstances, but I hope that I can return under happier circumstances."

Donning a green felt hat after his speech, Johnson walked over to the fence and began shaking hands with onlookers under what had deepened into a cold, driving rain. A dozen people in the crowd surged forward, and the fence holding back the public gave way. Secret Service agents and police wrestled it upright amid considerable shouting and confusion, while Johnson climbed into Governor

Karl Rolvaag's limousine for the trip to St. Paul's dike defenses at Shepard Road and James Avenue.

The rain intensified as the president's seven-car motorcade, accompanied by three buses loaded with Washington reporters and forty-one United States congressmen, pulled up at that intersection where the NSP plant sat isolated. Scores of police and Secret Service agents had cleared the area two hours before, but a crowd of 150 managed to slip through anyway. As Johnson stepped from his car, he put the green felt hat on his head again and an aide helped him into a trench coat. Flanked by Governor Rolvaag and Senators Eugene McCarthy and Walter Mondale, the president stood on a platform five feet from the swirling water. Pulling up his coat collar and tugging at the brim of his hat in the driving rain, he watched workmen piling sandbags around the NSP plant.

"Terrible, terrible," LBJ muttered.

A moment later, he turned and hurried back to his limousine. The motorcade and buses, with lights flashing, returned to the airport. Air Force One, after one hour on the ground, lifted off the runway at 12:38 P.M.

Barbara Wisdorf's boyfriend, Gary Venne, had tried to talk her out of going to Dennis's funeral, saying it would not be good for her, but she had insisted. So Wednesday morning just before ten o'clock, Gary drove her from North St. Paul to the Lake Mortuary in White Bear Lake. He stayed outside, waiting in the car, while she walked through the rain toward the mortuary's front door.

Barbara was a skinny, fragile-looking eighteen-year-old with a soft, delicate manner that sometimes shifted to something more venturesome, in those occasional moments when her wide brown eyes sparkled with a sense of fun. Because she was such good friends with Joanne—the daughter of Lois's eldest sister Eloise—Barbara during her midteens had hung out with the Zerwas clan three or four evenings a week, usually at the parents' house on Park Street in White Bear Lake. Those three years, 1962 through 1964, had been a new type of experience for a girl who'd grown up in a loving but strict Catholic home, the only daughter of a painting contractor. Barbara learned her lessons at Catholic schools from Franciscan nuns, and at home she minded her parents, so walking into the Zerwas home on Park was like entering another world.

Barbara marveled at the scene every time she came over. The front door led her right into the kitchen, with a large square wooden table in the middle. The living room, full of old stuffed furniture, branched off to the left. A torn, castoff sofa sat outside in the backyard, which looked like a dump. There were no rules in this house, no lines drawn between adults and children. Conversations, even dirty jokes, didn't stop when kids entered a room. The women smoked—even Joanne, in front of her mother no less. The Zerwas men flirted with any young single girls present, pinching and patting, pulling them to their laps. Barbara was so skinny she didn't get much attention, though, so she avoided trouble. *Loose* was the word that came to mind. This was a loose place. None of the aunts and uncles seemed to work, and no one seemed serious about anything. Jerome Zerwas confused her, being a police officer in this setting—Barbara expected him to arrest her for smoking.

In truth, although she thought these guys were losers, she didn't at all mind going to the Zerwas home, for she enjoyed the looseness. It was a place to go, a place she was allowed to go—because there were parents present, Barbara's mother and father assumed it was normal, okay. She couldn't just go hang out anywhere.

Barbara was surprised the first time Lois had appeared at the Zerwas house with Dennis, since she, like the others, had expected a newborn. What struck her most about Dennis that day was his physical energy and his mischievous, animated eyes. The second time Barbara saw Dennis over at the Zerwas home, Lois had him on the floor, trying to get him to walk. Barbara had never forgotten that scene.

Over and over, Dennis would collapse into a crawl, and Lois would pick him up and slap his bottom. Back and forth they went, a battle royal for fifteen minutes, the struggle escalating until finally Lois was yanking Dennis up by the arm and delivering sweeping hard smacks with an open palm, more blows than slaps. Barbara, sixteen then, looked around, feeling horrible. No one in the room was doing anything about it. The others watched, sat, ignored, talked. Other kids were crawling around, getting into cabinets, getting dirty. Dennis was crying but being stubborn, displaying both willfulness and spirit, going right back to his knees and crawling just as soon as she let go.

As her visits to the Zerwas home continued, Barbara saw more of Lois with Dennis, and she just didn't understand. She'd never seen this before. It was not simply the specific things Lois did to Dennis, but also her manner. Lois seemed to hate that kid. He was stupid, ugly, fat, clumsy. She tore that guy down all the time. Barbara would go home and talk to her mother about Lois's treatment of Dennis. She couldn't describe the whole scene, she couldn't tell her mom about the flirtatious men and dirty jokes and cigarettes, but she could tell her about Dennis.

One day six months after Dennis's first appearance, Barbara arrived at the Zerwas home to find Lois in the kitchen, feeding the toddler spoonfuls of mashed potatoes. He was sitting in a high chair, his hands bound by a dish towel, with Lois in a chair beside him, holding the boy's mouth open with one hand while pushing food in with a spoon. Dennis would spit it out, she'd spoon it back in, again and again. Finally, he gagged and vomited, but she kept spooning the food and the vomit. Dennis was screaming now. All the time, the other family members stood about, talking, gossiping, seeming to ignore this scene as it unfolded.

They know what's going on, Barbara thought. They talk about her, after all, when she's not here.

Barbara was not sure which she was most upset with, Lois or the family's reaction. Again, she talked to her mother. Her mom listened, but since there were other adults involved, she had a hard time believing what Barbara described.

In late August of 1963, after Barbara had turned seventeen, she accompanied Joanne and her mother Eloise on a camping trip to Gunflint Trail in northern Minnesota. The drive up was stirring, full of verdant valleys and forests thick with majestic pine trees. Lois and her two boys joined them for one night midway through the campout, and this made Joanne happy, for it meant help with the tents. Early the next morning, Lois decided it was time for Dennis to have a bowel movement. Barbara was awake and up already—she couldn't sleep, almost couldn't breathe, it was so suffocatingly hot and humid. Lois got the potty from her car trunk, then put it and Dennis in her tent. Barbara could hear Lois screaming and yelling at him. In the heavy, sticky air the tent shimmered before Barbara's eyes. It was so hot Lois had trouble breathing in the tent, so she'd come out, take a deep breath, then go back in, Dennis crying, she yelling. Barbara could hear noises that sounded like blows to a body. The scene seemed so bizarre to Barbara, beyond belief, this woman

forcing a bowel movement in this insufferable heat. After ten minutes, Barbara and Joanne, needing to get away, left on a hike. When
they returned, the Jurgens family had packed up and left.

Back home, Barbara had trouble sleeping she was so upset, and
her mother, finally believing her stories, told her to call the welfare
department. Her mother helped her with the phone number and sat
with her in their kitchen while Barbara placed the call.

I want to report child abuse, she said into the phone.

A voice asked for her name, age and the details. Barbara told her
story the best she could. Her biggest fear was not that they'd ignore
her, but rather that they'd go rushing out to the Jurgens home. Then
Lois and the Zerwas family would confront her, and she was afraid of
that moment most of all. The confrontation never happened, though.
Nothing came of her call to the welfare department. As far as she
could tell, the agency just never responded.

Barbara wasn't out at the Zerwas home very often after the camping trip. That part of her life was ending, for she was growing up and
falling in love and moving away from home. The last time Barbara
saw Dennis—it must have been in late 1964, she realized, when he
was just about to turn three—he was standing next to Harold at the
Zerwas parents' front door. In that moment, she realized the once
husky and exuberant baby was now terribly thin and covered with
bruises and strangely listless. He no longer had life in him—there
was no sparkle, no devil in his eyes. It just didn't look like Dennis.

Now, six months later, he was dead.

When she reached the front door of the Lake Mortuary, Barbara
found a crowd of Zerwas cousins gathered just inside—Joanne and
Theresa and Willem and Patty and Butch and all the others she hadn't
seen in some time. Everyone was quite excited.

She killed him, they were whispering to one another. *Lois killed
him.* They told Barbara the story as they understood it, although
it was unclear how they knew. Lois supposedly was making Dennis say the rosary. He would miss a prayer and she'd get angry, beat
him, make him kneel on a broomstick, put a clothespin on his penis.
Every time he'd miss a prayer, she'd start on him again. Harold wasn't
home, the story went. An autopsy has been done. There will be an
investigation. There were so many bruises. That, at least, was the
story going around.

Barbara looked about her. The Lake Mortuary was a one-story brick building with deep vertical windows covered by thick beige drapes and viewing rooms outfitted with sofas and overstuffed chairs. She had expected to embrace grief here, to see many people crying, but instead, everyone seemed excited, buzzing with talk. Lois stood amid the crowd, looking to Barbara like a regal ice cube.

Barbara moved to the viewing room and approached the casket. Jim Honsa had done his best, but Dennis was blond and fair-skinned, so the mortician's work couldn't hide all the bruises. Barbara saw the big one on his forehead, another on his right temple, one on his cheek, one on the side of his nose. A crown of white roses sat not on top of Dennis's head, but more over on his forehead, as if placed there to hide the bruises.

Others also noticed the markings. Lois's sister Beverly, who worked part-time doing hairdressing and makeup at funeral homes, counted six in all, and Harold's supervisor at Muska Electric, Walter Moore, saw them, too. Looking into the casket, Moore thought: This boy has been murdered.

To those at the funeral who had the nerve to raise the matter directly, Lois explained that the police had beaten up the child after taking him away. That, she said, was the reason he had so many bumps and bruises. For the most part, though, the matter was ignored. Barbara couldn't believe the atmosphere—it was almost like a party. In the corners of the room, kids were yakking about how Lois had killed Dennis, while Lois stood in the corner, out of earshot, like a queen. The room held no tears.

Barbara bolted from the mortuary, crying, rushing through the rain into Gary's car.

"My God," she whispered, "Lois killed that baby and they're not doing anything. This is horrible."

The moment only confirmed to Gary that Barbara shouldn't have come to the funeral, that it was too much for her to handle. Gary drove quickly to the home of Barbara's godparents, Ed and Delores Heroff, so he could get help in calming her down.

Barbara's mother, only forty-one, had died of cancer just three months before, and now her father was going off the deep end, disappearing, unable to handle matters. Barbara had started turning often to her godparents with her problems, so the current visit was not unusual. This day, the Heroffs felt Barbara was exaggerating, overreacting because of her own recent emotional trials. They soothed her and diverted her attention to other topics.

Barbara never heard about Dennis's death again. The police never approached her—Pete Korolchuk and Bob VanderWyst didn't know of her existence—and she didn't contact them. In time, she married Gary Venne and started a new life. The memory of Dennis stayed with her, rising to trouble her not every day, but often enough. She soon had her own children, four of them, blond and bubbly, and on occasion they would make her think of Dennis. Then Barbara Venne would mention to people that she once knew a witch who abused and killed her child, but no one ever believed her.

CHAPTER 14

Good Friday

Two days after Dennis's funeral, on Good Friday, April 16, word reached Pete Korolchuk and Bob VanderWyst that some of the people they'd already interviewed, members of the Zerwas family, wanted to talk to them again.

Once more, the officers' resulting reports were suggestive but sparse. Korolchuk wrote:

> On 4-16-65 Officer VanderWyst and I made a second visit to the following persons in regard to the investigation of the death of Dennis Craig Jurgens. Mrs. Gerald Dube . . . Mr. and Mrs. Kopp . . . Lorenzo Arsenal . . . Mrs. Eloise Bartholmy . . . The reason for our second visit was that we had learned some of these people wanted to talk to us again . . .
>
> Mrs. Kopp . . . gave us verbal statements which contained information regarding the case. This information consisted of acts allegedly committed by Lois Jurgens against Dennis Jurgens, with Harold Jurgens present at the time of the alleged acts. Mrs. Kopp told us she would sign a statement. Mrs. Kopp's information appears corroborative to signed statements we have received from Mr. and Mrs. Jurgens' relatives and neighbors. Mrs. Kopp also gave us verbal statements containing information of occurrences unbeknown to us at the time.

Mr. and Mrs. Lorenzo Arsenal also have now given us verbal statements which appear corroborative to other statements already signed.

Mrs. Eloise Bartholmy upon our second visit . . . stated she would sign a statement covering information she originally gave us.

Those mentioned in this report were all sisters of Lois and their husbands. Hours later, VanderWyst and Korolchuk spoke to another sister, Beverly, and to Lois's parents. Korolchuk wrote:

Officer VanderWyst and I also contacted a Beverly Zerwas, a sister of Mrs. Jurgens. Beverly Zerwas gave us verbal statements containing information new to us, and said she would sign a statement also.

Also, Mr. and Mrs. John H. Zerwas, parents of Mrs. Jurgens, talked with us. Neither of them had any new information, but did relate occurrences which did take place when Mrs. Jurgens was at one time in the Crestview sanitarium for treatment. I asked Mrs. John Zerwas if she thought Mrs. Jurgens was or appeared to be psychotic. She replied "definitely." Mr. and Mrs. John H. Zerwas each talked privately to us. Mr. John Zerwas said he thought his daughter (Mrs. Jurgens) needed help for a possible mental condition, and also expressed concern that Mrs. Jurgens may try to harm herself. Both Mr. and Mrs. Zerwas said they would give us signed statements.

Korolchuk and VanderWyst felt satisfied by week's end. The investigation was moving along quickly, and within days the case file promised to grow thick with witnesses' affidavits. Accordingly, Bob and Pete on Friday decided to pay a visit to the Ramsey County attorney's office.

The Mississippi slowed but did not stop its relentless rise on Good Friday, swelling to just under twenty-six feet. The expected crest at twenty-seven feet failed to come that day because below-normal temperatures during the previous three days had diminished the runoff. This was not good news at all. The crest still would arrive—in four days, the specialists now predicted—and because it was coming slowly, it also would leave slowly, hanging on to its high point for three to five days. There would be no respite for some time.

Despite the transportation problems and the holiday, an emergency meeting convened that afternoon in the Ramsey County courthouse in St. Paul. Three people—Beatrice Bernhagen and Paul Schroeder of the county welfare department and Bertrand Poritsky of the county attorney's juvenile division—had received phone calls at home at midday from Paul Lindholm, the assistant Ramsey County attorney who decided which cases warranted prosecution.

There's a case we need to work on right away, Lindholm told them.

They gathered in the prosecutor's small office on the courthouse's third floor late in the day, and the meeting began with a typical piece of Lindholm's macabre humor. As the four pulled their chairs about a conference table, he tossed on the table a gruesome eight-by-ten-inch glossy photo of a murder victim, an adult male riddled with bullets. Willy the Bird, a local hood, had met his maker. Lindholm collected such photos, kept a pile of them in his desk drawer, and he enjoyed showing them to people for the startled, flustered reactions they produced.

Lindholm was a big, beefy man with a deadpan expression, few polished edges and no illusions about his job or the legal system. Right and wrong, good or bad, guilty or innocent were not the issues—what you could prove in court was the issue. Cops and social workers had to give him a case, enough to move on, and it seemed to Lindholm they didn't do that nearly often enough. "Go back and work on it," he'd tell them gruffly. "Bring me something more."

Willy the Bird was not the reason for the Good Friday interruption. VanderWyst and Korolchuk, it turned out, had told Lindholm enough about the Jurgens case to arouse the prosecutor. There might or might not be a case to charge—that remained an open question—but another piece of business suggested immediate action.

They had been called down today, Lindholm explained, because a small boy had died in White Bear Lake from a ruptured bowel. From the police reports and a few relatives' statements, there was a fair showing that Dennis Jurgens had been abused. There was another boy still in the house, Robert, a five-year-old, and the investigating officers feared Lois Jurgens might turn on him. Should they get him out of there?

Lindholm looked about the table for reaction.

Poritsky was a bright, scholarly Columbia Law School graduate, but young and new to the prosecutor's office. Schroeder, the welfare department's liaison with the juvenile court, was equally inexperienced. So all eyes turned to Beatrice Bernhagen, the welfare department's director of social services. She was a short, squat woman full of the impatience that bright people often have for others. To get along with Bernhagen, co-workers found it best to be compliant and subservient, for she was demanding, decisive and often convinced she was surrounded by incompetents.

Bernhagen didn't hesitate. "Let's get the boy out," she said. "Right away."

Lindholm had already drawn up a petition asking the juvenile court for an emergency removal order. Schroeder would be the petitioner, and Poritsky would represent the welfare department before the juvenile court.

In Ramsey County in 1965, one man comprised—defined—the juvenile court. Early in the evening on Good Friday, Schroeder and Poritsky set out for Judge Archie Gingold's home.

They found Gingold not at his own house but at his mother's, the lower half of a stucco duplex on Summit Avenue in St. Paul. As the judge opened the front door, Poritsky eyed the heavily laden dining room table visible over his right shoulder. Gingold was Jewish and his wife Protestant, Poritsky recalled, so they must be celebrating both Good Friday and the Passover seder. Great, he thought. We've managed to break up both ceremonies with one knock.

Gingold didn't seem to mind, though. Come in, come right in, he said. He was a short fireplug of a man with a quick manner. Judge Gingold first insisted on introducing the two men to his family—his mother, his wife, a sister, three daughters—before settling in the den. Full of apologies, Poritsky briefed Gingold on the case as the judge studied the document before him. Schroeder sat tensely in his chair, for Gingold, although warm and gregarious, also could be testy and at times downright irascible. The judge usually put Schroeder to a tough test whenever he brought him petitions, and Paul had learned long ago always to be on his toes. I don't like this wording or that clause, the judge often would snap. He always wanted full information, a good set of facts, so he wouldn't be reversed somewhere later, far down the line.

The Jurgens petition raised no problems for Gingold, though. After studying it briefly, the judge pulled out a pen and signed his name at the bottom of the single sheet.

When Korolchuk and VanderWyst knocked at the Jurgens house on Gardenette less than one hour later, Harold opened the door. The two officers steeled themselves for what they expected to be a trying confrontation. If necessary, they figured, they'd call for backup help.

"We have an order signed by Judge Gingold to take Robert," Korolchuk said.

Standing at the door, Harold studied the piece of paper. He seemed almost in shock, stunned by the official-looking document and the officers' mission.

"I guess that's it," Harold said.

The officers could hear but not see Lois, standing just inside the house, behind the door. She was talking to Harold, but the conversation was too muffled to be heard from the front steps. Then, briefly, a few of Lois's words reached the officers' ears. "We better get some clothes for him," Lois was saying. "Just a minute, I'll get a paper sack."

Harold, waiting, turned back to the policemen. "I sure wish Doc Peterson would have looked Dennis over better," he said. "They must have beat him up at the morgue. Dennis sure didn't have all those bruises when he left here."

Moments later, Harold brought Robert to the front door and handed him over to Korolchuk. The scene seemed to be unfolding underwater, it was so slow and muted. No one was crying or yelling or expressing any emotion. Since VanderWyst had taken Robert to his own home five days before, the boy came to him now without protest. Just minutes after knocking at the door, the officers were walking down the driveway, their mission accomplished. The whole thing seemed to them surprising and odd.

"You going to blow me over?" Korolchuk said, looking at his partner.

"No, I'm waiting for you to blow me over," VanderWyst replied.

After they left Judge Gingold and handed over the signed order to the two White Bear police officers, Bertrand Poritsky and Paul

Schroeder could not shake a sense of depression. They felt drained and in need of catharsis.

"Come over for a drink," Poritsky suggested.

They reached Poritsky's two-story frame home in the McAlister-Groveland area of St. Paul at 7:00 P.M. Poritsky's wife Joanie was in the kitchen, cooking a beef roast, so the two men settled in the den with gin martinis—Gilbey's, very dry, as Poritsky preferred them. They drank and talked and refilled their glasses.

How could this happen, they asked each other. They felt sure this woman had killed her boy. The details seemed so gruesome and tragic—so upsetting, in fact, that they were hard to hold in mind for too long. Poritsky and Schroeder poured a third drink and the gin helped to dull the details.

From the kitchen, they could smell the beef roasting in the oven, beckoning to them, but suddenly an awkward thought occurred to Poritsky. Wasn't Schroeder Catholic? He can't eat meat on Friday night, certainly not Good Friday night. It would be rude to rise now for the dining room. So the two men poured a fourth drink and continued talking, until the hour grew late and the smell of burnt meat reached them.

"Why don't you stay for dinner, Paul?" Joanie asked precisely at midnight. As Friday turned to Saturday, the trio sat down to dine on charred roast.

Not until weeks later did Poritsky learn his concern had been groundless. Schroeder was a good, religious Lutheran.

When Robert was admitted at 11:00 P.M. that Good Friday night to St. Paul's Ancker Hospital, the social services department workers there found him unnaturally interested in religion for a five-year-old boy. He had with him rosary beads, a prayer book and a picture of St. Francis of Assisi, whom he knew all about. Dennis died of hunger, Robert told one caseworker. His parents called the doctor and the doctor called the "cops," and the "cops" took Dennis away, he explained. Robert also talked a good deal about his mother, and refused to eat candy offered by the nurses. "No, no," Robert said firmly. "My mother wouldn't like that."

CHAPTER 15

Riding a Dead Horse

The story as offered by Pete Korolchuk and Bob VanderWyst rarely varied. The two of them were sitting in the squad room—Thursday evening, April 15, they believed—when Jerome Zerwas arrived. His normal charm had worn thin—"he was completely changed, you might say almost sneering," VanderWyst would recall later. Jerome had something to tell them.

"He said to Sergeant Korolchuk and myself that he would do everything within his power to get Lois off, even if it meant his job," VanderWyst testified under oath a month later in a courtroom.

Again, Jerome's memory differs considerably. Also testifying under oath, he didn't simply dispute the words attributed to him, or their context—he flatly denied that the exchange ever took place in any form.

Perhaps, but if Korolchuk and VanderWyst once again imagined the moment, their imaginations were particularly vivid just then, for they soon began recounting their experience to others. VanderWyst told his colleague, Sergeant Howard Markuson, who told his neighbor, Donald Tomsuden. Korolchuk told Buzz Harvey.

"I could tell Pete and Bob were having problems," Harvey recalled much later. "I was told by them, Pete mostly, that Zerwas had warned them he'd do anything to protect his sister. I think they felt threatened physically. Jerome was big and had a title."

Korolchuk and VanderWyst also reported the incident to Assistant Ramsey County Attorney Paul Lindholm.

"They were apprehensive about Jerome having closed up Harold and Lois," Lindholm said years later. "They said Jerome was potentially interfering."

For whatever reason, over the Easter weekend VanderWyst and Korolchuk felt uneasy—they were anxious to get the Zerwas family's statements recorded and signed before people started retreating. It was a close-knit family, after all, and other than the Norton wing, those who did talk had seemed fairly hesitant.

Accordingly, at 2:00 P.M. on Monday they drove to Sharon Kopp's home, accompanied by VanderWyst's wife, Kay, who was to take shorthand notes. Lois's sister greeted them at the door—or rather, she blocked them at the door.

The officers' unease, it turned out, had been well-founded. In his report, Korolchuk wrote:

> On Monday April 19th, 1965, Officer VanderWyst, myself and Mrs. Robert VanderWyst at about 2:00 P.M. went to Sharon Kopp's home for the purpose of getting a statement from Mrs. Kopp . . . Mrs. Kopp (Sharon) met us at the door and told us that upon advice of their attorney they were not going to give us a signed statement. She said she would bring out all the facts that she knew about the case if she was called into a trial by a subpoena. She said that she didn't want any kind of signed papers around because if it came about that her statement was never used in a court trial, or if she were not subpoenaed, she maybe would be subject to being sued in a civil case at a later time. She felt that if she were summoned to testify in court by a subpoena there wouldn't be any possibility of her being sued later. Mrs. Kopp said that all the information she gave us was true. She also said that Mr. and Mrs. John H. Zerwas and Beverly Zerwas were going to follow this same procedure according to their attorneys' advice. Mr. and Mrs. Lorenzo Arsenal also are following this advice.

Korolchuk and VanderWyst now faced a tricky problem. They hadn't recorded Kopp's verbal accounts in their own reports because they'd expected to get a written statement. Needing at least their own summary of her remarks, they returned to Kopp's house later that same day.

Korolchuk wrote in his report:

At about 6:30 P.M. Officer VanderWyst and I went back to Sharon Kopp's residence. Mrs. Kopp (Sharon) was told that we would like to go over her previous verbal statements to be sure that we entered this information on our reports in proper sequence.

Mrs. Kopp told us that Mrs. Jurgens was very strict with Dennis Jurgens. Also that Mrs. Jurgens was very religious.

Mrs. Kopp related that during a telephone conversation with her sister (Mrs. Jurgens) she heard Mrs. Jurgens talking to Dennis about dribbling on his pants when he went to the bathroom, and Mrs. Jurgens said something to the effect that she had to attend to Dennis. Mrs. Kopp said she then heard on the phone what sounded like blows being struck and Mrs. Jurgens yelling. Mrs. Kopp said she could hear these sounds like blows for a long time, along with Mrs. Jurgens yelling and a child screaming. She (Mrs. Kopp) relates she could hear the child's voice during the screaming, begging not to be hit anymore. Mrs. Kopp relates that the sound of the screaming and begging affected her so badly that she dropped the phone and went into another room so that she wouldn't have to listen. When Mrs. Kopp returned to the phone she relates that the line was still open but Mrs. Jurgens was not back to the phone yet. After awhile Mrs. Jurgens did return to the phone and continue the conversation with Mrs. Kopp.

Mrs. Kopp also related that Mrs. Jurgens told her of an incident which at this time Mrs. Kopp stated she believes occurred about two weeks prior to Dennis's death.

As a method of discipline of some sort Mrs. Jurgens was supposed to have told Mr. Jurgens to put a clamp-type clothespin on the end of Dennis's penis and have Dennis kneel on the handle of a broom while the Jurgens were saying the rosary. During the rosary Dennis Jurgens was supposed to have been complaining that the clothespin was hurting him, and that he wanted Mr. Jurgens to take it off. The clothespin remained on the penis through the recitation of the rosary, and after the rosary, Mrs. Jurgens was supposed to have told Mr. Jurgens to let Dennis take the clothespin off of the penis by himself. Mrs. Kopp stated that her sister (Mrs. Jurgens) laughed about this as she was relating the incident to her . . .

Kopp's remarks were powerful, but still, they were paraphrased in the officers' own words, not sworn to or signed by Sharon. Bob and Pete could do no better, and later, Kopp under oath would deny ever having told them such stories.

So it went for VanderWyst and Korolchuk all that second week. They pushed on, adding an anecdote here and a detail there, but the well of information had dried up. Sharon Kopp, they discovered, was right—the other family members also had decided not to sign statements. Harold and Lois had retreated into silence behind a lawyer's shield, and those who did talk now had little to say. In the end, only the two couples in the Norton wing of the Zerwas family signed statements, along with one neighboring couple, Ivan and Gladys DeMars.

By now, the case was affecting VanderWyst's nerves. Although conscientious, he was not by nature a driven man. In late April of 1965, he started coming home so disturbed he'd need three or four hours of talking it out to Kay before he could calm down enough to sleep.

"Why doesn't someone stop this?" he'd ask his wife. "Isn't someone going to stop this?"

One morning in that week after Easter, Lois called Father Reiser at the Church of the Epiphany in Coon Rapids. She had a question for the priest: Would he write another letter of recommendation for them? They possibly were going to adopt another baby.

The Jurgenses' application, after all, was still before Norma Potter and the Ramsey County welfare department.

Father Reiser saw no reason now to alter the recommendation he'd first written in 1959. The death of their boy Dennis was a terrible thing, but still, he felt, any kids going into the Jurgens home would have a nice, ideal family.

"Yes, of course," the priest told Lois on the phone. "I very definitely will write a letter for you."

Lois, however, was being overly optimistic. Ramsey County was pliable, but not quite that accommodating. On the Monday after Easter, the welfare department's Beatrice Bernhagen briefed a middle-level supervisor on what she'd learned from the Good Friday meeting in Lindholm's office, and this supervisor in turn related the details to Norma Potter.

Later that Monday, Norma wrote in her log:

> Received information that on the basis of the investigation into the death of Dennis Jurgens, Robert Jurgens had been picked up and taken to Ancker Hospital. The coroner's office had pictures of bruises on Dennis's body and the county attorney had documented enough evidence of mistreatment to support the battered child statute. There was also evidence of mutilation of Dennis's genitals and ears.

A day later, on Tuesday, after another briefing, Norma recorded her closing entry:

> I received a more complete report on the death of Dennis Jurgens. In view of the suspicious circumstances surrounding the death of Dennis, and in view of the petition filed before the Ramsey County Juvenile Court alleging the neglect of Robert, we cannot further consider the Jurgenses' application for a third child and our home study will be closed and will not be reopened unless the matter now pending before the juvenile court is resolved satisfactorily. The case has been referred to intake for protective services on Robert. CASE CLOSED.

Norma Potter had tried to be as professional and factual as she could in her final entries, but she knew the file still presented quite a problem. An agency, after all, doesn't want one of its approved adoptive families to kill a child. These last paragraphs had been entered under what Norma called the "CYA program"—cover your ass—but of course they couldn't entirely obscure what had happened.

Norma's supervisor approached her soon after they closed the case. "Miss Bernhagen wishes she could eat that Jurgens record line by line," she said.

At 2:00 P.M. on Thursday of that week, a preliminary hearing convened before Judge Archie Gingold in the Ramsey County courthouse. On one side of a conference table, Bertrand Poritsky sat with the petitioners he represented, Paul Schroeder and

Beatrice Bernhagen. On the other side, an attorney named Joseph H. Rivard sat with the respondents he represented, Harold and Lois Jurgens.

The purpose of this brief proceeding was to let both sides state their basic positions, and to fix a date for a formal hearing on the county's petition asking for temporary legal custody of Robert due to neglect in the Jurgens home.

Rising to speak for the Jurgenses, Rivard denied all allegations and strenuously objected to the taking of Robert. Then he asked if the court, "in its own good judgment," until the hearing, would give temporary custody of Robert either to Harold's parents or to Mr. and Mrs. Jerome Zerwas.

"Mr. Zerwas is a lieutenant in the White Bear Lake police department," Rivard said. "I have known him personally for some fifteen years. I think he is a very high-type individual, very capable, as well as his wife who keeps a clean home. He has children . . . The status of the child at Ancker Hospital is . . . well, he is crying, he is very unhappy out there. We feel that if the court would allow custody to either Mr. Zerwas or the paternal grandparents, that it would be beneficial to the welfare of the child."

The welfare department can check out these proposed homes, Judge Gingold said, and if they decide the placement can be made there, the court would not oppose such a move.

Flipping impatiently through the county's petition like a man sorting trash, Gingold first surmised the case would take a full day to hear. Reading further, he changed that to two days, and set the hearing dates for May 10 and 11, 1965.

The judge appeared irritated as he eyed the Jurgenses' attorney. He looked like an unhappy bulldog.

"On the face of the petition," Gingold said, "I think we should all be interested in the same thing."

"Certainly, Your Honor, we have nothing but the best interests of the child—"

Gingold interrupted.

"I think we are going to get along," the judge said evenly. "Mr. Rivard has been up in this court several times. He knows the way we operate. I think he understands our philosophy. I don't think we will have any trouble. All we are going to try to do is to arrive at the truth in this case."

At the start of their third week of investigation, Korolchuk and VanderWyst, feeling they had exhausted their leads, decided to write a general overview and analysis of what they had. For two days beginning Monday, April 26, in the squad room and Jantzen's coffee shop, their spiral notebooks spread before them, they sorted through their reports and mapped out a blueprint of what they wanted to say. They listed what they'd learned, what they had, what they didn't have.

On Wednesday, Korolchuk settled in the station squad room with pen in hand. Centered across the top line, he first placed a title— "Analysis of Report Information from April 11 to April 26, 1965." He skipped a line on the ruled investigation report form, then composed his first sentence. "There appears to be a number of discrepancies in the information received by us from Mr. and Mrs. Jurgens," he wrote. He continued:

> The Jurgenses' attorney has been contacted and asked if he will bring Mr. and Mrs. Jurgens in for further questioning. He said that he would contact us, but to this date he hasn't called. Because of the communication lack between the Jurgenses and ourselves we have the following areas that are not clarified:
>
> Mr. and Mrs. Jurgens said that Dennis was up and around shortly before the time he died, that the boy said his "before meal prayers," talked to his father about a broken watchband, went to the bathroom and wiped himself after a bowel movement. Although we do not have a professional opinion at the present time covering the possibility of this sort of activity by a person afflicted with peritonitis, so short a time before death, it has been discussed by the investigating departments that activity of the sort mentioned by the Jurgenses would not be very likely to have occurred and if it did was very unusual.
>
> Another unclear area is that the report of coroner's deputy investigator Sam Pitera states that Dennis fell on the basement stairs. He says he got his information from Mrs. Jurgens. Officer VanderWyst, whose report information also came from Mrs. Jurgens, has it that Dennis fell on the basement floor. When Officer VanderWyst and I were at the Jurgens residence on April 11, 1965, Harold Jurgens pointed out a spot on the basement floor where Dennis was supposed to

have slipped and fallen when coming out of the basement toilet room. This area is some distance away from the basement steps . . .

There are quite a few areas of Mr. Jurgens's statements that require further exploration. Mr. Jurgens on April 11, 1965, said that a sore on the base of Dennis's penis came from a scalding last summer when Dennis was standing in the bathtub and turned on the hot water faucet. According to Dr. Roy Peterson's statement, he treated Dennis for this scalding, and his records show that it occurred August 21, 1963 . . .

Mr. Jurgens also said that one of the reasons he and his wife probably were not aware of numerous bruises all the time may have been due to the possibility of Dennis being insensitive to pain. At this time the possibility of insensitivity has not been supported by the Jurgens doctor. Other persons we have talked to said that Dennis appeared normal to them, and when he was injured or reprimanded he would cry the same as any other normal child . . .

Also during our conversation with Mr. Jurgens on April 11, when asked about the numerous bruises present on the body of Dennis, Mr. Jurgens said that Dennis was clumsy and appeared uncoordinated . . . Most of the relatives . . . stated that Dennis appeared to move about and was as well coordinated physically as any normal child. This is also supported by a statement of Dr. E. Dale Cummings . . .

When Mr. Jurgens was in on April 11 we also asked him about a bruise on the end of Dennis's penis. Mr. Jurgens related the scalding incident in the bathtub which left an unhealed sore at the base of the penis. As to the bruise at the end of the penis Mr. Jurgens had no explanation, and did not imply that he had any knowledge of this particular bruise. In regard to this particular bruise, there seems to be a relation here with a statement (verbal) given to us by a Sharon Kopp about a clamp-spring type clothespin being placed on Dennis's penis by his parents while he was kneeling on a broom handle and reciting the rosary. On this date 4-28-65 we received a copy of a letter by Dr. Robert Woodburn dated April 26, 1965. Dr. Woodburn is the pathologist who performed the autopsy on Dennis Jurgens. In this letter Dr.

Woodburn stated that both the marks on the penis could have been caused by focal pressure, such as would be caused by a spring-loaded clothespin . . .

Another unclear area of the day before Dennis died is why wasn't a doctor summoned to the Jurgens home, being that Dennis was so sick that Mrs. Jurgens was up with him on Friday night and Mr. Jurgens on Saturday night . . .

One other area of concern to us is that through some of the people we have interviewed regarding this case, it was brought to our attention by them that an attorney representing the Jurgenses had been visiting them. We learned that Mrs. John Zerwas had been instructed by an attorney to tell her children the less they said at this time the better it would be. We subsequently found that a number of persons who had intended to give us written statements were reluctant to do so, in fear of possible future action against them by the Jurgenses. These people also mentioned that they were indirectly informed that they better watch what they say or they may be in trouble. These same people, however, informed us they would give us verbal statements for our report use, and they would be willing to testify in court if subpoenaed.

On Thursday, Korolchuk and VanderWyst visited Chief Wayne Armstrong in his office to explain why their investigation was no longer yielding reports, and to hand him their seven-page analysis.

While Korolchuk talked, VanderWyst studied Armstrong. He didn't think highly of the chief. In fact, Armstrong reminded him of a dishrag that had been soaked in soapy water for a good number of days and then laid out in the hot sun. You tell him about something, VanderWyst thought, he turns it over to somebody else. You want a direct answer, you'll never get it from him. You go by his office, half the time he's sleeping, right in his desk chair. The station joke.

Armstrong did not display any indecision now, however. When Korolchuk finished talking, the chief told his two officers that without new leads or information, they had gone as far as they could. Their investigation was over.

Later that same day, on their own, Korolchuk and VanderWyst decided the Ramsey County attorney's office should have a copy of their complete file, including the final analysis. Climbing into a squad car, they headed for the courthouse in downtown St. Paul. When they were five blocks from their destination, their car radio crackled to life. Come back to White Bear, the dispatcher was saying. The chief wants you to turn around and return to White Bear.

Korolchuk and VanderWyst looked at each other. How'd the chief find out what they were doing? Korolchuk continued guiding the car down St. Peter as VanderWyst reached for the radio mouthpiece.

"We can't understand you," he said to the dispatcher. "We can't hear you . . . Reception is bad here . . . If you can hear us, we'll be out at the county attorney's office."

The officers ran up the three flights to Paul Lindholm's office, left their package on his desk, and bolted for their car.

"We knew you were calling us, but we didn't know what it was all about," VanderWyst explained to Armstrong later that day. "We were near tall buildings and just couldn't hear."

At that moment the matter of Dennis Jurgens's death passed from the hands of White Bear Lake to those of Ramsey County. Both the county coroner and the county prosecutor had decisions to make.

Only by a passing twist of fate did Dr. Thomas Votel even happen to be the Ramsey County coroner in 1965. Soon after he'd started his private practice in the suburb of Roseville in 1955, the county coroner had dropped by to say he needed a deputy in that region to make death pronouncements. Votel, soft-spoken, voluble and guileless, had shrugged and agreed. Four years later, when the coroner was led off to a mental institution after waving a gun and threatening a police chief, the office's chief investigator had approached Votel, asking if he'd take the job. Part-time, $5,000 a year, Tom Flaherty had explained. I do the investigating, the pathologist does the autopsy. You just rule on the cause of death.

The county was desperate, Votel reasoned. Why not help out?

That Votel had only brief experience as a general practitioner mattered little—the county was thankful they had a doctor of any sort. State law at the time required only that coroners be twenty-one and free of felonies, and in some counties these were the only qualifications the coroner could claim. Forensic pathology was in its infancy, recognized only since 1951 as a medical specialty. When

Votel first became coroner, there were no board-certified forensic pathologists working anywhere in the upper Midwest.

In Ramsey County, Votel soon discovered, there wasn't even much of a coroner's office. In the autopsy room, a pump that suctioned out fluids from the dead bodies deposited its waste through a hose stuck into a toilet. Attendants sometimes stacked a dozen bodies, like pancakes, in a cramped cooler of a size for four corpses. Decisions about causes of death at times were reached by the flip of a coin—natural deaths that weren't autopsied got signed out as *stroke* or *coronary* on a random basis. Votel soon began campaigning for a new coroner's building and revised policies, and in time he got both. At the next election, flush with his accomplishments, Votel prevailed over his strongest challenger, Bill Heinje, a used-car salesman from Long Cadillac.

The dead children troubled him, though. Infants and toddlers with ruptured livers, torn guts, cracked heads, and always the parents had explanations that didn't ring true. One kid supposedly fell over a pool cue and ruptured his spleen. Another, the boyfriend was playfully throwing the baby in the air when it slipped. In all, there'd been a dozen such cases in Ramsey County between 1961 and 1965, and in four of the twelve, the child had died of peritonitis due to an abdominal injury inflicted by another person.

Votel had tried flagging the county attorney, Bill Randall, on a few of these, but they never went anywhere. Randall wasn't so much uninterested as he was pragmatic. You know these cases are difficult to prove, the prosecutor would tell the coroner. We have to prove malicious intent. And we need an eyewitness.

Votel, neither a weak nor a forceful man, neither coward nor leader, found himself unable to act. No one wants to be the first over the parapet, and the coroner was no exception—where the prosecutor would not venture, Votel wouldn't either. In deaths where the facts seemed puzzling, where kids lay in caskets with busted insides, he began to write "deferred" on death certificates in the box reserved for mode of death.

So the little Jurgens boy on Palm Sunday had troubled but not shocked Votel. He'd seen this before and he understood this was an abused child. What to do about it was less clear. As the White Bear police reports flowed to the county, Votel received briefings from his chief investigator, Tom Flaherty.

Those who prefer conspiracy theories to the less glittering if more complex tales of human failure tend to eye the late Tom Flaherty with a certain relish when speculating about the Jurgens case. He was by all accounts a well-liked Irishman with a keen wit, an advanced taste for liquor and friends throughout Ramsey County, particularly among policemen. As it happens, he knew Jerome Zerwas, and the two were sometimes seen together. There are those who think it significant that a White Bear police officer twice received orders from the station dispatcher to pick up an inebriated Flaherty at the Bali Hai Bar on White Bear Avenue and take him to the Hilton in downtown St. Paul. Where the dispatcher got his orders, no one could say. What does seem clear is the nature of Flaherty's report to Votel.

Dennis Jurgens had fallen down a flight of stairs and also slipped on the basement floor, he told the coroner. The police were still investigating. He'd keep Votel advised.

An abused child's death could be caused by something other than the abuse, Votel reasoned. It was possible that a ruptured bowel could come from an accidental fall down fourteen steps to a concrete floor, particularly if the child hit something in the basement. He'd seen one ruptured bowel from a biking fall and another from a sledding accident.

Votel, deciding he wanted the White Bear police to resolve the issues before he ruled on the mode of death, put aside Dennis Jurgens's death certificate to await more information. The coroner was still waiting when he retired from office two years later, in 1967.

In the Ramsey County attorney's office, Paul Lindholm flipped through the file containing the White Bear police reports, the coroner's autopsy and the photos taken of Dennis's body just past noon on Palm Sunday.

Korolchuk and VanderWyst had come to him that first week, speculating over this case, acting as if they thought they had something special but weren't sure just what. Since he barely knew them, Lindholm had trouble reading the two White Bear cops. Those from the small towns didn't come by more than once every three months, and usually it was Jerome Zerwas who brought in cases from White Bear Lake. Body English counted in these meetings—if the cops pressed their case, Lindholm sometimes responded. This time,

Lindholm sensed the two officers wanted the case prosecuted if possible, but understood the legal problems.

As Lindholm saw it, there were indeed legal problems.

This new battered child syndrome thing just then getting written about wasn't a concept recognized in a court of law. It would do little good in court to trot out all the tales of Lois's abuse toward Dennis, even if the family members agreed to testify. They'd still need an eyewitness to tell how the child died. They needed to link the ruptured bowel to a specific act by Lois or someone else. Proving that Lois had abused Dennis at other times just wouldn't bring a conviction—they could show that the child was beaten up every Friday for six straight weeks, but if on the Friday before he died, they had no witness to a beating, they'd lose in court.

There was also the matter of people's attitudes. You don't judge a case in a vacuum, Lindholm knew that much. You consider how well you can sell this to twelve people in a jury box. Lindholm just didn't think he could convince jurors that middle-class families in suburban homes killed their children—not without an eyewitness, that was for sure.

Finally, there was the coroner's report. Votel's indecision wasn't binding on the prosecutor, but the defense attorney would zero in on this. If the doc can't figure this out, he'd say, well . . . how can we? If Votel had called it a homicide, at least that prospect would have been removed.

There was a custody hearing coming up over the fate of the Jurgenses' other boy, Robert, now living with his paternal grandparents. Maybe we can pressure them, smoke them out at this hearing, Lindholm reasoned. But right now, there's no case. You go after the cases you think you can win. Don't put your money on a dead horse—that was the rule in Lindholm's office. That was the rule in the prosecutor's office.

The end of April in 1965 was a time of good feeling in White Bear Lake.

On Saturday night, April 24, hundreds gathered in the White Bear Lake High School auditorium for the official All-America City award presentation. The evening opened at 7:30 with a half-hour concert by the White Bear Lake High School Stage Band, followed by greetings from the evening's master of ceremonies, George Rice of St.

Paul's WCCO-TV. Minnesota's lieutenant governor, A. M. "Sandy" Keith, spoke, as did assorted congressmen, state senators and mayors. A White Bear High student group performed a modern dance interpretation and local resident Arline Withy performed her much-acclaimed comedy sketch. Dave Farkell and Bob Eddy took the stage to present the full ten-minute, seventy-eight-picture slide show and narration that had swayed the judges in San Francisco. Mayor Milt Knoll followed them.

"We haven't resolved all our problems," he told the crowd, "but we have demonstrated something more important . . . Individuals from all segments of the community can work together for greater progress."

Knoll asked Bill LeVasseur to the stage so they could accept the All-America City award jointly. Grant Jacks, *Look* magazine's Twin Cities representative, and Raymond Black, from the National Municipal League, handed them their plaque before a flurry of popping flashbulbs. At ten o'clock, the crowd repaired to the armory for a gala late-night dance.

After relentlessly rising for eight days, the Mississippi River had finally started dropping in the week after Easter. The twenty-six-foot crest was still twelve feet above flood level and four feet higher than anything in St. Paul history, but weary volunteers now rejoiced all the same, and relaxed.

On April 30, a week after the All-America City award presentation, spring took hold in the White Bear Lake area. Amid fair blue skies and temperatures of seventy-five, the floods and the storms seemed a distant, blurred memory. Golf clubs and fishing poles made their first appearance of the year.

CHAPTER 16

The Custody Hearing

Camille Brass could not imagine who was knocking at her front door on South Gardenette Drive. It was a crisp, sunny morning in early May of 1965. The children were at school and her husband Bob was perched in his office on the platform overlooking the selling floor of the Ben Franklin five-and-dime. Moving from the kitchen to the living room, Cam could see through her front window a fleshy man in a dark suit standing on the porch.

He introduced himself as Ed Donohue, and said he was one of the lawyers representing the neighbors across the street, the Jurgenses.

Cam had wondered what was happening over at the Jurgenses'. After the hearse and the police and the doctor had pulled away that Sunday, they'd never seen or heard anything further. It was as though nothing had ever happened. She'd assumed the authorities were taking care of things. Certainly the authorities were dealing with this terrible event.

Donohue had a question: Had she ever seen Lois abuse her kids?

Cam considered. What she knew, she'd heard from Dorothy Engfer and the DeMarses. Cam herself had never directly seen Lois hurt the boys. Besides, these were private family matters. One day, a little girl had come to the school where Cam taught with a handprint on her face, but who was there to tell?

No, she replied, she had not seen Lois abuse her children.

Donohue thanked her, and departed.

This scene repeated itself on front porches up and down Gardenette Drive in the early days of May, and Ed Donohue soon had a long list of neighbors favorable to his case. Eventually, more than a dozen of these neighbors received subpoenas, calling them to testify on behalf of the Jurgenses at the custody hearing in Judge Gingold's courtroom.

Donna Neely, who lived next door to Cam Brass, felt terrified at the notion of testifying, for she'd tried once to confront Lois and the effort had only left her feeling jangled.

That encounter had started because each morning the neighborhood kids stood at the corner in front of Lois's house, waiting for the bus to St. Pius, and Lois would yell at them even though they weren't on her property. One day Lois called the school to complain, and the school called Donna Neely, who went over to Dorothy Engfer's house to confer. Finally, Donna had summoned the courage to dial Lois's number from Dorothy's house.

"Why didn't you call me instead of the school?" she demanded.

Donna was hoping to scare Lois, to bully her, but in this she failed. Lois responded with a string of mean, nasty comments about Donna and the children. Donna, reaching for a response, invoked what she'd heard from Dorothy and the DeMarses. "You're a bad mother," she told Lois. "We hear how you treat your children." Lois snarled in return, "I'll treat my kids any way I want. You can't tell me." By the end of the conversation, it was Donna who felt scared, not Lois.

Now here was this subpoena, threatening another go-around. She'd had quite enough of confronting Lois. And she felt intimidated by the police car that was regularly parked outside Lois's house. Donna knew it belonged to Lois's brother, the cop. She felt Lois had the law on her side. What did Donna know, anyway? What could she say to make a difference? There were much bigger, stronger people in the community. Why not the welfare people? Dr. Peterson? Or the Zerwas family?

Because Donna was pregnant, near full term, she had a way out. She called her doctor, who in turn wrote a letter to Judge Gingold, and soon after Donna was excused. She wasn't really needed, anyway, she figured. So many other neighbors were going to testify.

The two-day hearing unfolded in a thirty-by-thirty-foot room on the sixteenth floor of the Ramsey County courthouse. The gathering looked more like a conference than a courtroom hearing. Departing from the customary rules of decorum, as he often did in juvenile proceedings, Judge Gingold sat not up on the bench in robes, but rather, at a large floor-level table in a business suit. Before him, positioned three feet back, in cushioned straightback chairs with armrests, sat Harold and Lois Jurgens, their attorneys Ed Donohue and Joe Rivard, and assistant Ramsey County attorney Bertrand Poritsky. Court reporter Harry "Buzz" Dynes sat at the end of the table to the judge's left, and James Nelson, a young attorney appointed by the court to represent Robert's interests as guardian *ad litem* sat at the end to the judge's right. The welfare department's Paul Schroeder and Beatrice Bernhagen and White Bear police officer Robert VanderWyst watched from behind this group, in a row of chairs lined against the west wall. Windows on the east wall, behind Gingold, gave onto views of the Mississippi.

May 10 and 11 were hot, humid days in St. Paul, and the sixteenth-floor courtroom soon grew sultry and uncomfortable. There was no fan, and the windows remained closed to shut out the river and street noises below. The lawyers kept waiting for Gingold to say they could take their suit jackets off, but the judge never did.

Gingold had a tremendous ability to endure heat, and this was only one of the attributes that had made him something of a legend in Ramsey County. He was by all accounts a man of concern and compassion, with a deep commitment to the juvenile law system, a system he'd essentially created in Ramsey County when he assumed his position in 1960. Gingold's parents were European immigrants who had started life in America virtually penniless, peddling matches and making cigars, and Gingold had worked his way through school selling everything from newspapers and vegetables to janitorial supplies. He saw the juvenile court more as a substitute parent than as a source of punishment, which was one reason he sat at conference tables without judicial robes. At the same time, Gingold was a man who wanted to have his way, who preferred to run affairs without question or challenge. He could be absolutely charming and delightful, but he also could be curt and demanding and abrasive. Even as a defense attorney was in the middle of talking, Gingold might order a probation officer to take a child away. Or he might step out of the room and, as the hearing continued, make use of the adjacent bathroom, while the participants at the hearing pretended not to notice the judge's absence or hear the flushing toilet. Gingold liked to get things done.

Only one other person besides Gingold seemed impervious to the humid heat in the hearing room. Lois Jurgens wore a hat with a folded veil, and sat unflinchingly upright, staring straight ahead, throughout two twelve-hour days. Her rigidity and lack of any affect came to mesmerize others in the room. Early in the proceedings the unsettling autopsy photos were passed about the room, and Lois remained without expression when they reached her.

Moments after the hearing began at 8:30 A.M. on May 10, the Jurgenses' attorney, Ed Donohue, rose with an inquiry.

"Your Honor," he said, gesturing over Poritsky's shoulder, "I'd like to ask counsel to make a disclosure as to who this man is sitting behind him, for the record."

Poritsky identified the man as Patrolman Robert VanderWyst of the White Bear police department.

"I would move the court for an order excluding all possible witnesses from this hearing, including the officer from White Bear . . ." Donohue continued. "I understand that he has been conducting an investigation which is designed to enable the Ramsey County attorney's office to make a determination as to what course will be followed so far as any criminal action toward the Jurgenses is concerned. I think he should not be present, except to testify in this case."

Donohue had good reason to make this request. Ever since getting the case, he'd been worrying about a criminal prosecution. In fact, after looking at the evidence and the autopsy photos, he fully expected a criminal prosecution, and had so warned the Jurgenses. Donohue was a knowing, combative, convivial Irishman, part of the downtown St. Paul lawyers' network, recommended to the Jurgenses by Judge Bill Fleming in White Bear Lake. VanderWyst's presence in a private juvenile hearing caused him great apprehension.

"He is a police officer . . ." Donohue said. "There is no question in my mind if there should be any criminal action in this matter at a later time, that he would be one of the principal witnesses. I feel it is extremely unfair that he should be present in this courtroom . . ."

If counsel is worried about what Officer VanderWyst might find out, Poritsky pointed out, it's easy enough for the county attorney to order a transcript of this testimony and turn it over to him.

Such a notion raised even greater alarms in Donohue.

"Your Honor," he said, "we would ask that no one be permitted to have a transcript of this testimony for purposes that might be followed up by the county attorney's offices, particularly—"

The judge cut Donohue off in midsentence.

"The police people have been generally permitted to sit in this court," Gingold snapped. "I don't see any reason why I should change that ruling today and I'm not going to change it."

As it unfolded, the hearing proved to be a curious affair. Although it was a juvenile proceeding in which the county charged neglect and sought custody of Robert, most of the testimony focused on the life and treatment of Dennis.

Poritsky, presenting the county's case first, called upon those few neighbors and relatives who had talked openly to the White Bear police. He had just one neighbor couple, the DeMarses, and two couples from the Zerwas family—Lloyd and Donna Zerwas, Richard and Donna Norton.

On the witness stand, Ivan DeMars, then forty-five, seemed vague, almost befuddled, unable to understand when Poritsky asked if he had seen Dennis's appearance change over time.

"I thought he got a little thinner as time progressed . . ." DeMars said. "I don't understand the question, exactly what you're getting at."

"Did Lois ever remark about Dennis's mental ability?" Poritsky asked.

"Let's see, how was that?" DeMars responded. "We were by the house . . . I remember her saying . . . I believe the way she said that was, 'You can't even talk, you're so stupid. I don't know why we were saddled with you.' It was a remark, and it was made over the fence. We were speaking . . ."

Gladys DeMars was more precise. She'd observed Dennis's bruises "on numerous occasions." She'd seen Lois yank Dennis by the ears—"She kept going and he could barely toddle along on his little toes . . . She seemed particularly fond of taking the children by the ear. It seems to be her way of disciplining them." She'd watched Dennis's appearance wither—"He looked just terrible . . . his whole face looked just so old, like a little old man . . . He looked so sickly, so peaked and so sickly, very thin . . . His little face seemed too small, didn't appear normal to me . . ."

Lois's brother Lloyd also talked of bruises and black eyes and ear-yanking, as well as an episode of force-feeding on Thanksgiving Day of 1963.

"Dennis wasn't eating his meal like he was supposed to . . . I seen my sister take horseradish and make him eat this horseradish . . . I just seen her give him a forkful of it . . . She put the stuff and jammed it down his throat there, so he'd swallow it . . . Well, he choked on it and that's when I went into the other room . . . I didn't see anything from that point on . . . Oh, I heard him throw up . . . I heard after that she was supposed to have fed this back to him . . . Dennis had kind of a scared look on his face. He, to me, looked like he was scared half the time that I've seen him . . . It bothered me, really did . . . But I just didn't stick my nose into it . . . There was a time, yes, that I thought somebody should check it out."

Lloyd's wife Donna elaborated on the Thanksgiving Day dinner.

"[Lois] fixed TV dinners because she was sick in bed, she said . . . She was provoked with him because he wasn't eating and she said—she gave him the mustard because then he had to swallow his food . . . He didn't cry. He choked. [She said] 'If you vomit, you're going to eat it.' Because he was gagging. He was choking on the food . . . [Then] he vomited it . . . He had food in with the horseradish-mustard . . . [Lois] fed it to him . . . We went home shortly after that. . . ."

Donna also talked about Lois's toilet training methods.

"Quite frequently [Lois said] that he had a hard time going to the toilet and she had to help him go to the toilet. He couldn't pass his stool . . . She said she used her finger in his rectum . . . She told me—I was having trouble with my dog going to the toilet . . . And [she said] feed him his stool. That's what she did to Dennis . . . I didn't think she was kidding. Maybe she was . . . I didn't think so."

Having soon exhausted his supply of eyewitnesses, Poritsky called to the stand Dr. Robert Woodburn. The pathologist's testimony was unequivocal. Peritonitis would leave a person doubled up in excruciating pain. The fatal injury could only have come from external trauma applied to the bowel. There was no possibility that death came from a blow to the head, and scarce chance it came from a fall on a flat surface. Only five to ten percent of Dennis's bruises could have been caused by such a fall.

"It is essentially inconceivable to me, without a protruding object above the floor, that he could have been injured in this way," Woodburn testified.

Dr. Roy Peterson's interpretation of events, however, differed considerably from Woodburn's. In fact, although initially called by Poritsky, the family doctor ended up testifying mostly on behalf of the Jurgenses.

Q: Was there anything unusual about Dennis's condition as you viewed him as he lay in the crib?

A: No, nothing struck me, except for these bruises . . . The Jurgenses of course had many questions why he should die and all, and I talked to them about the causes of death in children, like this one, of there being the possibility of this quick pneumonia since he had a cold and fever and I also mentioned that it was possible that because of this fall that he had a blood clot in his brain . . . But other than that, nothing remarkable.

Q: Doctor, is it quite customary to see a little boy that has numerous bruises on his body?

A: It's not unusual. I have several children about that age now with this same problem. Active children that bruise easily, and the parents have questioned me about what can be done about it. So it's not real unusual.

Q: Was there anything unusual about that [genital burn] incident?

A: No, not in particular. He was a good patient . . . He seldom was fussy.

Q: In your opinion, was there anything unusual about this boy, Doctor, that you saw in view of the explanations as given you by Mr. and Mrs. Jurgens?

A: No.

The sixteenth-floor hallway in the Ramsey County courthouse grew crowded on May 11, the second morning of the custody hearing, for Ed Donohue planned to call a good number of witnesses to testify on behalf of the Jurgenses. Bob and Cam Brass bumped into Father Reiser.

"Bob, Camille . . . isn't this awful?" the priest said.

Cam Brass felt upset about testifying. "I don't know anything," she protested when the man had handed her the subpoena, but he'd just shrugged and said, "You got it, lady." Bob Brass felt perplexed. As a kid, he remembered his mother's friend once saying she'd been "taken advantage of" by her father—he knew what that meant—but the idea of a parent abusing a child was beyond him. Besides, what with the store and the All-America Cities campaign and the recent celebrations over getting the award, he hardly knew the goings-on in Gardenette Park.

Precisely at 8:30 A.M., Donohue started parading a string of witnesses through the courtroom—a dozen neighbors and another dozen relatives—all testifying they'd never seen the Jurgenses abuse their children. From Gardenette Park came Bob Hatch, Margaret Dahlberg, Raymond Zetah, the Latchams, Thomas Fischer, Leo Brown, Myrtle Brown. From the family came Lois's parents and her siblings—Lyle, Joseph, Donald, Eleanor, Jerome—as well as in-laws and nieces and Harold's mother. In fact, Donohue's sweep of the neighborhood had been so wide it had ensnared one fellow who didn't have a clue why he was there.

"Do you know Mr. and Mrs. Harold Jurgens?" Donohue asked Robert Edmund Buskirk, a sales manager for Diebold, Inc., who lived at 2161 South Gardenette Drive.

"No."

"You do not know them?"

"No."

"Do you know who they are?"

"No."

"Do you know anything about them at all?"

"Nothing."

"Have you ever seen these people before?"

"No, I wouldn't recognize them."

Donohue quickly hustled the man off the stand as Poritsky smirked behind his open palm.

Lois's parents proved more helpful to Donohue—their testimony now differed considerably from what they'd told VanderWyst and Korolchuk in the week after Dennis's death.

"I never heard anything about that," Lois's father said when asked about reports of mistreatment. "Never saw it."

"I should say not," Lois's mother added. "Their children are not neglected. If every child was taken as good a care of as these children were, there'd be a lot better children in this world . . . They have the most beautiful home . . . I have never seen those children dirty . . .

Come to pray, they never missed . . . We really got a charge out of the little children saying their rosary."

Soon it was the Brasses' turn. They'd decided just to answer the questions asked of them, no more and no less. Bob took the stand first.

Q: Have you ever noticed anything unusual about any activity in the Jurgenses' yard?

A: Nothing at all, sir.

Q: Have you ever noticed anything which would lead you to believe that Robert Jurgens was neglected in any way?

A: No, definitely not.

Camille followed her husband to the stand.

Q: Have you ever seen Mrs. Jurgens mistreat these children in any way?

A: No.

Q: Have you ever seen Mrs. Jurgens grab one of the children by the ears?

A: Never.

Q: Have you ever seen Mrs. Jurgens pick up the children by the ears?

A: No.

Q: Have you ever seen any conduct on their part or anything to lead you to believe that they have neglected Robert Jurgens?

A: No.

Father Reiser did not sound quite as unequivocal when Donohue asked him if he'd ever known the Jurgenses to mistreat their two boys.

"To the best of my knowledge, and like I say, we interview thousands of people, I can never recall ever hearing or ever having been told that they mistreated, mishandled or treated their children in any way but in a proper fashion," Reiser answered.

"Specifically," Donohue then inquired, "three persons, Lloyd Zerwas, Donna Zerwas, Mrs. Richard Norton—did any one of these people ever offer any complaint to you as to alleged mistreatment of the Jurgens children by either their mother or their father?"

Donohue had a particular reason for asking this question—he was responding to those three witnesses' testimony the previous day.

Just twenty-four hours before, Poritsky had asked Donna Zerwas: "Have you ever talked to [Father Reiser] about this problem? Did you ever tell him about Lois?"

A: Yes . . . I've talked to him several times.

Q: Did you talk to him or tell him about seeing the manner in which this boy, Dennis, was being treated?

A: Yes.

Q: You discussed this with Father Reiser?

A: Yes.

Q: After Thanksgiving 1963?

A: Yes.

Q: And you told him about this also?

A: Yes.

Q: Did you also tell Father Reiser that she would try to cause him to have a bowel movement by inserting her finger into his rectum?

A: Yes.

Q: Now, you're sure about this?

A: Yes.

Q: You're under oath and you're telling us that you reported these incidents to Father Reiser?

A: Yes.

Now, on the second day of the hearing, Father Reiser glanced at Judge Gingold as he answered Donohue's question.

"Like I say, all I can answer, and I think the court understands this . . . at this moment, I can't ever recall having been told that these parents mistreated these children. Like I say, I'm human and I'm fallible, but I don't recall ever having been told that they mistreated their children . . ."

Soon after, Jerome Zerwas marched to the witness stand.

Q: Did you partake at all in any investigation that may have been made by the White Bear Lake police department into the circumstances surrounding the death of Dennis Jurgens?

A: No, I didn't.

Q: Have you ever at any time over the past five years ever observed Lois or Harold mistreat either Dennis or Robert?

A: No.

Q: Have you ever observed anything unusual about Harold or Lois which would lead you to believe or suspect that they neglected either one or both of these children in any way whatever?

A: No.

Bob VanderWyst, standing behind the lawyers, was whispering to Poritsky as Donohue questioned Jerome. The lieutenant's threat, imagined or not, apparently was still occupying a corner of Vander-Wyst's mind. Poritsky took aim on cross-examination.

Q: Did you ever talk to anybody about this case after the time Dennis died and before the time of this hearing?

A: Sergeant Korolchuk and Officer VanderWyst.

Q: Did you talk to any members of your family?

A: Yes.

Q: Who did you talk to?

A: Oh, my wife and I talked a lot.

Q: How about the brothers and sisters?

A: No.

Q: Never talked to any of them?

A: There might have been a passing word or something. I don't know which ones. I couldn't give you any answer.

Q: Did you ever say anything to the effect that anyone who testifies might be in trouble?

A: No.

Q: Never made any threats of any kind to any of the witnesses?

A: No.

Q: Did you ever make a remark to the effect that I'm going to do anything in my power to get Lois off, even if it means my job?

A: No.

Q: Did you make a remark to this effect in the White Bear police station a week after the child died?

A: No.

Q: Nothing to that effect?

A: No.

Q: You're under oath and I'm asking you to search your memory to the best of your ability.

A: No.

Q: Lieutenant Zerwas, you never made a statement like that?

A: No.

Poritsky stared at Jerome.

"I have no further questions," he said.

The patrolman and the prosecutor were not inclined to let the matter drop, however. Later in the day, Poritsky told Judge Gingold he had a witness to call in rebuttal to evidence placed on the record by Donohue. Bob VanderWyst settled into the witness chair.

Q: During the week after Dennis Jurgens died, were you in the White Bear police station at any time in the evening with Lieutenant Zerwas and Patrolman Korolchuk?

A: Yes, I was.

Q: On this occasion, did Lieutenant Zerwas make a statement concerning this case?

A: Yes, he did.

Q: Will you tell us what that statement was?

A: He said to Sergeant Korolchuk and myself that he would do everything within his power to get Lois off, even if it meant his job.

As the second day of the hearing wound into the late afternoon, Donohue asked for a recess. He had saved Harold and Lois Jurgens for the end, and now needed to prepare his clients for their interrogation.

Lois took the stand first, wearing the pillbox hat and veil that had remained on her head for two days. At thirty-nine Lois was still attractive, but the years had toughened and thickened her features. She sat erect, her face stony and impassive.

In their private talks, Ed Donohue had found her terribly indignant at what was happening. She had flatly denied any responsibility for Dennis's death and insisted that she was a great mother. She was a strong disciplinarian, she'd told her lawyer, but she brought those kids up right so they would make something of themselves.

Donohue had to walk a fine line with his direct examination of her, selecting his questions precisely, wording them carefully. Poritsky, in his cross-examination, could only question Lois about matters raised on direct, so Donohue didn't want to open unwelcome doors. He would focus on Robert and stay far away from questions related to Dennis.

Cautiously, slowly, he began, walking Lois through her background and family history, then moving on to Robert's adoption and upbringing. Attorney and client talked of diapers and bottles and eating habits and methods of discipline.

"When he doesn't behave," Lois said, "I stand him in the corner or sit him in a chair or send him to his bedroom."

"Does Robert play in the backyard and around the neighborhood?" Donohue asked.

"Yes," Lois said. "Well, not around the neighborhood. He plays in his own backyard because on that street, there is a lot of hotrod boys going around and I don't want my children getting out in the streets, so therefore, I have the gate locked and they play in the backyard."

"Do you love Robert?"

"Very much."

When Donohue sat down, he felt satisfied he had kept the testimony away from dangerous topics.

Then it was Poritsky's turn. He tried to push through a door even though it had not been opened.

"When was Dennis adopted?" he began.

Donohue jumped to his feet.

"Just a minute now. I'm going to object to any questions on Dennis on the grounds that it's beyond the scope of the direct examination."

Gingold had to agree.

"Yes," the judge said, "the record may show that he asked her no questions about Dennis and that we will restrict the cross-examination to the areas that were covered in the direct."

A moment later, Poritsky tried a subtler approach.

"Do you feel the same way toward Robert that you felt toward Dennis?" he asked.

Donohue again jumped up.

"Just a minute. That's objected to on the grounds that it's beyond the scope of the direct examination."

"Your Honor," Poritsky responded, "he asked her feelings toward Robert and that's what this question is about."

Gingold thought Poritsky was one sharp attorney.

"I think we will take this question," the judge agreed. "We will allow this question to be asked."

Poritsky had found an opening. He was successfully maneuvering into critical territory, and Donohue knew it all too well. If the assistant county attorney could establish a similarity of background between Robert and Dennis—if he could get Lois to say she had much the same feelings for the two boys—he could argue that Robert faced the same danger as did Dennis. The only way Lois could escape this trap would be to acknowledge an animosity toward Dennis that she didn't have toward Robert. Such an admission might help prove that Robert was safe, but it would be fuel for a criminal prosecution over Dennis's death. With one deft question, Poritsky had constructed an inescapable box.

With the judge's approval, he began to repeat his question: "Do you now feel the same way toward Robert as you did toward Dennis, before he died—"

Donohue, frantic, moved to Lois's side and interrupted.

"Just a minute. I want to consult—"

"Wait a minute," Poritsky interrupted in kind. "He's got no right to go over there and prompt the witness."

"That's right," Judge Gingold said.

"Could I have an opportunity, Your Honor, to talk to this witness then . . .?" Donohue asked. "Privately, for a moment."

"No, you'll not be given that privilege now . . . Not during the period of cross-examination when a question is—"

"Your Honor—" Donohue implored.

". . . when the question is proffered to her," Gingold continued.

Donohue just could not let Lois answer the question.

"Then I'll instruct the witness at this time to refuse to answer the question on the grounds that it may tend to incriminate her," he said.

Raising a Fifth Amendment privilege in a juvenile custody hearing was quite unusual, even extraordinary, and Poritsky did not hesitate to point this out. What crime could be involved in her feelings toward her child? he asked. This was, of course, a disingenuous question, for everyone knew the subtext of homicide ran beneath the proceedings.

Gingold surveyed those before him. In truth, the judge didn't like Donohue. Gingold had presided at other juvenile cases where defense attorneys acknowledged their clients' problems. This son of a bitch Donohue should be doing just that, the judge thought. Sometimes, you get a case rotten enough, you tell the client to take the file somewhere else. Still, the law was the law, and he'd respect an attorney's advice to a client. Donohue had a right to raise the Fifth Amendment protections.

"I'll honor it," the judge said. "I'll honor it."

Harold Jurgens's time on the stand proved less fiery. His answers frequently rambled far afield of the questions—a description of the games he played with Robert turned into an elaborate discussion of their playful wrestling matches, which meandered into a survey of Harold's attitudes toward professional wrestling. For the most part, though, Harold talked simply of his love and pride and hopes for Robert. Poritsky did not try to corner him as he did Lois.

When Harold left the stand, Ed Donohue rested his case.

The specter of homicide hovered, but did not land, in Judge Gingold's courtroom in May of 1965. In the corridors during recesses, the lawyers among themselves acknowledged what lay at the core of the hearing, but much remained unspoken, at least for the public record.

"The deceased child during his lifetime was subjected to many incidents of cruel and severe actions . . ." Judge Gingold wrote in the findings he eventually entered into the sealed juvenile record. "The extent and severities of the injuries excluded that they were accidentally received, and left the court with the sole inference that Dennis died as a result of a beating or beatings by Lois."

That, however, was not the issue. That was not why they were gathered on the sixteenth floor of the Ramsey County courthouse. They were participating in a juvenile court custody hearing regarding Robert, not a criminal prosecution regarding Dennis. There was enough evidence to sustain child neglect charges, and that was all Gingold had to concern himself with. The judge hadn't let Donohue's parade of witnesses fool him, but homicide wasn't being charged.

"You see," Gingold would say much later, "I didn't have to go that far . . . The county attorney wasn't getting help from the White Bear police. Lois's brother was on the force. The welfare casework was flawed. Those people can't treat and blow the whistle at the same time. Lots of people were lined up on Lois's side. The doctor out there also had problems, a typical doctor, they just can't believe their patient was killed. Many babies were buried without notice then . . . This was all part of the picture, my friend. Nobody gave a shit then. I don't think Harold wanted to face who Lois was, any more than other people did . . . I was quite certain it was a homicide, quite certain, but it was a different time, a different time."

When the second day of testimony ended early in the evening on May 11, the judge, sitting at the conference table and without further deliberation, delivered his ruling.

The Jurgenses, he said, "are very honorable people. I think they're both people of very good intentions. I think their best thinking is not to hurt anybody." However, on the basis of the evidence received at the hearing and the findings he would soon enter, "We are going to find that a condition of neglect does exist."

The Ramsey County welfare department would keep temporary legal custody of Robert, who could continue living with his paternal grandparents. Gingold, though, hoped "we can develop conditions in the immediate future where these people can have their child back again, who I know they love."

Gingold felt it would be helpful to him if Harold and Lois consented to a psychiatric evaluation, "which the court will take into consideration at the first date that this case is continued to." At that next hearing, "the court will decide whether at that time or at any reasonable time in the future after that, the court can transfer the custody of the child back to the mother and the father."

With that, the hearing adjourned. Being a closed juvenile proceeding, no one was present to observe the conclusion other than the principal participants. The St. Paul newspaper had never followed up on the two brief reports published in the days after Dennis's death, and the local *White Bear Press* had never reported his death at all.

In the Ramsey County attorney's office, Paul Lindholm had kept his options open in case the hearing yielded fresh evidence, but now, after Poritsky told him nothing new had emerged, Lindholm officially decided there would be no prosecution of the Jurgenses for Dennis's death. Tom Votel that very day, May 11, wrote the word "deferred" in the mode-of-death box on Dennis's death certificate and signed his name. The word *homicide* remained unspoken publicly. Dennis lay in the ground at St. Mary's Cemetery, no name given to his death.

The hearing did yield certain repercussions, however.

In the days following its conclusion, the two couples in the Zerwas clan who had testified against Lois—Lloyd and Donna Zerwas and Richard and Donna Norton—began receiving angry, threatening phone calls, often in the middle of the night. Later they would claim the caller was Lois. *I'm going to burn your house down*, is the way they remembered her words. *I'm going to burn those little fuckin' bastards in your house.* Well past midnight, the families sometimes would hear a car drive slowly past their houses, and late one night Richard Norton's daughter Karlene heard a sharp noise on the back porch outside her window. The calls continued for several weeks, finally driving Norton to consult an attorney.

Then, a month or so after the hearing, Lieutenant Jerome Zerwas called Patrolman Bob VanderWyst into his office at the White Bear police station and pointed to the pile of overtime slips filed by VanderWyst for the hours spent at Robert's custody proceeding.

"We can't pay you for that," Jerome said.

VanderWyst grew upset and threatened to appeal to Chief Armstrong, but Jerome felt there was nothing he could do. "If you go somewhere on a voluntary basis because you want to hear what's going on," he said, "you shouldn't turn in overtime. After all, we have to operate according to the rules and regulations."

Life otherwise followed its usual patterns in White Bear Lake that summer of 1965.

The VanderWysts piled all eight children in a motor home and, with friends, caravaned north to a campsite at Two Harbors, near Duluth, a region of water and lush abundance that ranks among Minnesota's most beautiful spots. Later, back home on Hinckley Avenue, the friends circled their campers on the VanderWysts' front lawn and continued the party. The women wore jeans cut to their knees and scarves wrapped around their heads, while the children—eighteen in all—poured across the street to play in Ramaley Park, the boys with crewcuts and dirty T-shirts. They sat out on summer nights eating meat loaf, hamburgers, baked potatoes and chocolate cake, until finally the wives, rebelling at all the cooking and dishwashing, went on strike, picketing with signs that said "We Demand Equal Trailer Time" and "No More Food Until Mothers Recuperate" and "Father's Day Is Only Once a Year" and "Unfair to Mothers."

White Bear continued its All-America City celebration. The All-America Cities committee appeared on a special St. Paul television show sponsored by Polar Chevrolet. Three citizens—in adult, junior high and elementary school categories—won an American flag and an All-America City flag for writing winning essays on "Why White Bear Lake Is a Great Place to Live." A White Bear Lake All-America City Spectacular on Friday and Saturday, June 18–19, offered a virtual phantasmagoria—an automobile show with sport models from Polar Chevrolet and Tousley Ford, a teen dance featuring the Elites band, an outdoor concert and a giant barbecue involving forty twenty-pound turkeys cooked on a sixty-foot spit over six hundred pounds of charcoal. Turkey sandwiches sold for fifteen cents, cartons of milk for a nickel.

For a full week in mid-July, St. Paul's KSTP-TV showcased White Bear Lake. The high point came on Saturday, July 17, when, beginning at 11:15 A.M., a caravan of convertibles containing KSTP personalities and city officials, escorted by two police cars and one firetruck, rolled through downtown White Bear, stopping three times to provide autographs. Precisely at noon, the caravan reached the Holiday House on Highway 61, where, after luncheon for three hundred, chamber of commerce president Bill LeVasseur thanked KSTP for "showing what a wonderful place White Bear Lake is to live, to work, to do business, to play and to educate our children."

Harold Jurgens's employer, the Tony Muska Electric Company, held its annual picnic during the third week in July at Carver Lake Park. Harold and Lois attended, bringing with them Robert—the county allowed such Sunday visitations—and their twelve-year-old nephew, Dennis Donald Zerwas. The nephew's parents told him he was going because the Jurgenses now lacked a child, and didn't want Robert to be alone.

Dennis Donald had mixed feelings about this venture.

He was sort of wary of Lois, to tell the truth, for there'd been some weird moments. In 1963, when Dennis Donald was nine, Lois had come into the kitchen at his home on Murray Avenue, unbuttoned her blouse and urged him to "feel her firm breasts"—Dennis Donald's young curious hand was on the way up when his own mother intervened. Early in 1965, his father, Donald, came home one day, telling his wife that he'd just been over to the Jurgenses', where Dennis had come walking out of his bedroom wearing nothing but a T-shirt and a clothespin attached to his penis. Just this morning, driving over to the picnic, Lois, dressed in slacks, had announced, "I decided to wear pants today because I do wear the pants in the family, don't I, Harold?"

All the same, Dennis Donald liked the Jurgenses very much, mainly because whatever their oddities, they still seemed to him much better than his parents or the other adults he knew in the Zerwas clan. Playing in the backyard games during the Sunday gatherings on Park Avenue, he'd never seen Lois's treatment of Dennis, but he'd felt the back of his own dad's hand often enough. In truth, whenever he used to see the Jurgenses, his heart would turn. To him, in comparison to what he knew, they were like the ideal families he saw on TV—just like the "Leave It to Beaver" family, he thought. They'd be dressed up so nice on Sunday, he recalled, Harold holding hands with his boys. Dennis Donald would be happy if his dad just carried him to the car when he was asleep—he'd fake being asleep to get that much close attention. The Jurgenses were different. They were into music, the cello, the piano. Harold would show him his coin collection when he visited and their two boys would sing. Dennis Donald longed to be part of such a family.

At Carver Lake Park, he soon discovered he loved the Muska picnic, which continued for hours. As always, old Tony Muska, natty in his pure white suit, ran about handing out silver dollars to the squealing children. Under a warm, penetrating sun, there were games and drawings and three-legged races and tables groaning with food. Harold held his son Robert's hand as they walked through the park, and Lois, dark and voluptuous, was pretty enough to catch the eye of Harold's supervisor, Walter Moore.

Late that afternoon, the Jurgenses dropped Dennis Donald at his house, then took Robert back to his grandparents before returning alone to their home on South Gardenette Drive.

Watching from her window across the street, Camille Brass surmised that Lois still did Robert's laundry, for she could see children's clothes drying on the Jurgens clothesline. Cam was right. In fact, Lois had kept both Dennis's and Robert's rooms intact, their clothes and toys undisturbed from the time when they both lived there. Dennis's tap dancing shoes rested at the head of his bed, polished and neatly aligned, as if he were going to use them again at any moment.

CHAPTER 17

A Little More Baling Wire

At the close of the May 1965 custody hearing, Judge Gingold had requested a psychiatric evaluation of Harold and Lois, and for this the Jurgenses' attorney did not turn to a stranger. Ed Donohue told his clients to make an appointment with Dr. James T. Garvey, a psychiatrist who had been a senior consultant to the Hennepin County District Court in Minneapolis since 1955, regularly advising judges on matters ranging from child protection to murderers' sanity.

By the time the Jurgenses arrived at Garvey's office on Golden Valley Road in Minneapolis at 2:45 P.M. on September 7, the doctor already knew a good deal about his visitors, for Bert Poritsky had phoned days before, then followed that with a letter and a copy of Gingold's findings. Together, the documents piled on Garvey's desk provided a detailed summary of the abuse Dennis had suffered, as well as the judge's "sole inference" that the boy had died as a result of a beating by Lois.

Sitting in the doctor's office, however, Lois denied everything. She was strict, she allowed, even harsh, but she hadn't killed Dennis. She'd sometimes punished Dennis for his own good, but Dennis had died after falling down the stairs.

That was all she or Harold had to say. Garvey probed and prodded, asking questions about their boys and their own childhoods, but gleaned little more. He thought Lois's responses flat and lacking in affect, with no hint of grief or guilt, and he judged her a cold, self-righteous woman who couldn't tolerate being wrong. He had to admit she just wasn't a likable person.

None of this, however, was central to the point of the examination. Garvey's task was to answer specific questions posed by Judge Gingold and relayed through Poritsky's letter:

Was the mistreatment of Dennis caused by a mental illness or an emotional disturbance?

If so, would psychiatric help be beneficial?

If not, is there a definable cause of the mistreatment?

For example, is there any evidence of feelings of hostility toward Dennis, the deceased child?

Is there any evidence of feelings of hostility toward Robert, the surviving child?

Is there any other information you can give the court that will aid it in dealing with this family?

In order to form his response, Garvey gave both Harold and Lois the Minnesota Multiphasic Personality Inventory, the most widely used psychological test in the world, administered annually to millions in all languages. The result was unequivocal—Lois simply did not test psychotic. She no doubt was a troubled lady full of problems, Garvey reasoned, but she wasn't clinically psychotic. It was a fine but quite distinct line. There were plenty of competent, nonpsychotic people walking around, people on the borderline who functioned normally but drifted back and forth, breaking under moments of stress. Garvey just couldn't explain what happened on Gardenette Drive by saying Lois was crazy. In fact, he had no psychiatric explanation at all.

On September 29, the psychiatrist wrote a letter to Poritsky.

"I will attempt to answer your specific questions," he began, "but generally speaking, I did not find psychiatric illness in either Mr. or Mrs. Jurgens . . . I do not feel that psychiatric help as such is definitely indicated. I do feel that any reason for keeping the child, Robert, out of the home would have to be on other than psychiatric reasons . . . There did not appear from a psychiatric point of view to be any definable cause for any severe maltreatment of the boy . . ."

It is fair to say this evaluation complicated matters inside Judge Gingold's courtroom when the Jurgens case reconvened at 2:15 P.M. on October 14. The lawyers and judge, stymied within their own legal system, had hoped the psychiatrist would resolve matters for them.

He hadn't, and now two particularly troubling questions left many in the room plainly puzzled: If Lois wasn't crazy, how could they explain what had happened to Dennis? And if Lois was neither crazy nor a proven child-killer, how could they justify Robert's removal?

The county expressed a desire to retain custody of Robert for a year while weighing such issues.

"I hope within this year's time that we can find something which will have explained Dennis's mistreatment," Poritsky said. "Perhaps sooner than within the year, we can work on a plan for restoration of the boy back with them . . . We don't know anything about the mistreatment of Dennis. Neither the parents nor the psychiatrist have provided any indication."

The subtext was almost audible. Tell us what happened to Dennis, the prosecutor was saying, and maybe we'll let you have Robert.

Judge Gingold seemed to agree.

"I'm not satisfied that there is an explanation . . . There is a lot yet to be known in the science of this whole darn subject on child battering that I don't know . . . Let's not build up some fiction that now we have done everything we should do . . . The doctor hasn't said she didn't do it . . . He just can't explain it psychiatrically . . . I don't know, but I don't intend for the time being to take any chances. I want to know more . . . I am not going to make it a year, as the welfare department is asking. I'm going to make it six months. In this period of time I want the welfare department to measure the entire casework picture, to work with these people . . ."

Donohue felt dismayed, for the welfare department meant Beatrice Bernhagen. There she sat behind them in the courtroom, fierce and grim and mannish. In home visits all summer, she'd been clashing with Donohue and his clients as she vainly pressed Harold and Lois to talk about Dennis. Donohue cringed at the thought of the Jurgenses' fate now resting largely in the hands of such a person.

The attorney cleared his throat. He had the greatest respect for Miss Bernhagen, Donohue told the court, but we all have our faults and shortcomings. There is something in the relationship between Bernhagen and the Jurgenses that rubs each the wrong way. Might Miss Bernhagen consider withdrawing from this case and assigning the home visits to someone else?

When Poritsky rose to respond, his words reflected the decision made by Paul Lindholm months before. The Jurgenses shouldn't worry about Bernhagen, Poritsky volunteered, for they no longer were in danger. "I'd like to point out, Your Honor, that our office is not interested in a prosecution of these parents at this time," the assistant county attorney said.

Gingold took that cue, and the focus of the hearing shifted discernibly from the events of Palm Sunday.

"No one here is being punitive," the judge told Donohue. "We have tried to deliver the message to you. We want this thing to win. We are on the same side. Want it to work. We are all interested in the same identical thing, but we want to be sure."

Gingold continued the welfare department's legal custody of Robert, and scheduled a new hearing for April 14, 1966, six months down the road.

During that half year, Beatrice Bernhagen visited the Jurgenses a number of times. In a home study later presented to the court, she noted several unusual characteristics of their household, among them Harold and Lois's habit of keeping special clothes for Robert to wear during his Sunday visits. "They undress, redress and return him to the original clothing on return to his foster home," she observed. "The Jurgenses say they want him 'perfect' when he attends church with them . . ." Bernhagen thought the marital situation difficult to understand, with Harold passively giving in to his wife and Lois regularly belittling him for his infertility. There appeared to be severe emotional blocking related to Dennis's death, Bernhagen reported. "Mrs. Jurgens still 'knows nothing' of the injury . . . Mrs. Jurgens does not believe Dennis was neglected or abused. She does not recall any bruises . . ."

Bernhagen regarded Dr. Garvey's written evaluation of the Jurgenses, derived from one afternoon's visit, as unsatisfactory and unhelpful, particularly in its conclusion that Lois showed no sign of hostility to Dennis. So in early March, Bernhagen consulted with Dr. Richard Teeter, the chief of psychiatry at St. Paul–Ramsey Hospital and a doctor whom Judge Gingold happened to admire greatly.

Teeter, studying the by now voluminous Jurgens file, expressed regret that in such a serious case there'd been no inpatient evaluation at a hospital. Without seeing the Jurgenses, he said, he couldn't provide a written recommendation.

"Would Robert be safe in the home or not?" Bernhagen asked.

"I simply don't know," Teeter replied.

◆   ◆   ◆

When the Jurgens matter next came before Gingold after lunch on April 14, 1966, the prosecutor, following Dr. Teeter's suggestion, asked that the welfare department's legal custody of Robert be continued for another six months, while Lois Jurgens submitted to an inpatient examination by a psychiatrist approved by the county. The Jurgenses had played their doctor, now the other side wanted its turn.

Donohue exploded in anger, pacing about the courtroom as he orated and argued about the perfidies of this now unconscionably extended process.

"You may be seated," Gingold told him at one point.

"I'd just as soon stand if you don't mind, Your Honor . . ." Donohue responded. "We feel very strongly about this."

Gingold eyed him.

"I'm glad you do," the judge said. "I do too. I've got some strong feelings about the case too, some very strong feelings. You're not the only one worried about this child."

In truth, Gingold's words just then suggested confusion along with those strong feelings. He displayed no doubts about what had happened to Dennis, but he seemed unable to connect the horribly abused dead boy with the apparently decent couple sitting before him in the courtroom.

"There isn't any evidence that we are dealing with any people who have any demonlike motives . . .," Gingold said, laboring to get his bearings. "We are dealing with people of very high motives . . . These are very honorable people. They are very religious people. They are very good people . . . You have to distinguish a search for truth, a search for safety on the one hand, and any attack of any kind being made against your client on the other . . ."

In the end, Gingold, like the county authorities, wanted a psychiatrist to tread where he found himself unable to venture and to act where he felt incapable.

"The threat of a criminal prosecution that you were so worried about long ago is way by the boards now," the judge told Donohue. "So that isn't involved. She can get a much better examination today. All these special protections won't have to be set up . . . I just want to put a little bit more baling wire on this thing here for everybody's protection, a little bit more baling wire. This guy Teeter is a great guy . . . I like Dr. Teeter . . . I have a great respect for his recommendations. I like his courage . . ."

To Donohue, though, Teeter was a no-win deal. Lois might say something to the doctor that could be used in a criminal prosecution, an event Donohue still feared despite the reassurances from the judge and county attorney. Accordingly, the Jurgenses' attorney now rose to announce he was going to order a transcript of all the testimony in this case—an unsubtle message that he intended to appeal the judge's rulings.

"You can order the transcript from the reporter, out of the courtroom," Gingold snapped. "You don't have to do it on the record. I'm still making the same decision—to continue for one month . . ."

The six-month extension requested by Poritsky apparently was too long for the judge.

"During this time," Gingold continued, "the court is recommending your clients involve themselves in the type of evaluation that Dr. Teeter is currently recommending."

Fine, Donohue decided. If the court wants the type of inpatient exam Teeter was recommending, he'd provide one—but the exam would be conducted by Dr. Garvey. On May 8, Lois began a four-day stay at Glenwood Hills Hospital, where Garvey was chief of the psychiatric section. By the time the Jurgens matter once again came before the judge at 2:00 P.M. on May 18, Garvey had reached a firm conclusion.

"We have not found signs of mental disorder in Mrs. Jurgens or of sadistic traits," the psychiatrist testified. "It would be my opinion that it would be safe for Robert to be in the home."

In a sense, Garvey's judgment represented a fitting extension to the judicial system's handling of Dennis Jurgens's death. The homicide was never openly acknowledged in Gingold's courtroom and now, like an unwelcome guest, it was being equally ignored in the psychiatrist's evaluation. Garvey quite simply had chosen to judge Lois in a vacuum, without considering the details of Dennis's treatment and demise.

In his cross-examination, Poritsky highlighted this circumstance with vigor.

Q: Did you ever discuss with Mr. and Mrs. Jurgens the events surrounding the death of Dennis?

A: They said that the child had been injured in a fall . . . She in talking with me denied that she had been, shall we say, mean or had been injurious to the child . . . She felt that she was not directly responsible for his death.

Q: Did you have an opinion on how the child died?

A: Frankly, I don't know how the child died.

Poritsky stared at the witness.

Q: So your opinion will be based on facts which don't include the circumstances surrounding the death of the deceased child?

A: Well, it includes the circumstances, but I don't know if there has been a definite opinion by anyone on that, as to the direct cause of death, I mean . . . I don't think this is my—even if, if we knew, I don't think this is my position to make that judgment . . . My judgment is on the basis of my contacts with Mrs. Jurgens, my clinical evaluation of her . . . This would be what I would be basing my opinion on.

Poritsky was incredulous.

Q: You would rely on what she told you about Dennis's death?

A: I have no other information.

Q: Your opinion on the safety of Robert will be based on Mrs. Jurgens's statement that she was in no way responsible for the death of Dennis?

A: Certainly, if I could know the exact situation, it would be helpful, but I think my opinion now will have to be based purely on my study and on observations of Mrs. Jurgens and not on what transpired previously . . . The assumption that I have to make is that we really do not know specifically . . . I just don't know what the cause of the death of the child was.

Q: Did you receive the court's findings that I sent you last September?

Here, of course, was the tricky crux of the matter. The lawyers, unable or unwilling to press charges or prove guilt, were still hoping the psychiatrist would solve their problem through a nimble extrapolating of those findings. This doctor was not so inclined.

"There had been a finding as to giving temporary custody, but I didn't feel there had been a definite finding as to the cause of death . . ." Garvey replied. "As I understood it . . . there never had been a judgment as to the exact reasons for the death . . . I did not find psychiatric illness here and it was my feeling that if the child was not going to be returned, it could not be on the basis of a psychiatric finding. It would have to be on some other basis."

◆   ◆   ◆

When Garvey left the stand, Donohue asked that Robert be returned to the Jurgenses, but it was no use. The tug of war had reached a standstill. The county attorney wouldn't charge a murder, the psychiatrist wouldn't let the judicial system off the hook by labeling Lois a dangerous psychotic, and Ed Donohue wouldn't expose his clients to a possible prosecution.

Gingold tried once more: "I am still very insecure in coming to any conclusion that would return the child. I would like to again continue the matter for a couple weeks . . . so you and your clients might make arrangements to participate in an examination under the direction of Dr. Teeter."

No go—Donohue just wasn't going to let Harold and Lois see Teeter. "I've discussed this at great length with the Jurgenses," he informed the judge, "and they have instructed me to have this matter reviewed by a higher court."

"I understand," Gingold said.

After that, the Jurgens matter appeared before Gingold regularly if briefly at six month, then later at full year intervals. As in a ritual reunion, the same handful of people gathered on the sixteenth floor of the Ramsey County courthouse in June of 1966, October of 1966, April of 1967, October of 1967, October of 1968. Each time, the Jurgenses reported they had not agreed to see Dr. Teeter, and each time, Gingold continued the matter, hoping they would change their minds. Robert Jurgens remained in the custody of Ramsey County, living in a series of relatives' homes, visiting with Harold and Lois only on Sundays, in accordance with welfare department regulations.

Be it the strain of the extended custody proceedings, or the memory of Dennis's death, or simply her temperament taking an ever firmer hold, Lois during this time began to suffer increasingly from anxiety and depression. She saw Dr. Garvey now on a regular basis, and several times—in December of 1966, June of 1967, August of 1967—he felt it necessary to hospitalize her at Glenwood Hills. To remedy her chief complaint, he began to prescribe the barbiturate Tuinal. Lois was suffering from chronic insomnia. She could not sleep.

CHAPTER 18

Revolution

On several occasions in late 1959 and early 1960, two doctors, one a pediatrician and the other a psychiatrist, found themselves crossing paths in the hallways of Colorado General Hospital, which is affiliated with the University of Colorado in Denver. Stopping to chat, they made an odd pair. The pediatrician, Dr. C. Henry Kempe, then thirty-seven, was an animated man with a hurried, kinetic manner, while the psychiatrist, Dr. Brandt Steele, then fifty-two, was reflective and almost patrician.

Kempe's line of conversation was always the same on these occasions.

"I've got another one of these beaten babies in here," he'd tell Steele. "I can't find out much about it, nobody can tell me much about it. The mother says this and the father says that, but it looks to me very clear that they did it, and I don't understand why. I don't understand why people would do this."

Then chairman of the department of pediatrics, Kempe's own expertise was in the field of infectious diseases and virology—broken bones, skull fractures and puzzling stories from parents were not something he'd encountered during his field studies in India. Accordingly, in these hallway encounters Kempe never failed to push a request at Steele: Would he, being a psychiatrist, go talk to these parents, people whom Kempe thought were responsible for their children's injuries?

"I can't get the child psychiatrist in our department to see them because he only handles children . . . I can't get anybody to see these people, and I want to find out what's going on here."

Time after time, Steele would put him off. He thought Kempe's concern was an interesting problem, but just then he was directing an adult psychiatric division, and wasn't supposed to be doing anything with pediatrics—the medical center, after all, already had a child psychiatrist assigned there.

Then, at 3:30 one afternoon, Kempe happened by chance to catch Steele strolling down the hospital corridor with nothing to do. "We've got another one, just admitted, please take a look," the pediatrician implored. The psychiatrist, seeing his colleague was not to be denied, finally succumbed.

The baby was three months old, lying in a crib with a cast on a broken femur and bandages wrapped around the head, following an operation for subdural hemorrhaging. Steele stood on one side of the crib, a pleasant and attractive young woman on the other. Mother and doctor fell to talking, and Steele found the twenty-one-year-old woman warm, friendly, open, verbal, very nice—and clearly responsible for the baby's injuries. It was obvious, plain common sense— things seemed to happen when she was alone in the house with the infant, and a three-month-old can't beat up its own head.

Steele felt distressed and angry, but also extremely curious, so for two hours that afternoon, he sat and listened as the young mother talked on about her feelings and memories of a troubled childhood. She was telling him something he'd never heard before. He'd known plenty of people, of course, with bad childhoods, but he'd never seen anybody with a bad childhood who was attacking her own child. That is, he'd never put the two together before. It was as if somebody had yanked a set of blinders off his eyes.

That night, Steele left a note on Kempe's desk. "This is a very interesting problem," he wrote. "We should try to collect some data together. Maybe it would be worthwhile at some time to publish something about this."

What was to rise out of this pivotal moment in a Denver hospital would, in the following months and years, produce something close to a revolution in an entire country's awareness of and response to child abuse. As it happens, Dennis Jurgens's death, and the puzzled wrestling by lawyers and doctors in Judge Archie Gingold's courtroom, were events unfolding just as this revolution was coming to life. Dr. Garvey's inability to explain Lois's actions in standard psychiatric terms had a distinct context.

What seemed a revolution might more fairly be called an evolution, actually, for Dr. Kempe's team in the early 1960s was working against a backdrop of past steps, hesitant steps, taken by doctors uncertain of just what they were seeing or saying.

A shy, quiet pediatric radiologist named John Caffey, who seemed to prefer greatly his Columbia University X-ray laboratory over the society of other people, had been the first to notice, in infants he examined, a curious link between multiple fractures of the long bones and chronic bleeding under the skull. How could leg fractures be a complication of subdural hemorrhaging? In a seminal 1946 paper Dr. Caffey offered six case studies and suggested the origin of the injuries was traumatic, but he stopped there, reluctant to draw the obvious conclusion: "The fractures appear to be of traumatic origin but the traumatic episodes and the causal mechanisms remain obscure."

After that, a scattering of articles began to appear, which in their words and titles reflected the slow, reluctant realization by doctors that they were not facing nature's disorder or a person's carelessness, but something far darker and harder to understand. Under titles like "Roentgen Manifestations of Unrecognized Skeletal Trauma in Infants," physicians tried at first to concentrate upon the physical condition of the child rather than the origin of the trauma, but the effort was in vain. Doctors educated to fight illness and treat patients, doctors who carried with them certain beneficent assumptions about human behavior, were being forced by the evidence of their own eyes and the rigor of their training to acknowledge something they would prefer to evade. They were finding it necessary to look unflinchingly into the way people truly thought and felt and acted.

In a 1953 paper, one of Caffey's protégés, Dr. Frederic Silverman at the University of Cincinnati, ventured to suggest that those caring for babies might be unaware of injuries they'd inflicted carelessly and might deny injuries they'd inflicted deliberately. Two years later, a pediatrician-radiologist team at Children's Hospital in Detroit, Dr. Paul Woolley, Jr., and Dr. William Evans, Jr., put it more bluntly if pedantically: "It is difficult to avoid the overall conclusion that skeletal lesions having the appearance of fractures . . . are due to undesirable vectors of force." Thus encouraged, Caffey in 1957 wrote about removing "abused youngsters" from their traumatic environment and punishing their "wrongdoers." By the late 1950s and early 1960s, articles with such titles as "Fractures among Children: Parental Assault as Causative Agent" started appearing, but these still were scattered, isolated and largely unnoticed voices. A paper on child abuse submitted by Henry Kempe to the Society of Pediatric Research's annual gathering in 1959 was read by title and summarized in a one-paragraph abstract, rather than published, because it wasn't considered sufficiently important.

Kempe was not long to be denied in this fashion. Born a Jew in Breslau, Germany (now a city in Poland called Wroclaw), he fled the Nazis in 1937 at the age of fifteen, going to England under the auspices of a Quaker program while his parents went to South America. A year later a rescue organization brought him to the United States and settled him in California, where he enrolled at the University of California at Berkeley, graduating from its medical school in 1945. Later, Kempe wouldn't talk of his early years, but his colleagues couldn't resist speculating. His wife Ruth, a child psychiatrist, thought it likely his adolescence "accounted for his courage and ability to know so well what he wanted. He had learned early on that there was no time to waste . . . Henry's view of the world [was] as a place to be freely explored, befriended and enjoyed. He also viewed it as a place in which one does have responsibility, wherever one can, to do the best one can." For whatever the reason, Kempe, just thirty-four when invited in 1956 to take over as chairman of the University of Colorado medical school's pediatrics department, seemed a force of nature.

"It was as if a storm had struck us and an emergency plan had been put into action in a disaster area," one of his colleagues there, Pierre Ferrier, later recalled. "Dr. Kempe's first statement to us house officers was that he wanted to be respected and did not care to be popular. In the same breath he added that the safety and the well-being of the sick children came first, and therefore he was doubling the number of interns and residents on hospital call at night in pediatrics . . . On the other hand, and as a sort of reward, Dr. Kempe was able to recruit a whole platoon of new attending physicians . . . Dr. Kempe seemed to be able to obtain more of everything: more nurses, more laboratory space, more lab technicians, more material of all sorts, more social workers, more money for research and more researchers. It was constant happening, something else, something new every day . . . He was like the wind and we were like tumbling weeds behind him. During my last two years with him in Denver, I never saw him walk down a corridor normally. He walked so fast that the people with him had to run . . ."

Kempe's advice to others tended toward such thoughts as "when something has to be done, forget about your principles and do what's right." Requesting work from others over the phone, he'd interrupt their protests by simply saying, "You've got to do it!" then hang up. Once, in a moment of frustration after receiving one of Kempe's blue-ink scribbles to "take care of this," his colleague Ray Helfer barged into his office, exclaiming that he had students in the clinic, patients waiting, sick children in the wards and residents needing consultations. How in the world could he "take care of this"? Helfer demanded. Kempe answered without looking up. "One at a time," he said.

Kempe couldn't help noticing the nature of the injuries afflicting children in his wards. At first, his interest was more intellectual than humane. Day after day, while making rounds at the University of Colorado medical school, he'd see children with diagnoses that he felt just didn't make sense—diagnoses that clearly seemed the product of a physician's denial and fear of dealing with difficult implications. This annoyed him, for he'd always held a visceral dislike for sloppy thinking in diagnosis and treatment.

Here were children who had thrived for seven months and then developed "spontaneous subdural hematoma" and hairline fractures—children that Kempe felt certain had been shaken or bashed. Here were children with "multiple bruises of unknown etiology" who had normal test results, no bleeding disorders, and didn't bruise on the ward even when they fell. Here were children with "osteogenesis imperfecta tarda" who had normal bones by X-ray except that they showed many healing fractures that could be dated. Here were children with "impetigo" whose skin lesions clearly were cigarette burns. Here were kids with "accidental burns of buttocks" that were in a symmetrical form that could only occur from dunking a child who'd soiled into a bucket of hot water for punishment.

Kempe had seen abused children as a student on the public wards at San Francisco County Hospital, but his teachers there had dismissed them as products of a drunk father or inadequate mother. He'd never seen such things in a middle class setting, and he didn't fully understand. "What are you doing about this?" he'd asked Jack Giphens, the pediatric department's acting director when he had first arrived, and Giphens would explain that they weren't doing anything, really couldn't do anything. Puzzled and concerned, Kempe thought to turn not to a specialist in bruises or bones, but to an expert in minds and emotions. In the end, the psychiatrist, Brandt Steele, was no more able than anyone else to turn aside the persistent pediatrician who had begun stopping him whenever he walked through the hospital's corridors.

That first afternoon, talking to the young, pretty mother of a battered three-month-old, Steele was struck with how normal she seemed. The daughter of an assistant police chief and wife of a senior engineer, she was poised and natural and feminine, not unlike many other Denver housewives he knew. Her story, though, was unsettling, haunted by a mother who'd regretted her birth and regularly expressed this feeling through fists, razor strops, wire coat hangers and whatever else was handy. In the following weeks and months, talking to other parents who abused their children, Steele quickly grasped the obvious pattern. His was a clientele quite different from those described in reports coming out of welfare departments and public hospitals. Here were mainstream, affluent members of the Denver community, white collar and upper middle class, doctors and doctors' wives, lawyers, stockbrokers, members of the country club. The details differed but not the essence—as children they'd been severely abused, and as parents they now were abusing their kids.

As a psychiatrist, Steele was fascinated but also stymied, for it seemed apparent to him that his patients weren't suffering from a psychiatric illness in the usual, accepted sense of the term. Their condition could be understood in psychological terms, but was not an acknowledged syndrome—it wasn't included in any of the psychiatric diagnostic manuals. Listening to his patients, Steele couldn't get away from the fact that these people were simply repeating what they'd learned was the correct way to treat kids when they were growing up—they were following righteous principles that they'd absorbed early on.

This insight was disturbing to Steele. There was a certain comfort to be derived from considering child abusers psychotic, after all. It was much more distressing to realize that sane, normal people could do such terrible things. Adolf Eichmann, for instance. The psychiatrist who examined him during his trial had found him sane, and Steele thought this sanity the most frightening part about the whole business. Eichmann was carrying on his work in perfect consonance with the dictates of his superego—in his own context, he was a very moral man. He was listening to the voice of his own conscience, the echoes of the parental commands of his own childhood, just like the rest of us. So too were parents who hurt their children, Steele came to believe. They weren't psychotic, and they didn't show an appropriate sense of guilt over their actions—they were just following the dictates of their consciences. They were doing only what was right and necessary by their standards.

It is commonplace now to explain child abusers by saying they were themselves once abused, but it wasn't in 1960, when Steele began listening to the patients on Henry Kempe's ward. In fact, it was in large part through Kempe's team that the notion became so familiar.

They began first in their own hospital, meeting as a team—Kempe, Steele, the radiologist Fred Silverman, the pediatrician Henry Silver, and social workers—discussing the week's cases, going over all fractures involving children under the age of two. They finally reached the startling conclusion that a full ten percent of all their emergency room trauma visits for children were due to abuse. On one single day in 1961, they realized they had no less than four child abuse cases in their ward. Aroused, Kempe's team turned to other arenas.

In the fall of 1959, a senior medical student named William Droegemueller, drawn to Kempe's dynamism, had come looking for a research project in the pediatric department, and Kempe gave the eager student the task of surveying dozens of hospitals and district attorneys across the country about child abuse. When Droegemueller graduated in 1960, he left the data behind in two shoe boxes. Soon after, Kempe retrieved them, collated the information, and, in consultation with Steele and others at the medical school, began preparing to publish a paper.

For their debut, Kempe chose the American Academy of Pediatrics' thirtieth annual meeting, held at the Palmer House in Chicago from September 30 through October 5, 1961. Having been a member of that group's program committee for five years, by rotation he was its chairman that year, and one prerogative of that position was the planning of a morning plenary session. Kempe scheduled his symposium for 9:00 A.M. on October 3, in the Palmer House's Grand Ballroom, with Silverman as the chairman and he and Steele on the panel, along with a professor of social work, a health law expert and a juvenile court judge. Searching for a title that would grab the pediatricians' attention and fill his ballroom, he manufactured a name for what his Colorado team had been observing—"The Battered-Child Syndrome." Thus did a new concept enter the medical and legal worlds. The symposium bearing this title drew a full house.

In a private letter years later, Kempe recalled that morning: "The presentation went all morning and the room with well over a thousand people was totally quiet; nobody seemed to leave and after we were done a great many doctors came up and for the next two hours talked of cases in their private practice which they had missed . . . The press and radio picked it up from there."

Nine months later, on July 7, 1962, the *Journal of the American Medical Association (JAMA)* published the Colorado team's landmark paper, "The Battered-Child Syndrome," coauthored by Kempe, Steele, Silverman, Silver and Droegemueller. Where others in earlier reports had offered passing, hesitant, oblique references, Kempe's team now spoke boldly.

"The battered-child syndrome is a term used by us to characterize a clinical condition in young children who have received serious physical abuse, generally from a parent or foster parent . . ." the article began. "It is a significant cause of childhood disability and death. Unfortunately, it is frequently not recognized or, if diagnosed, is inadequately handled by the physician because of hesitation to bring the case to the attention of the proper authorities."

The authors continued:

> A marked discrepancy between clinical findings and historical data as supplied by parents is a major diagnostic feature of the battered-child syndrome . . . Beating of children is not confined to people with a psychopathic personality or of borderline socioeconomic status. It also occurs among people with good education and stable financial and social background . . . There is also some suggestion that the attacking parent was subjected to similar abuse in childhood . . . Often

there is complete denial of any knowledge of injury to the
child and the maintenance of an attitude of complete innocence on the part of both parents . . . In addition to the reluctance of the parents . . . there is another factor which is of
great importance . . . That is the fact that physicians have great
difficulty both in believing that parents could have attacked
their children and in undertaking the essential questioning
of parents . . . Many physicians . . . attempt to obliterate such
suspicions from their minds, even in the face of obvious circumstantial evidence. . . .

Kempe's team had not discovered a new drug or therapy or law
of science, but it was as if a light had been turned on in a darkened
room. The reaction to the symposium in Chicago and the *JAMA* article was immediate and overwhelming. Two major conferences were
held in 1962, one sponsored by the Children's Bureau of the United
States Department of Health, Education and Welfare, the other by
the Children's Division of the American Humane Association, which
after a year-long study published in 1963 a pamphlet entitled "Guide-
lines for Legislation to Protect the Battered Child." In the following
three years, forty-nine states adopted specific statutes that required
physicians and others to report cases of injury or abuse to children.
Kempe's team, now inundated with invitations to deliver speeches,
began offering annual training workshops every May in Colorado,
and a continuous flow of articles on child abuse filled the scholarly
journals—some three hundred by 1966.

The popular press also paid attention. The *Saturday Evening
Post*, citing Kempe's work, published a multipage spread in October of 1962 on "Parents Who Beat Children." *Life* followed in June
of 1963 with "Cry Rises from Beaten Babies," *Good Housekeeping* in
1964 with "The Shocking Price of Parental Anger," *Time* in January
of 1965 with "Saving Battered Children," The *Wall Street Journal* in
July of 1965 with "Medical, Legal Drive Aims to Spot, Reduce Cases
of Child Abuse." In 1963, a television episode of "Ben Casey" about
child abuse was broadcast by some two hundred affiliates, and similar plots soon appeared on other weekly programs, including "Dr.
Kildare" and "Slattery's People." By early 1965, the battered-child
syndrome had become a distinctive, widely recognized condition.
For a while, Kempe seemed almost a household name.

Minnesota, as it happens, was with California the first state to take notice of all this. In late May of 1963—exactly three months before Dennis appeared at Mounds Park Hospital with burned genitals and a bruised body—the state legislature made it mandatory for doctors and other health care providers to notify the local police or sheriff, by both phone and letter, of injuries arising from child abuse. In St. Paul on December 7, 1963, a symposium on "The Battered Baby" was presented as part of the annual meeting of the Minnesota Civil Liberties Union. In response, a few University of Minnesota law professors started writing about the legal implications, while in Ramsey County, the redoubtable Judge Archie Gingold began keeping a file of child abuse articles published in the *Juvenile Court Judges Journal*, the first being a January 1963 piece entitled "'The Battered-Child Syndrome'—A Now Recognized Medico-legal Complex."

In early 1965, the Minnesota state legislature started considering an amendment to its existing law, one that would require health care providers to report abuse to welfare departments as well as to the police. As part of these considerations, a state house committee on health and welfare, meeting in St. Paul on Tuesday, February 23, 1965, heard testimony on the battered-child syndrome, then fell to debating the available options. Three months later, the legislators managed to agree upon a bill that required health care providers to report suspected abuse to both the police and the welfare department, both orally and in writing. Responsibility for investigating complaints of abuse and offering protective services would fall to the county welfare departments, and anyone making a report in good faith would be immune from civil or criminal liability.

The state legislature, sitting in St. Paul, adopted Minnesota's pioneering new statute on May 25, 1965—six weeks after Dennis Jurgens's death and two weeks after Robert Jurgens's custody hearing.

CHAPTER 19

Stone Hill

In the months after the police took him away from Harold and Lois on Good Friday in 1965, Robert Jurgens saw more than one home. The time at Ancker Hospital passed as if part of a dream, he sitting on the edge of a bed while doctors tapped his knee with a rubber hammer. His father visited, but never his mother. Then one day a strange man appeared. You're going to be staying with me, he said.

Robert, about to turn five, shrank back into his bedsheets. No, I want my dad, I don't wanna stay with you, he said. I just wanna go home and be with my dad.

Well, the man coaxed, I have a helicopter.

Robert sat up in bed, his eyes wide. The prospect of a helicopter made him eager to go with this man. They drove in a fancy car, Robert in the backseat, until they reached a large white house with a big pine tree spreading across the front yard. This was the Hinz residence, a foster home. Robert spent most of his time in a small bedroom upstairs, even eating meals there, never seeing a helicopter. He did not like the place, and within days the Hinzes had had enough of him too—Mrs. Hinz thought Robert "odd," and she tired of the unscheduled, unauthorized telephone calls and visits by the Jurgenses.

At Harold and Lois's request, the welfare department next placed Robert with his paternal grandparents, Bob and Irene Jurgens, who lived on the east side of St. Paul. Lois's relations with her strong, dominant mother-in-law were still strained but much improved from years past, so Harold and Lois visited there often—too often, for their abuse of the visitation rules prompted the welfare department to write a letter and call a meeting. In July of 1965, the Jurgenses requested that Robert be moved again, from the grandparents' to the home of Lois's niece, Bonnie Welsch, who lived closer to them in White Bear Lake. This request was not granted immediately. Then tragedy struck. One night in November of 1965, while Robert was hospitalized with pneumonia, his grandparents' house burned down, the blaze trapping and killing Harold's mother. Soon after, Robert went to live where the Jurgenses had wanted him, at Bonnie and Mike Welsch's home on East County Road D.

To Beatrice Bernhagen, evaluating him in April of 1965 for the welfare department, Robert had seemed more an adult than a little child. Now, months later, in late 1965, a school report from Harrison Kindergarten said Robert "displayed some emotional difficulties, he did not make friends easily . . . He seemed to know there were certain subjects he should not discuss and often had to talk himself out of a situation when he realized he had said too much . . . He had a slight nervous blinking of the eyes, and when he used scissors, he became very tense."

Robert liked it at the Welsches', though. His dad would come by to take him bowling or to a movie or a restaurant. He turned six, and slowly warmed to his world. The report of March 1966 from a new school, Hazelwood, declared the "tall tales to be lessening . . . Robert is making friends easily and has excellent ability for logical reasoning." That May, Bernhagen thought Robert well-adjusted—instead of speaking about St. Francis of Assisi and the Bible, he now talked of baseball.

The sojourn at the Welsches' ended after a year and a half, however, for reasons not entirely clear. In July of 1967, Lois approached another relative, her cousin June Bol, asking if she and her husband Richard would keep Robert for two weeks at their home in Stillwater, while she and Harold finished getting the boy back from the courts, an event they then felt was imminent.

"We think you're such good parents," Lois explained.

June Bol did not know what to say. Her blood connection to Lois was indirect—it was Richard who actually was Lois's cousin, his mother the sister of Lois's father—but June had known Lois since high school and liked her. She'd seen Dennis only once, at Lois's sister's funeral in January of 1965, where she remembered those two little boys kneeling and saying the rosary so loudly and beautifully. She'd heard rumors about Lois, and there were times when she could tell the woman was on tranquilizers, but June felt forgiving, for Lois was always so nice to her.

Of course, June Bol liked just about everyone. Then forty, she had a round, full face and sunny, amused eyes. Sitting at her kitchen table, light pouring through the window, a phone at her elbow, checkbooks and mail and notes strewn about, she seemed, in her natural chatty ease, sprung more from a television family than from real life. She'd lived in the same North St. Paul house all during her childhood, her mother a model of even tranquility. Then at twenty she had married the boy down the block whom she'd been dating since she was sixteen. They lived in St. Louis while Richard trained at Washington University to be a chiropractor, then moved to North St. Paul and had four children before settling, in October of 1965, on fifteen acres in a rural region near the towns of Lake Elmo and Stillwater.

Their home provoked stabs of yearning in others. The rambling ranch house stood on a rise overlooking their land and the rolling valley beyond, fronted by a sloping, capacious lawn densely treed with blue spruce, weeping willow, maples and poplars. The Bols' view remained lushly green half the year and pure white the other half. Out the back door, at their stables, Richard cared for nine horses, the Tennessee walkers he raised and rode and showed. Out the front door, the kids in winter tobogganed straight from the porch down an undulating snowy slope. They called their spread Stone Hill, the name engraved on a wood sign at the base of the long winding driveway that curved up from Nolan Avenue.

Before her own family started growing, June had taught second grade in public schools for seven years, something she'd known she wanted to do ever since she was a girl. She'd always carried a dream with her—someday, she told herself, she'd have a place where she'd stick a big sign, a sign saying if you don't want your babies, you can leave them here and I won't ask any questions. After she had her own four boys, she'd asked her husband if they could adopt one child, for she wanted that experience. They applied through Catholic Charities in 1966, and the people there soon called to say they had a little girl, three months old, with big eyes and no hair, who wants to come and live with you. June said yes, oh yes she can. Well, the lady on the phone responded, why don't you first come down today and see her, take ahold of her and see if she feels just right. No, June replied. No one did that when I had my other children, no one said hold him and see if it's right. I want to come down right now and get her. So that's just what they did, driving to St. Paul with clothes and blankets, just as when June had her own little ones. When they got there, the baby was crying. They put the clothes on her and took her home and called her Carolee, and it felt to June exactly like when she had the others.

June did not take long to consider Lois's request. "Of course we'll take him," she said. That would have been her answer even if she'd known the two-week visit was going to stretch to two years.

Robert was seven when he came to Stone Hill in July of 1967, and even though much improved, he still seemed to June so afraid and withdrawn—afraid of fire, afraid of getting dirty, afraid of doing something wrong. She had to teach him how to get muddy—her other kids helped there. When he spilled milk at the table, she had to convince him accidents were okay. Once Robert knocked a bike over outside and was in the house apologizing to June's husband before the bike hit the ground. One day when Robert grew frightened of a garter snake crawling about the yard, June steeled herself—she didn't like snakes either—and picked the snake up, shuddering inside as she reassured Robert it was harmless. She would sit him down at times with a metal pie tin and teach him how to light matches. He was leery, but she'd insist—at seven, she'd say, you have to know how to handle matches, to understand that they're good and bad but not be scared.

Once when June, following Ramsey County requirements, took him to visit a psychiatrist at the Bureau of Catholic Charities, Robert drew a picture of a house with locks on all the doors—a lock in the kitchen, a lock in the living room, a lock everywhere. On vacations in their camper, Robert often kept the family awake at night, grinding his teeth, and sometimes he sleepwalked. June would sit at the side of his bed then, reassuring him everything was okay. When people asked June how many children she had, Robert loved it when she included him and answered six, but June had to be careful not to say that when Lois and Harold were near.

Even with time, though, June never fully melted the certain guarded reserve that enveloped Robert. They hugged often, but their talks had limits. Gingerly, June would try to probe. Did you ever see Dennis get hurt? she'd ask. Robert would never say anything then. He seemed scared, as if he were trying to remember what to say, and a good many "I don't knows" filled his conversation.

The Jurgenses came every weekend to take him for their visitations, usually keeping him longer than the rules allowed, but June was not inclined to object. At first they drove out from White Bear Lake, but then one day they announced they were moving to the Stillwater area and would be neighbors.

Be it to get nearer to Robert, or to escape the past, or both, Harold and Lois in late 1967 sold their home on South Gardenette Drive and bought a frame house that perched hidden on a wooded rise just one half mile down Nolan Avenue from the Bols.

After that, Lois, seeing Robert on the road as he stood waiting for the school bus, would note whether he had his hat on, or his mittens, and call June with her complaints. June decided early on she just wasn't going to let that bother her. Well, thank you for telling me, June would say back, because I certainly want Robert to wear mittens. One day Lois stopped on the road and asked Robert if he'd had breakfast. No, the boy said, he'd risen late that day and hadn't eaten. Lois began calling the relatives, and soon June's phone was ringing. Robert came home from school crying, asking whether he was supposed to say something else. No, June told him, that's just fine, I teach you to tell the truth. You didn't have breakfast, but lots of people get late sometimes and don't have breakfast, it's no big deal, I'm not in any trouble for that.

Beneath her breezy response, though, June felt afraid. She was thinking of the more serious confrontations the future might bring. Don't let Lois get to you, she reminded herself. You don't have to outscream her. You're not going to outscream her. But maybe you can outthink her.

CHAPTER 20

This World Stinks

In the summer of 1967, as the hearings in Judge Gingold's courtroom continued sputtering along at six-month intervals, a new Ramsey County social worker found herself involved in the Jurgens affair. Marion Putnam was twenty-six, four years into her job after earning a bachelor's degree in sociology, when her district supervisor handed over the thick file. "We want you to reinvestigate," Donald Tomsuden said. "Talk to the family and see if you can come up with any reason why Robert should not be returned to the Jurgenses."

Marion, knowing nothing of the case, began by reading through the file. What she learned took her breath away. Here was the whole story, reaching back to Gerane Rekdahl's early visits, Dennis's placement, the burn, Norma Potter's experiences, Dennis's death, the autopsy, the ruptured bowel, peritonitis. Marion just couldn't believe they had left Dennis in that home. It was so apparent—Lois never liked him, never wanted him there.

When Marion drove to the White Bear police department, and there read Korolchuk and VanderWyst's police reports, her feelings only deepened. It seemed obvious to her these were all inflicted injuries. Lois was lying, and Harold and the family were covering up. Her brother being on the police force, Marion thought, had to have an influence.

She called the Ramsey County attorney's office to say she wanted to read the Jurgens file. When she arrived, though, no one allowed her past the front desk. Instead, a blunt, gruff man emerged from an office. "We can't find the file. I guess it's been lost," Paul Lindholm told her, turning and disappearing. Marion stood by the receptionist's desk, the blood rising to her face, intimidated and angry all at once.

"I just can't believe this," she said soon after, stomping into Donald Tomsuden's office. "How could the county attorney just lose this file? How could this lady have not been prosecuted for Dennis's death? What is happening here?"

Tomsuden eyed the high-strung young woman before him. He liked Marion, considered her a friend, but he felt she did tend to go off on tangents. She was impulsive and idealistic and not compliant at all, a difficult caseworker to manage. Tomsuden couldn't believe Marion had tried to get the county attorney's file—a social worker just did not do that. How could he explain this case to her? How could he tell her all that he knew?

When he'd first heard about little Dennis Jurgens's death, Tomsuden was not in his office, but on the driveway beside his house. Tomsuden, as it happened, lived on Floral Drive in White Bear Lake, just around the corner from Gardenette Drive. The Jurgenses were his neighbors.

Born in Brooklyn, with the accent and manner to match, he had driven to Minnesota in 1952 and bought a house in White Bear Lake two blocks from the water, amid open fields and gravel roads, for $14,000. White Bear Police Sergeant Howie Markuson lived across the street, and their families became friendly—they played cards and worshiped at church together, their kids were playmates, their wives close chums. When Markuson found someone in town who needed the help of a social worker, he'd call his neighbor and Tomsuden would go knock on a stranger's door and sit over coffee for forty-five minutes.

One morning days after Dennis's death, Tomsuden had encountered his neighbor as he walked down his driveway. Markuson looked disturbed.

Boy, do we have a terrible case, the sergeant said. Terrible . . . kid fallen downstairs . . . bruises . . . beaten up . . . ruptured bowel . . . peritonitis . . . apparently been going on for some time . . .

As the days and weeks passed, Markuson and Tomsuden on occasion talked about the investigation, the sergeant sounding increasingly agitated. Markuson had no role in the case himself, but he was friendly with Bob VanderWyst, so heard a fair share about their problems. Years later, Markuson would claim a murky memory— "whatever I heard was just gossip"—but Tomsuden would recall that most of the problems described by his neighbor involved Jerome Zerwas's desire to protect his sister.

Tomsuden also heard about the Jurgens case at work, for Beatrice Bernhagen brought it up at staff meetings. Tomsuden volunteered what he knew from the neighborhood, substantiating reports more than providing new information. Gradually, in his management role, Tomsuden began to see how the case was going to be played. It was going nowhere. The county attorney was unresponsive, the case-workers young and inexperienced, Bernhagen brilliant but so abrasive she was creating resistance in her department superiors.

To Tomsuden, the transplanted New Yorker, Bernhagen seemed like Bella Abzug in appearance and manner. At staff meetings, she held forth about the Jurgens case, highly indignant, full of anger at the parents, second-guessing caseworkers, impatient with an investigation where it was clear from the start the mother killed the boy. Normally, Bernhagen trampled over those in her way, just took over a case and pushed, but here, this time, she ran into a brick wall. There was the problem of evidence—of proving what exactly had happened in the Jurgens house when Dennis died—but Tomsuden also saw something else, something more typical of the small jealousies that fill bureaucracies. Bernhagen was getting blocked by her superiors, Tomsuden believed, because to them her aggression represented a threatening power play.

The notion made Tomsuden laugh out loud with bitterness. This world stinks, he told people. This world so full of manipulating, opportunistic careerists. Still, you couldn't respond to it with impulse and idealism, he knew that much. Tomsuden's edgy, unvarnished manner seemed out of place in this muted, contained world colored by stoic Scandinavian roots, but it was here he had settled, and here he had to work.

Tomsuden nodded at the young woman before him. "Yes," he told Marion Putnam, "you're right, this case really is something. But there's nothing that can be done in the legal system. They don't have the right evidence. It can't be prosecuted."

Marion began to protest, but Tomsuden waved an impatient hand.

"Marion, will you please settle down. Robert is your client. You're supposed to see if there is any problem or mistreatment with Robert. Just concentrate on that."

So Marion set about her assigned task. She tracked down some dozen Zerwas family members, asking each if they knew of Robert being mistreated, or any other reason why he should not be returned to the Jurgenses. Some she talked to were hostile, and all were unhelpful. No one knew anything.

Then she arrived at Stone Hill, for the first of half a dozen visits with the Bols spread over twelve weeks. A smiling woman with twinkly eyes met her at the door and led the way to a split-level living room with a high, pitched ceiling. "Well, I'm June Bol," the lady said, "and this is Robert." Marion looked to where a thin, slight boy with blond hair cowered in a corner, wanting more than anything, it seemed, simply to stay out of the way. Marion spoke mostly to June, and thought her warm and motherly.

"Is Robert getting along okay?" she asked June after Robert had left the room to play outside. "Do you know of any mistreatment, or any reason why he shouldn't go back to the Jurgenses? Is there anyone else I should talk to?"

June now grew uncomfortable and hesitant, her eyes for a moment losing contact with Marion's. No, she knew of nothing, but maybe he shouldn't go back just yet. "Maybe after a while," June suggested.

Marion sensed there was much on this lady's heart, much she would like to say, but when June didn't offer anything more, Marion also held back. Despite her impulsiveness, she was not the sort of person who could set a different tone from those around her—June was being polite and discreet, so she was too. The two women sat talking about Robert, by silent agreement stepping around the matter of Dennis's death.

Gradually, over the weeks, through small moments rather than sudden soul-baring, the two women learned to know each other. Marion Putnam and June Bol were fourteen years apart in age and quite different in character, but they found their common bond—a concern for Robert. Neither woman seemed inclined to let Robert go back to the Jurgenses. One day, Marion came to June with excited news of a breakthrough. At the end of every visit, Robert always asked the social worker "When can I go home?"—something Marion thought sounded like a trained, memorized ritual—but at the last visit, Robert, happily playing with the other kids, had forgotten his lines. June and Marion giggled over this coup.

In January of 1968, writing an employee evaluation, Marion's most immediate supervisor, Larry Goodspeed, noted her accomplishment:

> Mrs. Putnam's work with Robert Jurgens has been both demanding and delicate. Robert was recently moved by the Jurgenses to the Bols home, a distant relative of the Jurgenses. Although the Bols initially identified with the Jurgenses concerning the death of Dennis, they have been helped to realize why our agency has intervened. The Bols have now formed a relationship of trust with Mrs. Putnam and are jointly protective of Robert's interests. They have now reached the point of sharing information and leads which could assist the agency at a subsequent termination hearing.

After Goodspeed's boss Don Tomsuden countersigned this evaluation, the two supervisors talked frankly for a moment about the Jurgens case. Goodspeed raised the same question voiced by his caseworker.

"Why wasn't this Jurgens case ever prosecuted? Even now, why can't we take this to court?"

Tomsuden shook his head.

"There's not enough evidence . . . The county attorney won't prosecute."

After that, feeling vaguely uncomfortable, Goodspeed kept the Jurgens file locked in a drawer of his own desk, from time to time pulling it out to leaf once again through the pages of evidence.

Then one day in 1968 the file disappeared from his locked drawer—it just wasn't there when he looked. Goodspeed felt shocked and paranoid. He told someone in the office—years later, he couldn't recall who—but nothing ever happened. Goodspeed assumed there were people who didn't want him to ask questions about the Jurgens case, so after that, he never did. A year later, he left the Ramsey County welfare department, but as the years passed, he never stopped wondering about the file he had once kept locked in his office desk.

Marion Putnam also drifted away, never filing a final report on the Jurgens case. Soon after the favorable evaluation by her supervisors in January of 1968, she transferred to a new job, taking with her only memories. Years later, after her marriage fell apart, after she stopped drinking away that pain, after she was reborn and remarried and renamed Marion Dinah Nord, after she was settled happily on a farm in southeastern Minnesota, she still harbored those memories. In the Caledonia Health Care Center where she worked, she would tell her fellow caseworkers about the strange, disturbing case she once handled, and they would listen silently, full of wonder.

CHAPTER 21

Colorado

In early May of 1969, an intriguing letter arrived on the desk of Judge Archie Gingold. Dated May 1, it was signed by Dr. Homer D. Venters, head of the department of pediatrics at St. Paul–Ramsey Hospital and Medical Center.

Dear Judge Gingold:

Your interest in and involvement with the problem of child health, particularly in the neglected, abandoned or abused child cases is well known to and appreciated by the staff of our department as well as those other departments here in the hospital. Therefore, I wish to call to your attention a course which is being given in Denver later this month which Dr. C. Henry Kempe is conducting on the Diagnosis and Care of the Battered Child. I am attempting to coordinate the participation in this course by a group of interested professional people. The Welfare Department will be sending a supervisor, the County Attorney's office will be sending one of their men, and two social workers as well as Doctors Teeter, Mayerle and myself will be attending from this hospital.

It may well be that this short notice precludes the attendance of any of your staff at such a meeting, or perhaps you as ourselves find departmental funds extremely difficult to come by for such a course. However, if any of your staff would

be interested in attending, the enclosed brochure describes
the course.

Dr. Venters, a thoughtful physician with a gentle, soft-spoken
manner, had graduated from medical school in 1951 and interned
in Atlanta before coming to St. Paul–Ramsey in 1963. In his clinical work over the years, he'd often seen a particular type of injury
in children, a puzzling one that produced a fracture along the long
bone shaft of the leg. Frequently, the same child would have bleeding under the skull. It just didn't make sense to Venters. What could
cause these two together? A type of cancer? In the early years of his
training and practice, Venters just did not know. Then along came
Henry Kempe's team and sudden enlightenment. When the brochure from Colorado crossed Venter's desk, he'd wasted no time.

His letters to Gingold and other Ramsey County officials drew
immediate interest. The historic evolution in awareness of and
response to child abuse had affected Ramsey County as much as any
region of the United States. County officials in 1969 were sensing the
need for sweeping new programs and policies, and Kempe's workshop in Colorado promised to provide a wealth of new ideas.

For some in Ramsey County, though, there was another reason
why the Kempe conference beckoned—for some, it seemed a way to
deal with the unceasing memory of Dennis Jurgens.

The case had not stopped haunting the Ramsey County welfare
department. "We all felt guilty that we didn't protect Dennis. We
talked about it for years, trying to understand why," Paul Schroeder
said years later. Nor had it left Judge Gingold with much peace. To
friends and colleagues, the judge often expressed his anguish about
the system in general, and the Jurgens case in particular. "I know
that boy was killed," he would say. "I just can't do anything about it."

Instead, Gingold had vented his feelings on other fronts. On July
15, 1965, just weeks after Robert's custody hearing, the judge, invok-
ing the public's right to know, had angrily authorized the county
attorney to release sealed juvenile information about a four-year-old
boy who had been critically injured by his mother the week before.
That same month Gingold also began talking frequently and with
feeling about the battered-child syndrome, publicly calling for the
creation within the welfare department of an investigative program, separate from caseworkers, to deal with child abuse cases.

The difficulties of assembling evidence in such cases, he said, require people with police backgrounds. Caseworkers and doctors are oriented to helping and counseling people, not questioning parents as though they were investigating a crime.

"It is rare that parents are willing to admit child battering," Gingold told a *St. Paul Pioneer Press* reporter in late August of 1965. "This means that by the adversary process in our court, quantitative and qualitative proof must be submitted which would establish the allegation of the battering. Unless this is established by competent evidence the court is powerless to act." Ten days later the St. Paul newspaper published a lead editorial enthusiastically endorsing Judge Gingold's proposal.

Now, with Dr. Venters's letter before him, Gingold would not even consider the doctor's suggestion that he send a member of his staff to Kempe's conference in Colorado. The judge intended to go himself.

Two social workers and the St. Paul police department's child abuse specialist, Lieutenant Carolen Bailey, also signed up. So did Dr. Teeter, a young assistant Ramsey County attorney named John Tuohy, and Shirley Pierce from the St. Paul–Ramsey Hospital mental health center. In all, Dr. Venters ended up leading a group of ten to the Kempe workshop in Denver on May 21–22, 1969, easily the most from any state other than Colorado.

The Minnesota delegation checked into the Writer's Manor motel on Colorado Boulevard in Denver on the evening of Wednesday, May 21. Part of their interest was indeed professional—Carolen Bailey for years had pushed child abuse cases and read Kempe's papers in frustrated isolation—but for one of them it was more personal. John Tuohy, the assistant county attorney, thirty-one and less than a year out of law school, knew nothing about child battering then and didn't particularly care about the topic. The Kempe conference in Denver intrigued him primarily because of its proximity to the Arapahoe ski basin. When the brochure about the workshop and a request for volunteers passed through the county attorney's office in early May, Tuohy first called to verify that Arapahoe was open before signing up for the two-day course.

Looking back much later, those who went to Colorado talked of the trip as the time they "got to know each other" and "built a base of trust," which was another way of saying they spent half their time having fun. Soon after they checked into their motel on Wednesday night, Carolen Bailey received a message from Gingold summoning her to his room—the others in the delegation were already there, a party underway. Denver was a late-night, wide-open town compared to St. Paul, and the visitors took full advantage. Bailey recalls sitting in a striptease club watching a woman hanging her ample breasts over Gingold's head. Tuohy remembers retreating from his raucous colleagues to his hotel room after an evening of unbridled drinking, only to have Bailey and Gingold bang on his door, calling "Tuuuuuohy, Tuuuuuohy."

The taxi driver taking them to the medical school shortly before eight o'clock the next morning got lost, and stopped to get directions. The question arose whether they knew precisely where they were at that moment.

"We think we are in Denver," Gingold roared from the rear of the cab.

The taxi finally dropped them before the medical school's entrance, under a bridge on the south side of East Ninth Avenue. The Minnesota delegation rode an elevator to the third floor, then pushed through doors directly opposite the elevator that led them to the lobby of the Humphreys Postgraduate Center, where they registered. At nine o'clock, just as they settled into their seats in the main auditorium, a vibrant man with a round, broad face and high forehead appeared before the audience. Venters leaned forward to catch his words.

"Good morning," the man was saying. "I'm Dr. Henry Kempe."

The Minnesota delegation's merriment soon evaporated amid photos of brutally battered children, X-rays of long bone fractures, and unflinching profiles of abusive parents. Here were new, startling, discomforting insights. As first Kempe, then Brandt Steele and the others talked, Venters furiously scribbled notes in the small red unlined notebook provided by the medical school.

"In our work with parents we are constantly reminded that the battering parent, as a rule, loves his child very much," Kempe said. "By and large, the parents are *not* psychopaths, drunkards or just 'plain mean.' Out of a hundred, perhaps only two or three are psychotic . . ."

"Doctors' livelihoods depend on not telling their patients they're no good, and doctors also don't want to go to court," Steele said. "I understand, but it's a sad thing, to not do your duty, what's right, because you don't want to go to court. There are two things psychiatrists like a lot—to be admired and to make money. Abusive parents don't provide either . . . Instead of trying to associate child abuse with a specific type of psychiatric disorder, we search for a consistent behavior pattern. These parents expect a great deal from their infants, and not only is the demand great, but premature. Their attitudes are not rare, but rather are a variant, extreme form of patterns pervasive throughout human civilization . . . Without exception in our study group, there is a history of having been raised in the same style which they have re-created in rearing their own children . . . It is so important to expose these parents somewhere along the line to a warm, caring person, a model. If they get that, they can be cured, and it needn't happen in their own early childhood, it can happen any time. My own patients tell me, you were the first caring Mom I ever had—I still get letters and cards . . . We are strongly opposed to punishment for the abusive parent, for it tends to reinforce the pattern of rejection . . ."

To the Minnesota delegation, the presentations were eye-opening. Here they were, sitting at the feet of the guru himself, listening to something right on the cutting edge. No longer was it just a hospital or police or welfare department problem, but something shared.

"This was important," social worker Shirley Pierce said later, "because everyone had been reluctant to be alone, to be the first to say something . . . There is an element of insecurity in caregivers, and a sense of disbelief that such things could happen. We all needed the Colorado conference to assure us . . . to tell us that people like us are hurting kids."

The conference adjourned at four o'clock on Friday, May 23. John Tuohy rented a car the next morning and drove to Arapahoe for a day of skiing, but returned to the Denver airport that night disappointed, for the snow under a hot sun was hard as cement. The others, choosing not to spend a weekend savoring the grandeur of the Rockies, had already boarded a Western Airlines flight for home. They were returning to Minnesota with a mission in mind.

Venters soon began his own clinical tests at St. Paul–Ramsey Hospital, set plans to write a paper for an international conference in Vienna, organized workshops and, with Dr. Teeter, started visiting high schools and community groups, giving talks about abuse, diagnosis and reporting laws. Within weeks of returning from Colorado, Judge Gingold, pushing the power buttons as only he could, began urging the formation of a multidisciplinary battered child response team in Ramsey County to assess all suspected cases of abuse.

By September, just three months later, the team was in full operation, involving representatives from the welfare department, the police department, the mental health center, the family nursing service, the juvenile court and the departments of pediatrics, psychiatry and social work at St. Paul–Ramsey. With Shirley Pierce as full-time coordinator, the team established twenty-four-hour hotlines, protocols and procedures, a schedule of regular meetings, pathways for referral.

"The next step," Pierce said in a local newspaper interview just then, "is to convince physicians in private practice that they no longer stand alone when they report cases. The team will take over."

In the publicity surrounding the team's creation, Judge Gingold garnered most of the credit. "He kept drumming the idea every chance he had for the past four years," one county official explained.

To community groups and newspaper reporters, Gingold himself repeated the same arguments he'd been offering since the summer of 1965: Social workers feared jeopardizing relationships with parents . . . Relatives and neighbors were reluctant to testify . . . Police focus was strictly on a prosecution . . . Doctors lacked the confidence and sense of security needed to report . . . No one saw the child beaten, parents would insist the injuries were accidental, the doctors by nature found it hard to believe that a parent could be so brutal . . . The court was faced with horrible cases, but little evidence, and the court needs evidence to act.

The legacy of Dennis Jurgens's death echoed clearly in Gingold's words just then. This echo made the timing of events that month all the more curious. In September of 1969, just as the Ramsey County child abuse team was springing to life, the judge closed the Jurgens file for good. That month, Archie Gingold decided to return Robert to the Jurgenses.

CHAPTER 22

Robert Returns

By 1968, Lois was spiraling even more into a restless torment, worrying and lying awake at night and turning increasingly to drugs such as Tuinal and Equanil, a tranquilizer prescribed for relief of anxiety and tension. Three times that year—in February, April and July—Dr. Garvey felt compelled to hospitalize her at St. Mary's.

In a letter to a consulting doctor dated March 28, 1968, Garvey described Lois as "an obsessive-compulsive neurotic lady" who does not handle pressure very well. Because of the way she'd responded to the past year's events, he had "serious doubts as to her emotional stability for standing any type of prolonged stress."

In mid-1968, a worn out Ed Donohue withdrew from the custody battle and referred the Jurgenses to a new attorney, William Fink, who wrote to Garvey in October, asking for a thorough assessment of the case. Garvey's response in November sounded even bleaker than before.

Lois Jurgens was a difficult person to understand, he began. He'd hospitalized her several times over the last three years, but she had remained basically the same—the usual diagnosis was chronic neurotic type with anxiety and depression, plus schizoid personality. Lois was self-centered and lacking in insight, and Garvey thought she would remain so the rest of her life. "I would certainly have serious doubts at this time whether the child should be returned to the home," Garvey concluded. "It is my feeling that she has been gradually becoming more seriously neurotic and unable to face the stresses and strains of raising a young boy . . ."

Bill Fink, of course, needed quite a different type of letter if he was to prevail with Gingold, so he asked Garvey to reconsider. As a result, the doctor saw Harold and Lois twice, on May 22 and May 27, 1969, and apparently found something in those sessions that enabled him to oblige Fink. Writing on the very day of the second meeting with the Jurgenses, just six months after expressing a gloomy view of Lois, Garvey composed another letter that seemed to reveal a change of mind.

Lois Jurgens had improved over the past year, he reported. She now is more relaxed, less rigid and neurotic than she had been over the past few years. "It is my opinion at this time that Mrs. Jurgens . . . is able to control her emotions, and that she would not be physically dangerous to Robert . . ." he concluded. "There does not, at this time, seem to be any serious danger in Robert returning to the Jurgens household."

There are those, of course, who would link Garvey's swift, striking change of heart to his role as the Jurgenses' hired psychiatrist. More generous observers might find it simply puzzling. It is hard to say whether Garvey's explanation for his reversal, offered twenty years later, would diminish their confusion.

"Robert got older, so he wasn't in physical danger as a little kid would be," the doctor said. "Harold was wishing Bobby home, and in a position to watch and protect. There was no reason to say no— Lois was rigid and obsessive, but not psychotic, and there are lots of mothers like that raising children. If you remove the kids from all of them, half our kids would be in foster homes. It's a little scary to consider whether Big Brother has the right to take children out of homes. It's a matter of judgment. She being so rigid and punitive, I felt Lois killed Dennis by accident, that she got carried away, went overboard, but I didn't think it was planned or was intentional. And remember, she was never charged."

Days after receiving the psychiatrist's opinion, Fink wrote back on June 6, thanking the doctor for his letter and outlining his present plan. This new lawyer, not inclined to fight the battle Ed Donohue had been waging for years, was going to accept Gingold's terms.

"I would like to have the Jurgenses examined by Dr. Teeter at St. Paul–Ramsey Hospital because the judge of the juvenile court seems to want that," Fink wrote to Garvey. "I was thinking of sending a copy of your report to Dr. Teeter first to pave the way . . . Have you any objection to this?"

To his colleagues, Richard Teeter seemed laid-back and pragmatic, not the least dominated by Freudian concepts and unlikely to be snookered by patients. With Dr. Venters, in the wake of the Colorado trip, he had started speaking before assorted community groups. "The battering parent frequently is neither an alcoholic nor a psychotic person . . ." St. Paul–Ramsey chief of psychiatry would explain to his audiences. "Sometimes the parent is quite religious . . . And these cases are not just from poverty areas. They happen among professional people, college graduates, the well-to-do . . ."

Dr. Teeter met the Jurgenses just two months after he returned from the pioneering Kempe workshop, interviewing Harold and Lois separately, for two hours each, on July 28 and August 4, 1969. On September 18, he settled at his desk to compose the letter that Judge Archie Gingold had been seeking now for four years. What he produced, however, was not exactly what the judge had expected.

Dr. Teeter wrote:

At the time of the interviews, neither Mr. or Mrs. Jurgens were considered to be psychotic or in any other way suffering from major mental illness . . . Mr. and Mrs. Jurgens were both of average to above average intelligence. Specifically no evidence of mental retardation or deficiency was evident . . .

Mrs. Jurgens, age 44 . . . is a person predominantly aimed at overcoming or compensating for the cultural, educational, economic and esthetic deficiencies of her background. As such she is bent on a high degree of the ordering of the physical environment and conventional beauty, and a firm hold on religion, and family budget. This is a cohesive, well-ordered system which tends occasionally to bar the experiences and advice of others from influencing her. It also provides a well regulated household. This type of personality organization is frequently labeled as compulsive and rigid and the trait is very strong in Mrs. Jurgens . . . At times when she has been severely thwarted in her aims in the past . . . she has decompensated enough to" require psychiatric treatment. Mrs.

Jurgens is a person who would expect obedience and con-
formance of other people close to her, and who has difficulty
in accepting the imperfections in those people close to her
. . . Mrs. Jurgens has had and could be expected to have difficulties accepting the social and personality imperfections
of an infant or a young child (before the age of six). A child
after the age of six would be less vulnerable to this effect and
would be more compatible with Mrs. Jurgens in that he is a
trained, more socially compliant individual . . .

Mr. Jurgens is a receptive person who shares the ide-
als of his wife, is able to be a strong follower and supporter
in the marriage. He is well organized but has considerable
resilience, warmth and tolerance toward others. As such, the
marriage is well balanced and durable. He appears to have a
warm, tolerant but expectant relationship with his son, Robert. He has been very persistent in planning a future for his
son in spite of the obstacles between them . . .

Lois, in short, was a troubled, difficult, middle-class woman from
a deprived background, but not crazy, and accordingly, Teeter in the
end was no more inclined than anyone else to pronounce her dangerous or homicidal. Robert's older age and Harold's stability most
certainly were critical factors in the doctor's judgment, but so too
were the times. Despite the Kempe team's pioneering work, Lois still
did not fit within the framework of diagnoses known to psychiatrists
in 1969, any more than she fit within the established boundaries of
the legal system—Kempe's first textbook had appeared only the year
before. Professionals just those few years ago generally believed a
person had to be psychotic to beat a child to death. A decade later,
doctors, having fixed on a new diagnostic category of mental disorders, would be calling a person like Lois a "borderline personality,"
and judges would be sentencing some of them to prisons or treatment centers.

The Jurgenses should continue seeing their private psychiatrist
and the welfare department should continue regular visits, Teeter
concluded, but if those recommendations are followed, he saw no
reason to stand in the way.

"Strong consideration should be given toward returning Robert
to his adoptive home," the doctor wrote.

Judge Gingold felt helpless. For years, he'd held out for Dr. Teeter's opinion, and now that he had it, the judge found his own favored psychiatrist agreeing with the Jurgenses' doctor. What's more, no one else was fighting this battle anymore.

Beatrice Bernhagen had died of cancer a few months before, and caseworkers in the welfare department had turned to other matters. "The fight was out of it," Paul Schroeder recalled years later. "We had agonized and agonized, trying to get a fair psychiatric evaluation, and that's finally what we got from Teeter. We were all by then bored. The case had dragged on four years, an awful long time. You had to terminate or give him back. Each time the case got transferred, new people would have the same shock we all had when we first opened the file. But it did not have the same wallop for me in the late sixties that it did in 1965."

Bertrand Poritsky had left the county attorney's office for private practice, and those who followed him felt less aggressive. "When I first got involved, I cared very much," said Pete Lopez, the assistant county attorney who had the Jurgens case in 1969. "But then the judicial process takes place, the psychiatrists get involved, time goes by . . . You're not as involved in the horror, in the details, as you once were."

Another consideration affected Gingold. As it happened, the Jurgenses' new attorney, Bill Fink, was his close friend. He wished his buddy hadn't taken the case. Because of their bonds, Gingold announced one day in court that he would not preside if this matter went to another hearing.

It never did. On September 25, 1969, one week after Dr. Teeter wrote his letter, Judge Gingold ordered that Robert be returned to the Jurgenses, subject to a six-month probationary period. Why he did so was a question the judge wrestled with forever after, never finding an entirely satisfactory answer.

"I had no choice, my friend," Gingold said years later. "I finally reached the point . . . I'm a human being . . . What could I do? I never felt happy about that case . . . I never forgot that case."

June Bol baked a cake the day Robert was to leave her home. We'll try to celebrate, she figured, because it's either that or the opposite. "We live so close, we're always going to be friends," she told Robert as they worked in the kitchen. "You're going home. Isn't that exciting?"

Robert stirred the frosting bowl. He'd been seven when he came to the Bols, a second-grader; now he was nine and in the fourth grade.

Then Harold and Lois appeared, full of broad grins. June had a thought.

"Now, Lois," she said, "Robert's used to these five children, and Carolee being so little, he plays with her and loves her up a lot. So it would be kind of nice now if you would bring him over, or my kids could come to your place, once or twice a week . . . then gradually cut it down, so it would be easier for Robert to not be with the children . . ."

Lois shook her head, four sharp, firm swivels of the neck in all.

"No," she said. "We've waited a long time to be alone with Robert and we don't want anyone else around."

June felt all mixed up inside. She knew they'd gone to court and proved it was all right for him to go home, but in her heart, she wasn't secure with that.

The Jurgenses now were through the front door, heading across the driveway, Stone Hill's manicured lawn and a wall of long needle pines stretching out before them, everything an abundance of green and orange-rust in late September. June ran after them, swallowing, fighting a rising panic. What if she heard that something happened to Robert like what happened to Dennis? No, she told herself, he'll be all right. Richard said he's big enough now, he can protect himself. Harold is not going to let anything happen to him.

"Harold."

June called to him on the driveway, and he turned back. They looked at each other. June blinked back tears.

"Harold, you watch him. I mean it, you watch him, Harold, you take care of him."

Harold's eyes were blank and mild.

"Of course," he said. "What do you think?"

After that, Lois wouldn't let June see Robert. When the Bol children stopped by, Lois would say Robert couldn't come out. When they'd call Robert on the phone, she'd say he was too busy. On two occasions, driving by the Jurgens home, June encountered Robert out by the mailbox. They talked, but Robert kept looking over his shoulder at his parents' house, and June sensed he was in a hurry, that he didn't want to be caught talking to her.

In truth, Robert felt conflicted. At first he'd wanted to go home to his parents—they had bought him a fancy new chest of drawers and welcomed him warmly. Within days, though, the initial glow had worn off. Lois told Robert she didn't want him to have anything to do with the Bols, nor did she want him going out much with other friends. The contrast to the Bol house, always so full of kids and things to do, gnawed at him. The Jurgens home was quiet, and Robert began to feel terribly lonely.

Twice, sneaking in a roundabout route through the backwoods, Robert came bursting through the Bols' door. He'd run through the house, drinking in the sights, the way it had been. He'd run up to his old room and look around, then turn and bolt for the door, saying he had to go. June would watch as he again turned into the backwoods rather than walk directly down Nolan Avenue.

June and Robert had made a deal before he left. Every day, as the school bus passed, June stood on her hill overlooking the road, waving so Robert could see her. He'd stick his head out a window at the front of the bus, then slowly, as the bus rolled down the street, he'd move toward the rear, his head reappearing at different windows, waving back until there was nothing more to see. That was the only regular contact they had, and the routine could not last forever. In time, June stopped appearing on the hill, for she needed to get on with her life and back to her own five children. Gradually, it got so she did not miss Robert as much.

Robert's return, so long pursued, still did not provide Lois peace or grace. That fall of 1969, she grew ever more tense as the life she so adamantly imagined and wanted to create continued to elude her. At forty-four, her once voluptuous body had started to turn to fat, and the delicately pretty face had hardened into a fixed mask. Lois still could not sleep.

In October, she sent a note to Dr. Garvey.

"I'm wondering why the sleeping pills I take at bedtime only provide me with five hours' sleep . . ." she said. "I have to resort to the third sleeping pill as I just don't get enough rest otherwise . . . Maybe you can come up with a solution. I would appreciate any advice at this time."

Garvey scribbled a thought in his log: "I was wrong on this case. She really should not have the boy."

On October 25, just a month after Robert's return, the psychiatrist hospitalized Lois again. After four days of tests and observation, Garvey fixed on a diagnosis of "anxiety reaction" to Robert's return, and discharged her with prescriptions for a mild tranquilizer called Vistaril and Ritalin, a stimulant that is sometimes used to treat depression.

His official evaluation, however, remained optimistic. "The overall adjustment appears to be going quite smoothly," Garvey wrote Fink on November 25. "There is some tension with Mrs. Jurgens, however, in general, I feel they are adapting well to their new situation and that Robert especially is getting along quite well at home."

When Dr. Teeter agreed—after reviewing Robert's school reports and interviewing the Jurgenses again, he saw no problems—Gingold was convinced. On March 5, 1970, one week after getting Teeter's follow-up evaluation, the judge officially ordered dismissal of the case entitled "In the Matter of the Welfare of Robert Gerard Jurgens."

Almost five years to the day after Dennis died, the repercussions from that Palm Sunday at last seemed to be growing still.

PART TWO

CONSEQUENCES

CHAPTER 23

Kentucky

Just as Lois Jurgens was winning her long battle to regain custody of Robert, another mother in another state was trying equally hard to give her kids away. Kentucky and Minnesota's capitals are a good 570 miles apart, but events in each region were soon destined to reverberate in the other. The failure to charge the Jurgenses with Dennis's death would prove to have lasting consequences for four other young children.

Alice Lou Howton apparently was not much inclined to being a mother anyway, which made all the more puzzling the fact that she'd borne seven children in the twelve years between 1954 and 1966. The father in most cases was thought to be Lewis Wayne Howton, a truck driver whom Alice Lou married in 1954 and divorced thirteen years later after several extended periods of separation. Social workers in Hopkins County, Kentucky, had considered the Howton home questionable since January of 1968, their thinking influenced considerably by Alice Lou's habit of leaving the house without arranging for the care of her children. By early 1969, the social workers were receiving a number of calls from people reporting that a mother had approached them, offering to give her children away. One such call, from the principal of the grade school the younger Howton children intermittently attended, revealed that Alice Lou, then thirty-six, had appeared there one day asking a teacher and a lunchroom worker if they'd like to have some of her kids.

In late March of 1969, social workers filed a court petition to remove the children from their home, a petition that for assorted reasons dealt with the two eldest and the youngest child separately from the others. On April 8, after a hearing, the Hopkins County juvenile court ordered the removal of the middle four—Renee, Grant, Michael and Ricky, ages nine, eight, six and four, respectively.

Immediately after this hearing, Kentucky state foster worker Jacqueline Lee Oliver drove to the Howton home to pick up her new charges. Oliver, forty-three, was the sort of warm, gracious southern lady whose lilting accent masked a sharp mind and strong will. She was married to a Kentucky state trooper, had worked with people all her adult life, and knew how to make her point when it was needed. The children's parting from their mother was not as emotional as Oliver had expected. Renee and Grant cried some, but they all appeared more afraid of the unknown than of the actual separation. Alice Lou kissed each one and told them to be good children.

Once in the car, the children grew quiet, staring at the passing scenery with wide eyes. Jackie Oliver stopped in the town of Princeton to buy them clothes, for their belongings were meager and beyond use. The children marveled at the idea of having new clothes to wear, but remained well-behaved in the stores despite their excitement. Grant, protective of Michael and Ricky, helped them try on their pants and shirts, and Renee, bubbling with delight, thought each little dress more beautiful than the one before.

By the time they arrived at their foster home, the children were tired and hungry, but not apprehensive. They were in the town of Fredonia, in Caldwell County, and waiting on the front porch were their foster parents, Cherie and Michael Colling. The four were soon scrambling through the house, exploring each room, trying to figure out where each would be sleeping.

Over the next two months, as Jackie Oliver visited the Colling home often to evaluate the placement, she grew increasingly close to, and admiring of, the Howton children. Jackie kept waiting for an explosion, they were so well-behaved. Renee and Grant praised the food and helped with the dishes, Mike took out the trash and they all picked up their clothes and made their beds—the older ones helped the youngest, Ricky, with his chores. Jackie thought them sweet beyond words. She had never seen four more affectionate children—they were starved for attention, and would not let her leave without an abundance of kisses and hugs.

All were wholesomely good-looking, with plump apple cheeks, light brown hair, medium fair complexions, and deep blue eyes. Renee, with long eyelashes and a body just filling out and gaining shape, was terribly sensitive and emotional and cried easily, but she adored all her new clothes and the permanent Cherie Colling applied to her hair. Grant was easily disciplined, for he so wanted to please. Mike appeared more fearful than his two older siblings, but it was Ricky who had the most problems. At first he seemed afraid that every move he made was going to bring punishment—once, when he accidentally stepped on a tulip, he began crying hysterically, begging Cherie to understand it was an accident. Soon all four were calling the Collings Mommy and Daddy. Renee, stopping Jackie at the door one day as she was leaving, kissed her and thanked her for bringing them to such a good home.

The Colling house, however, was just a temporary boarding facility. Jackie needed to find a more permanent solution, and by mid-1969, she had set herself a difficult goal, for she'd decided she couldn't split up these four children.

"They are precious," she wrote in a report that June, "all bearing a very striking family resemblance, and I have already put in a bid with the higher power that if these children are not to be returned [to their natural parents] that somewhere in the state we have a home ready to take all four at the same time."

The higher power did not soon respond to Jackie. The number of prospective adoptive homes in Kentucky willing to embrace the Howton package—four older children, Catholic, living on welfare—was not large. Six months passed, then a year. In April of 1970 the Howton children were still living at the Collings' foster home. They were happy and contented there, but that was just the problem—Renee and Grant were now expressing a desire to stay with the Collings forever. We're not going anywhere else, they'd regularly insist.

In truth, they couldn't stay. Cherie Colling had talked to Kentucky officials about permanently adopting all the Howtons, but just then her marriage was foundering. Cherie was the type of large, gentle woman who seemed deeply maternal by instinct, but the state wouldn't consider placing four children with a single mother. There could be no negotiation on that issue.

So Jackie handled the Howtons' feelings as best she could. This boarding home is a bridge and not permanent, she'd remind the children. There will be one more move, and then no more. She couldn't tell them where they were going, though, or when, and this pained her.

"The worst thing for these children is the fact that they are dangling in midair," she wrote in a memo that April. "They are affectionate children, each one as handsome as the next, and I think it is tremendously unfair to them if we don't get them settled this summer."

But the summer came and went without a resolution.

Renee was now a lovely feminine girl, sensitive and affectionate, protective of her younger siblings and sometimes bossy toward them. Grant was a quiet, obedient daydreamer with a talent for drawing and a passion for animals, sports, hunting and fishing. Mike was the family clown—an affectionate, outgoing and outspoken show-off who loved sports and the outdoors. Ricky's nightmares and fears had faded away over time, leaving an uncomplicated, happy-go-lucky little boy who looked forward eagerly to starting the first grade. All of them slept and ate well and handled their chores without complaint.

Three more months passed, then six, then nine, still without a permanent adoptive home. On June 21, 1971, Jackie typed up for the Howtons a five-page "presentation summary of children for adoption"—a document that fairly can be likened to a discreet, understated sales brochure aimed at possible adoptive parents. She passed her report and supporting documents to a regional supervisor, L. C. Wolfe, and a state adoption specialist, Sue Howard, who was another genteel but strong-minded southern woman.

"We wish to consider only placement keeping the children together," Jackie wrote in a cover memo. "The worker will cooperate with any effort to make a suitable placement, including an out-of-state referral."

Three more months passed without a connection. In early October, a Kentucky couple, responding to the photographs of the Howton children distributed by the state, expressed some interest, and for a time, adoption workers thought they had solved their extended problem. As the adoptive study proceeded, however, this couple gradually decided that four children would be a bit too much for them. Two or three children, several years younger than the How-tons, would be more like what they could handle.

Disappointed, Sue Howard continued her search for a home in Kentucky, but as she did so, she also thought of one other possibility— a private, out-of-state adoption agency that in the past had placed several large family groups for Kentucky. Perhaps, Howard reasoned, they could help again. In mid-October, Howard referred the Howton file to Lutheran Social Service in Minneapolis, Minnesota.

With this move, success at last seemed within reach. Lutheran Social Service, matching Sue Howard's query with adoptive parents' applications on file, responded within two weeks, sending Kentucky officials an adoptive home brief on a Minnesota family willing to take four children. With just one boy in the house and four bed-rooms, a Harold and Lois Jurgens of Stillwater seemed to offer the answer to a prayer.

Four months before—in fact, on precisely the same June day that Jackie Oliver had written her sales brochure for the Howton chil-dren—Harold and Lois had filled out Lutheran Social Service's appli-cation for adoption, apparently believing that this agency would be more receptive than the Bureau of Catholic Charities or the Ramsey County welfare department. Robert by then had been back almost two years, and the Jurgenses once again wanted more children in their home.

Their application painted an encouraging portrait. They attended the St. Francis of Assisi Church in Lakeland. Harold earned $16,000 a year at Muska Electric, carried an $8,800 mortgage on a house they valued at $35,000, owed a credit union $5,000 and held life insurance policies totaling $5,500.

Where asked to list their children, the Jurgenses had written Robert's name and birth date, June 22, 1960.

Where asked, "Have you previously adopted a child?" the Jur-genses had written "Yes."

Where asked the year, the Jurgenses had written "1960."

And that was all. Harold and Lois had made no reference to Den-nis. On their application, he didn't exist.

In Kentucky, Sue Howard, her supervisor, L. C. Wolfe and a social worker named Peter Crego were interested, but wanted to know more about the Jurgenses. On November 4, Crego—young, newly arrived in the department, taking over Jackie Oliver's caseload—wrote a letter to Robert M. Lageson, the Lutheran Social Service caseworker in Minneapolis who had referred Harold and Lois. "I am quite certain in my mind the home is acceptable," he explained, "but . . . more information will be needed."

On November 23, Lageson wrote back to Crego, sending photos of the Jurgenses and several documents.

"I can be very enthusiastic about Mr. and Mrs. Jurgens . . ." Lageson reported. "Mr. Jurgens is a man with many interests and enjoys life . . . Mrs. Jurgens is an attractive and feminine woman who has a very good self-concept. Being one of sixteen children, she feels, had a real part in making her the kind of person she is . . . I recommend this family . . ."

With his letter, Lageson enclosed two handwritten essays, each two pages in length, one written by Lois, one by Harold, both responding to the agency's request that they describe themselves, their backgrounds and their interests.

Harold's handwriting slanted across the page, the lines rising as they approached the right edge, some bunching too tightly, one atop the other, and others widely spaced. Many sentences included parentheses, much like Harold's often meandering conversation. He seemed uncomfortable talking directly about himself, and preferred to guide his comments to other topics or ramble wherever his mind might take him.

His father was a playing manager of a fast-pitch softball team, Harold began, so growing up, his neighborhood was well supplied with bats and balls, and all the kids played often on the many vacant lots. He was an only child, and his grandmother on his mother's side often cared for him, taking him to ball games on ladies' days—"I vividly remember my aunt pulling a straw hat by the brim over a man's ears because he didn't agree with an umpire's decision in our favor." He began piano lessons at seven and tenor sax at fifteen, and had his own band in high school. His present hobbies included baseball, hockey, swimming, camping, fishing, music and nature, "but as everyone says, the days are never long enough . . ." He was particularly interested in hockey because his son Robert liked ice skating and played the game at school. "I assist in Scout work as time allows and enjoy working with children . . ." he reported. "Neither my wife, Lois, or I feel children are a burden, as some people say . . ."

By contrast, Lois's handwriting flowed evenly across the page, each line level and balanced, filling all the space between the left and right edges of the paper. Her tone gave no hint of hesitancy. "This description of yourself and your situation could include what now seems important to you," the agency form had said, and Lois, at forty-six, responded warmly to the invitation.

She has always loved dancing and music, she said. Also biking, walking, reading, sewing, knitting, painting, gardening, cooking, baking and swimming. She loved the outdoors because as a child she lived in the country with a close family full of lots of siblings and pets. She had "loads of friends," and was a "very generous person who liked to make people happy."

"Children are always loved and welcomed in my home . . ." she concluded. "Our home is just that, a home. It's not always spotless, but it's a place where one feels relaxed. It's a happy place. We all enjoy . . . just plain letting our hair down and singing while my husband plays the piano . . ."

Kentucky officials responded warmly and quickly to these communications, thanking Lutheran Social Service for "finding this wonderful home for our children." Excitement filled the Collings' foster home. Peter Crego visited the Howton children six times in December, preparing them for their move to the adoptive home in Minnesota. The children seemed apprehensive at first, but grew more enthusiastic as the days passed. They did not want to leave the Collings, but at least the long, uncertain wait was over.

Or so it seemed.

Late that December, following normal procedure, Lutheran Social Service sent a copy of its five-page Jurgens study to the adoption unit in Minnesota's department of public welfare, the body that must approve out-of-state placements involving private agencies. There a caseworker, following routine, opened a new file under the name Jurgens but also crosschecked to see if the state already had a record on this family.

This inquiry came back positive, for the Jurgenses were in the state registry. So was someone not mentioned on any of the present adoption forms—a small boy named Dennis.

The state would not have had a record of the Jurgenses but for one circumstance. Dennis was placed out of Scott County, which because of its smaller size is not, like Ramsey County, licensed to handle its own adoptions. The state had matched Dennis in Scott County with the Jurgenses in Ramsey County and approved their union.

When the caseworker saw the contents of the older, existing Jurgens file, she bundled it with the new paperwork from Lutheran Social Service and carried it over to Ruth Weidell, supervisor of the state's adoption unit.

"I think you'd better look at this case," the caseworker said, dropping the package on Weidell's desk.

Weidell, a brisk and precise woman capable of reciting various state codes from memory, grew increasingly alarmed as she turned the pages. It was not her unit's task to investigate adoptive homes—that was what they licensed county and private agencies such as Lutheran Social Service to do. All the same, this looked disturbing. What's more, the Jurgenses had omitted any reference to Dennis or his death when completing their forms and talking to the private agency.

We just cannot approve this adoption, Weidell decided.

When Bob Lageson got the news, he visited the state department of public welfare office in St. Paul to review the records for himself. Then he contacted the Jurgenses to hear their side of the story.

They had not informed anyone about Dennis, Harold and Lois explained, because from past experience they were aware of how social agencies used information against you. Besides, they had never abused Dennis or been charged with anything or done anything wrong.

After talking to Lageson, the Jurgenses called their attorney, Bill Fink, who provided the Lutheran social worker with copies of two letters written by psychiatrists for the Ramsey County juvenile court, one by a Dr. Garvey, the other by a Dr. Teeter.

By the time these conversations and exchanges were completed, Lageson had embraced both the Jurgenses' worthiness and a rescue plan devised by Fink. A memo Lageson wrote to his supervisor on January 2, 1972, spelled out the results of his investigation:

> Mr. and Mrs. Jurgens erred in not sharing this past information with us. They explained that they in no way had been responsible for Dennis's death and had not been abusive to

him. If they had problems in this area they would not want to add to their family and jeopardize these children . . .

Newspaper clippings in the DPW file stated Dennis had died of a ruptured bowel and peritonitis. Mr. Jurgens said he had been playing with Dennis about an hour before they found him dead and had no idea that anything was wrong. He said they had been concerned about Dennis because he seemed not able to experience pain . . .

Mr. Fink felt he had gotten to know Mr. and Mrs. Jurgens quite well and did not feel that they would harm children . . . He thought it could be a very good thing for these children and these parents to have each other. If he felt otherwise he would not be supporting them . . .

Mr. Fink asked that I make an appointment to meet with Ruth Weidell. She refused to meet with us, said her decision was final and that she felt responsible for these children. I offered that I did not want to proceed with a plan that was to be bad or one that was harmful to these children but wanted a decision based on more material than she had and not to decide on fear. After lengthy discussion she agreed to review the pending evaluation and then reconsider.

Mr. Jurgens has contacted Dr. Teeter, who is chief of psychiatry at St. Paul–Ramsey Hospital and also, I believe, on the child abuse team. He has agreed to submit an evaluation and will set up an appointment.

Despite all this, Lageson apparently did not feel optimistic, because on January 6, he called Peter Crego in Kentucky to say the Jurgenses would be unable to adopt the Howton children, since the commissioner of public welfare in Minnesota wouldn't give permission.

"It seems that the Jurgenses had a child abuse case brought against them regarding their adopted son," Crego wrote in his log later that day. "The child died, but the Jurgenses were acquitted. Details are incomplete at the moment, but it is rather doubtful that the children will ever be placed in the Jurgenses' home."

Harold and Lois, however, were just beginning their fight. Lois was even talking about the Kentucky children to her psychiatrist. This interest in another adoption alarmed Dr. Garvey, for Lois now was so dependent on prescription drugs, particularly Tuinal, that he felt she should be hospitalized for a month to cleanse her system.

"She can't sleep," the doctor wrote in his log. "Now they want to adopt four kids . . . She will never change."

On January 12, Bill Fink wrote Crego, enclosing a copy of Dr. Teeter's psychological evaluation from 1969 and promising a new one shortly. The Minnesota department of public welfare is going to reconsider this matter, he reassured the Kentucky social worker, as soon as they get Teeter's updated report.

"I personally thought there was a lot of undue excitement about the original child battery case," Fink observed. "Not everyone who is accused of child battery is guilty. However, because the offense of battering a child is so heinous, once the charge is made a lot of feeling is engendered . . . I happen to know quite a bit about the Jurgens family . . . I have no hesitancy in vouching for them . . . Robert Lageson, a social worker for the Lutheran Social Service, agrees with me on this matter . . ."

Fink apparently was as convincing with Crego as he had been with Lageson. On February 3, Crego wrote a memo to the Kentucky adoption specialist Sue Howard, updating the Howton case. In part, it read:

> Mr. Fink sent me a psychiatric evaluation on the Jurgenses. It was a very thorough evaluation written by a psychiatrist who specializes in child abuse cases. It was by his recommendation that Robert . . . was returned to their home. At the present moment this psychiatrist, Dr. Teeter, is . . . consulting with the Jurgenses and will be making a report . . . There were quite a few unanswered questions regarding the child abuse case. Mr. Fink handled this case and reported to me there is a brother-in-law involved who made the charge and is considered to be mentally ill. Mr. Fink vouches for this family's suitability as parents. Because of the interest shown and inconclusiveness of the charges, I am still holding out in support of the Jurgenses.

Crego, however, was not able to spread his enthusiasm to his superiors. Sue Howard and Jackie Oliver expressed strong opposition to the Jurgens placement—so strong that on the same day Crego composed his memo to Howard, he found it necessary to write a letter of warning to Bill Fink.

"We are having difficulty with our main office over this case," Crego reported. "They want answers to questions we don't have. Of particular interest is the manner in which this trial was conducted. Was there a jury present, or was a decision made by the presiding judge? Also, were the Jurgenses acquitted on a technicality or because of insubstantial proof? Our central office would probably be happy with a court transcript of the proceedings. I must be honest with you in stating that there is at the moment strong opposition from our central office."

Almost four weeks later, on February 28, Fink responded to Crego's questions with a two-page letter and several documents.

> First of all, there never was a trial . . . The Jurgenses had adopted another child, and the question was whether or not this child should remain in their home . . . The matter involving the welfare of Robert Jurgens was dismissed. It was not dismissed on a technicality but after substantial proof was submitted on both sides. The transcript of the proceedings is a heavy book of 798 pages. I have a copy of it, and I will be glad to send it to you if you think it essential . . . It of course contains evidence supporting the charge, and it contains evidence against the charge . . . The charges in the petition are heinous. They were all explained by the parents, and many of them were denied. Many of them were not substantiated by proof. Enclosed is a partial copy of the transcript—some of the testimony . . . To make charges is one thing. To substantiate them is quite another. It is quite obvious that the court would not have restored Robert Jurgens to his parents if the court felt that he was in danger of any great bodily harm . . . Should we not be more interested in the reality of the present than speculating about the past?

The eleven pages of transcript Fink chose to send Crego happened to involve the testimony of Dr. Roy Peterson. They were not consecutively numbered pages, but rather, a precise selection that skipped from one moment of the hearing to another. Since the Jurgenses had refused to discuss Dennis's death in Gingold's courtroom,

Fink was offering Peterson's summary of the account the Jurgenses had provided him—seasoned with the doctor's own embrace of his patients' story.

Here Crego could read of Dennis slipping on the basement floor and falling down the basement stairs. Here Crego could read of Lois finding Dennis on Sunday morning gasping his last breath. And here Crego could read of Dr. Peterson finding nothing unusual in Dennis's physical condition or manner of death: *No, nothing struck me . . . nothing remarkable . . . It's not unusual . . .*

In early March, Fink followed up this package with two newly written letters of recommendation, both solicited by the Jurgenses. One came from Father Reiser, the other from Dr. Teeter.

"This is to inform you that I have known Mr. and Mrs. Harold Jurgens for the past twenty years . . ." the priest wrote. "They are people of excellent character and fine religious convictions. I would judge them to be most worthy to be adoptive parents. I recommend them to you for the adoption of Renee, Grant, Michael and Richard Howton. I am sure these children would be given an excellent home with good character and religious training."

Dr. Teeter was no less supportive.

Mr. and Mrs. Jurgens are a stable family with positive motivations to receive the four children, he reported. From a social, educational and financial point of view, they display an impressive capacity to raise more children. "Mrs. Jurgens . . . is, if anything, more sensible and contented now than when I examined her originally," he concluded. "She appears from her own comments, as well as her husband's and her son's, to have matured to a more relaxed attitude . . . It is my opinion that the Jurgenses are suitable risks for the adoption of children."

Crego by now was unabashedly campaigning for the placement. He'd been visiting the Howton children two or three times a week, and had even allowed Lois to start phoning and writing the children, mainly Renee.

"Believe me, we're as anxious as you are to settle this matter," he wrote Fink on March 14. "Adults can rationalize a given situation, but children are not so apt to grasp meanings other than 'am I wanted.' I'm beginning to run out of excuses, too."

For the states of Minnesota and Kentucky, Ruth Weidell and Sue Howard were still resisting, but the bases for their opposition were weakening. On March 17, Fink sent to Weidell copies of the new letters from Father Reiser and Dr. Teeter, and at month's end he arranged shipment to Howard of the full record on Robert's foster stays from 1965 to 1969. He never did send the full transcript of Robert's custody hearing, though, and Kentucky never repeated its original request.

Weidell finally felt the pressure. She had waved the first warning flag, but she was much more the reliable state employee than a quixotic maverick in the system. She valued facts and statutes, and played most matters straight down the middle, with no wobble to the left or right. The Jurgenses had been allowed to adopt two children already, she reasoned. All the psychological evaluations were favorable, as was the letter from their priest. Even if they had been involved in child abuse five years ago, couldn't they be okay now? What's more, the Howtons were older, bigger children—couldn't they protect themselves? Besides, the information they had was only an accusation. The Jurgenses had never been charged criminally in Dennis's death.

With some trepidation, Ruth Weidell decided to approve the placement.

On April 10, Webster C. Martin, Jr., director of the division of social services, acting under authorization delegated by Minnesota's commissioner of public welfare, signed four notarized documents giving consent and approval for Lutheran Social Service to bring the Howton children into the state, for the purpose of placing them in the home of Mr. and Mrs. Harold Jurgens in Stillwater.

Kentucky held out somewhat longer, largely because Sue Howard and Jackie Oliver still vehemently opposed the placement. Theirs was a losing battle, though. Here was a couple willing to take all four Howtons, children who had been living unwanted for two years in a boarding home, supported entirely by state welfare payments. The Collings were now divorced; Cherie and all the kids were living with her parents. Lutheran Social Service was considered state of the art in the adoption field. In mid-May, after several departmental meetings in Frankfort, Howard and Oliver's supervisors decided to overrule their objections.

The Jurgenses received the news by telephone from Bob Lageson.

"You can go to Kentucky," he said. "You can go get your four new children."

Harold, Lois and Robert Jurgens arrived in Fredonia too late at night on Thursday, May 18, for their scheduled visit with the Howtons. The next morning, they met first with L. C. Wolfe, who reviewed with them various background and placement information. The Jurgenses asked several questions about the Howtons' natural parents, but seemed more concerned about recent events, especially the divorce of the foster parents.

Wolfe felt impressed with Harold, Lois and their son. Robert was a typically awkward twelve-year-old, but he looked healthy and participated freely in the discussion. Lois Jurgens seemed a little more tense at first than did Harold, who immediately struck Wolfe as being quite likable—relaxed, warm and very genial.

Wolfe drove the Jurgenses to the house of Cherie Colling's parents, the Buchanons. The Howtons and Cherie were still away at school and work, but the Buchanons embraced the Jurgenses at the door and settled them onto the living room sofa. Soon after, when the Howton kids arrived home, the three boys rushed directly to the Jurgenses, while Renee hung back, for she'd been crying as she bid farewell to her classmates. Taking the initiative, Lois approached her, and Renee, now twelve, responded. The Jurgenses gave Grant a new basketball and shirt—this day, May 19, happened to be his eleventh birthday.

The Jurgenses, Buchanons, Howtons and Cherie Colling spent three hours together, eating lunch and visiting. The two older Howton children, Renee and Grant, thought the gathering quite pleasant, with everyone acting so comfortable and loving. In letters and on the phone, the Jurgenses had talked of all they could offer them, and now, sitting in the Buchanons' living room, Harold and Lois continued in this vein, emphasizing in particular the music lessons and instruments they'd buy and the trips they'd take and the big house they owned. Renee and Grant were sad about leaving the Collings, but at the same time, they felt excited about entering a new, promising home where they could all stay together permanently.

After a life of poverty, the Jurgenses also looked good to Grant because it seemed they had money. In relative terms, they did, for the Jurgenses' income was twice that of the Collings. Talk of buying things and taking trips sounded marvelous to Grant, like entering a fantasyland.

When L. C. Wolfe returned later that day, the packing was underway, and it seemed to him everyone felt satisfied. The Howton boys were hanging all over Robert, teasing and playing, and though he was apprehensive about sharing his parents' attention, Robert also felt happy to have siblings.

"We like them," the Howton children whispered to Wolfe in private. Harold and Lois said much the same.

Late that day, Cherie and Wolfe and the Buchanons stood outside, waving good-bye as they watched the Jurgenses' brown Buick Skylark, stuffed with children and suitcases, pull away. Cherie wanted to stop them, to raise a voice in protest, but she felt there was nothing she could do, for she was divorced now, and the adoption had been approved.

L. C. Wolfe felt more satisfied. Returning to his office that evening, he composed a memo for Sue Howard.

"The placement was made this afternoon and appears to me to be a very promising one . . ." he wrote. "I feel very comfortable. . . ."

The drive north to Minnesota from Kentucky took two and a half days. The Jurgenses stopped at restaurants and motels and places to sightsee, and the Howtons thought the trip quite pleasant. Renee looked forward to seeing their new home and what the Jurgenses had to offer—finally, they were going to have real parents after all this time.

Only one odd, brief episode marred the journey. Late in the afternoon on the second day, Harold pulled into a small town and started asking the children which motel along the street they preferred.

"Well, kids, want to stay here tonight, or over there, or over there?" he asked, pointing out the options.

"No, Harold," Lois snapped, her voice suddenly rising, harsh and unpleasantly hostile. "We're staying here at this one."

Grant caught his siblings' eyes, then looked away. They had never known such an angry woman before. For a moment, Grant wondered just what kind of situation they were getting into. The thought quickly passed, though, and soon the children were scrambling out of the Buick, racing each other toward the motel door.

CHAPTER 24

Stillwater

Historical markers at the north and south ends of Stillwater's Main Street welcome visitors to "The Birthplace of Minnesota," but the signs are misleading. Orange Walker, a tanner from Vermont, leading some dozen pioneer loggers, built Minnesota's first commercial sawmill upstream at the town of Marine in 1839, four years before John McKusick and three other eastern transplants, all in their twenties, established a second sawmill on the west shore of Lake St. Croix. Contemplating the serenity at his mill's doorstep, McKusick named his settlement Stillwater. Surrounded by a stunningly lush valley and conveniently located on the rugged lower St. Croix River, which feeds into the Mississippi below the Twin Cities, Stillwater soon flourished as the region's headquarters for the lumber industry.

Some 120 years later, Stillwater and the surrounding St. Croix Valley were still doing well, although for different reasons. The town's upscale shops, trendy restaurants and restored inns were now a magnet for tourists rather than for whiskey-soaked loggers, and the interstate highways had transformed the surrounding virgin region into an attractive alternative for those tired both of the Twin Cities and the orderly suburbs.

This reach of rural land was where the Jurgenses had settled upon leaving White Bear Lake in 1967, and the setting seemed a fantasy to the Howton children on the day they first arrived—what they imagined summer camp might be like. The last five miles of the journey from Kentucky to the Jurgens home were the most exciting, for now they were curving and turning on a narrow country road through abundant farmland and thick stands of elm and oak. The Howtons couldn't see their new home until Harold pulled the Buick Skylark all the way up their steep dirt driveway, for a forest of elms surrounded them. The Jurgenses had no neighbors here.

Life for the Howton children at first seemed much as they had hoped. Harold and Lois bought them everything they'd promised—new clothes, sports equipment, baseballs, bats, gloves and, above all, musical instruments. Grant got a set of drums, Mike a trumpet, Ricky a guitar, Renee a piano, and they all began music lessons at the local school. They and Robert soon formed their own group, the "Jurgs 5," and with their name emblazoned on their speakers, took to playing at nursing homes and weddings, often lipsynching to records, sometimes singing their own songs, even winning third place at a state fair talent show. Harold promoted his beloved hockey—he scrimmaged with the boys, drove them to their practices, attended all their games, took them to see the professional North Stars.

Bob Lageson, making his early postplacement visits for Lutheran Social Service, felt satisfied. "The Jurgenses and their five children are doing real great," he wrote Sue Howard in Kentucky on June 2. "It has every indication of being a real success at this point."

The changes in Lois did not come all at once. When they had been there three months, she started showing the Howtons how to clean the house. "You kids must learn responsibility," she'd say, sounding serious but not mean. She'd get down on her knees to demonstrate. Beds had to be moved when vacuuming, she explained, so you can get under the legs. Soon the Howton children and Robert were dusting and vacuuming and wiping windows with precision.

Some of Lois's requirements were odd, though. She insisted, for example, that the boys scrub the steps descending into the basement until not a single shoe mark could be seen. In their bedrooms, she'd run a finger behind the furniture and across the baseboards, looking for dust. Curtains had to be tied back with precision, hangers ordered precisely in their closets, with none crossing.

The music playing, at first fun, soon acquired certain burdensome requirements as well. Lois made them practice one hour every weekday, two hours each Saturday and Sunday, and four hours if they messed up. "Do another hour," Lois would say when their playing did not sound right to her. Grant practiced standing up, so as the sessions stretched on, the pain in his back would bring tears to his eyes.

They thought all this strange, but for a while they tried hard to please. Maybe, they reasoned, this is what real parents are like. Maybe it's part of what families with money are like.

On October 17, half a year after the Howtons arrived and just one month after they had started school in the Stillwater district, an elementary school counselor named Mike Hedloff called Bob Lageson at Lutheran Social Service to express concern about the Jurgenses' treatment of their children.

Mrs. Jurgens, Hedloff explained, had not permitted Mike to go on a field trip, and there also had been other problems. Such incidents concerned the teachers, Hedloff said, because they adored these Kentucky children—some found them so appealing they were prepared to take them to their own homes in a minute.

Lageson called Lois two nights later to relay what he'd been told. Lois thought some of the school counselor's points were "picky." She had intended this punishment involving the field trip as a one-time thing, and had so assured the teacher, she said. She was glad to hear that the school felt the children were good kids.

Lois had another matter on her mind. She and Mr. Jurgens had been thinking, she said. They wanted to adopt another child—a little girl.

Lageson, the memory still fresh of his laborious struggle to push through the Kentucky adoption, was discouraging. The prospect of once again opening the Jurgens file to the Minnesota DPW's scrutiny left him weary. Any child from out of state, Lageson told Lois, would almost be impossible.

In truth, Lageson had his own mildly mixed feelings about the placement he'd now been monitoring for half a year. Mrs. Jurgens was trying extremely hard to be a good mother, he felt, but she did have a tendency to get involved too much with the children, to control them more than she should. All the same, the kids exuded happiness and security—they were confident and outgoing in a situation where they could easily be anxious or tense.

When the probationary period ended half a year later, Lageson had not revised this judgment, and ultimately saw no cause for alarm. On April 27, 1973, he received the official decree formalizing the Jurgenses' adoption of the four Howton children. Lageson placed the original in his own file and sent a copy to the state department of child welfare. In his log, he wrote the words, "Case closed."

As the weeks and months passed, however, the Howton children, try as they might, were finding they could not keep Lois satisfied. Beginning that first fall in 1972, and continuing in ever stronger waves during 1973 and 1974, Lois would express her displeasure through increasingly powerful explosions of anger. Harsh reprimands evolved into unrestrained screaming, then into body blows, first with the hand, then a belt, finally a belt buckle and a cedar board. Desiring a child's presence or attention or obedience, Lois often grabbed his hair or ears. Yanking the boys by the short hair on their sideburns seemed one of her favored techniques. The children soon discovered that anything could trigger her—a single crossed hanger, a streak on the bathroom mirror. Once, when he had failed to remove an empty hanger from his closet, Lois grabbed Grant by the ears and ran his forehead into an exposed two-by-four stud in the wall.

Lois required all five children to clean their own socks and underwear on an old-fashioned scrubbing board, using strong laundry soap, much as she had done as a child. More than once, when they failed to wash the stains from their underwear, Lois required the boys to wear their dirtied shorts inside out on their heads while in the house and out in public—at the kitchen table, shopping in stores and, once, while attending Renee's softball game.

When she felt Ricky had not properly cleaned his ears, Lois would dig deep into them with her fingernails until the boy bled and screamed out in pain. Sometimes she'd make Mike and Ricky lie on their beds, their pants pulled down, while she spanked them with a metal pancake spatula.

When Renee started menstruating, Lois required her to wrap her soiled napkins in toilet paper and store them in a paper sack until her cycle ended, when she was to carry the bag out back for Harold to burn. One month when Renee forgot to dispose of the bag, Lois discovered it and angrily dumped the contents before the family, then required Renee to stand outside without shoes in the winter snow. Other times, she called Renee a whore, and forced her to drop her underwear before the boys while she administered a spanking.

Robert received some of the abuse, but less than the others. As a result, even though Grant and Renee were friends with Robert and close to his age, there was some competitiveness and jealousy among the three over relations with their parents. The Howtons thought Robert was favored. It seems likely that out of survival, Robert long ago had learned how to please his mother. Still, even he operated at times in dangerous territory.

"Is that what you did to Dennis?" he would snap at his mother when she yanked at his ears.

The Kentucky children hardly knew what Robert was talking about. They understood the Jurgenses had a boy who died years before, and three or four times they visited his grave, but that was all. Although a picture of this child sat framed on an end table in the living room, the children were rarely allowed in that room. Lois kept plastic on the furniture in there, and cleaned the room herself. One other room remained off-limits—Lois kept her bedroom door locked at all times, the key pinned to her pants. That door happened to have rusty hinges, so when they heard its loud squeak, the children grew fearful, knowing Lois was emerging.

Once, after Lois had whipped him with a belt buckle, a school counselor and coach noticed big purple welts on Grant, but he explained he had gotten them falling down the driveway. If I tell, they'd just send me back to Lois, he figured.

Over time, the children became scared even to come home from school. When the school bus dropped them off each afternoon, Mike would look up the steep driveway to see if Lois's Buick Skylark was parked by the house, relaxing if it was gone, cringing if it was there. Standing in the driveway, Renee would look with apprehension at her bedroom window—when the curtains weren't visible, she'd know Lois had ripped them off because the ruffles weren't tied back perfectly. If Lois was not home, they had to sit outside and wait, often in the chill of winter—Lois wouldn't give them keys to the house or allow them to go to a friend's home—but even that ordeal seemed preferable to her presence.

Once inside, Lois would set them all to their cleaning routine, followed by music practice, homework, their baths and supper. Before bed, they'd gather in the TV room to recite the rosary on their knees. After everyone else had gone to sleep, Lois would walk through the house and down into the basement until she found something wrong or out of place. Mike and Ricky, in bed in their shared room, would dread hearing her call their names, for they knew then that something wasn't right, that something had not pleased her.

Sometimes Harold tried to intervene, but the children sensed he too was afraid of Lois, and in any event, he was ineffective.

"Now, Lois, let's not get all worked up, they didn't mean it," he'd say, but she'd just turn on him. "Shut up," she'd snarl. Now and then, he would try physically to restrain her by grabbing her arm, and once he even punched her when she threw a cup of coffee over him, but usually she'd scratch and claw until he gave up. One night she swung at him with a frozen fish.

On occasion, when one of the boys misbehaved and Lois was otherwise occupied, she would tell Harold to take him down to the basement for a whipping. Down the stairs they'd go, settling in chairs, Harold commencing to whack noisily at his own leg while instructing the child to holler loudly. One time, back upstairs, Lois complained because she saw no tears in Ricky's eyes. "You can't whoop him no harder than that?" she asked Harold.

Harold seldom reprimanded them and never lost his cool. When Lois tore into the children, however, he often would leave the room, and sometimes the house. When he could, he would take the children with him to escape Lois's tirades—they'd go out to breakfast, or a movie, or a McDonald's. Once when they returned, they found Lois sprawled on the floor, beer and pills strewn about, the scene so staged that even Grant knew her suicide was faked.

Sunday mornings were nice, for Harold alone took them to the St. Francis of Assisi church, Lois now preferring to practice her religion privately in her bedroom. On these occasions the children sometimes tried to talk to their father.

"God, she's beaten us for dust on the shelf," Grant would say. "Everything's always our fault."

Harold would agree that Lois was overdoing things, but there was a line he would not cross. "You did screw up," he'd say. "You kids know what happens with her when you screw up, so why screw up?"

Lois had her own response to their complaints, one she voiced regularly.

"This is what I was made to do as a child," Lois would insist. "This is the way my mother did it, and I'm going to bring you up like my father and mother brought us up. You think this is strict? You should have been living back when I was a child."

She threw that thought at them all the time: "I'm going to bring you up like my parents brought me up."

Lois by now was regularly calling Dr. Garvey for refills of her Tuinal prescription, and the doctor was obliging, although he was concerned. Lois's efforts to break her drug dependency always ended after two or three days, so she and the doctor had long talked of taking stronger action. Finally, on August 3, 1973, Dr. Garvey admitted Lois to North Memorial Hospital, where she planned to withdraw from the various medications she'd been using since 1965.

Harold drove her to the hospital, then talked to the social worker who was preparing Lois's admissions paperwork. In her report, this social worker summarized what Harold had to say about the current situation:

> During the last year, the patient's husband has noticed changes in the patient. She has become much more short-tempered and the smallest things would upset her. She cannot admit she's wrong and she continually picks on her husband . . . She has lately been very short with the kids even though she is aware of what she is doing and doesn't like it. She criticizes her husband for being too easy on the children although he says that he thinks she is too strict with them and so is kind of a buffer between the patient and them. He said he does not approach her sexually very often because she continually is degrading and putting him down. He just sits and takes her criticism and doesn't let it bother him, so he says.

Lois stayed at North Memorial for two weeks, leaving on August 17. Dr. Garvey thought her "improved," but considered the prognosis "guarded." At her discharge, he categorized Lois as a patient who had been taking too many medications over a number of years, especially sleeping pills. While in the hospital, he said, she had managed to reduce greatly her use of pills. "The patient, I feel, basically was not intellectually and emotionally honest with me; however, she did improve . . ." he wrote. "The patient herself recognizes that she is far from well at this point and that she will require further treatment . . ."

Whatever the value of Lois's hospitalization, it did not alter the mood or events in the Jurgens home. Harold grew so overwhelmed that in early February of 1974, half a year after Lois's stay at North Memorial, Dr. Garvey found it necessary to hospitalize him. After a week, though, the doctor could find nothing wrong with him other than his wife.

At his discharge on February 9, Garvey described Harold as a fifty-two-year-old man whose wife had created a great deal of stress for him. During his stay in the hospital, the doctor reported, Harold adjusted well. "It was felt that he very definitely had to learn to express himself . . ." Garvey concluded. "It was felt that this man's basic stress was his sick wife and that he should receive counseling with her."

So twice, on Sunday evenings, Harold and Lois drove their children to Coon Rapids for family counseling sessions with Father Reiser. First the whole family would sit together in a room, talking to the priest, then the children would gather in another room alone with Father Reiser. "You need to do better," the priest would say, and the children would agree, fearing if they said more Lois would find out. On the second visit, though, the Howtons apparently felt secure enough to tell Father Reiser about the hangers in the closet and underwear on their heads. Memories vary on this point, but the priest later told police investigators he'd heard from the children about these incidents and had raised the matter with Harold and Lois. After that second visit, for whatever the reason, the family did not come to Coon Rapids again for a counseling session.

Once so ebullient, all four Howton children, and Robert too, now felt filled with pain and fear almost all the time. They could not understand how they had fallen into such a world. The tirades and beatings came every day, without relief or escape. They were not allowed to attend school dances or other functions. Renee regularly sneaked tearful phone calls of complaint to Lois's niece, Bonnie Welsch, and on occasion Lois's sister, Sharon Kopp, both of whom had befriended her at family gatherings. In school, they all felt humiliated by other kids, for Lois now bought their clothes at Goodwill, just as her parents had done with her as a child. Comparing themselves to others, they came to realize they were not living a normal life. Talking to classmates, they discovered that some kids never got spanked.

The phone rang in June Bol's kitchen one morning in the spring of 1975. Lois's eldest sister Eloise was on the line, her voice uncertain and trembling.

"Renee has been calling and saying that Lois is abusive to them," Eloise said. "They're frightened and need help. If they ever need to run from her, can they come to your house?"

Eloise had hesitated to get involved, but she knew her cousin June was a darn good person, and lived just a half mile down from Lois.

"Will you help if they need you?" Eloise asked again when June didn't answer promptly.

June was caught by surprise. She'd seen Lois's new children only a few times, and didn't even know them well enough to distinguish one from the other. It was also odd for Eloise to be calling, since Lois's sister, like a number of the Zerwas women, was usually afraid to get involved in anything. One time years before, when the Bols had members of the Zerwas clan over for an evening of playing the game charades, Eloise had trembled so badly that June, noticing, finally rose and said, "Well, I'll do your turn for you." Whenever June had raised the question of Dennis to the Zerwas family they'd retreated, insisting they knew nothing about anything. Now here was Eloise, venturing to call about these Kentucky children.

"Well, I guess so," June finally answered.

In the years since Robert's return to the Jurgenses, June's relations with Lois had improved—enough at least for the families to visit on scattered occasions—and June didn't want any more trouble. Still, she was not about to have something like Dennis happen again. She couldn't possibly say no to Eloise. They could come, but she wasn't going to get involved.

Not long after that call, the Bols by coincidence received one of their infrequent invitations to visit down the road at the Jurgenses' home. There they spent the evening listening to the children's "Jurgs 5" band play their numbers while Lois stood before the performers, waving her arms about like a conductor, insisting that they continue, forbidding them to stop.

"Play more, we want to hear more," she'd say when they hesitated.

June, knowing how kids are in front of company, sensing they didn't want to continue, tried to help them. "Oh, that's enough," she said. "I'm sure they're tired."

Grant looked at this short, plump stranger with thankful eyes.

A moment later, when Lois left the room, June approached him. She didn't want to interfere, but she felt obliged to communicate. "If you ever need a place to go, come to my house," she whispered.

♦   ♦   ♦

That same spring, on a Sunday morning in late April, Harold took the children out to breakfast while Lois stayed alone in her bedroom.

"I'm thinking of putting your mother into a clinic," he said. "Do you think it's a good idea?"

Yes, the kids said. Yes, they did.

Lois's sister Beverly received a call from Harold on the last day in April. Would she come over? he asked. He needed a favor.

Bev drove to the Jurgens home that afternoon and knocked on the door, but no one answered, so she retreated to her car and backed it down the steep driveway, figuring she'd wait on the road for the kids to arrive home on the school bus. When they came, she honked her horn and they all piled into her car for the ride up the driveway. This time, Lois opened the door when they knocked. Beverly saw what appeared to be a large bottle of catsup thrown on the floor, thick red sauce and shattered glass strewn everywhere.

"That's Renee's job to clean up," Lois informed Bev.

When Lois turned away a moment later, Harold appeared and quickly, secretly, slipped her a note. Bev retreated to a bathroom to read his message.

I'm taking Lois to a clinic tomorrow, Harold had written. Will you take care of the children?

The next morning, May 1, 1975, the Jurgens family piled into the family's Buick Skylark for the forty-five-mile drive north along the bank of the St. Croix River to the Hazelden Foundation, the renowned drug and alcohol rehabilitation center in Center City, Minnesota. The Howtons recall this as the day they "committed" Lois to Hazelden, and certain police and welfare department reports prepared later also refer to a "commitment," but the matter remains unclear, for other available records suggest she was being admitted voluntarily. Whatever the basis, Lois was going to Hazelden in yet another effort to rid herself of a prescription drug dependency. As the children gazed through the car windows with wonder at emerald green fields, pristine canyons full of ocher and sandstone, and a densely wooded river basin, Lois sat silent and stony-faced in the front passenger seat.

Then, nearing Center City, Harold turned up a private road and suddenly they were amid the manicured lawns and stark modern buildings of Hazelden. Only as she climbed out of the car at the entrance to the main building did Lois turn back to the children and speak.

"Now you do your chores or there'll be hell to pay when I get back," she said.

For the five weeks Lois stayed at Hazelden, the children savored their life. For the first time since they'd come to the Jurgenses, Grant felt they were living like normal kids. They did their chores, but they also roamed the countryside and missed supper and went fishing and skipped practicing their music.

Then one day, Harold called them all together.

"Your mother is coming home," he said. "Better clean up the house."

The children felt scared, for they were sure Lois would find things wrong, but they set to work, nursing the hope that she might have changed.

When Lois came home on June 6, she marched straight to her bedroom without bothering them. Renee thought she'd cooled down a bit from her old ways. Maybe they gave her a pill, Grant figured. Whatever change they saw, though, did not hold. Within hours, Lois was raging at them again about everything from dust to hangers.

In truth, Lois had not responded well to the Hazelden program, and had discharged herself without staff approval.

"Lois denies and represses a great deal . . ." a Hazelden counselor wrote in a letter days after she departed. "In counseling and in group therapy Lois never became amenable to treatment, denying her need to change. She consistently blamed her childhood experiences, her mother and father, her husband and in-laws for her angry behavior. When she left treatment she continued to feel she had the 'right' to feel the way she does. In general, it was felt that the patient's response to treatment was unsatisfactory . . ."

What happened next is known but some precise details are uncertain, for the children's memories of those days remain blurred and the available juvenile records incomplete.

Robert apparently gave up first. He could see right away that Lois hadn't changed, and the disappointment and frustration he now felt consumed his remaining hope for a family. He was fifteen, and had experienced enough. Ten days after Lois's return, on June 16, Robert appeared before the Washington County family court on a delinquency-runaway petition. The judge there continued the matter for investigation and placed Robert under the custody of the Washington County welfare department, which settled him in a foster home in the nearby town of Newport. Almost six years after the Jurgenses had regained custody of their boy, Robert once again was beyond their grasp.

It remains unclear whether authorities at that time investigated the other children in the Jurgens home or evaluated Harold and Lois as parents. Almost certainly, they did not link the current problems with the thick juvenile file in neighboring Ramsey County. It is known that Renee and Grant soon began plotting their own escape. Grant remembered the lady who'd been so nice the night they were playing music, and looked up her number in the phone book. He sensed they'd be safe with her—she wouldn't make them go back to the Jurgenses.

Renee and Grant, now fifteen and fourteen, told their younger brothers they were going to leave, but Mike and Ricky, twelve and ten, were afraid to join them, fearing that if they were forced to go back to Lois after fleeing, she'd beat them.

"We'll come back to get you," Grant promised.

On July 9, Renee and Grant did not get on the school bus after summer school let out at Stillwater High. Instead, Grant, standing at a pay-phone booth, pulled a scrap of paper from his pocket and dialed the number he'd hastily scribbled down that morning. June Bol's phone rang three times before it was answered, and then it was not June, but a male voice who finally said hello to Grant.

June was away, teaching a Weight Watchers class, part of her own program for slenderizing. Her son Todd had answered the phone.

"We're at school," Grant said. "We don't want to go home. We want to come there."

When June arrived home later that afternoon, Renee and Grant were sitting in her kitchen. She reached for the phone to call her local priest. He could handle the matter, she reasoned, and she wouldn't get involved, she wouldn't have any problem. The priest was away, though, so that plan fell through. June settled in a chair across from the two children and studied their faces. She didn't even know the boy's name, there being three of them.

"We don't want to go home," Grant said.

◆   ◆   ◆

Returning to the Jurgens home from summer school that day with-out their older siblings, Ricky and Mike felt more scared than they'd ever been since leaving Kentucky. Apparently sensing something was wrong, Lois met them at the door. She'd never done that before.

"Where are Renee and Grant?" she demanded.

"We don't know," Ricky answered.

Lois exploded. "You know, you know," she shouted, grabbing and yanking their hair, pulling them by their scalps out the door and across the side yard to the car, slapping and screaming all the way. Driving to their summer school, she continued boxing them in the head and face, reaching over to them as she kept one hand on the steering wheel. "You know, you know," she kept saying. "I'll find out where they are one way or another."

At the school, Lois stormed around to teachers and counselors, but could get no answer. As far as anyone knew, Renee and Grant had climbed on the bus and gone home.

That night, Lois came looking for Renee and Grant at June Bol's house. The two women settled at the kitchen table.

"Where did they go?" Lois implored. "I'm mad at them."

Lois appeared a little angry to June, but also concerned—really more concerned than angry—and this made June feel like a rat. Actually, she felt like a scared rat. She was not so much afraid of Lois as she was of a confrontation, for June was no good at confrontation. Looking at Lois sitting so erect and stiff-necked, staring at her across the table, June wished she wasn't in this situation. Coming from such different backgrounds, it was hard to understand this woman who, like herself, seemed so much to want children. June knew only that she had never wanted to be Lois's enemy.

Renee and Grant, however, were hiding upstairs behind a closed door in June's bedroom, deathly afraid, praying for her help. An image of them cowering under the bed crossed June's mind.

"Where are they?" Lois demanded. "Did they come here? Are they here?"

June swallowed and looked Lois in the eye.

"No," she said. "No, they're not here."

CHAPTER 25

An Example Could Be Made

June Bol grew up in modest surroundings, but never considered her family poor, for her mother, baking and cooking and sewing, shielded her three children from discomfort and distress. June's father provided unbending support too, but it was of a less tranquil sort, considering the nature of his job. For twenty-two years, Herb Partridge had served as chief of police in North St. Paul. June grew up a cop's kid.

For this reason, she did not hesitate for long after Renee and Grant fled to her house. Early the next morning, July 10, she led them to her car and drove directly to Washington County Sheriff Ed Westphal's office in downtown Stillwater.

"I'm Herb Pattridge's daughter," she said to the receptionist, and that got them into the sheriff's office immediately.

"What's the matter, kids?" Westphal asked after they had settled into chairs around his desk.

Glancing at June for encouragement, Renee and Grant began to talk, their manner at first slow and halting, then increasingly animated. They told of the beatings with belt buckles, the underwear worn on their heads, the hair pulling and ear yanking, the hangers and dust. The sheriff began taking notes, his frown deepening as the stories continued. His notes spilled over to a second page, then a third, then a fourth.

When the children finished, Renee pulled a small envelope from her purse and handed it to Westphal. Looking inside, he found a clump of human hair. Then he noticed the writing Renee had scrawled on the outside of the envelope. "My hair that Mom pulled out January 3, 1975." The sheriff reached for his phone and started making calls.

We've got something going here, June thought. She looked longingly at the door, for now that the sheriff was involved, she yearned to back quietly out of the room and leave the whole matter to the authorities. All the same, she remained still in her chair.

Late that morning, the phone rang on the desk of Carol Felix, a level two social worker for the Washington County welfare department. The clerk of the court was calling.

"A Mrs. June Bol is down here," the clerk said. "She has some children in an extreme abusive situation who need protection. Judge Albertson wants you to get over here right now."

In Carol's experience, such a call was quite unusual, even singular. She'd learned over time that most people are afraid of the system and won't meddle in abuse cases. Despite the growing recognition since Henry Kempe's early writings about child abuse, despite the publicity and new laws, Carol had not seen a dramatic change in how folks responded to evidence of a battered child. And those few who did report a problem got snarled in a sluggish bureaucracy. If they managed to get through on the phone, the information still had to be written up, then sent to a supervisor, then assigned to a caseworker, who might or might not go out the next day to investigate.

As she drove the two miles from the welfare department office to the courthouse, Carol marveled at what was happening. Wow, she thought. This June Bol must have some pull.

She met Judge Howard Albertson outside his chambers. Albertson had been so disturbed by Sheriff Westphal's phone call that he'd chosen to step beyond normal channels and intervene directly with the welfare department.

"These kids are in trouble, but leave me out of it," he told Carol.

The social worker found June, Renee and Grant sitting in a small conference room off a hallway in the courthouse. June spoke first, calmly, and again Carol found this odd. She usually encountered people full of emotion and anger and manipulation, grinding personal axes, using kids as pawns in struggles of their own. Why was this lady involved?

Only gradually, as the conversation continued, did Carol relax the skepticism she'd acquired with experience. She had reason for her hesitant attitude. Felix came from an upper middle class family in the Chicago suburbs, but even within that comfortable milieu she'd been exposed as a child to alcoholism and emotional abuse, and the experiences had taken their toll. She'd come to social work late, just five years before, at the age of forty-six, after a life that included teaching, two babies, a fair amount of fiddling, a spell as a widow and a second marriage. She understood her clients because she'd been there too, and in this she felt isolated from others in her agency.

The two children were sitting quietly, depending on June to do the talking, but after sketching the background, June insisted they tell their own stories to the social worker. Carol thought Renee and Grant quite charming and physically attractive, both healthy looking with light brown hair and bright eyes, Renee's deep blue, Grant's more a greenish-blue. Speaking with the slight southern accents they had carried with them from Kentucky, they again told their story.

Carol recognized the pattern immediately. An angry mother, perfectionist, controlling, not pleased with much of anything. In her work Carol had encountered far too many like this. The children talked readily, spontaneously, in a fashion that convinced Carol they weren't manufacturing their story. These were not just rebellious teenagers.

Such a risk they were taking, Carol thought. They had no reason to trust adults, none at all. Grant and Renee didn't seem to Carol naive or foolish—they simply had figured this was the best choice available. In Carol's experience, most kids wouldn't be here—those without a June Bol run off and end up being called delinquents.

The youngsters talked warmly of their earlier lives in a Kentucky foster home, and over and over, they pleaded with Carol to look into Ricky and Mike's situation.

"We honestly tried to be good kids," Grant said.

"We're so scared about our two younger brothers," Renee said.

Carol looked at them. "You'll have to go into court," she said. "It will be difficult, but you can expect to get fair treatment from me and the judge."

Actually, Carol felt she was blurring the truth, for over time her faith in the workings of the juvenile system had diminished considerably. On the other hand, she believed this case would be a snap compared to others, for Judge Albertson would listen to what June Bol brought in. This case had that edge. Carol didn't think she'd have to fight upstream.

That same day, to get the legal process started, the social worker filed a dependency petition in the Washington County family court division on behalf of Renee, Grant, Mike and Ricky. Continuing the matter for investigation, Judge Albertson placed Renee and Grant in temporary foster care under custody and control of the Washington County welfare department, while Mike and Ricky remained in the Jurgens home under the welfare department's protective supervision.

Again, blurred memories and available documents offer only a general picture of what happened next. It is known that Grant eventually went to live at June Bol's home and Renee to Bonnie Welsch's in St. Paul. It is less clear just what type of protective supervision Washington County provided Mike and Ricky in the Jurgens home, or how their lives fared. It can be said with certainty that by August, after more than one preliminary hearing in Washington County family court, the four shaken Howton youths were scattered in three different houses. The Kentucky officials' extended effort to keep the children together was now only a failed vision.

Grant, at least, had finally found a home. During his early weeks in the Bol house, he slept tightly curled in a fetal position, waking up in the middle of the night in a cold sweat. June, not unlike her way years before with Robert, would rub his back to relax him and assure him he was not in physical danger.

Lois apparently contained herself in the face of these events, and did not openly display anger to June, for a court hearing was pending. But she managed to communicate her message all the same. Asked to send over some of the children's clothes, Lois delivered a meager sack that included, among other items, a piece of lead pipe and dirty socks. One night soon after, Lois called and asked June how the kids liked their clothes.

June figured she wasn't going to outbite this lady.

"Well," she said, "they found a lot of things that they were looking for."

The task of investigating the Jurgens case and preparing a report for the court had fallen to Carol Felix. Her initial move was to interview

Harold and Lois, and this she did for the first time just days after Renee and Grant fled their home.

The afternoon she gunned her car up the Jurgenses' steep driveway, the Minnesota summer was at full force—the temperature near ninety, the bright sun filling a clear blue sky—but the Jurgens house, surrounded by its shield of tall elms, remained insulated in its own dark, cool pocket. At the door, Lois, her guard held high, was only minimally polite. At least she opened the door and let me in, Carol told herself.

Harold stood in the entry area, looking scared. Carol could feel his fear, and knew he didn't want to talk. If he's afraid of me, she thought, what about Lois?

Harold soon receded into the background, and Lois quickly seized control of the conversation, telling Carol what she was doing all around the house. A long and difficult reupholstering project, it seemed, was just then occupying much of her time and energy.

Carol looked around the house, which appeared to her large and beautiful, quite well furnished and cared for. Floral ornaments and Early American fixtures filled the rooms, as did Lois's handiwork as a seamstress. Jesus was also much in evidence—there was a cross or picture in almost every room.

She's not just sure of herself, Carol thought, but also of God. At least of Jesus, anyway—they're very close, that's apparent.

The two women were just one year apart in age, and Carol thought Lois at fifty was very pretty, a little overweight and matronly but dark and buxom, reminiscent of Liz Taylor. Lois's manner, however, was rigid, without even a hint of expression, her anger palpable. As they talked, Carol found her defensive, wary, imposing and aggressive. Lois had an unusually bright glare in her eye, a look that suggested to Carol a "touch me and I'll kill you" attitude.

That's okay, Carol thought. I'll have my way in court no matter what Lois does now.

Asked about the reports of abuse, Lois talked instead of all the things she and Harold had done for the kids, expressing particular pride in the music lessons and clothes and Stillwater life-style. Lois guided Carol through a tour of the entire house. It all was very lovely, so Carol complimented Lois, which pleased her greatly. Over and over, Lois emphasized her industriousness and talked of how hard she worked.

As the visit wore on, Lois gradually began to express her feelings more freely.

"These kids don't appreciate anything," she said suddenly, while moving from room to room.

"I can't get these kids to do anything," she added a few minutes later.

Lois's odyssey just then veered outside to a shed and storage area.

"Look at what a mess this is," she said. "They're lazy. They don't want to do their jobs or keep things neat."

A full barrage followed soon after.

Grant and Renee are selfish and greedy children, Lois said. They enjoyed the many things we gave them but are thankless and unappreciative of our good care. It's grown more and more difficult to handle these children. They won't take on the responsibilities assigned them without a lot of forcing.

Renee seemed a particular thorn to Lois. She wouldn't wear the clothes they bought, Lois complained. She wouldn't respond at all. She tries to take over Lois's role as mother with her younger brothers.

Carol avoided much discussion about Mike and Ricky, for she wanted to talk with the boys first, and they weren't home. Instead, the social worker again raised the matter of physical abuse, and Lois angrily dismissed her.

"It's discipline," she insisted. "Kids don't know what that is, but they need it, so I'm giving it to them. They don't understand, but they need the discipline."

Carol next visited Robert. He was not her main concern for he had his own caseworker, but the court had folded his runaway case in with the others so Felix needed to include him in her report. She found Robert adjusting well to his foster placement. She thought him exceptionally serious and responsible for a fifteen-year-old, able to talk with maturity and detachment about his parents.

Although he felt a strong attachment to the Jurgenses, Robert said, he could no longer endure the tension and fights. He didn't want to hurt his parents deliberately, and he knew that they loved him in their way, particularly his father, but he had given up on the idea of living in their home.

Carol had seen hundreds like this one. Years later, in fact, she couldn't remember Robert. There were so many of them—children from abusive problem homes who run away but in truth love their families even while hating them. Robert seemed as ambivalent as any of them. The less interference the better in these cases, Carol had decided. You can't intervene in such parent-child relationships, you can't alter the dynamics of these relationships. You just help the kids into foster homes where possible and try to keep them afloat until they're eighteen and out on their own. Carol quickly decided she'd support Robert's desire to remain in a foster home.

In a way, Mike and Ricky were the toughest to figure. Carol visited them twice in the Jurgens home. Alone in a room without Lois present, both insisted they wanted to remain with Harold and Lois. Speaking to Carol separately, though, both used almost precisely the same words, so the social worker wondered how much weight to put on their statements.

Puzzling out the case, Carol found herself spending hours over at June Bol's house. She came there partly because her job involved visiting with Grant, but she had another reason as well—she wanted to see June. The Bol house was so normal, so much the way things should be, but never were, in the world Carol saw in her work. June provided direction. When Carol had reached a particular judgment or decision, she'd check it with June, and if they agreed, the social worker knew she was on the right track.

One day, June had a suggestion for Carol: Why didn't she read the Ramsey County file on the Jurgenses? She might find interesting material there.

So Carol set aside half a day and drove the twenty miles to downtown St. Paul. The file brought to her in the Ramsey County welfare department was stuffed with documents—a far thicker package than Carol had expected. She settled at a spare desk and started reading. As she turned the pages, the blood rose to her head until she felt dizzy. The details of Dennis's placement and death, all news to her, were assaulting her like a burst of needles.

Lois had streamrolled her way through as people looked the other way. Carol knew this was a murder—there was no doubt in her mind that Lois had killed Dennis. Robert's eventual return four years later didn't shock her in the same way—social workers were always under pressure to get a kid back in the family, and it was standard for things to get watered down over time.

Carol made photocopies of the file. You poor people, she thought as she worked the copier and looked around the welfare department's office. You don't know what you're giving me.

Back at her own office in Washington County the next morning, she slammed the file down on the desk of her ally and colleague, Marsha Wilensky. "Look at what I've got here," she said.

Wilensky was a calm, contained woman, just the opposite of her explosive friend, but as she turned the pages in the Jurgens file and listened to Carol's story, her eyes grew round. Wilensky was as detached as ever, but absorbed.

Soon after, through Lutheran Social Service and her own department, Carol also got her hands on part of the Kentucky files, and began to unravel the ways that the four Howton children had come to be placed at the Jurgenses. She called Jackie Oliver and Sue Howard and Peter Crego in Kentucky, but couldn't find Bob Lageson, for he'd left the Lutheran agency and adoption work. Oliver confirmed what she'd surmised—Kentucky had jumped at the placement because the Jurgenses were willing to take all four children.

Then, in August, Carol met the children's original foster mother. Cherie Colling, remarried after her divorce, now Cherie Riley, came to Minnesota.

June Bol had suggested to Renee and Grant that they call their Kentucky parents, since they seemed to care so much for them. The children had no phone number, but they remembered that Cherie's parents owned a store—Buchanon's Tile and Carpet—in the small Kentucky town of Eddyville. June instructed them how to dial for long distance directory assistance, and minutes later, Renee was talking to her foster grandmother.

Donna Buchanon was fit to be tied when she learned all that had happened since she'd last seen the Howton kids. She and Cherie flew to Minnesota the next day, rented a car and drove directly to June's house. The tearful reunion soon gave way to a fact-finding session. Renee told of letters she wrote to Cherie that Lois had intercepted before they could be mailed. June talked of Dennis's suspicious death. Both Renee and Grant described life in the Jurgens home, their hands curling into fists and their shoulders stiffening as they spoke.

From the Bols' house, Cherie Riley and Donna Buchanon drove the half mile down Nolan Avenue to visit Mike and Ricky at the

Jurgenses. Again, the two younger boys insisted everything was fine, but their eyes were jumpy, touched by fear.

Cherie felt shocked, at this and what she'd seen over at the Bols'. These four kids, once so open and loving, now seemed like frightened animals, thinking solely of survival. What a change in three short years.

As she was leaving, Cherie leaned over to Ricky and Mike. "You should try to run away," she whispered.

It was later the same day that Cherie and her mother met Carol Felix. The social worker showed them the piles of reports, and a gruesome photo of a dead child, a boy who had once lived in the Jurgens home. As the three women talked over the matter in hushed voices, Carol felt a loving bond with these big, wide southern women, both so upset just now, and she felt compelled to act.

No longer was this just a juvenile custody petition. She wanted punishments exacted, justice delivered, wrongs made right. Carol wasn't thinking of a murder prosecution, for she was out to expose the system, not Lois. Her anger was aimed at the people and agencies who had allowed all this, who would, if not uncloaked, keep spitting out other damaged or dead kids. Soon letters and phone calls were flying from her desk. She wrote to Lutheran Social Service, she wrote to the Ramsey County welfare department, she called Shirley Pierce, head of Ramsey's child abuse team. Pierce recalled the case—"Yes," Felix later remembered Pierce saying, "we goofed on that one, we were just starting out then"—but that was the only response Carol ever drew. She could find no one interested in digging up what she considered to be a scandal. Her own supervisor was not encouraging.

Then a thought occurred to Carol: Why should any of these people be willing to reopen all this? These are their mistakes, after all. Instead of turning to them for remedy, Carol decided she'd look to the court. She would put everything she'd learned into the report she was preparing for Judge Albertson.

And that's just what she did. The whole sorry tale, combined with her present assessment, required seven pages, single-spaced.

"My outrage in looking at this matter in hindsight is such that I feel Lutheran Social Service and the Kentucky agency should be chastised for gross negligence in making this placement," she concluded. "The matter is now three years old, it is true, but I feel that an example could be made in this case in the hope that such negligence might be prevented in the future."

After several continuations, the dispositional hearing in the Washington County family court division unfolded on September 19, 1975. Cherie Riley and her new husband Jerry attended, as did June Bol, Bonnie Welsch and Carol Felix. Lois and Harold came with Ed Donohue, the same attorney who'd battled for them before Judge Gingold.

There was to be no repeat of those scenes, however. Donohue, veteran barrister that he was, still couldn't believe this was happening all over again. He'd urgently advised the Jurgenses not to fight this time, and they had agreed. The kids were much older now, he reasoned, so could battle back. The attorney, of course, had an even more compelling reason for his reticence. Donohue feared a contested hearing now might very well reopen what he'd labored so long to keep closed—the 1965 death of Dennis Jurgens.

June Bol had to testify with Lois sitting right before her, a task that made her cringe. More than once, Lois responded to what was said on the stand by making a noise and shaking her head at her lawyer. When Cherie Riley looked over at her, Lois stuck her tongue out. Other times, Lois cried. Her sobs were so wrenching they made June feel terrible, for she hated to hurt someone in that way.

"I'm not worrying about her," the judge reassured June in chambers. "I'm not here to take care of her, I'm here to protect these children."

That made June feel better. Albertson, in appearance, reminded her of a little toad, but she thought him a wonderful judge.

In her report, Carol Felix had recommended that the court interview Mike and Ricky privately to determine their true desires, so now, near the end of the hearing, Albertson invited them into his chambers. When the judge asked where they wanted to live, Mike and Ricky looked at each other, hesitating, scared, saying nothing.

It's now or never, Ricky finally decided. "Yeah, I wanna be moved, but me and Mike are gonna stick together. We've always lived together." He turned to his brother.

"Okay," Mike said.

Back in the courtroom, the two young boys were sitting on Harold's knees when the judge revealed the children's wishes, and despite everything, Ricky felt bad for his adoptive father. Minutes later Albertson placed all the children in the custody of Washington County.

For the time being, Grant ended up living at the Bols', Renee with Bonnie and Mike Welsch, Mike and Ricky in a third foster home, Robert in yet another. Soon after, Mike and Ricky moved to Kentucky and rejoined Cherie Riley's family. A half year later, on March 19, 1976, following further evaluations and another hearing, the judge permanently terminated the Jurgenses' parental rights to all five of their children. Lois Jurgens's persistent dream of creating a family had finally come to an end.

In his ruling, however, the judge displayed no inclination to right distant wrongs. He never addressed the history so emphatically detailed by Carol Felix. And years later, he refused even to discuss the case, adamantly insisting he had no memory of it at all.

Oh, well, at least I was right, this one was a snap, Carol told herself when it was all over. Funny, really—I have Dennis's death to thank for the ease of this case.

CHAPTER 26

The Bubble Bursts

No one now can say precisely when the street parties ended in Gardenette Park, but by 1967, when the Jurgenses moved away, time and events had subdued the once-vital White Bear Lake neighborhood. Unexpected and untimely death now was visiting other homes on Gardenette Drive—for a while it seemed as if an epidemic of premature dying had taken hold in the neighborhood.

There was, first of all, Leslie Manley, just thirty-six, mother of four young deaf children, the youngest only two. Camille Brass and the other neighbors thought it might have been a suicide, but as they understood it, even after an autopsy the authorities never could decide on a physical cause of death. One of the deaf boys, talking through an interpreter in his low, halting, drawn-out voice, told the neighbors, "My mother died of a deep depression," which just amazed Cam, for she knew people didn't die of depression. Cam had visited her neighbor just the day before, and Leslie had shown off her freshly painted pink kitchen and her new dress and the coffee table her son had made. Her oldest boy, Eddie, came home from school the next day and found her on the floor, the TV turned to "As the World Turns," the little two-year-old running around, a cheese sandwich and tomato soup on the table for lunch. Eddie ran by Camille's house yelling "Mother . . . floor . . . blue." Cam and the other neighbors hurried over, but were so unnerved they couldn't find the telephone. Finally Jim Lane, a White Bear police officer, came by and shook his head. The Shriners brought her husband Larry home. Leslie wore her new dress in the coffin.

Not long after, Helen Barson, also just thirty-six—what was it about that age?—died of a bleeding ulcer, leaving another bunch of kids motherless. Then there was Dave Strathman, a good-looking youth in his late teens. He'd walked through Cam's yard just the week before, and she thought him so handsome. Cam wasn't sure whether it was carbon monoxide in the garage or something else, but after the suicide, she'd see Dave's father walking up and down the block, back and forth, evening after evening. Soon he and his wife divorced and moved away. Bill Newson, so young and smart, also killed himself around then. This one Cam knew for sure was carbon monoxide, up on White Bear Avenue. As Cam understood it, he just couldn't stand all the evil in the world.

The world did seem full of trouble, if you let it get to you. All around the Brasses, friends and colleagues were suffering midlife crises, leaving wives, changing jobs, turning with just a little too much relish to their evening cocktails. The ranks of the local Alcoholics Anonymous chapter were growing at a rapid clip.

The strange, untimely deaths left some of those remaining in Gardenette Park feeling uncomfortable, as if their neighborhood was haunted. Maybe it was that thought, some allowed later, that hastened their own departures. Not much more than a year after the Jurgenses left, the Brasses too moved from Gardenette Drive, buying a somewhat larger house eight blocks farther south. Then the Jurgenses' old next-door neighbors, the DeMarses, also relocated, moving to a house almost directly across the street from the Brasses' new home. When Dorothy Engfer's husband Howard died, she took off for Florida. Donna and Tom Neely moved to a new home built in an open reach on the outskirts of town.

In truth, it was not just Gardenette Park where people scattered and aspirations dimmed during the late 1960s and early 1970s, but all of White Bear Lake. The town's energy and hopes, rising out of the promise of the postwar boom, had collided with the more difficult realities then taking hold throughout the country.

A generation before, White Bear's citizens, eager to forge their lives, had happily put memories of a monstrous war behind them, but now the horrors of combat once again demanded their attention. Local boys, their sons, were dying in Vietnam, and the bitter debate over the United States's involvement intruded insistently on the town. At 8:00 P.M. on October 13, 1967, some six hundred people jammed the White Bear Lake High auditorium for a panel discussion on "Vietnam: Pro & Con." Congressmen and Veterans of Foreign Wars figures, introduced by Mayor Milt Knoll, argued far into the night.

A month later, White Bear citizens, after years of unwavering support, for the first time voted down a school bond issue, rejecting a requested $5.8 million for a new high school and assorted other facilities.

The next spring, the town's changing attitude toward the schools spread to the teachers. A salary dispute grew acrimonious, with the teachers demanding a $6,650 beginning salary, the school board offering no more than $6,000. In April, angry and frustrated, White Bear teachers resigned all their extracurricular jobs at the schools, and parents retaliated by signing petitions supporting the school board and urging its members not to go higher. In time, after students staged a walkout on behalf of the teachers, a compromise was reached, but concerned citizens wondered how the deal would affect their taxes.

They had reason to worry, for homeowners comprised almost all of White Bear's tax base, and this lurked at the heart of the dispute.

The town had never grown nearly as large as its leaders had expected and planned. Despite their All-America City award, the chamber of commerce boosters—Bill LeVasseur and Bob Brass and all the others—had never attracted the commerce and industry they needed. Nor had they captured the adjoining land they coveted— Gem Lake and Vadnais Heights and the unincorporated townships resisted repeated efforts at annexation. The Reynolds aluminum plant, once seen as the beginning of an industrial park, shut down in 1968 because of a strike by the machinists' union, then was shuttered for good in 1969 when the Hamms Brewing Company in St. Paul decided to make its own cans. The town's population, projected to reach 70,000, stopped growing at 22,000 and never started up again. In time, schools built in the late 1950s and early 1960s fell vacant, and teachers were laid off. By 1971, there was talk again of a "downtown redesign," and Dave Olson of Dave's Courtyard was named chairman of a study committee on the annexation issue. In truth, though, White Bear had become a bedroom community, part of a contiguous stretch of suburbs connected to St. Paul by the new interstate highways.

The regional shopping centers to the south had prevailed. At his Ben Franklin store, Bob Brass cashed far more checks from people living in the lightly populated region north of town than he did from White Bear's own affluent, densely settled southern half. With a sprawling chain supermarket now claiming a full city block in downtown White Bear, Bill LeVasseur in 1967 closed his family's historic fifty-five-year-old grocery store. Jantzen's Motel and Restaurant, started by Bill Jantzen as a few cabins on Goose Lake in the early 1940s, became a Best Western.

During this period, the White Bear Lake police force experienced its own particular transition.

A new young city manager arrived in 1967. Steve Bernard, twenty-seven, had a master's degree in city management and a preference for dynamic leaders. Police Chief Wayne Armstrong did not satisfy this penchant. The city manager thought Armstrong was trying his best to do a good job, but simply wasn't up to the challenge of making decisions or managing people.

In late February of 1969, after Armstrong had repeatedly declined Bernard's invitation to resign, the city manager suspended the police chief, pending a hearing before the town's police civil service commission. The hearing proved unnecessary, for days later, on March 5, Armstrong submitted his written resignation, citing "differences in approaches and personalities."

Lieutenant Jerome Zerwas served as acting chief for the next six months, but his legendary aversion to taking written tests—the mere thought seemed to produce the shakes—precluded him from competing for the permanent job. In late August, after sifting through thirty applicants, Bob Brass and his two fellow police commissioners named Scotty Kline the new chief.

Kline was quite unlike Armstrong. A veteran of World War II, Korea and twenty-two years on the Minneapolis police force, the last five as deputy inspector, he was, at fifty, both streetwise and a good handshaker. He soon reorganized the twenty-two-man force, drafting new rules and regulations, spotting the good and bad policework, rearranging assignments. In 1970 he appointed Pete Korolchuk his administrative lieutenant. Jerome Zerwas, needless to say, no longer ran the department. He took to calling Kline "the longshoreman" and found he had nothing good to say about the man.

Jerome's reach was also contracting for physical reasons. In January of 1968 he injured a knee, striking it against the door of a squad car when he slipped on a patch of ice. He returned to work in five days, without X-rays being taken, but the discomfort persisted for years—periodically, the knee would lock so badly Jerome couldn't walk. In January of 1973 Jerome finally visited an orthopedic surgeon. After X-rays revealed a bone chip the size of a lima bean, Jerome underwent surgery on January 29, leaving the department on what he believed was temporary disability. Ron Meehan settled at Jerome's desk, thinking he was assuming the chief investigator's role for three or four months, tops.

Jerome's surgery, however, proved problematic. He emerged with a circulation problem in his left foot, and spent six months in a wheelchair and six more months on crutches before moving on to therapy and a cane. When his doctor finally said he "thought" Jerome could return to work, Steve Bernard did not appear overly inclined to welcome him back. Jerome visited him on June 13, 1974, bearing a letter of endorsement from his surgeon, but Bernard asked that he see a doctor of the city's choice. This Jerome did, obtaining a second letter that repeated the first physician's judgment. Still dubious, Bernard wanted Jerome to take an agility test. Jerome objected. He was then forty-six, a twenty-four-year veteran of the force, with more seniority than any other city employee. The agility test, he argued, was unfair and irrelevant to his job.

Just then, the White Bear police force underwent yet another change in leadership. In late August, Scotty Kline resigned to join the Washington County sheriff's office, and on September 13, Bernard appointed Korolchuk acting chief. Pete was now Jerome Zerwas's boss.

Since Korolchuk had once worked for him, and as a boy had lived in the Zerwas home for two years, Jerome had reason to expect a certain consideration from the new acting chief, but this was not forthcoming. There had been chilly relations between the two men in recent years. In fact, their strained feelings had been noticeable to others in the department since 1965—since the spring of 1965, to be precise. Korolchuk apparently was not inclined to intervene on Jerome's behalf.

In early October, Jerome filed a complaint against the city, charging White Bear Lake with discrimination for preventing him from returning to work. He had complied with the request to see a doctor, Jerome told the local newspaper. "Now I want to go back to work."

Asked for comment, acting chief Korolchuk said the dispute involves "city policy, to be handled by the city manager's office." City manager Steve Bernard told the newspaper it was a "complex situation" and an "internal personnel matter." He also said: "The city has to test a man to see if he is still fit for the job."

The dispute ended the next month, when Jerome agreed to take the agility test. Half a dozen men gathered early one chilly November morning in the parking structure of the First National Bank building in downtown St. Paul. While Bernard, the city's doctor and the city attorney watched, Jerome, still lean and muscled a month short of his forty-seventh birthday, easily sprinted up and down a ramp, tossing an inflated tire rim about as if it were a balloon.

"The test wasn't really that bad," Jerome told the local White Bear reporter afterward.

"All it took was to determine if he could pass the test," Bernard said. "We're happy to have him back."

Jerome returned to work on Monday, November 25, twenty-two months after leaving. He did not, however, resume his old job as chief investigator. Due to a "structural change" and Kline's resignation, Korolchuk explained, "we no longer have the investigative lieutenant's post." Jerome instead had an inside desk job, his office a cramped cubbyhole without a window.

"This is something new for Jerry," his wife Rose told the local newspaper. "He's inside a lot but he's glad."

Jerome lasted just seven months behind the desk. When he sat for extended periods, his leg locked on him worse than if he were running the parking ramp. On July 1, 1975, Jerome left the White Bear force on permanent disability, and a year later moved thirty-two miles north to Elk River.

After two or three more shuffles of personnel, Pete Korolchuk in December of 1976 became the permanent chief of the White Bear Lake police force, a position he held with honor until his retirement in 1983.

Bob VanderWyst by then had long since drifted away from police work. When his father died in 1970, he took over the family's dry cleaning shop, but after that business faltered in the wake of the wash and wear trend, VanderWyst turned to dairy farming in the Wisconsin country-side, in time running 120 cows on 640 acres. His pals on the force still came around, plugging in a radio or a phonograph and holding barn dances. At one New Year's Eve party, Korolchuk walked around with a hair net over his head, while Ron Meehan and VanderWyst playfully hawked what they billed as hangover pills, supplied by Doc Peterson, that made everyone pee purple. One moonless night in the fall of 1973, the whole gang hooked a wagon to a trailer and took a hayride through VanderWyst's pastures. The cows came around, so they shut down the engine and sat quietly in the sable stillness, the night and the black heifers together so dark no one could see them.

VanderWyst loved such moments, but in truth, he was not all that oriented to running a business. Breeding records and feeding schedules became confused, milk prices plummeted, and the debt on machinery rose. VanderWyst grew tired of rising at four in the morning and working until ten at night, and none of his eight chil-dren expressed an interest in taking over, so in 1978 he sold out and took a job driving a long-haul truck.

Sometimes over these years, he'd wake up in the middle of the night thinking about Dennis Jurgens. He had grown accustomed to such moments, for they were not uncommon. He had long tried to wipe the case from his mind, but he'd come to believe there were some things you just couldn't forget.

Passing through White Bear Lake one day in the spring of 1979, VanderWyst on an impulse dropped by Dr. Peterson's office unan-nounced, simply to visit. Peterson still had his old-fashioned store-front on Fourth Street, but the years had brought changes, just as they had for everyone else. There'd been a divorce from his wife Lau-rie and a second marriage. There'd also been some trouble with the Minnesota board of medical examiners over the doctor's liberal atti-tude toward his prescription pad. On December 16, 1977, Peterson had signed a stipulation with the state board, agreeing to an order that prohibited him from prescribing, administering or dispensing any schedule II amphetamines or controlled substance anorectics, as listed in Minnesota statutes. Those in White Bear seeking speed or diet pills were now obliged to look elsewhere.

When he walked in, VanderWyst found Peterson's office full of waiting patients.

"I'd just like to talk to the doctor for a moment," he said. "I live out of town now and I'm passing through, so I'd like to say hello."

The nurse looked dubious. "He's awfully busy," she said.

Just then Peterson emerged from an examination room and came walking down the hallway. He was graying now around the temples, but appeared as kinetic and hurried as ever. When he saw VanderWyst, he changed course and walked to his side, greeting him with a handshake.

"Well, Bob, what do you want?"

"I just wanted to say hello. I don't get in town too often anymore and just wanted to say that everything's fine."

Peterson looked down the hallway at his five rooms full of waiting patients, then put his hand on the small of VanderWyst's back. "Come on to the back," he said.

The two men settled in chairs in the doctor's office and talked warmly of the past. Their conversation meandered easily, without a pointed direction, touching on memories of friends and family. Peterson wondered what kind of work VanderWyst now was doing, and asked after his children and wife. They talked about trucking and farming and doctoring. They smoked cigarettes—VanderWyst one after another, Peterson spacing his out, rewarding himself at intervals.

After forty-five minutes, they rose and shook hands, vowing to keep in touch. VanderWyst turned down the hallway and walked out the front door onto Fourth Street. He felt glad he had stopped by, for the doctor had been bubbly and animated, clearly happy to see him.

Neither man had mentioned anything about the events of Palm Sunday 1965.

CHAPTER 27

The Loss Case

At 3:45 P.M. on Saturday afternoon, March 13, 1971, a six-month-old baby boy named Lance Running arrived in the emergency room of St. Paul–Ramsey Hospital, carried in the arms of a frantic St. Paul policeman. A hospital resident, pediatrician Dr. Sharon Libit, rushed to their side and leaned over the infant as the officer placed him on an examining table. The baby, average-sized with sparse light brown hair, was wearing a blue and white terry cloth sleeper over a diaper, plastic pants, and an undershirt. He had a tannish bruise about one centimeter in diameter on his forehead and a purplish bruise about two and a half centimeters in diameter on the top of his skull over his left ear. His skin was pale and mottled, his pupils dilated and fixed. Lance had neither pulse nor breath.

Dr. Libit, realizing the infant was in full cardiorespiratory arrest, began emergency resuscitation, which proved successful for the moment. Within an hour, Lance, hooked to a respirator, had been transferred to the pediatric ward. Between seven and eight o'clock that evening, a physician there contacted Dr. Homer Venters, head of the hospital's department of pediatrics, who promptly assumed control of the baby's case, ordering X-rays and a spinal tap.

Studying the results that came from the radiologist, Venters felt weary. The X-rays revealed fractures of the midfront to left region of Lance's skull and of the long bones in his left leg. The lumbar puncture yielded bloody spinal fluid. The baby was hemorrhaging blood under his skull.

Venters leafed through the admitting forms. According to the history provided by the parents, Lance had been well until one week before, when he developed a moderate respiratory infection and received treatment from the family physician. This morning, on the day of admission, he'd appeared somewhat sleepy, and had taken only one-and-a-half ounces of pineapple juice. This afternoon, the father said, he'd put Lance to bed, then minutes later had discovered he no longer was breathing. The father—a young man named Danny Loss, not married to the baby's mother—had called the fire department rescue squad and police, and Lance was at the hospital within fifteen minutes.

Venters slapped the reports on his desk.

It's amazing to see how patently false some parents' stories are, he thought.

In the early 1950s, he knew, this case would have been an enigma. They would have thought it didn't make sense, but they wouldn't have made the real connections. It was all just common sense, but they'd needed Kempe's workshop in Colorado to convince them that parents really did kill their kids. The Denver experience had dissolved their worries of being vigilantes. Even though they were the parents' confidants, Kempe taught them, their patient was the child. Since coming back from Colorado two years before, Venters and his department had handled more than one hundred battered-child syndrome cases. Skull and spiral long bone fractures were the most frequently encountered of all injuries in battered children—Lance was a textbook example. What just a few years ago had been a source of puzzlement was now something all too familiar, and not only to the experts.

Venters knew Lance's fate, but figured he'd wait the night out and give nature a chance.

By half past eleven the next morning, Sunday, March 14, there seemed little point in further effort. Examining the baby, Venters noted a fresh purple bruise over the left side of the forehead, which suggested the bleeding under the skull was continuing. The infant was flaccid and unresponsive to light or deep, painful stimuli. Venters could see hemorrhages in his eyes. A consulting neurosurgeon suggested that Lance was brain dead, and Venters had to agree—the baby, for all practical purposes, was being kept alive by artificial means. At 12:20 P.M., doctors took him off the respirator, and when he did not start breathing on his own, they vainly attempted resuscitation. Venters pronounced Lance dead at 12:40 P.M.

There was no question in Venters's mind about this baby. For cause of death, he wrote "brain injury, secondary to battered-child syndrome." The more problematic question, as always, was how to handle such a case, but it was not as thorny an issue as it once had been. Just six years after Dennis Jurgens's death, another child's murder in Ramsey County was about to draw a considerably different response.

The resulting prosecution, *State of Minnesota v. Daniel Alan Loss*, would eventually yield a landmark Minnesota Supreme Court decision, one that would fundamentally alter the way the judicial system approached matters of child abuse. In later years, judges such as Archie Gingold would regularly hail *State v. Loss* in speeches, and county attorneys would cite it in arguments. *State v. Loss's* influence would reach into the past as well as the future. The Loss case would provide prosecutors the opportunity to look once more at the events of Palm Sunday 1965.

Minutes after Lance died, Dr. Venters reached for his phone, and soon St. Paul police lieutenant Carolen Bailey's car radio sputtered to life. Go to St. Paul–Ramsey, fourth floor, the dispatcher said—the pediatrics department.

Knowing where the call came from, Bailey reported to Venters's office. "What do we have this time, Homer?" she asked as she marched through the door and settled in a chair.

For years in St. Paul, Bailey had comprised all there was of the police department's child abuse team. She'd worked in child protection for the Ramsey County welfare department from 1957 to 1961, before joining the force in the juvenile division. The early sixties had been a frustrating time for her. She'd refer cases to the welfare department and the county attorney, but could get no reaction, even though she was a forceful woman with a confident manner and a penchant for getting things done. People simply were not interested in her type of cases. Once Bailey listened to a mother not only confess to suffocating her infant with pillows and cellophane, but also to smothering two other babies. Investigating further, Bailey discovered the mother had already admitted all this to a St. Paul–Ramsey doctor, who had dismissed her confession, saying she was delusional.

Such working conditions finally changed for Bailey after she attended Kempe's workshop in Denver, even though smart and caring people still, on occasion, had trouble acknowledging what parents did to their kids. Recently, Bailey had rushed a two-year-old boy to the hospital who looked as if he'd been run over by a truck or thrown out a six-story window. When she called Dr. Venters to voice her suspicions, he seemed aghast. "But the mother has been pacing the hallway all night. I can't believe she'd beat him to death," the doctor had said. "Homer," Bailey had responded, "you know better than that." As it happened, the mother had just confessed to Bailey that she'd walloped the boy with a wooden hanger, and had supplemented her confession by producing the hanger.

Presented with a brief summary of Lance Running's death that Sunday afternoon, Bailey swung into action. By the end of the next day, she'd taken photos of the body, run a records check on Lance's parents, consulted with county child abuse team coordinator Shirley Pierce and interviewed half a dozen people—emergency room doctors, the pathologists who conducted the autopsy, Lance's family physician, Lance's mother, Lynn Running, and Lance's father, Danny Loss.

What Bailey heard could have been echoes of the accounts gathered by two other police officers as they drove through White Bear Lake six years before.

The pathologist, Dr. Wayne Schrader, told Bailey the skull fracture he'd seen during the autopsy could only occur from a drop or fall to a hard surface, or from a blow by a blunt instrument. Assorted bruises on the baby's head and forehead were of varying colors, indicating some older, some fresh.

The family physician, Dr. William Watson, told Bailey he'd never seen trauma on Lance or evidence of child battering. Just a week before he'd seen Lance for a swollen, discolored left foot, and had accepted the mother's explanation that "the puppy got ahold of it," although he could see no teeth marks. The baby that day had been clean, neat and healthy, the mother cooing and hugging and loving up her infant. The baby's leg had not been fractured then, the doctor said, but he might not have observed a skull fracture if it existed.

Bailey, finding Lynn Running at her parents' house on Herschel Street, took her into a bedroom to talk alone. Lynn was a good-looking young woman of nineteen, visibly overwhelmed by the events of the past few hours. She had been living with her parents when Lance was born, and had moved into an apartment with Danny only in the previous month, after he was legally judged to be the baby's father.

Lynn had never seen Danny hit the baby, she told Bailey, "but I know it irritates him quite a bit when the baby is crying." He swears at the infant and shouts such things as "Goddamn, go to sleep." When Lance was crying in another room with Danny, Lynn at times heard the baby suddenly cry harder. Loss had a "hot temper," Lynn allowed, but she was very much in love with him. They planned to marry in July when he had enough money to buy a trailer home.

The Ramsey County child abuse team, at its regular Tuesday meeting two days after Lance died, concluded this was beyond doubt a battered-child case. Soon after, Dr. Venters drafted a letter to Captain Ernest Williams, head of the St. Paul police homicide bureau. It was concise and direct, quite unlike any document or judgment produced on the occasion of Dennis Jurgens's death.

"Enclosed please find a copy of my hospital report on Lance Running, who . . . on evaluation was found to be a battered child," he wrote. "The injuries noted on examination of this patient . . . are, in my opinion, such that (they) could not have happened by accident. Therefore, we made a diagnosis of battered-child syndrome."

Despite such an unequivocal statement, the authorities had a problem. However obvious the matter seemed to Dr. Venters, Lieutenant Bailey and the child abuse team, the evidence in the Loss case was entirely circumstantial, and would require a jury to make one or two sizable inferences. Danny Loss had been alone with the baby, but there simply was no direct proof of what he had done, or how the fatal injuries were inflicted.

For this reason, Carolen Bailey had carefully framed her questions and composed her reports, purposely including information related not just to the facts of the death, but also more generally to the battered-child syndrome. For some time, the county child abuse team had been looking to set precedent, and the details of the Loss case—Danny's personality, his temper, certain incidents with the baby—seemed to provide a fitting opportunity, especially since two veterans from the Colorado conference, Bailey and Venters, were involved with this one.

When she completed her investigation, Bailey carried her file to the charging attorney in the Ramsey County attorney's office. Times hadn't changed that much since 1965—Paul Lindholm once again would decide whether a child's death merited prosecution.

Bailey considered Lindholm typical of the county attorneys—they were, she felt, more concerned with their won-lost record than anything else—so she knew she had to give him more than enough to move on. Lindholm, in turn, tended to look with skepticism at files Bailey brought him, for he felt she often let her enthusiasms and emotions color her judgment of cases. The two squared off one morning in late March in Lindholm's small office.

Bailey first spelled out the hard details of the case, then began to paint a word picture of all they'd learned in Denver two years before. The policewoman talked of twisted long bone fractures and subdural hematomas and battering parent characteristics. Reaching into a second file, she spread before Lindholm articles by Drs. Kempe and Steele and others.

Lindholm considered. The battered-child syndrome, if not yet a household phrase, was by then nine years old and no longer obscure. All the same, there was no telling how it could be used in court. As Lindholm mulled this issue, he recalled that one of the young attorneys who reported to him, John Tuohy, had wangled a free skiing trip to Colorado by signing up to attend Kempe's conference. This Loss case, Lindholm reasoned, might be a chance to collect on that trip. Tuohy should know all about the battered-child syndrome.

On April 6, Lindholm took the case to a Ramsey County grand jury, which that same day indicted Daniel Alan Loss on two counts—third-degree murder and first-degree manslaughter. Loss pleaded not guilty at an arraignment on April 23.

John Tuohy began to prepare his prosecution. Sitting at his desk, he spread before him the Loss case reports, the materials he'd brought back from Colorado and a scholarly essay by a University of Minnesota professor—something Tuohy had found while rummaging through his old law school materials. Tuohy couldn't remember reading this article while studying law from 1964 to 1967, even though the author was a professor at his school, but then again, in

1965 he was a young man without children of his own, and the topic hadn't been important to him.

On a legal-size ruled yellow pad, Tuohy began taking notes and drawing lists. He'd come to law after first training as an accountant, and his inclination toward ordered precision was apparent.

Under "Essence of the Case," he compiled three items.

There was the syndrome itself—typical battered child injuries, including twisted long bone fracture, subdural hematoma and bruises of various ages.

There was the battering parent profile—traits such as immaturity, instability and poor emotional control.

Finally, there was the strictly circumstantial evidence—a father alone with a child, the injuries inconsistent with the history provided.

Tuohy stared at his list. The problem, he concluded, was that he couldn't show a pattern of abuse. There were no repeated injuries because the baby hadn't been repeatedly exposed to the father—Danny had only moved in with the mother a month before.

Tuohy leafed through his materials until he found Dr. Kempe's definition of the battered-child syndrome. It begins with the pattern of injuries to the child, Kempe had said, but it is really descriptive of the pattern of conduct of the parents. When an emotionally immature person in any stratum of society suffers pressures, the child just becomes the focus for generalized frustration or anger.

Tuohy leaned back in his chair. Okay, he reasoned, I'll show the profile of the batterer instead. He would go after Danny Loss's nature and conduct—his emotions, temper, release mechanisms and reaction to annoyance. Tuohy would document Loss's attitude toward everything from children and pregnancy to Lynn, work, his parents, school, friends.

Putting pencil to his pad, the prosecutor wrote "Ask Lynn Running," drew a line under those three words, then began another list: Diagram bedroom . . . measure height of bed . . . where bed located . . . type of floor covering . . . covers on bed . . . type of bed . . . what baby wearing . . . where pillows . . . size pillows . . . what pillows filled with?

"When defendant first talked to you after the incident, what did he say?" Tuohy wrote on his pad.

"How do you know the defendant was irritated by the baby's crying?" he added.

"What was the pattern of the defendant's conduct?"

Below that list, Tuohy drew three outlines alongside each other, one cataloging battered child injuries, another battering parent characteristics, a third, Lance's precise wounds.

He compared the three columns.

The baby had been okay just the week before. Only Loss was present when he stopped breathing and his explanations didn't fit the clinical evidence. Loss fit the pattern of a child batterer and the baby had the typical injuries of a battered child.

Tuohy's mind raced.

He could put Dr. Venters on the stand both as an expert about the battered-child syndrome and as the doctor who treated Lance. He could, through the doctor, couple a complex and unfamiliar medical concept with the particular circumstantial evidence of this child's death. He could, through the doctor, ask the jury to infer that Lance Running's death was an example of the battered-child syndrome, and Danny Loss an example of the battering parent.

Yes, Tuohy thought, that would be his case.

There was just one problem. The entire prosecution rested on the concept of the battered-child syndrome, but this was a medical, not a legal notion, and had never been recognized in a Minnesota court of law. In fact, one judge had thrown out an entire case because he found use of the term "inflammatory." There was no reason to assume a judge would allow Dr. Venters to testify as an expert in this field. In fact, there was no reason to assume a judge would allow the term "battered-child syndrome" even to be uttered in his courtroom.

Tuohy needed to speak to the judge.

In the dead of a Minnesota winter, the journey from the prosecutor's office to the Ramsey County courthouse would involve a circuitous route through the enclosed skywalks that connect buildings in downtown St. Paul. During the summer months, though, the trip is one short block in the open air. Following that familiar course one morning in mid-June of 1971, Tuohy gathered himself in preparation for his appointment with the Honorable John W. Graff, then chief judge of the Ramsey County district court.

A creaking elevator that seemed frozen in time slowly carried him to the courthouse's thirteenth floor. Tuohy turned right, then left in the dark corridors before finding Graff's chambers. The judge greeted him at the door, and the two men groped for their opening words.

Tuohy then was thirty-three, not yet three years into his job, and Graff was all white hair and jowls and furrowed brows, a courthouse veteran now nearing retirement, deliberate and calm and hard of hearing.

"Well, let's go in and sit down," the judge said. "Would you like some coffee?"

Tuohy declined, not needing a further jolt to his system just then. Leaning forward in his chair, he began to explain the details of the Loss case. When he finished, he slid without a pause to the more general topic of the battered-child syndrome. He talked of conferences and papers and the Ramsey County group's visit to Colorado. He spoke of Dr. Kempe and child abuse teams and patterns of behavior. He explained what he hoped to do in the Loss case and what he needed—Dr. Venters on the stand, testifying about the battered-child syndrome.

As he talked, Tuohy kept his eye on Graff, but he couldn't tell from the judge's expression how he was faring. Tuohy never could read Graff—in conferences and trials, the judge always remained impassive.

The prosecutor found framing his argument difficult, for he was pushing something bordering on the legally exotic before a blunt, hard-eyed jurist who'd been presiding in courtrooms for most of his adult life. A generation later, other lawyers would do much the same with strange new forms of evidence such as DNA fingerprinting.

What's more, he was bucking Henry Kempe's own feelings. By the time the Loss case rose in St. Paul, the famed Colorado doctor had decided the "battered child" term should be discarded. When first used in 1962, the words he coined had done their job—they'd drawn the attention of pediatricians and the public, and generated reporting laws in all fifty states within six years. But Kempe believed that the term, which described only a narrow part of the syndrome, often was used in misleading and unfair ways. "It has no place in court because it is prejudicial and may arouse anger," he wrote in 1969. Kempe thought the term "nonaccidental injury" preferable, or maybe "failure to give reasonable care and protection."

Tuohy, though, needed a good deal more than "nonaccidental injury" for a jury. As he pleaded his case before Judge Graff, the young lawyer decided he might as well complete his presentation with a direct appeal.

"We have these situations, Your Honor," he said. "Babies are dying. Courts can't keep asking us to have witnesses because there never are witnesses in these child abuse cases. It's not a tennis match. Why let these cases go by the boards because there wasn't an audience? The only way we can prosecute is to do what I propose."

Graff's poker-faced reserve remained, but he appeared to be weighing Tuohy's comments. The judge and prosecutor sat across a desk for a moment in silence before Graff finally spoke.

"Okay," he said. "Go ahead and try it."

When the trial began June 22 in courtroom 1301, Tuohy, in his opening statement, immediately drew the jury's attention to the unique nature of the coming evidence.

"The whole case will principally be a medical investigation, which is unusual," he said. "This will not be a police investigation, for the most part . . . Through the course of this, we start to see the medical people starting to infer that this is not an ordinary injury. In fact, this is what they will call a battered-child syndrome and you will get to know that term, I think . . . This will be circumstantial evidence because the facts will bring out . . . that when this occurred, the father was home alone with the baby. In other words, there are no eyewitnesses, and, of course, this is a six-month-old baby who couldn't talk if it wanted to and in fact died. So what we have to do is infer through circumstantial evidence."

Tuohy then began to call witnesses to establish the facts—the men from the police and fire department and rescue squad who responded to Loss's call, the family physician, the pathologist who conducted the autopsy. Once they testified, Tuohy turned to those witnesses who would carry the heart of his case—Lynn Running, Lieutenant Carolen Bailey and Dr. Homer Venters.

Lynn took the stand first. After guiding the dead baby's mother through a retracing of the day Lance died, Tuohy began his march into uncharted legal territory. He needed to focus not on what Loss did, but who he was.

Had she observed Dan Loss with his parents? he asked. "Did he talk to you about his relationships with his parents?"

Loss's lawyer, John Wylde, Jr., jumped to his feet with an objection.

Wylde, working in a firm headed by one of St. Paul's most noted criminal defense attorneys, Doug Thomson, had assumed the case with a certain degree of confidence. The prosecution had no direct evidence, and Wylde didn't think they'd get anywhere with this novel, curious piece of business about a battered-child syndrome. He was not sure what Tuohy was after just now, but he didn't want him to get started.

"Your Honor," Wylde said, "I think I'm going to object to this on the grounds of materiality. I don't see any relevance to this proceeding."

The lawyers approached the bench to argue, away from the jury's earshot.

"Your Honor," Tuohy said, "my purpose is to try to bring out certain characteristics of a battering parent as a part of the battered-child syndrome . . . I believe she will testify that he felt in a sense he was a battered child. And I think that the medical people will testify that this is typical and that this is passed on from parent to child . . ."

Wylde, seeing the thread, sputtered with incredulity.

"I'm going to strenuously object to this line of questioning . . ." he said. "It doesn't make a whit of difference what his psychological makeup is or what his relationship with his parents is. Medical opinion along these lines would be completely improper anyway . . ."

Graff looked at Tuohy.

"Do you have any authority on this proposition?" the judge asked.

Here was the crux of the matter, and where they would depart from the past, if they were going to do so at all. Tuohy had no precedents, nothing to cite from the law books. There were no appellate cases dealing with the admissibility of medical opinion on the battered-child syndrome.

"My only authority would be to our showing of his mental state, the tendencies he would have at the time," Tuohy said.

"How far back do you intend to go?" the judge asked. "You going to take him all the way back to the time he was a baby?"

Tuohy swallowed. Yes, he allowed, he was. Loss had told Lynn he was not the favored child growing up, that an older brother was better loved. As punishment, his parents had made him crawl on the floor, something he greatly resented.

"Your Honor," Wylde said, "he's not accused of committing any crime with respect to his parents . . ."

"She's simply going to relate medical conversation," Tuohy interrupted. "It will be up to the medical people to state the characteristics of a battering parent . . ."

The prospect of doctors on the stand talking on this topic alarmed Wylde even more than the idea of Lynn testifying. He could not imagine that the doctors' general opinions about battering parents would be at all admissible in court, and without those opinions, what would be the point of Lynn testifying about Loss's childhood?

"This is a battle which is going to have to be fought," Wylde said, "when the so-called experts are brought in here to testify to such an obscure conclusion . . ."

Graff looked back and forth at the two attorneys, troubled and uncertain. It was only 10:30 A.M., and they were already sinking in a swamp. After a moment, the judge spoke.

"Gentlemen, it's a little early for a morning recess, but frankly, I'm bothered by the thing and I would like to discuss it further with counsel and I'll do that in chambers and give the jury a little bit longer recess."

The three men talked alone for twenty minutes, Tuohy advancing his arguments and Wylde objecting repeatedly to the whole notion behind the prosecution's strategy.

A doctor testifying about battering parents just is not material, Wylde argued. If doctors testified about the presence in a child of this so-called syndrome, they would be giving their opinion as to guilt. That would deny due process. Whether a particular injury was intentionally inflicted was a question for the jury and, in fact, was the entire purpose of the trial.

When the lawyers had finished, Graff ruled.

Counsel for the defense could object as he wished during the course of the testimony, the judge said. But the testimony would be allowed.

"The objections are overruled," Graff said.

With that, Tuohy was off and running on a clear field.

Questioning Lynn Running and then Carolen Bailey, he introduced a detailed profile of Dan Loss's character and behavior. Lynn talked of Loss's temper, anger, emotions and nerves, telling how he once pushed her across a room. Bailey testified that Lynn had told her that Loss handled the baby roughly, grabbed his legs when changing diapers, and grew disturbed when the infant cried.

Dr. Venters took the stand just after lunch on the third day of the trial—Thursday, June 24. He was not unaccustomed to courtrooms, but Tuohy's request that he testify about the profile of a battering parent was something new. Venters hoped it would work, for getting the battered-child syndrome recognized in the legal system would take physicians off a big hook—judges often tended to ask the doctors "who did it," seeking an answer the doctors did not feel they should provide outside of a medical context.

Tuohy began slowly, first establishing the notion of the battered-child syndrome and his expert witness's credentials in that field, then moving to questions about patterns of physical abuse to children and patterns of behavior among battering parents. To link the general with the specific, Tuohy finally guided Venters to the baby named Lance Running. After walking together through the tangible details and history of the case, the prosecutor stood before the doctor, ready to ask the central questions.

"Based upon the history, Doctor, and based upon your experience and learning, what was your conclusion regarding the history?"

"I regarded the history as incompatible with what we found clinically and by X-ray."

"And for what reasons?"

"The state of the infant and the X-rays led, in my opinion, to a diagnosis of battered child."

"And as far as this particular case, the injuries to the child and the history taken, do you have an opinion based upon your experience and learning as to whether these injuries were accidental?"

Jack Wylde rose to object, arguing that the answer was beyond the competence of the witness. Graff brushed him aside. "He may answer," the judge said.

All eyes turned to the doctor.

"I think the injuries we saw in the child . . . could not have happened by accident."

Tuohy was finished. The doctor left the stand at 3:24, not quite an hour and a half after he had begun.

The jurors required more than seven hours to reach a decision, not returning to the courtroom until 9:20 P.M. on Monday, June 28.

Daniel Loss, they'd decided, was guilty of first-degree manslaughter in the death of Lance Running.

Appeals were filed that fall, and argued before the Minnesota Supreme Court one year later, with the Ramsey County attorney's appellate specialist, Steve DeCoster, replacing Tuohy as the prosecution's advocate. On February 2, 1973, almost two years after Lance Running died, the state high court handed down its opinion.

In prosecutions relating to injuries or death of minor children, the justices concluded, it is proper to introduce medical testimony relating to the battered-child syndrome and the battering parent syndrome. Prosecutors no longer needed to link a specific act by the accused to the precise cause of death.

"This case presents to our court for the first time the use of the medical terminology 'battered-child syndrome' and 'battering parent syndrome' . . ." wrote Justice John Todd. "Medical authorities have recently expanded their investigation into this field, which has developed from a series of conferences beginning in the late 1950s and early 1960s . . . We hold that the establishment of the existence of a battered child, together with the reasonable inference of a battering parent, is sufficient to convict defendant herein in light of the other circumstantial evidence presented by the prosecution. It is very difficult in these prosecutions for injuries and death to minor children to establish the guilt of a defendant other than by circumstantial evidence. Normally, as was the case here, there are no eyewitnesses . . ."

Daniel Loss's conviction was affirmed, and the precedent established for all manner of similar prosecutions. The legacy of Dr. Kempe and the St. Paul group's pilgrimage to his workshop had yielded rich fruit. Prosecutors in counties across the country—New York, Virginia, Connecticut—now wrote, called and journeyed to St. Paul to seek Dr. Venters's advice or expert testimony for their own battered child cases, ones that usually lacked eyewitnesses or direct evidence. It was a satisfying time for those in Ramsey County who, out of personal concerns, had first stirred back in 1965. No longer would they have to suffer the frustrations they'd endured just those few years before.

No longer, for example, would they have to look the other way when little children such as Dennis Jurgens died. If they'd had the principles established by the Loss case, lawyers in the Ramsey

County attorney's office later took to saying, they might very well have been able to prosecute someone for Dennis's death.

Of course, that was all pointless speculation. The Jurgens case had been closed years before. That bulging file now rested, dusty and yellowing, in a cardboard box stacked high in a basement storage room, somewhere in downtown St. Paul.

PART THREE

VOICES FROM THE PRESENT

CHAPTER 28

It Never Entered My Mind

Despite the many and varied events that shaped her life after her teenage years in the Sauk Centre Home School for Girls, Jerry Puckett Sherwood never forgot the baby boy she'd borne, and lost, when she was seventeen. Every December 6 she'd grow moody, knowing this was his birthday. She would count the years since 1961, calculating Dennis's age. She would study her four other children and wonder which one Dennis looked like. Did he take after her, or his father? Was he happy?

Jerry's own life had not been all that joyful. She never could figure out why a mother would walk away from her husband and three young children. The photo left behind yielded no answers—in the picture, Jean Puckett, young and pretty with long, dark hair, sat cradling three-month-old Jerry in her right arm, her left hand draped across the backs of the two older children. Without a mother, growing up in assorted small towns of Missouri, Jerry's family life had been tenuous at best, what with her father driving long-haul trucks for a living. One stepmother arrived, then, some years later, following the family's move to Minnesota, another. Jerry endured abuse from the first and tormented the second. She was ten the first time she ran away from home, and by her early teens she was in open rebellion, defying her parents, skipping school, sassing everyone— including the social worker at the Minneapolis juvenile center her parents had turned to for help. When at thirteen she shoplifted from the local drugstore and ran away one weekend, her parents finally hauled her to court, where she was declared an incorrigible and placed in a foster home.

After that, she bounced often through the Twin Cities region, fleeing foster homes when they grew intolerable, only to be placed in another, until the court finally committed her, at the age of fourteen, to the Sauk Centre reform school. She soon learned there that in daily life her choice was to remain passive or learn how to survive, and with little hesitation she chose survival. Not long after coming to the institution, she joined a riot, tearing up a cottage and breaking windows before fleeing the school with eight other teenage girls. The authorities came after them with dogs, and Jerry ended up in solitary confinement for thirty days, occupying a closet-sized room that contained a bed, a porcelain pot and a Bible.

After eleven months at the reform school, a review board released her to a new foster home on a farm in Waterton, Minnesota, but when the old man there tried to molest her, she fled again and was returned to Sauk Centre. Some time later, the authorities sent her to another foster home, and again she fled, ending up back at the reform school. Sauk Centre was getting to be like home to Jerry. She'd learned how to deal with that system.

"You know, I don't think I can deal with living in the Cities," she told her caseworker one day. "I want to go to a small town."

This time, they sent her to a foster family in St. Cloud, and that was where she met Dennis McIntyre. At school, he was the boy every girl wanted, lean and handsome and manly. Jerry at sixteen was fairly popular herself, for she had blossomed, her long blond hair and voluptuous body stirring considerable interest. Three months after they started dating, Jerry invited Dennis over one night when her foster parents were out. She'd heard sex was fantastic, but it wasn't that first night, and soon after, Dennis drifted away. When her foster parents started harping at her, Jerry fled again. This time the police hauled her back to Sauk Centre in handcuffs. The customary admitting examination there yielded unexpected news—Jerry was two months' pregnant.

Jerry had never considered the possibility that she could get pregnant the first time. "It just never entered my mind," she explained later.

She first felt her baby move on a Sunday. She was reading a *Saturday Evening Post* propped up on her stomach when suddenly the magazine jumped up into the air. Jerry thought this was kind of neat. She no longer was alone.

Dennis was born that December 6 after nine and a half hours of labor. When she first got hold of her baby, Jerry undressed him and counted his fingers and toes as she studied his body. He was big and strong, with fat cheeks, a round face and blond peach fuzz on his head. During the few days they stayed together in the hospital, Jerry arranged to have Dennis baptized a Catholic, like his father. Then the Scott County authorities took Dennis away and placed him in a foster home.

Jerry never could devise a plan to keep her baby that suited the county people. She then had a job caring for a woman's two children, and the woman had said she could have a room in her house as pay. Jerry's caseworkers didn't think that would work. Jerry's sister would take them in, although she was due in three months herself. The caseworkers didn't think that would work either. In time, Jerry gave up.

Four months after Dennis's birth, when the authorities brought her to court to sign the papers relinquishing her parental rights, Jerry started to cry.

"The baby will have everything," the caseworker said. "The baby will have a mother and a father. He will have the kind of life that you could never give him. He will be happy. He will have everything that there is to give in life."

Jerry picked up a pen and signed her name.

She saw Dennis for the last time that day, in a room off the courthouse basement. Jerry stood him on her lap and he held onto her fingers, smelling of baby powder and laughing as he swayed back and forth. Then he was gone.

Soon after, Jerry learned she was pregnant again by Dennis McIntyre. Once more she ran from a foster home, and again she was brought back to Sauk Centre, for she was still seventeen. This time, when she gave birth to her daughter Misty, Jerry refused to sign any papers, and the authorities eventually found a foster home in Shakopee that would take both mother and baby.

Months later, on June 22, 1963, while Dennis was still in the Jurgens home on a probationary basis, Jerry married Dennis

McIntyre. The couple had three more children following Misty, two girls and a boy—Jerry named him Dennis too—and then divorced in 1970. After that, Jerry scrambled as best she could to support four kids. She packed metal pipes in a warehouse, she managed an apartment building, she drew AFDC welfare assistance. For several years Jerry danced at Alary's Club Bar in downtown St. Paul, using the name Rhoda and working in bikini bottoms and pasties on a stage suspended high in the air. After that, she later told some of those who came to chronicle her story, she turned to prostitution. The once lonely neophyte had toughened into a street-smart survivor.

In time, Jerry got married again, to a maintenance company superintendent named Richard Sherwood, but in 1976 that union also ended in divorce. Jerry counted the years. She purposely waited until December of 1980 before starting the search for her firstborn. He would be nineteen then, and she thought that made him the age of legal consent.

"I'm a realist, I don't live in a fantasy world," she told those who inquired. "I'm prepared for his rejection. But I want him to know he has blood relatives."

One morning, days after another passing birthday had left her with an unshakable depression, Jerry called the Scott County welfare department. She explained who she was and provided details— where and when Dennis was born, his name, her maiden name, the hospital.

"I have a right," she said. "I have a right to know what happened to him."

The voice on the phone said he'd do what he could, and get back to her.

The letter arrived six weeks later, from Ramsey County, not Scott. Jerry's hands shook as she opened the envelope.

"We are very sorry to inform you that Dennis died April 11, 1965, of peritonitis . . ." the letter began.

The typed words continued across the page, something about a ruptured bowel, and Jerry vaguely assumed this meant Dennis had died because of a diseased appendix. It did not matter—Dennis was gone, again. She began to sob, while her four children gathered about, uncertain what to do. As Jerry saw it, the system once more had taken Dennis from her. Dennis had died at three-and-a-half,

Dennis had been dead all these years. She'd been prepared for rejection, but not this. She reached for a breath, and words.

"It never entered my head that he was dead," she said.

Days later, after gathering herself, Jerry called the man at the Ramsey County welfare department who had written the letter. From him, after some pressing, she managed to glean two facts. Dennis was buried at St. Mary's Cemetery in the town of White Bear Lake, and his adoptive last name had been Jurgens.

For two months, Jerry thought about what she'd learned. What could she do? He was gone, and she'd given up her rights long ago. She wanted at least to visit the grave, but she had no means of transportation, no way to get to this small town ten miles north of St. Paul.

Then, one day in February, a male friend came visiting who did have a car. "Let's go to the cemetery," Jerry said.

Soon they were driving up I-35E toward White Bear Lake, accompanied by Jerry's middle daughter, Dawn. They found St. Mary's Church first, but the cemetery lay more than a mile to the northwest, on the town's outskirts, abutting a new housing project rising on reclaimed marshland. Small and surrounded by these modern, wood-decked homes, the cemetery suggested a neighborhood park both in size and character.

Climbing from her friend's car, Jerry pulled her coat tight against the midwinter chill, and walked through an unlocked black wrought-iron gate, flanked on each side by a multicolored stone and cement pillar topped with a small cross. Directly to her left stood a large, solitary poplar. All was quiet but for the sound of a tractor laboring at the park's edge, cleaning leaves amid a stand of bare oak trees.

Jerry and her companions walked up and down the rows of tombstones, studying the inscriptions. They had a name and the dates of birth and death, but in the overcast gloom they still couldn't find Dennis's grave. Jerry's friend suggested they check with the mortuary where they kept the records.

So they retraced their route back to Lake Mortuary, which stood across the street from St. Mary's Church at Fourth and Bald Eagle, side by side with a car repair shop and the White Bear Lake Oil Company. The one-story brick and stucco building looked much as it had on the day of Dennis's funeral some sixteen years before. A man with a long, craggy face greeted the three visitors in the reception area.

"Did you bury a Dennis Jurgens back in 1965?" Jerry asked.

Jim Honsa knew right away what she was talking about. By early 1981, he'd been the mortician at Lake for some twenty years, but had never forgotten that one. He didn't know who this tall, ample blonde with the angry blue eyes might be, but he willingly brought out his old registers and files.

Jerry turned the pages. Some of the burial records were accompanied by yellowing newspaper clippings, and Jerry paused in dismay over a photo of a motorcycle crushed like an accordion. Then, flipping another sheet, she found what she was seeking: *Jurgens, Dennis Craig*. She traced the name with her finger and studied the attached certificate. A moment later, her eye drifted to the bottom of the page. Someone had pasted in a small newspaper clipping, just three paragraphs in all, now curled and faded.

"Tot's Death Due to Peritonitis," the headline said. The date was April 13, 1965.

Jerry continued reading:

"An autopsy on the body of 3½ year old Dennis Jurgens, son of Mr. and Mrs. Harold R. Jurgens, 2148 S. Gardenette Dr., White Bear Lake, showed he died of peritonitis caused by a ruptured bowel, Dr. Thomas W. Votel, Ramsey County coroner, said today. The body also bore multiple injuries and bruises, Dr. Votel said. White Bear police and the coroner's office were investigating the death . . ."

Jerry felt as if something was exploding inside her. She began to cry. "My God," she said out loud. "They beat my baby to death."

The trio drove back up Bald Eagle to the cemetery and resumed their search for the grave, but even with their new knowledge, they couldn't find the right tombstone. A tractor still growled in the background, and now Jerry's friend turned to consider the groundskeeper perched on its seat, who just then was talking to two other men standing amid the oak trees.

"Let's ask him because he takes care of the cemetery," the friend suggested. "He may know where he's at."

Jerry approached the tractor. "I'm looking for Dennis Craig Jurgens's grave site," she said.

One of the men who'd been speaking to the grounds-keeper turned toward Jerry. He was tall and slender. "It's right over there," he said, pointing. "Right over there."

Jerry looked about, puzzled. "Where?"

"I'll take you over."

They turned left, then right, walking midway down a row.

"There," the man said.

The grave was bare of flowers or adornment. The figure of a cherub was etched into the left side of the small headstone. To the right were four brief lines:

OUR LITTLE ANGEL
DENNIS C. JURGENS
DEC. 6, 1961
APR. 11, 1965

Their guide suddenly cleared his throat.

"Dennis was my sister's son."

Jerry never would learn which of the Zerwas brothers this one happened to be, for in her surprise she neglected to ask. The question instead came from him.

"Who are you?"

"I'm the natural mother," Jerry replied.

"That boy was so happy and spirited," the man began, waxing almost lyrical. "My sister Lois loved him and gave him everything— musical instruments, tap shoes, whatever. They could afford that. Her husband Harold's an electrician, works at Muska Electric."

Jerry stared at him. "Well, what about the numerous bruises and injuries that I read about in the paper?"

The man turned and walked away.

Back in her apartment, Jerry huddled with her friend and daughter, plotting strategy.

First she called the Ramsey County welfare department again, reaching the person she'd talked to before. She spoke with feeling.

"You know, the system took my son away because I couldn't take care of him, and yet my son is dead and my four other children are alive. I want some more information about what happened."

The man on the phone put her on hold for a moment, then returned to the line. "I've checked with my supervisor and I'm sorry, I can't give you any information. I should never have given you what I did."

Jerry heard a hard click. The man had hung up his phone. She next dialed directory assistance.

"Jurgens residence," Jerry said. "Harold and Lois Jurgens in White Bear Lake."

The operator could find no such listing, of course, for the Jurgenses had moved to Stillwater fourteen years before. Jerry's friend had an idea. That brother at the cemetery said Harold Jurgens worked at Muska Electric, so why not call there?

In a trusting town like St. Paul, it was not terribly difficult to coax a home phone number from the shop by pretending to be a family friend. Within minutes, Jerry was dialing the Jurgens house.

"Hello." The voice sounded kind and grandmotherly.

"Mrs. Jurgens, please."

"This is Mrs. Jurgens."

Jerry introduced herself, explaining who she was. "I just found out Dennis had died," she said.

"I thought you'd been informed long ago," Lois replied. She sounded pleasant and polite.

"No, I wasn't . . ." Jerry swallowed. "I was calling now to find out what kind of little boy he was."

Lois talked freely. Dennis was a good, sweet, happy boy, she said, so cute and healthy. Of course, that's not the way he was when he first came from the foster home. Then he was filthy, infested with worms and lice, and covered with cradle cap.

"I wish you could have seen him before and after."

His death was mystifying, Lois explained. When they found him dead in his crib, he had dark blotches all over him, kind of like star bursts. She had no idea where they came from.

Jerry asked for a photo of Dennis in the baptismal slip she'd bought him during their days together in St. Michael's Hospital. Lois readily agreed to send one, along with the baptismal slip itself. Jerry provided her phone number and address and hung up, feeling calmer than she had in some time. Perhaps her mind had been running away from her, she reasoned. Lois Jurgens seemed to her a fantastic person.

Six weeks later, when nothing had arrived in the mail, Jerry once again dialed Lois Jurgens's number, but in vain. The Jurgenses' phone number had been changed, and the new number was unlisted.

It is difficult to say just how Jerry Sherwood felt at that moment. Her family then was living on welfare assistance, she would explain later, and she feared the consequences of challenging the authorities.

She also, of course, had not been an entirely mainstream member of society over the years. If you buck the system, she was fond of saying, it bucks you back. Besides, adoption records are confidential, and she—as everyone reminded her—had given up her rights.

For whatever the combination of reasons, Jerry at that moment stopped her quest. In late 1980 and early 1981, she glimpsed the past, but then backed away. Jerry Sherwood decided there simply was nothing more she could do.

Years passed—three, four, five. On occasion, sitting with pals at a bar or visiting a friend's home, Jerry would bring up the matter of her firstborn's death, and the people around her would respond with anger and sympathy before turning the conversation to other topics. One evening in early September of 1986, Jerry was telling her story yet again, to a new friend who'd come visiting, but this person reacted differently from the others. He grew visibly shaken as Sherwood voiced her suspicions and fears.

"Don't be afraid of the system," he urged. "They can't control you . . . To hell with your legal rights. What about your moral rights?"

So, after five and a half years, Jerry now gathered herself for another effort. She sent her son Dennis Craig to the public library to scour newspaper files in search of articles on his namesake brother's death, and she sent her daughter Ronda to the county courthouse to get a copy of his death certificate. Ronda's mission proved the most fruitful. She returned with a document that looked strange to Jerry.

The death certificate didn't seem entirely complete. In the "mode of death" box, the coroner had written the word "deferred."

Dennis Craig now took to the phone under his mother's guidance. He called the coroner's office, where Jim Essling explained they would need a court order to see their files. He called the county attorney's office, where Jim Konen suggested he contact the police department that had conducted the original investigation. He called the White Bear police, where his message landed on the desk of Lieutenant Buzz Harvey.

Buzz Harvey studied the Jurgens file now sitting before him.

Wants to talk about his brother's murder, Heidi had said. *Dennis Jurgens.*

Buzz found it difficult to believe this case was resurfacing after twenty-one years. It hadn't been his business then, but now it was. Unwelcome memories filled the room.

"Ron!" Harvey shouted at the burly figure passing by his open doorway.

Ron Meehan turned and retraced his steps. More than thirteen years had passed since he'd settled at Jerome Zerwas's desk and assumed the role of chief investigator.

"Ron," Buzz Harvey said. "Do you remember the Jurgens case?"

CHAPTER 29

A Horse to Ride

It cannot be said that events unfolded rapidly after Jerry Sherwood's turbulent meeting in Buzz Harvey's office on September 18. Conferences were held, phone calls exchanged, memories prodded, but those involved seemed to be poised in a suspended state, waiting for a course of action to make itself apparent.

What little motion there was came from Ron Meehan, who carried the Jurgens file to Jim Konen in the Ramsey County attorney's office the very next day.

"Buzz Harvey called me about this," Konen offered. The head of the criminal division was grinning, and inhaling a Winston bummed from Ron. Apparently he'd heard quite an earful from Buzz. "Yeah, Jerome sure screwed this one up in 1965," he said.

Meehan wondered where that comment came from, and how to respond, for his own thoughts about Jerome Zerwas were conflicted. He considered Jerome quite an operator, but all the same, he liked the former lieutenant and thought him an exceptionally personable man.

In truth, they'd been good friends. Meehan was struggling to get by when he first arrived on the force in 1960, a twenty-six-year-old cop with three kids and a $400-a-month salary, and Jerome had helped wherever he could. The two cops had shared a particular appreciation for the art of boxing, since both had a pair of fists. Meehan had fought amateur matches in the Marines, but still had to admire Jerome's devastating left, for the lieutenant on several occasions had dropped angry, drunk bullies with three or four punches. One night, after a couple of drinks together, Jerome and Ron had ended up behind the police station sparring, just goofing around, but Meehan took satisfaction in staying with the lieutenant, particularly when he realized Jerome was setting him up for a knockdown.

They'd also taken their pleasure together in bars. Ron and Jerome could be spotted on more than a few nights tossing back screwdrivers at the 617 Lounge on Fourth Street. Let's go down and have a drink, Jerome would say as they got off work. Okay, Ron would agree, but just one. Liz wants me home. Five screwdrivers later, they'd still be sitting there. Meehan couldn't help himself. He'd almost fall out of his chair laughing as he watched Jerome leer at the waitresses and customers.

"Yeah, Jerome sure screwed this one up in 1965."

Ron felt Konen was inviting a response, but he was not inclined to provide one.

"I don't know," he grunted.

Let the prosecutors tell us if we have a horse to ride, Meehan figured. He backed out of Konen's office and soon was gliding north on I-35E toward White Bear Lake. There was a phone call he wanted to make.

Pete Korolchuk had retired as police chief just three years before, in 1983, and now lived in Hackensack, a small Minnesota town some 150 miles to the northwest. He answered Meehan's call on the first ring.

"Hey, Pete," Meehan began. "Ron here." He plunged in without further courtesies.

"Do you remember the Jurgens case? The natural mother has looked into things and come up with stuff. What do you remember?"

"The natural mother?" Korolchuk sounded surprised.

"Yeah," Meehan said. "Whatever happened to this one?"

The line remained silent, but for the two men's breathing. The typical Pete Korolchuk thing, Meehan thought. Taking time to think, sorting things out before he talks. Just like when he was chief.

Korolchuk and Meehan had taken the civil service test and joined the police force together back in 1960, both coming out of construction work, and Meehan had watched the other man rise systematically through the ranks. He considered Korolchuk to be methodical and conscientious, but not particularly open or demonstrative. As chief, he was not the sort of man who would come out of his office to slap Meehan on the back and say nice job. He'd write a note instead. Once, instead of calling a meeting when he wanted to praise the whole department, he presented a plaque that included everyone's name.

Korolchuk seemed a little vague now as he responded to Meehan's question.

To the best of his recollection, he said, he and Bob VanderWyst took the case down to the county attorney after they finished investigating. He recalled a hearing of some sort at that point. He thought it was a grand jury, or maybe a coroner's inquest. He remembered that the Jurgenses' attorney—Donohue, was it?—had objected to questions put to his clients and had advised them to take the Fifth. After the hearing, Korolchuk thought the file was left with the prosecutor as a chargeable case, but Paul Lindholm couldn't get the statement he wanted from Lois Jurgens. The county attorney instead took the file to juvenile court and had the other son, Robert, removed from the house.

That was all Korolchuk could offer.

Meehan reviewed what he'd just learned. Even though there hadn't been a prosecution, if Pete was right there'd been a proceeding of some sort back then, a proceeding not hinted at in the twenty-odd pages of reports written by VanderWyst and Korolchuk.

Those pages provided Meehan with all he knew of the case, and they left him feeling uneducated. The file wasn't just thin—it was incomplete. Certain pages clearly were missing. Pete and Bob's reports referred to statements they'd taken from the Jurgenses' neighbors and relatives—specifically, from Ivan and Gladys DeMars, Lloyd and Donna Zerwas, Richard and Donna Norton—but none of these statements was in the packet Heidi had pulled from the station's record room. Nor were there any photos. There should have been some pictures in a case like this.

"What about the photos and statements?" Meehan asked Korolchuk. "They're missing now from the file."

Korolchuk again measured his answer before replying. To the best of his recollection, he said finally, the last time he'd seen the photos and statements they'd been down at the county attorney's office.

When Meehan hung up the phone it was almost four in the afternoon—the end of his shift. There was nothing more he could do just then anyway. It was up to the county attorney's office to say whether they had a dead horse or not. All this was so long ago.

As Meehan drove home, memories of life back then filled his mind. The late-night parties at Bob VanderWyst's house, the camping trips, the bars and boxing matches—they'd been so young then. Wasn't 1965 the year the Mississippi was at its highest, the year of the big rain and floods, the year they had all the problems and had to pump the streets and work overtime directing traffic in the south of town?

In 1965, in fact, he'd almost always been scrambling. With three kids and another on the way, he worked two jobs—up at half past six every morning for a shift at the Montgomery Ward on University in St. Paul, then off at two o'clock and home for a quick shave and shower before reporting the police station at three for a tour of duty that ended at eleven at night. Weekends and days off, he took security guard jobs at armory affairs, weddings, Rod and Gun Club parties, wherever they had a dance. He didn't mind—he had energy and felt proud to be a cop. Life had changed, of course, as the years slipped by. Meehan was fifty-two now, still firm and strong, if thickening in the neck and gut, but at times he toyed with the notion of retiring to Santa Rosa, in California, where a relative lived and where it always seemed warm.

Once home, Ron described the day to his wife, Liz.

"Talked to Pete today about this case from twenty-one years ago. The natural mother started asking questions, so we're trying to figure out what happened. The Jurgens case . . ."

Liz looked at her husband. "Don't you remember?" she said.

"Remember what?"

"You came home from work the third night after that boy died and told me Lois Jurgens had killed her kid."

A door to the past once more had opened partway, and now it hung poised, frozen for a moment. In late September of 1986, the Ramsey County attorney's office and the White Bear police held the puzzling Jurgens file before them, a batch of pages that hinted at other, missing sheets. They talked and reread the reports and wondered what to do. Then Jerry Sherwood, impatient and distrustful, visited Jim Essling at the medical examiner's office and called

Brian Bonner at the *St. Paul Pioneer Press Dispatch*. With those final pushes, the door swung wide.

The county medical examiner, Michael McGee, had opened up lots of little babies, a fact he didn't hesitate to tell those who inquired. When he saw multiple bruises and a bowel full of pus, he thought bad thoughts. To him, this Jurgens case involved no medical mystery, wasn't even a close call. It wasn't an aberration, either—he'd been doing his job too long to think otherwise. The case was unusual not for what happened in 1965, but for what was happening now.

Just to confirm his own judgment, McGee showed the Jurgens file to a friend and colleague with even more specialized training than he—Dr. Janice Ophoven, a pediatric forensic pathologist—who within minutes agreed this was a homicide, and a particularly malignant one at that. The child suffered terrible pain for many hours and could have been treated, Ophoven pointed out. This did not need to be a fatal injury. The withholding of care shocked Ophoven as much as the brutality of the assault.

The post office was not speedy enough for McGee. The morning of October 7, he sent Dennis's revised death certificate to the county attorney by courier.

The phone call Brian Bonner placed to Lois Jurgens two days later, on Thursday, October 9, in preparation for his upcoming Sunday article, unnerved her considerably.

On that fall afternoon in 1986 Lois was sixty-one years old, and her delicate, youthful beauty had long since vanished into anger and disappointment. Eleven years had passed since all her children fled in that agitated summer of 1975, and time had not proven soothing. Lois had grown ever more obsessed with religion. One week she attended a shrine in Wisconsin where the Blessed Virgin Mary was said to have been sighted, then returned to Stillwater with rosaries, crucifixes and all manner of ornaments. She put religious bumper stickers on her car and sent pious literature to Zerwas family homes. At a family funeral she walked about holding a cross before various guests, proposing to remove the devil from them. At a family dinner one evening she suddenly spoke of Dennis—*I've seen him, he's fine, he's grown up*—then rose from the restaurant table and wandered into a rainy night. Lois now often stayed in her bed most of the day with newspapers and magazines strewn about the room. On occasion, she'd go on a buying spree and spend so much money it distressed Harold enough to complain to his priest. Their once neatly maintained home had deteriorated into a disheveled mess.

On the phone, the newspaperman's voice was pulling Lois into the unwelcome past.

"Well, who's doing this?" Lois responded. "I'm very much surprised . . . I can't understand what's going on. This seems really farfetched to me."

The next day, alarmed and confused, Lois turned to the one person she thought could help. She called the son who'd fled her home more than a decade before.

Robert Jurgens, as it happens, had grown up to become a policeman. Then twenty-six, he was working in Crookston, a small town of eight thousand in the far northwest reach of Minnesota, just across the border from Grand Forks, North Dakota, a good four-hour drive from the Twin Cities area.

That Robert had ended up on the law's side of a prison cell was a circumstance of some wonder. After fleeing the Jurgens home in June of 1975, he'd bounced among several foster homes, running away from one after another. He'd turned to drugs—marijuana, angel dust, acid—and dropped out of school in the eleventh grade before Washington County authorities intervened in mid-1977, placing him in a local chemical dependency treatment center. He fled once, ending up in the Stillwater jail for ten days, but when the court returned him to the center, he decided to stay and confront the dread and anger that had come to envelop him. From the treatment center he went to Shanti House, a halfway home on Hennepin Avenue in Minneapolis, and then to a group home in Cottage Grove. He was seventeen when he emerged, and free of drugs.

Two years later, after passing a high school equivalency test, he began his career in law enforcement. He worked for four and a half years at the Golden Valley County sheriff's department in Beech, North Dakota, then a year and a half for the U.S. Marshal's office, before coming to Crookston in early 1986. By then he had a wife, Joanne, and a three-year-old son, Joshua.

Throughout the years, Robert had maintained contact and relations with Harold and Lois. He wanted to put the past behind him, but he also felt the need for family and roots, and the Jurgenses were the only parents he'd known. Such was the power of this impulse that Robert from time to time had even entrusted Joshua to the Jurgenses. In fact, when he and Joanne were making the move from Bismarck to Crookston in early 1986, they left Joshua with Harold and Lois for three full weeks.

On the phone now, Lois sounded scared. She'd been contacted by a reporter for the *St. Paul Dispatch*, she told Robert. They're saying they're going to reopen the case of Dennis Jurgens.

"That's absolutely ridiculous," she said. "How can they do this? What are they trying to do here?"

Robert felt queasy. He realized something serious was happening, for the only way the case could now be reopened was if it involved a murder charge. Any other offense, he knew from his training, was well beyond the statute of limitations.

"Robert," Lois implored, "they're not going to take me away, are they?"

Her tone, and the meaning behind her question, chilled Robert. He'd always wondered what happened to Dennis. Nobody had ever told him anything other than that Dennis had gotten sick and gone to heaven, and Robert had never asked for more. In the family photo albums, when he'd see pictures of himself standing with an arm around this smaller, stockier boy, his parents would just say, "Oh, you guys were so nice together." Robert could recall certain other details on his own, but they were details that he didn't want to face.

"No," Robert answered. "There's nothing they could be reopening unless they were charging some type of murder here."

Lois was not appeased.

"They can't take me away, can they, Robert?"

"No," Robert said firmly. "No."

After talking to Lois, Robert called Jim Essling in the Ramsey County medical examiner's office. "What's the deal here?" he asked. "Why are you bugging my parents? Why are you bringing this back up?"

They reopened the file, Essling explained, because the biological mother had come around checking on Dennis. They found the death certificate had been left in a deferred status. After Dr. McGee examined the file, he changed it to homicide.

Robert held the receiver in his hand, absorbing Essling's words. The man was telling him his brother was murdered. With all his expertise, after reviewing everything, the doctor was saying Dennis had been murdered.

Okay, Robert told himself. There's a murder here. There's a homicide. Who did it?

Robert knew. Without a doubt, he felt he knew who killed Dennis. He called Harold at Muska Electric.

"Hey, I just talked to the medical examiner, and he said this is being investigated as a homicide . . ." he began. "Was she ever formally charged?"

"No, she never was," Harold replied.

"Well, how long after his death was I taken away?"

"Five days," Harold answered.

Robert had never known that. Five days.

Later that evening, he talked on the phone to Harold and Lois at their home. They now were cautious and tight-lipped. Don't believe anything you hear, his parents urged, and don't say anything to anybody. We've retained the services of a very good attorney. He says if our lips are moving, we're saying too much. Don't say anything to anyone.

His parents' words made Robert angry. How could they sit there and not have the balls to tell him what happened? They could at least lie, or tell their side of the story, or whatever. Why did he have to be quiet? What was there to hide?

Despite his anger, though, Robert was uncertain what he should now do. His relationship with his parents in recent years had turned good, very good, particularly since his marriage. He wanted to find out exactly what had happened, but he didn't want to damage this connection. He also worried about what could happen to his parents if he gave voice to his memories.

Still, those memories pulled at Robert. He remembered Dennis. Early on, he recalled, Dennis used to cry and try to get away when he'd get hit or yanked around, but later on he didn't do as much crying and he didn't do any running away. He'd more or less submit and just kind of whimper and not cry much at all.

The next day at work Robert went to his boss, Lieutenant Douglas Qualeey. It was Saturday, October 11.

"I need help," Robert said. "I need someone to talk to. I want to know what I should do."

Brian Bonner's article appeared the next morning, followed by several evening television news stories, and in the following twenty-four hours, even though the reports hadn't mentioned the Jurgenses by name, Ron Meehan received five phone calls.

One came from the Washington County caseworker, Carol Felix. One came from the Ramsey County caseworker, Marion Putnam, now Marion Dinah Nord. One came from Lois's brother-in-law, Richard Norton. One came from Lois's niece, Pam Docken, daughter of Richard Norton. And one came from Barbara Wisdorf—now, after years of marriage, Barbara Venne.

"You may think I'm crazy," Barbara told Ron, "but when I was a teenager, I knew a woman who I felt killed her adopted son. His name was Dennis and her name was Lois."

Barbara paused. She couldn't remember Lois's married name.

"Her maiden name was Zerwas," she offered.

"We're talking about the same person," Meehan said.

Barbara felt relieved. Just eighteen when she attended Dennis's funeral as a friend of Lois's niece, she was forty now, with four grown children, and from her house she operated a Ramsey County emergency shelter for troubled youths. Dennis's funeral—the crown of roses, the bruises, the gossip—was hard to think about. That, in fact, was exactly what she used to tell her mother about all of Dennis's treatment. Life is hard to think about, her mom would answer. If so, maybe her mother shouldn't have protected her the way she did before dying so young, so early. The Franciscan nuns in Barbara's Catholic school had been cruel, frustrated, frigid women, but it seemed they'd better prepared her for the reality of life than her mother had. Barbara hadn't thought consciously about Dennis when she'd started her emergency shelter, but maybe without really knowing it, Dennis was behind that choice. There were times over the years when she'd felt crazy—maybe she'd imagined all that about Dennis, maybe her memory was playing tricks on her. Then she'd seen the television newscast Sunday night about a child's death being reopened. She called the White Bear police not so much to bear witness as to verify her own well-being.

Now, with Ron Meehan's affirmation, she felt sane. She could prove to her husband she wasn't crazy.

In the wake of Bonner's article, the Ramsey County medical examiner's office also received phone calls, a half dozen in the first twenty-four hours, and these were from people with no connection to the

Jurgens case. They were people who'd harbored suspicions over the years about other children who'd died, children they'd known or loved or seen from afar.

For example, Lori Jetter, twenty-four, from the town of Hastings, called to talk about her brother. In the late 1960s, they had been split apart by adoption agencies when he was three. Later she'd learned he'd died in Wisconsin, but she never knew how. He had perfect health, Lori Jetter said. Why would a healthy child die?

It soon would emerge from a check of the files that thousands of Ramsey County deaths had never been classified. *Undetermined* or *deferred*, the certificates said, where the coroner was supposed to indicate whether the death had been natural or suicide or homicide or accident. Within days of the initial calls, a stunned Michael McGee ordered Jim Essling to begin a review of every unresolved Ramsey County case between 1958 and 1978.

Closeted in a conference room with two assistants, Essling began flipping through red-bound volumes of death records, each containing 1,500 deaths—morphine overdoses, starved kids, gunshots to the abdomen, gunshots to the head, a one-year-old with brain-stem damage. Essling was looking for all unresolved deaths, but focused particularly on those involving children and physical trauma. Page after page, puzzling cases became apparent. A two-year-old girl collapses and dies while seated at the dinner table. A sixteen-month-old boy drowns in a bathtub. A six-year-old girl dies after apparently being hit by a car. The attached newspaper accounts offered few details: "Police were told by a baby-sitter that she left the apartment bathroom for about ten minutes after placing the youngster in the tub with water and soap. She said when she returned the child was under water." Nothing more.

For 350 of the most suspicious cases, Essling pulled the complete files from a basement storage room and began poring through autopsy reports, police reports, toxicology reports, photographs. He doubted much would come of his labors, though. Most files didn't contain enough information for McGee to rule on, and prosecutions for those that did seemed unlikely. Aggressive defense attorneys would jump all over the matter of old evidence, extended delays and a coroner initially unwilling to call the death a homicide.

"We just don't know what we have until we get into them," McGee told reporters. "They're kind of sad."

With calls inundating the police, Ron Meehan needed help, so Buzz Harvey added a second policeman to the nascent Jurgens investigation, a juvenile crimes specialist named Greg Kindle.

The Jurgens affair had happened before Kindle's time—he'd joined the force in 1969—but Greg had heard of the case. Once, in his rookie year, while debating the pros and cons of police work with one of the station's older sergeants, that seasoned veteran had leaned toward Greg, almost whispering: *If you don't think people can commit murder and get away with it, you're nuts, because Jerome's sister did just that.*

Ron and Greg made for an unlikely duo. Kindle, forty-one, looked ready to ignite if a lit match were tossed his way. He stared at people as if he were trying to see through them or find hidden agendas—his flat, fixed eyes appeared almost menacing—and he tended to sneer at anyone in a tie or fancy office. He lived in the woods twenty-two miles to the northeast of White Bear, and most days rode a Honda 500-cc motorcycle to work. Meehan thought Kindle made a fine partner.

"Greg and Ron are one plus one equals three," Meehan told others. "We don't always agree, and Greg's got different attitudes, but this is going to take a lot of work and I need somebody to stick with me on it."

The two detectives knew where they wanted to begin. Just after lunch on Monday, October 13, they left the White Bear police station in an unmarked squad car and headed east on I-94, traveling through the soft, rolling prairie so typical of the upper Midwest. Approaching the Wisconsin border, the road suddenly descended and the prairie opened to the spectacular horizons of the St. Croix River valley, a vista that never ceased to amaze Ron whenever he came this way. Here was Minnesota at its luminous best, north country more than Midwest—the lines of sight so long and wide, the sky immense, the bluffs rising from the river full of color, the thick stands of maple and white-barked birch rich with yellow-green leaves, a vivid contrast to the darker oaks and evergreens.

Crossing the St. Croix River and entering Wisconsin at the tranquil river town of Hudson, Ron and Greg watched a dozen sailboats off to their right gliding through a wide, slow-moving bend of the St. Croix, one of the cleanest riverways in the country. The detectives drove on for forty-five miles, now once more amid the rolling Midwest prairie, before leaving the interstate at Menomonie. They turned into a neighborhood of small, worn frame homes that gave way, on their left, to a trailer park. They cruised the park's narrow lanes until they found trailer number seventy-six, small and light green in color. An elevated wooden porch, decorated with three potted plants, led to the entrance.

Bob VanderWyst, now fifty-five, had come to live out his life in this setting after falling ill with bone cancer the previous March. Meehan and Kindle found him in considerable pain.

VanderWyst shuffled more than he walked through the compact trailer, wincing when his body protested. He was egg-shaped, with an ample belly hanging over his belt, a wide, full-moon face, and a high forehead gleaming with perspiration. He smiled at his old colleagues, though, and his clothes—an orange-striped shirt, blue plaid slacks and black-gray-red suspenders—suggested an off-duty clown taking his ease in a circus dressing room.

The three men, supplied with coffee by VanderWyst's wife Kay, settled in cramped quarters at the trailer's kitchen table. As they talked, Meehan smoked Winstons, Kindle tucked a wad of Copenhagen under his lip, and VanderWyst inhaled Dorals, one after another, stopping only long enough to choke out a hacking cough or pour a spoonful from the quart jar of liquid morphine he kept at his elbow.

Meehan handed VanderWyst the Jurgens police file from 1965. As he leafed through the pages, reading the reports, the memories returned.

Oh, yes, VanderWyst mumbled as he studied his writing from twenty-one years ago. He recalled that interview, this meeting, where they were, how people acted. When he finished turning through the sheets, VanderWyst looked up at Meehan and Kindle.

"There's stuff missing here," he said. "There are statements missing . . . We talked to the DeMarses and the relatives. Kay came with us and took their statements. None of that's here. Everything that wasn't a report directly written by us is missing."

"Bob, at the time of the investigation, where did the reports go?" Meehan asked. "What did you do with them?"

"They all got locked up in Wayne Armstrong's office," VanderWyst said.

An unhappy thought crossed his mind, and the pained look on VanderWyst's face now seemed to come from more than his physical problems.

"What, Bob?" Meehan asked.

"I smelled something fishy, so I made a duplicate copy back then of everything we did. Kept a full extra set of the file. Brought it home and put it in a gray fireproof box . . ."

Meehan and Kindle started to grin.

". . . but two weeks ago I began going through my things. Didn't want my kids or anyone to see this stuff, it was just too horrible, and I didn't know how much longer I'd last. So I threw it all away. Tore it all up fine as I could and tossed it in the garbage."

The three men looked at each other blankly. A hacking cough took hold of VanderWyst. When he regained control, he shook his head.

"Just two weeks ago . . . I kept that file for twenty years and nothing had ever been done. I figured they weren't going to do anything with it now . . ."

"Bob, could you go through our file real slow and jot down anything that comes to mind while you're reading?" Meehan asked.

VanderWyst poured out two teaspoons of the morphine, then lit another Doral. He was tired now, his forehead drenched with perspiration, his breaths coming in rapid, shallow gulps. The past seemed beyond reach.

"It would be real helpful if I could get together with Pete Korolchuk," he said.

Meehan wanted to make one more phone call before he retired that night. At eight o'clock, he dialed a number in Elk River. His old friend Jerome Zerwas answered on the second ring.

"What can you tell me about this, Jerome?"

The years had taken their toll on Jerome's bad knee, but not his manner. He sounded as forceful and certain as ever.

Harold had called them at ten o'clock that Palm Sunday morning with the news of Dennis's death, Jerome said. He in turn had called the police station and asked that the reporting officer, VanderWyst, stop by his home after clearing the scene. VanderWyst had shown up later that morning, saying only that Dennis had a bruise on his forehead the size of a dime. (The original nickel apparently had shrunk.) The next day Jerome had gone to the station and told Chief Armstrong he didn't want anything to do with the investigation, since his sister was involved. He preferred that the chief assign the case to a Ramsey

County investigator. He had never read any of the reports prepared by Korolchuk and VanderWyst because he wanted to stay as far away from the process as possible. He had nothing to do with the case.

Meehan had a question about those reports. He'd spent hours at the station, poring through all the felony files for 1965, and every case looked undisturbed but for one. Only case number 651514, the Jurgens death, seemed incomplete.

"There's missing statements, Jerome. Do you know where they went?"

"I don't know anything about that. I never saw those reports."

All the same, Jerome wanted to be helpful. He provided Meehan with a list of relatives' names and phone numbers, adding his suggestions on which would be the best interviews. He told him where he could find Wayne Armstrong, who was now raising horses in Colorado.

"I'm conducting an investigation on the homicide," Meehan said before they hung up. "I'll be getting back to you so you can review the statement you've given me for accuracy."

"That's fine," Jerome said.

The next morning, Tuesday, October 14, Jim Essling called Ron Meehan. A Robert Jurgens phoned the medical examiner's office, Essling reported. From up in Crookston. Thought you'd want to know.

Meehan dialed the number for the Crookston police station but Robert wasn't on duty. Not until 7:30 P.M., after several missed messages, did Ron finally reach him at his home.

"This is Ron Meehan, White Bear PD," he said. "I understand you talked to the coroner's office and I'm just doing a little follow-up. I wanted to talk to you about the case and anything that you remembered from back in 1965."

Robert had been expecting the call.

"Why wasn't it prosecuted at the time?" he said. "Who covered it up? What happened?"

"That's why I'm investigating the case," Ron answered. "At some point down the road I should have some answers."

Robert drew a breath. He'd reached a decision.

"I'm coming down to the Twin Cities soon to take care of several matters. I'd like to stop by the White Bear police station and give a statement . . . If they take this to court, I'll testify."

After he hung up, Meehan nearly jumped across the hallway to Kindle's office. It was now 8:30 P.M.

"Greg, we're going to go on this one. This guy is really going to open it up."

Early the next morning, Wednesday, October 15, Kay Vander-Wyst drove her husband to the White Bear Lake police station, and soon after, Meehan, Kindle and Bob VanderWyst left the station in an unmarked squad car, heading northwest on U.S. Route 10. The drive to Pete Korolchuk's house in Hackensack took just over three hours. At 2:15 P.M., both pairs of investigators, from past and present, sat down together for the first and only time to discuss the topic that provided them a common bond.

Meehan looked at his old colleagues. They were not much older than he, but both looked unwell—heavy and pale and short of breath. Pete had a bad heart, and Bob could hardly get around. Sitting side by side for the first time in years, however, seemed to rekindle or at least encourage the two retired officers' memories on this Wednesday morning. They now talked more freely, and with greater detail, than they had in their earlier conversations with Meehan and Kindle.

The case really started when John Norton called a sheriff's deputy who called Tom Flaherty that Palm Sunday night, Korolchuk told the younger officers. They'd staked out the Jurgens home several times and had seen Jerome there. Dr. Peterson's first death report had been so inadequate, the coroner's office had called for a revised version.

Jerome had threatened them in the squad room during that first week, saying he would do anything to protect his sister, Korolchuk told Ron and Greg. They'd informed Wayne Armstrong and put it in a police report—a report that also was missing from the file—but the chief had just gotten upset and called them liars.

They were under "extreme pressure" from Zerwas and Armstrong, VanderWyst agreed. "No one will ever know" what he and Pete went through. They had a direct order from Wayne not to take the case to the county attorney, but they did anyway. Some reports were missing even before the end of the investigation.

As the others rose to leave, Korolchuk shook his head.

"I'll never forget what Lois told me the day Dennis died," he said. "'All that training down the drain.' That's what she said."

◆   ◆   ◆

At 9:45 the next morning, Thursday, October 16, Meehan and Kindle were driving south on I-35E, headed toward a meeting in downtown St. Paul with the top guns from the White Bear police department and the Ramsey County attorney's office. Greg was not enthusiastic. "Bunch of suits sitting around," he snorted. "Administrative muckity muck bull." Ron merely grunted at his partner.

The two officers walked through the revolving doors at 480 St. Peter just before ten o'clock. Directly before them, through a pair of double doors, was the receptionist and main office for the county attorney's juvenile division, but they turned to their left and walked into a conference room that branched immediately off the lobby. There, waiting for them, were six people. On one side of a long, rectangular table sat Chief Phil Major and Lieutenant Buzz Harvey from the White Bear Lake police department. On the other side sat Ramsey County Attorney Tom Foley, his juvenile division chief, Ann Hyland, and two of his top charging attorneys, Jim Konen and Chuck Balck.

The meeting's purpose was to decide just what to do with the Jurgens matter. With an aroused birth mother and an alerted news media, the police and prosecutors now were fully involved, concerned, thinking of a possible prosecution. They wanted to do things right this time.

Their determination didn't diminish when a commotion outside the conference room revealed the nearby presence of some dozen journalists. Local Twin Cities reporters and camera crews had somehow learned of their meeting, and now were milling about in the waiting area just outside the conference room door. As the police and prosecutors turned to look, a TV camera suddenly appeared at the narrow cubbyhole window in the conference room door, its glowing red light indicating they were all being filmed. For a moment everyone froze, until someone rose and covered the small window with masking tape.

How could the news media have learned of their meeting? Tom Foley wondered. Here they were trying to be so careful, to do everything right, and now cameras were everywhere, watching them. There were plenty of times when Foley welcomed media attention, but this was not one of them.

The county attorney was an earnest, careful man whose looks and demeanor were just photogenic enough to promise even higher elected positions in the future. From a politically active Minnesota family, Foley had run unsuccessfully for county attorney in 1974, at the tender age of twenty-six, before capturing the office four years later. Once installed, he'd created two tiers of management between himself and his small platoon of attorneys, a move that had managed to alienate some of his staff. In late 1986 he'd been prosecutor for eight contentious years, and talk had him jockeying for appointment as state attorney general if the current AG, Skip Humphrey, Hubert's son, won a U.S. Senate seat.

The police and prosecutors continued their meeting in a sub-dued, edgy mood, studying lists of possible witnesses, weighing possible directions for investigation, analyzing assorted legal strategies. The conference stretched into a second, then a third hour, still with no resolution. They'd have "one dickens of a time" unraveling a twenty-one-year-old murder case, the prosecutor in adjoining Hennepin County had been quoted in the newspapers as saying, and the Ramsey County crowd couldn't disagree.

There was a neglect petition and a custody hearing in the weeks after Dennis's death, involving the Jurgenses' other boy, Robert, Ann Hyland reported. She'd found the file, but no transcript, no record of what had gone on. They knew only that Robert eventually had been returned.

"I'm prepared to assign two guys full-time," White Bear Lake Police Chief Phil Major told Foley. "I've checked with the city manager and gotten the okay. But will you commit to this? Are you going to do search warrants if we give probable cause?"

Yes, he would use search warrants, Foley replied. But the police would have to do more legwork before the prosecutor could commit himself fully.

Ron Meehan cleared his throat. He was not much given to talking in groups, but he also wasn't inclined to wait for Robert Jurgens's trip to White Bear Lake, so he had a point to make. His rumbling nasal bass filled the room.

"I think that Robert Jurgens is going to open a lot of doors here and I think he is going to be a real key to this case . . . We ought to go up to Crookston immediately and talk to him. If he sounds in person as good as he did on the phone, we have the nucleus of a case."

A direction and a decision, at last—everyone agreed Ron and Greg should go to Crookston. That would be the start. From the conversation around the table, Ron sensed they were talking about, maybe, a two-week investigation. Fine, that should be enough, he reasoned—by next week they'd have the case wrapped up.

As the meeting drew near its end, Ann Hyland placed a large envelope on the conference table.

"I have the photos of Dennis's body," she said. "They're pretty bad."

She pulled the six eight-by-ten glossies from the envelope and passed them down the table. When the photos reached him, Ron stared. These weren't just recollections or representations, that was for sure. Ron found drawing a breath difficult.

"Boy, we owe it to this little kid to put somebody in jail," he said.

Ron Meehan and Greg Kindle felt sure of one thing, at least. Now they had a horse to ride.

CHAPTER 30

Crookston

At five o'clock on the morning after their meeting with the county attorney's team, Ron Meehan and Greg Kindle left their homes for the drive to Holman Field, a small local airport in St. Paul. It was chilly and still dark, but they weren't complaining. Chief Phil Major had found them a Minnesota highway patrol pilot who was flying early that morning toward the northwest, hauling a load to the Cross River at East Grand Forks, just a short hop from the town of Crookston.

The single-engine Cessna four-seater lifted off the runway at half past six. The highway patrol pilot was an amiable Minnesota farm boy, full of talk about crops and flying. He didn't ask where the White Bear cops were headed until they were well on their way.

"We're going up to interview a possible witness in a homicide," Kindle told him. "Something that happened a long time ago."

The pilot shrugged and turned back to his discourse on farming.

For two hours, they flew at just five thousand feet. It was Friday, October 17, and the reddish-gold colors of fall blanketed the rolling fields before them. After a while, the three men fell silent, staring at the sights out their window.

They were headed toward Greg Kindle's roots.

He'd grown up in North Dakota around Fargo and Bismarck, following a father who worked in radio. Kindle had enlisted in the army out of high school and served thirty-one months in Germany between 1963 and 1966, long enough to demonstrate a propensity for brawling. He didn't have much patience for people who said things he disliked, and this tendency convinced his mother he needed a bit more education and another go-around at the Christian attitude—a judgment that led Kindle directly from the army to Harding Christian College in Arkansas, where he found himself residing in a dry county, surrounded by giggling eighteen-year-old girls. At twenty-one, Greg was thirsty and didn't like girls who giggled, so he summoned his lady friend from North Dakota, married her and left school for Minnesota. He was loading lumber at Andersen Windows when the White Bear police advertised an opening. Kindle took the civil service test and joined the force in 1969, in time gravitating toward juvenile cases.

Kindle thought of his father as the plane carried them toward North Dakota. He'd been a pretty well known North Dakota radio personality, but one day he just up and quit when the station owner fired his good friend. There's such a thing as loyalty, Larry Kindle always told his son.

Shortly after 8:30 A.M., the highway patrol pilot landed his Cessna at a small airport three miles outside of Crookston, not far from the North Dakota border. After promising to meet his passengers there later that afternoon, he once more took to the air, just as Lieutenant Doug Qualeey from the Crookston police department greeted Ron and Greg at the edge of the short runway. In the car during the brief ride into town, Kindle asked Qualeey for his impressions of Robert Jurgens.

"How's he doing? How mentally tough is he? Does he really understand what's going to be coming down the road if this unfolds the way we think it's going to?"

Qualeey expressed no doubts. He had full confidence in Robert, he said. He was a sharp, bright young man. Qualeey was running for county sheriff in a couple of months, and if he won, he wanted Robert as one of his investigators.

At the Crookston police station, Qualeey led his guests into an empty conference room. Kindle swung his heavy attaché case on the rectangular table, and from it Meehan pulled out a tape recorder, blank tapes and a microphone. Greg began assembling the various parts.

Qualeey left the room, then reappeared moments later. With him now was a young man in full, crisply pressed uniform, including a revolver holstered at his hip. Robert Jurgens was of moderate size—Kindle judged him to be 140 pounds and five feet eight inches at best—but he looked well-muscled, like a compact weight lifter.

A lot in a little package, Kindle thought. And neat as a tack. Clean and pressed from head to toe.

Robert looked right at them, too, without side glances or averted eyes. Robert's eyes were so penetrating, in fact, that Kindle thought he was trying to read their minds. Greg liked that.

The two White Bear cops introduced themselves and explained why they were there. Greg always enjoyed this part of an interview. You soften up your guy, you lay out the whole ball of wax, you get conversational.

Robert listened. He looked boyish, with blond hair and a mustache that seemed not more than thickened peach fuzz, but there was a guarded reserve to him also, a reserve that bordered on seeming cold. He appeared to be hesitating.

He'd been doing a lot of thinking, Robert explained, and a lot of talking on the phone to his mother. He had several loyalties—one to his parents, another to the police and the law. He had a lot to lose, including his parents. He had a good feeling toward his father, particularly. Still, his parents would never tell him what happened in 1965. He'd heard lots of rumors about his mother, but only knew he was out of the house for five years and then moved back in again. Now they had a lawyer who said no one should even be moving their lips. He couldn't help thinking that he might have ended up like Dennis. He had a real fondness for his dad, but as a police officer and a citizen and a human being, he had a duty.

Robert spoke softly, almost gently, suggesting a kind of uncomplicated integrity that the White Bear detectives found unusual. Time to test this guy, Greg figured.

"We're investigating a homicide and we really don't care who the bad person is," he said. "We're going to cut them off at the neck."

Robert didn't even hesitate.

"I can tell you who it is," he said evenly. "It's my mother."

Kindle nodded, and turned on the tape recorder.

The interview began at ten o'clock. Greg asked the questions and Robert talked freely, growing more animated as time went on. Listening, Ron felt transported to Gardenette Drive in the early 1960s.

Greg: When Dennis moved into the family, did you notice that Dennis was treated any differently than you were?

Robert: Yes, quite a bit differently . . . As little kids, there was always toys we would fight over, or someone would do this or someone would leave the door open or this or that . . . Dennis was the one that got the brunt of the punishment. He was always the one that got reprimanded more so than myself.

Greg: What was your mother's normal form of reprimanding when it came to Dennis?

Robert: Well, pulling of the hair, pulling of the ears, slapping, I recall a belt . . . I recall being spanked with kitchen utensils, like a wooden spoon type deal. I recall . . . a rolling pin . . . Things of that nature.

Greg: Let's talk about the events you can remember concerning what you saw happen to Dennis . . . Do you remember any specific things that happened to Dennis?

Robert: There are two events that occurred involving Dennis that have stood out in my mind for several years . . . It's something that's always been fresh in my memory . . . The first event that I recall quite clearly is being in the basement of the house, sitting on a small wooden type trike, and observing my mother punishing Dennis by means of lifting him up . . . grabbing him by the ears . . . there was a laundry tub, the side by side one which would return the soap from the washing machine. And I recall her grabbing him by the ears and submerging his head under water several times. Putting his head under the water, holding him under, lifting his head back up and putting his head under the water . . . I just remember seeing him in that position, sitting on her knee, which was propped up against the laundry tub, grabbing his ears and submerging his head in the water several times . . .

Greg: Okay, there was another incident that you also recall?

Robert: The other incident that I recall is being on that trike again in the basement and observing Dennis falling down the stairs and landing at the bottom of the steps and then being picked up and hollered at and slapped at the base of the stairs . . . I was unable to see who in fact threw him down the stairs; however, Mother was the first one that was down the steps after his fall, picking him up and slapping him again . . . hollering at him.

Greg: Okay, do you want to relay to Detective Meehan and myself what you remember about April 11, 1965?

Robert: Yes. What I recall, and again, this is a memory that has been brought back up several times during my life, for whatever reasons—

Greg: Can you talk about what those reasons might be? What gives you occasion to recollect your childhood?

Robert: Well, as my profession, being a police officer and having investigated child abuse offenses, having taken photographs of children's arms that have been broken and legs that have been broken and multiple bruises. Having to photograph these children, working with the social service, interviewing the parents, so on and so forth . . . And prior to that would be times during my childhood, I believe in the seventies, where I had additional brothers and one sister and the abuse that took place at that time . . . And prior to that . . . I would hear about it from my relatives. My relatives questioned me about the events that took place with Dennis. They were always asking me questions. I have seen several psychiatrists. I have seen several social workers. I've been placed in several different group homes . . . Somebody [was] always asking questions about this. So this is something that I've dealt with all my whole life . . . and probably will never forget.

Greg: Okay. April 11, 1965 . . . Can you relate to Detective Meehan and myself what you remember about that particular date?

Robert: From what I recall, I went to bed. Well, we all went to bed. And then, I believe that night it was storming. I just happen to remember thunder, which kind of scared me at the time . . . I then recall the bathroom light or something being turned on and my father taking Dennis to the bathroom. I believe I even saw them in the bathroom, my dad helping Dennis go to the bathroom. Something woke me up, whether it be the thunder or the lights in the bathroom, but I do recall that plain as day . . . The next thing I recall is hearing some screams in the bedroom and it now was morning . . . I don't know if they were from Dennis or from my mother. However, I remember going into the bedroom and my mother looking over Dennis and she was hitting him on the back and grabbing him and shaking him . . . it seemed like quite some time. I wasn't asked to leave the room. I stayed in there and observed this. She was very upset. She was actually angry, from what I recall. Then she picked Dennis up and held him and then started to pound on his back several times. I don't recall my dad being around or seeing him in the room . . .

Greg: And was Dennis crying?

Robert: No, there, there was nothing. He didn't make no noise, he didn't do nothing. He was just limp . . . There was nothing coming from Dennis at all . . .

Greg: Okay, now, was there anything that happened before, the night before . . . between your mother and Dennis . . . Did she get mad at him the night before?

Robert: To the best of my knowledge . . . it's been over the years, but I thought that the event of the laundry tub and the stairs preceded that event in which he was found in the bedroom. In other words, this may have happened the night before he was found in his crib. It may have . . . Those three events tie together very closely. Those three events always flash through my mind . . . That is why I believe they could be so close and fit to that exact same time.

Greg: Okay. After Dennis died, in April of 1965, did your parents ever talk to you about the fact that he had died . . . Did they . . . sit down with you and clarify in your mind the events of the night?

Robert: Nope, never happened. That's, I guess, basically a grudge that I've held. All these years I've asked my dad, "Why haven't you, after what she's done . . . why in all these years after what she's done to our family, what she's done to you"—and believe me, my dad goes through pure hell every day because [of] the living conditions that he has to put up with, and he bends over backwards for her and I don't know why—but in asking him this, I just said, "Why didn't you ever divorce her? Why didn't you ever get us out of this? Why did this go on?" And we've never really sat down and I've never really brought anything up about Dennis as far as how he died until they called me and told me that the *Dispatch* was bugging them . . . Then I called Dad at work . . . and he didn't wanna talk much about it at all . . . I guess what pisses me off now is they call back and act like it's no big deal . . . "Don't believe anything you hear and we've got an attorney." But that's what's pissing me off right now . . . Hey, this is a homicide . . . I mean, they're telling you that Dennis was killed . . . Without a doubt, without *even* a doubt, she's the one that killed Dennis!

Greg Kindle needed to know they were not dealing with a passing, momentary wave of emotion. He chose his words carefully.

"Bob, at this point in time, you understand that this information you are giving us could necessitate your testifying in a court of law if charges are brought against your mother? Are you willing to testify concerning this information that you've given us today?"

"Yes . . . I've made up my mind that this is something that I want to do . . ."

It was 11:35 A.M. They'd been talking for one and a half hours. Kindle reached over and turned off the tape recorder.

When Doug Qualeey rejoined the trio, the four officers walked down Crookston's main street to the local police hangout, The Viking Room. Over burger baskets, the cops' conversation turned to shop-talk. They compared the type of calls they got in Crookston and White Bear, and the duties of a patrolman. Robert relaxed a bit, but remained guarded, even apprehensive.

Why not? Kindle thought.

Robert again asked the question he'd first raised on the phone: "Why did this happen? Why wasn't this prosecuted?"

"We're going to find out," Greg promised. "When we do, we'll let you know."

Robert had another question: Did Ron and Greg know his Uncle Jerry? Jerry Zerwas used to be a lieutenant in the White Bear police, he said. He used to see a lot of Uncle Jerry. Thought pretty highly of him.

Meehan nodded.

"Yes," he said. "We know your Uncle Jerry."

By the time Meehan and Kindle landed back in St. Paul and pulled away from Holman Field in Kindle's Pontiac, it was 4:30 P.M., the shank of the rush hour, or what passes for one in a town of 261,000. Lost in thought, hemmed in by three lanes of bumper-to-bumper traffic, Kindle missed his interstate on-ramp and had to circle back around. What a difference between my childhood and Robert's, Greg thought. Yet we both end up on the same side of the fence. If my parents beat my brains out every day of the week, what would I be like?

Shortly after five o'clock, they reached the White Bear police station. When they said good-bye for the evening, they'd been on the go for twelve hours.

The traffic jam out of St. Paul had concerned Ron Meehan because he was fighting the clock. He needed to get home, collect his wife, and be at his sister Marlene's home in Apple Valley, twenty-five miles to the south, at six o'clock.

Every month his family got together like that at someone's house—his two sisters, a brother, their spouses, Mom and Dad. At the most, they let six weeks go by without convening for a lunch or a supper. They'd eat and play penny-ante poker and shoot the breeze. They'd been doing this now for fifteen years.

Meehan made it to supper with minutes to spare. After eating, he sat talking to his father, a retired Montgomery Ward manager.

Russell Meehan had been the number-two man in the St. Paul store and once had a shot at an even bigger job. The Ward's people had wanted him to go to Chicago for two years, with the family, but his children had been teenagers and hadn't wanted to move. The fellow who took the shot instead came back as head guy at the St. Paul Ward's. Ron Meehan thought his father a leader and a Christian, nothing like himself—at least, not the way he'd been when he was younger, when he was brawling and drinking in the years before he got out of the Marines. Since then, Ron had to admit, he'd calmed down—he'd even picked up college credits, a year here, a quarter there, until he was just on the verge of his degree in business administration. He found math and accounting a piece of cake. The calming down had brought him closer to his father.

"Dad, this case I was on today is probably the biggest thing I've had in my entire life," he said. "Boy, some of the stuff I heard today, you wouldn't believe . . . The kid put us right back in the God-blessed house in 1965."

Ron knew he shouldn't talk about a case under investigation, but he couldn't stop now. "I have to get it out of me," he told his father.

Meehan did not, however, brood over what he and Kindle would do next. That much was clear to him. They were going to reconstruct. They were going to track down all the old witnesses. They were going to find out just what happened, and why. They were going to rebuild this one brick by brick.

CHAPTER 31

The Prosecutors

Melinda Elledge was sitting on her bedroom floor, watching the TV news with her husband and three-year-old son Tim, when she first saw the image of Jerry Sherwood on the screen. The newsman was saying something about a twenty-one-year-old murder case and Mike McGee, the medical examiner.

A twenty-one-year-old murder—what problems that promised.

"I sure hope I don't get that case," Mindy said, turning to her husband.

Then thirty-eight, Mindy had been an assistant Ramsey County attorney in Tom Foley's office for ten years. She began her career as a journalist, but after her experiences with unpleasant lawyers convinced her their work couldn't be all that hard, she enrolled at the William Mitchell College of Law in St. Paul. In the Ramsey County courthouse, she soon became known for her sharp tongue and her intensity—traits that earned her admiration from some, distaste from others. On occasion she snapped at opposing attorneys, and her unrestrained fervor seemed to some a case of bad nerves, but she was bright and committed and almost always got the job done. She was not among the office's established stars, and in late 1986 had never taken a murder charge to trial, but out of a thousand cases she'd handled in a decade, she'd lost only two.

In late October, some days after the decisive meeting with the White Bear police, Tom Foley handed the Jurgens case to Mindy. He did so with mixed feelings. Mindy, he felt, was hard to manage, for she tended to go off in her own directions, and what's more, she'd campaigned openly for Foley's opponent in the 1982 election. On the other hand, she was a good and experienced criminal trial lawyer who'd handled many child abuse cases, and most certainly would be sensitive to the issues involved in Dennis Jurgens's death. Mindy, as it happened, was herself an adopted child. As a young unwed teenager, her natural mother—like Jerry Sherwood—had given her baby up soon after birth.

Mindy groaned inwardly when she received the file from Foley. All that time away from the family, she thought. And Jim Konen had told her it was a "fall on your sword before the grand jury case." Apparently they had little to go on.

"Why can't juvenile take care of its own problems?" she snapped.

Foley shrugged and turned away. He knew there was friction between Mindy and Ann Hyland, head of the juvenile division. Mindy, he believed, felt she should have gotten that division. She was older and more experienced in court than Ann, but Hyland had a good, sharp mind, so he had chosen her. He couldn't please everyone.

Alone in her small office, Mindy's attitude changed when she opened the Jurgens file. She studied the six photos of Dennis's body, one by one. Her boy Tim was almost precisely Dennis's age. This is a homicide, Mindy thought. And we're going to win.

After conferring with Jim Konen, she enlisted the aid of another assistant county attorney, her good friend Jeanne Schleh. Together, they began the painstaking task of figuring out just how to mount a prosecution in a twenty-one-year-old homicide. They showered subpoenas on all sorts of people, gathered what they could from the Ramsey and Washington county welfare files, conferred with the White Bear police, studied old records, questioned an FBI behavioral science expert, called doctors and pathologists and medical examiners. They drew up lists of potential witnesses and questions they should be asked. *State v. Loss*, now thirteen years old, was never far from their minds, for what their colleague John Tuohy had pioneered was now the standard. Mindy and Jeanne began carefully cataloging all evidence of the battered-child syndrome.

Then Mindy met Jerry Sherwood for the first time, and the encounter, in a conference room at the county attorney's office, turned out to be a rocky affair. Jerry couldn't stop sobbing, and her son, Dennis Craig, spoke in what Mindy considered to be a surly snarl. Jerry and her son didn't seem all that confident the prosecutors were going to act.

"If you don't take this to the grand jury by December first," Jerry informed Mindy, "I'm going to march on this office with fifty people."

Mindy tried to explain that they needed time to prepare a case. "You need to have faith in us," she said.

These words did not appease Jerry. The lady appeared so distraught, Mindy thought she was going to have a breakdown.

"You also need to take care of yourself," Mindy added.

Those words provoked Jerry even further. "You're treating me like a child," she snapped at Mindy.

The women's visceral dislike for each other was understandable. Jerry saw in Mindy the system that she felt had so ill-used her, and Mindy saw in Jerry a birth mother who had given up her baby for adoption. Such a chemistry could sustain only a few minutes of conversation.

"You're not going to do a goddamn thing for us," Jerry finally announced, terminating the meeting.

Moments later an assistant county attorney named Clayton Robinson, Jr., happened to walk by the conference room. Looking through the open door, he noticed Jerry sitting alone at a table, shaking with sobs.

"Jerry, how're you doing?" he said.

Clayton, as it happened, knew Jerry. He once had interviewed her family about a robbery case he was prosecuting, a case in which Jerry and her son Dennis Craig eventually testified as witnesses. Even before that, he'd met her socially through mutual friends—one night in 1984 when Clayton found himself with a group at a bar, Jerry had joined their table. Falling into conversation that evening, Clayton had asked about her children, and Jerry had mentioned that she once had a boy who was adopted out, a boy who died. She hadn't elaborated, but when Clayton read the first *St. Paul Dispatch* article about the reopened murder case, he thought this might be Jerry's kid. Now here she was in the county attorney's office. The stormy, disordered look in her eyes gave him pause—Clayton too thought Jerry seemed agitated and emotionally overwhelmed, near a nervous breakdown.

"I'm not doing well, Clayton," she said.

Clayton, hoping he might be able to calm her down, suggested lunch, and they agreed to meet the next day.

Smoothing the waters was not a foreign activity for Clayton. At thirty-four, he was a polished prosecutor with a composed, polite manner that bordered at times on the orotund. A lawyer since 1979, with Ramsey County since 1982, Clayton had become known in the courthouse for his pleasant, unflappable style and his dignified closing arguments. He won accolades from his supervisors in 1985 for getting a conviction in the Tia McBroom murder trial, a case many prosecutors thought unwinnable.

Clayton, the only black lawyer working in the forty-five-person Ramsey County attorney's office, took considerable pride in the distance he'd traveled from the Chicago projects where he grew up, the son of a cop shot and killed while making an arrest. After his father died, a Chicago civic organization had paid his way through college and then the Drake University law school in Des Moines. Law school had opened his eyes to a world he'd never before imagined.

He met Jerry for lunch on November 19 at the Baker Square coffee shop on Ford Parkway in St. Paul, near the border with Minneapolis, close to the apartment building she then was managing and across from a Ford truck manufacturing plant. Jerry no longer appeared agitated. She was simply angry, and distrustful of the prosecutor's office.

At least she knew Clayton. He'd even dated one of her daughters for a while, as it happened. And he was a black man—that helped, that mattered to Jerry. She'd learned in her life to trust the black community in the Twin Cities area more than the white one. The sight of a blue-eyed blonde of Danish-German extraction sharing bar stools with black men was not an altogether familiar sight in downtown St. Paul, but Jerry didn't mind.

"The one thing I have to say is that it was like white people didn't care," she explained later. "Maybe a lot of people don't think too highly of the black race, but if you were on the run and you went to a white person's house and wanted to take a bath and wash your clothes, they would tell you you couldn't do it. But you could go to a black person's house and take a bath and they'd wash your clothes and give you a hot meal and send you on your way."

Sitting across the table from Clayton now, Jerry spoke bluntly. She didn't trust Mindy Elledge. She didn't think the woman could do a good job. She'd done some checking on her. Why, just recently an appellate court had overturned an aggravated drunk driving case Mindy had prosecuted. The system had wronged Jerry before, and she wasn't going to stand by and let it happen again. The news media was on to her now—the reporters were her allies.

"Mindy's a bitch. I don't trust her and I don't like her." Jerry offered this judgment at regular intervals over lunch.

Clayton considered the angry person before him. Jerry Sherwood was a hard woman, he reasoned, and she was talking irrationally, making conclusions without fact. She clearly disliked Mindy partly because Elledge wouldn't share with her information from their investigation. Jerry also had a habit of blaming "the system" for all her life's unhappiness. "Didn't the system think this baby might change my life?" she'd tell people who asked about Dennis. "Didn't they think that this wild and unruly girl might settle down if she had a baby to love, and to love her?" Words like that. All the same, Clayton respected Jerry Sherwood—she was streetwise, and Clayton valued that quality. Streetwise and determined. Dennis Jurgens couldn't have a better mother for the current purpose of seeking justice. To Clayton she was like a dog who wouldn't let go of a bone, like a dog who'd bite if you tried to grab it away.

"Mindy's a bitch. I don't trust her. I don't like her," Jerry repeated.

Clayton paused, gathering his words into full, rounded sentences.

"The present county attorneys are not the same people who failed to prosecute in 1965," he explained. "I am offering my personal assurances that this case will be handled properly."

Jerry was not appeased. She demanded they take the case to the grand jury immediately. Clayton again tried to explain. "We can't do that until we've built a case."

His efforts weren't working, though. Jerry was growing angrier, not calmer.

"Okay," she said suddenly. "I'll accept your reassurances—but only if they put you on the case . . . You tell Foley to put you on the case, or else I'm marching down there with a picket line of fifty women."

Jerry no longer seemed a friend, or even an acquaintance. Her manner was all business, cold and hard.

Clayton felt uncomfortable. He'd come to calm her down, to be a mediator, and now Mindy would think he had betrayed her. It would appear that he was horning in on the case. Still, he had to admit it was a terrific case.

Back at the office, he briefed Jim Konen and then Tom Foley on what had just happened. Summoning his courage, he also visited Mindy in her office. As he figured, she was furious.

Foley needed just twenty-four hours to consider the prospect of fifty mothers picketing his office with placards accusing him of being soft on child abuse. On November 20, Konen met alone, separately, first with Mindy, then Clayton, revealing Foley's as yet unofficial decision. Later that day, Mindy, now feeling the urge to document events in the Jurgens prosecution, summarized the encounter in a personal log:

"Meeting with Konen 11/20/86. He told me Jeanne would be taken off the case and Clayton would be on it because Jerry Sherwood does not feel comfortable with me on the case, but would if Clayton Robinson, a personal friend, assisted."

Clayton began immediately to acquaint himself with the Jurgens file. Four days later, at noon on November 24, Mindy and Jeanne met together with Konen to get the more official word.

"Konen says it has been decided that Jeanne is off, Clayton is on the case," Mindy wrote in her log that day. "Jeanne is very angry. I am very angry. Konen tells Jeanne she can stay on the case 'for the rest of the week' (two days—Thanksgiving holiday). We tell him that it will set the investigation back at least a month and ask if our talking to Foley would help. We are told 'no.'"

Mindy stormed into Clayton's office, making no effort to hide her feelings. She was very angry, she said. She'd been working well with Jeanne. This was shabby treatment of Jeanne. She might just drop out of the case.

Clayton understood. Mindy is intense, he reasoned. She takes the weight of the world on her shoulders. Now she feels betrayed.

The next day, November 25, emotions had calmed enough for Mindy, Jeanne and Clayton to meet all afternoon, figuring out how to bring Clayton up to speed and make the transition.

"We all realize that this change has been detrimental to and has slowed the investigation," Mindy wrote in her log. "I will have to learn all that Jeanne was doing and Clayton will need to go over the entire case."

That night, Mindy drafted a memo addressed to Foley, Konen, Clayton and Jeanne that expressed her concerns about the investigation and Jerry's success at making demands. The next morning, she had it typed and distributed. To eliminate any question about when or if the memo was sent, she mailed a copy to herself as well.

It was now Wednesday, November 26, the last working day before the four-day Thanksgiving weekend. Clayton had been reviewing the Jurgens file all week, but Mindy and Jeanne had purposely held back the photos of Dennis's body until he'd absorbed the facts. Late in the day he came to Mindy's office. Jeanne was present.

"I'm ready," he said.

Mindy unzipped her briefcase and pulled out the six eight-by-ten glossies.

Clayton in his career had seen pieces of bodies, motorcyclists hurtled head first into trees, guys shot four times, but he'd never seen anything like this.

"This woman needs prosecuting real bad," he said.

Returning after the Thanksgiving holiday, Mindy and Clayton met with Tom Foley on Monday, December 1. The county attorney was less than delighted with Mindy's memo.

"Foley not too happy about my memo," Mindy wrote in her log, "and said 'why is it every time I assign you to something you need help?' I said this case *needs* two people on it . . ." She continued:

> He said he wanted to know what my memo meant. I said I wanted to let him know that I thought his decision to take Jeanne off the case was very detrimental to the case because it set the investigation back by a month and that she and I both felt it had been going well. I also told him I was very concerned about the appearance that Jerry Sherwood was calling the shots. I explained that, even today, she was making additional demands. She called Clayton and told him that Ron Meehan had promised her a photograph of Dennis from one of our files . . . (She also continues her slanderous attack on me.) I told Foley that she is very good at playing people against each other and that, as with the press, only one person should be designated to talk with her. Tom and Clayton agreed. Clayton will talk with her. She told Clayton today that she is planning to talk with *People* magazine in January, even

though she told Clayton and Tom that she would quit talking to the press if Clayton got assigned to the case. Clayton
told her, in my presence, that he couldn't stop her, but that it
would hurt the case a lot . . .

Foley also wanted progress report, seems more interested
in knowing if we can "get" Jerome Zerwas for messing up
investigation. I said I doubted it.

Two days later, on December 3, Mindy and Clayton again met
with Foley. The topic once more was Jerry Sherwood. Mindy summarized the conference in her log:

Clayton talked with Jerry Sherwood. She was very angry that,
now, she was directed by White Bear PD to go to Clayton for
info. She told Clayton that she no longer trusted him. She also
said she demanded to know when case would be presented
to grand jury. Clayton said he was trying to get familiar with
the case and that that had delayed it and that he couldn't see it
being presented before late January or early February. She said
that was *not* acceptable and that she would "have to do what
she had to do." I told Tom that, as I predicted, she would be
making more demands. He said she would be making *no* more
demands, he had gone as far as he would go. I said I thought
Mrs. Sherwood did not care whether Mrs. Jurgens ever was
prosecuted successfully, that she was getting far more attention
by telling everyone that she got screwed by the system and was
still getting screwed by the system. Tom agreed.

Although he was not showing it, Clayton too was concerned
about Sherwood now. His approach to the problem differed from
Mindy's, however.

Soon after the meeting with Foley, Clayton arranged for St. Paul
attorney Ray Harp to represent Sherwood. You need a lawyer protecting your interests, Clayton explained to Jerry.

A sharp lawyer like Harp could complicate matters even more,
but Ray, as it happened, also was Clayton's good friend. Easier to talk
to a clever lawyer than an angry Jerry Sherwood, Clayton figured.
Maybe this would control her. He hoped so.

CHAPTER 32

I Want to Talk to You

In late October, the prosecutors and detectives had spent a day together drawing up a list of the most important witnesses, those Ron and Greg should go after first. Geography dictated some choices, but above all, the police wanted to find the people who had talked the most and provided written statements in 1965. In VanderWyst and Korolchuk's reports, Lois's sister Sharon Kopp seemed to have had plenty to say, so Ron and Greg started there.

Finding five Kopps but no Sharon in the local directories, Meehan visited the city utility department, the county abstract clerk, and the warranty deed department before learning that a Charles D. and Sharon T. Kopp had sold a piece of property in June of 1965. After two days of work, Ron had an address for Lois's sister in the town of Wyoming, Minnesota.

The interview there on the evening of October 20 started off well enough. The Kopps' home was newly built, rustic in design—worth at least $125,000, Meehan figured. Charley, he'd heard, was either an electrician or plumber. The couple greeted their visitors with a pleasantness bordering on the ingratiating. The niceties ended, though, when Greg started asking Sharon about the stories she'd told Korolchuk twenty-one years before.

No, Sharon said, I don't remember making those types of statements to Sergeant Korolchuk.

She was leaning forward, her jaw set, staring Kindle straight in the eye. Sharon reminded Ron of all the Zerwas gals he knew.

Greg pulled Korolchuk's reports from a file and began reading the sergeant's words from a report dated April 20, 1965: "Mrs. Kopp said she then heard on the phone what sounded like blows being struck . . . Mrs. Kopp relates she could hear the child's voice . . . begging not to be hit any more . . ."

At the time of the incident, Sharon explained, she thought that quite possibly her sister was being too hard on Dennis, but in the years since she'd become a parent herself, and there have been times she had to discipline her children in ways that might sound to others, on the phone, worse than it actually was.

Greg kept reading from Korolchuk's report: "Ear pulling . . . clothespins on Dennis's penis . . . toilet training . . . blows with a drumstick . . ."

No, Sharon responded, still looking right at Greg, I never saw any of that and don't remember making any such comments to Korolchuk. Maybe Pete had a bad memory or misconstrued the facts or lacked police expertise. I never said those things.

Greg was getting aggravated. Did the Kopps think Korolchuk was dead and couldn't discount what they were saying? Did the Kopps think he and Ron were the two dumbest people they'd ever met? Well, he'd have to change their minds about that—

Just then Kindle felt a kick under the table. Ron, his eyes blank and averted, said nothing.

Let them just go ahead and talk, tell you whatever they want. That was the advice Ron always gave Greg. You don't have any way to shoot holes in their story until they've told you what their story is.

Three nights later, on the evening of October 23, Ron dialed a phone number in Bullhead City, Arizona. The conversation that followed also started in a friendly manner, for Ron knew Lois's brother Lloyd Zerwas from their younger days in White Bear Lake. He liked him, in fact, and considered him the best of the Zerwas brothers. Years before, when he'd worked for Strauss Skate Company, Lloyd was the man the cops came to when they wanted their guns nickel-plated. Lloyd's wife Donna grabbed an extension phone as the two men started talking. Although pleased to hear from Ron, the couple sounded hesitant.

They'd already testified once against Lois in juvenile court in 1965, Lloyd and Donna said. They'd been outcasts in the Zerwas family ever since. They'd left Minnesota partly to get away from the family, and now they were living the good life in Arizona, where Lloyd had a job with the phone company. Two thousand miles wasn't far enough away. They really didn't want to get involved again. They'd given Pete Korolchuk long written statements right after Dennis's death. Why not use them? Those statements should be on file with the White Bear police.

Yes, Ron thought, they should be.

"Why wasn't this prosecuted in 1965?" Lloyd asked. "Since then, my sister has suffered the pains of hell, and now suddenly the case has been reopened and is on her doorstep . . . Lois should never have been allowed to adopt any of the children . . ."

We don't know what happened back then, Ron explained. We're trying to find out. We sure could use your help now.

"It's not going to go anyplace," Lloyd said.

"Hey, look, there's no doubt in my mind we're going to get charges and we're going to get her convicted, going to put her in jail," Ron said.

"That'll never happen, Ron. It's been too long."

"Well, Lloyd, let's give it a shot."

By the close of the conversation, Lloyd seemed to relent a little. At some point down the road, he said, if Ron and Greg wanted to come on out to Arizona, maybe they'd give another statement.

Ron had one other question. They were trying to locate the four other children the Jurgenses had adopted, the ones from Kentucky. Did Lloyd or Donna know their whereabouts?

Lloyd knew they went by the name Jurgens in years past. But no, he didn't know where they were now.

When Lloyd and Donna's daughter Nancy learned her parents had been talking to the White Bear detectives, she passed the word that she too wanted to speak to them, so Greg called her one day at her home in Chattanooga, Tennessee.

Nancy, thirteen when Dennis died, was thirty-four now, a long-legged blonde with four children. There was something she wanted to say.

She'd heard the news of Dennis's death as she was sitting on the steps of her family's front porch, waiting for her parents to finish dressing for Palm Sunday church services, she told Greg. Right away, she'd figured this was no accident. She'd heard the adults talking about all the abuse to Dennis.

"I was around everybody when they were talking . . . And I heard everyone talking of everything that she did . . . I don't care how many in my family want to talk. They all know what she did . . . I don't understand why the family doesn't want to see her helped . . . they should have done this years ago. They should have made sure that she was put in and helped . . . Why my uncles and aunts didn't say anything I, to this day, will never know. I don't understand it. And if they're not saying anything today I don't know why because they do know . . . They're older than I am and they seen these things as an adult."

Late in the morning on October 24, Robert Jurgens and his wife Joanne, a paralegal, met Ron and Greg at the White Bear police station. They settled in chairs in Ron's office while Robert reviewed and signed a typewritten transcript of the interview conducted the week before in Crookston.

Robert seemed as certain and self-possessed as he'd been at their first encounter. In fact, he had a plan to help the investigation.

If he got his father alone, he said, he thought Harold would tell the whole story. He thought his father would level with him. What did they think of setting Harold up?

"Are you talking about bugging the place?" Greg asked.

"Yes," Robert said.

The two detectives glanced at each other. They'd been thinking of just this sort of deal themselves, but had hesitated to bring it up for fear of its effect on Robert. Now Robert was volunteering. He'd done his soul-searching before giving the statement in Crookston, the detectives reasoned. Now he's starting to think almost the same way we are about the case.

"Well, we're certainly not in disfavor of that if you want to do it," Greg said.

They worked out a plan. Robert would arrange to meet Harold for a cup of coffee at the Holiday Inn on Highway 12 in the suburb of Maplewood. Afterward, he'd invite his father up to his room. Greg and Ron, renting the adjoining room, would have the place bugged.

"You set it up with Harold, and we'll line up the rest," Greg said.

As rapidly as the White Bear detectives were working, so too were several Twin Cities reporters. In fact, Ron and Greg soon realized they were competing with parallel investigations launched by three different local news organizations. Brian Bonner at the *St. Paul Pioneer Press Dispatch*, Dennis Cassano at the *Minneapolis Star and Tribune* and Frank Mann at KSTP-TV—all eager to expose a possible whitewash, all sniffing malfeasance in the air—were busily tracking down witnesses and seeking documents. The police and the prosecutors began to feel under siege by the press and compelled to move quickly, for the journalists' operating assumption seemed to be that the authorities once again would drop the ball.

On October 30, Ron and Greg delivered sealed search warrants to Washington County officials, collecting probate, adoption and police files on Renee, Grant, Michael and Richard Howton Jurgens. Culling information from those papers, Ron on November 3 called the Howton children's natural father at a number in Dawson Springs, Kentucky. Might he know his offspring's present location? Meehan asked.

Louis Wayne Howton proved to be chock full of hillbilly talk. He felt the urge to review with the White Bear policeman his lifetime of "horseshit luck," and Ron felt obliged to listen. Only after they had chewed on that lamentable history for a time did Ron manage to extract what he needed. Three of the kids were living in Carrollton, Georgia, Howton said. He seldom heard from the fourth, Grant, but thought he lived in the St. Paul area. If Ron called back in four days, on November 7, he'd have a phone number and address in Georgia. Howton understood the kids had gone through "holy hell" at the Jurgens house, and he felt sure they'd have things of interest to tell the police.

Conferring with Mindy and Clayton after this conversation, Ron made plans to deliver additional search warrants to Lutheran Social Service and the state adoption unit. They were, he believed, now on a roll.

Whatever sense of accomplishment he felt, however, evaporated the next morning when he picked up the local newspaper. On page one, with a five-column-wide headline, the November 4 edition of the *Minneapolis Star and Tribune* carried a story by staff reporter Dennis Cassano.

"A couple whose adopted child's death in 1965 recently was ruled a homicide also adopted other children," the lead sentence began, "but lost four of them when a judge ordered the youngsters removed from the home, some of them said."

Cassano had found the three Kentucky children in Georgia, and had interviewed them at length about life in their adoptive home. He'd also talked to Cherie Riley, the youngsters' foster mother in Kentucky. The Jurgenses still were not being mentioned by name, for they hadn't been charged.

"Ramsey County officials last week obtained the Washington County juvenile court records regarding the adoption and removal of the four siblings," Cassano continued, "but the three who were interviewed by the *Star and Tribune* said police have not contacted them. Investigators also have not interviewed the woman who was the foster mother for the four before they were adopted."

Ron wanted to tear the newspaper apart, but kept reading.

Renee, Mike and Ricky told about getting beaten and slapped and yanked about. They told of their adoptive mother ramming Grant's head against a wall. They described her tantrums when a curtain or a hanger wasn't straight. They explained how their adoptive mother inspected the house with white gloves after they cleaned, and beat them with a metal pancake spatula if she found dust.

While the White Bear police were still figuring out who could pay for an out-of-state trip, other news organizations were en route to Georgia. That very night, watching the evening TV news on KSTP, Ron saw the eldest Kentucky youngster, Renee, being interviewed in Carrollton by Frank Mann. She was now twenty-six, vivacious and bright-eyed.

Have the police interviewed you? Mann was asking.

No, sir, Renee was saying. I haven't heard from any of them.

Ron felt like throwing a shoe at the television screen. They're making a big monkey of us, he thought. On top of that, they're screwing everything up. What lousy timing.

As it happened, Robert was planning to meet Harold at the Holiday Inn in Maplewood the next day—he was down in the Twin Cities area that night. Ron felt sure these news stories would louse up the deal.

He was right. Late that night the Jurgenses' attorney, alarmed by the news reports, reminded his clients to trust nobody. Early the next morning Harold broke the appointment with his son, and Robert, after borrowing meal money from Greg Kindle, began the long drive back to Crookston.

Soon after, Jerry Sherwood called Ron and Greg to complain. Why, she demanded, hadn't they interviewed those kids in Georgia?

For all the trouble they brought, the newspaper article and TV broadcast also yielded a helpful dividend. At 4:50 P.M. on November 6, two days after the stories appeared, Lois Jurgens, alone at home, troubled by what she'd heard and read, called her son Robert in Crookston.

How are you doing? she asked.

Fine, how are you doing? Robert responded.

As he talked, Robert began taking notes, preserving the conversation on a legal-sized ruled yellow pad.

"I'm sure you're not feeling too well because of the coverage that's taking place . . ." he said. "Did you see Renee on TV?"

Lois grew angry and coarse.

"Yeah . . . that lying bitch . . . She looks like a little whore on TV . . . I'm not taking this sitting down . . . I'm going to get stuff on her . . . I'm going to start telling people about when Renee and I were down in the basement, she was asking how big your cock was and if it was bigger than Grant's . . . I'm not taking any of this shit lying down. I'm fighting back. I'm going to dig up everything I can on those kids . . ."

Moments later, she changed course.

"Robert, what is this shit about a white glove? I never used a white glove to go around and check stuff, did I?"

"Well, you did a couple of times," Robert replied. "You came around with a white glove."

"Yeah, well, maybe I did once or twice . . ."

Lois began reading out loud from a recent *Stillwater Gazette* article that summarized the results of Dennis's autopsy. The article talked of peritonitis and a ruptured bowel and facial bruises.

Robert figured this was a good time to dig, to see what he could find out.

"Well, were there any facial bruises?"

"Yes," Lois said. "That kid was always falling down . . . He fell down the stairs several times . . . He never felt it . . ."

Dennis had a medical problem with feeling pain, she explained. One time when he fell down the steps, he had a big crack on his forehead and ended up with a soft bump on his head. She called the doctor and the doctor told her not to worry or get nervous, just keep an eye on him.

"Another time," she said, "I remember hearing a real loud noise and I thought you kids were in the basement playing with a ball . . . And when I looked, there was Dennis laying at the bottom of the steps . . . I ran down and I picked him up . . . I got a little excited . . ."

So my memory is right, Robert thought.

"Yeah, Mom, I remember him falling down the steps. I remember you picking him up and screaming and hollering . . . You got pretty excited . . ."

Robert guided the conversation to the morning of Dennis's death, and Lois retold the same story she had offered so many years before. Dennis was okay at eight o'clock, sitting on the toilet talking to Harold, then dead an hour and a half later.

This also fits, Robert thought. Something about his memories didn't make sense, though.

"God dang, Ma. What's weird about this whole thing is I remember Dennis talking to Dad in the bathroom. And he seemed fine. He wasn't in any pain . . . And then he was put to bed and an hour later we find him dead in his crib . . . That is strange as hell . . . How could he just be so fine and die all of a sudden?"

Lois didn't know. The only thing she could think of was Dennis slipping the night before on the wet concrete floor in the basement.

"Well, Ma, maybe it wasn't that. Maybe it was when he fell down the steps . . . He took a pretty good fall . . ."

No, Lois said. That happened about a week before he died.

She feels no remorse, Robert thought. No tears, nothing in her voice. It was just kind of weird now to finally hear her version after all this time.

"You know, I'm sure you're pretty close with Uncle Jerome," Robert said. "I'm sure you've, you know, talked to him about the matter."

"Yeah," Lois replied. "We've talked and he just can't believe this is going on . . ."

Lois began recalling her childhood.

"Well, when we were growing up we were taken out to the barn and we were whipped and beat up there . . . Every one of us turned out just fine . . ."

She went on at length in this vein until Robert guided the conversation to the time when Dennis's genitals got burned.

"I remember there was a time when Dennis wasn't around the house. I think he was in the hospital or something. I remember you or Dad saying he wasn't going to be home for a while . . ."

"I don't want to talk about that," Lois said quickly.

Instead she started reminiscing about Dennis in other ways. "He was so very hyper," she said. "He never wanted to eat. All he wanted to do was drink out of a bottle. He had worms and couldn't be toilet trained. . . ."

Just the opposite of me, Robert thought. I behaved.

She had to dump Vaseline on his head for cradle cap, Lois was saying now, and tape a quarter on his belly to push in his protruding belly button. She called the doctor but the doctor said don't worry about the belly button.

"Well, geez, Ma, you shouldn't have anything to worry about, then. All these incidents just happened. It's just a mere fact of getting Dr. Peterson . . . You should be able to testify that you were always on the phone with him . . ."

Lois had a question.

"Robert, we never mistreated you, did we? You can't honestly say that we ever abused you or mistreated you."

Robert answered without thinking: "Well, I guess not. I'm still alive, walking and talking." As soon as he said that, he knew he'd offended her.

"That wasn't very nice to say," Lois responded.

"Well, you know how I am," Robert said. "Sometimes I don't use much tact. I just say what's on my mind, and that's what came to mind and that's what I said."

Just then, Lois heard Harold coming through the front door.

"Oh, shit, now he's gonna be pissed off as hell that I'm talking to you," she said.

Time to back down, to work off that subject, Robert thought. Can't let Harold hear her voice so tense . . . Maybe he could get something from Harold, too.

"Ma, I was gonna tell Dad a little joke here . . ."

"Well, what's the joke?"

"I was gonna tell Dad that when I send his birthday card to him, I wanted to know if I should send it to the attorney."

"Robert, don't say that . . . Just a second. I'll put him on the phone."

When he picked up an extension phone to join the conversation, Harold sounded ebullient.

"Hi, how you doing? What's the joke?"

Robert couldn't stop himself: "Should I send your birthday card to the attorney?"

The phone line seemed to go dead for five seconds, then Harold forced a laugh. "Well, yeah, maybe you should."

Robert, wanting to keep the conversation going, began to read Renee and Mike's quotes from Dennis Cassano's *Star and Tribune* article. The words drew the expected response. Lois grew loud and angry—she's still got that tone of voice she used years ago, Robert thought.

"Oh, I just can't believe what a lying little bitch she is—"

Harold stopped the conversation.

"We're done talking now," he said. "I gotta get off the phone. That's enough. No more—no more talking."

"Geez, Dad, you know, I suppose you didn't care for that joke but you know . . . I sure know where I stand . . ."

"We just gotta keep our mouth shut," Harold said.

"I realize that, but goddamn, the only time I've ever wanted to sit down and talk with you, you shut me off because of your goddamn attorney . . . I can understand where you're coming from . . . But it sure made me feel bad. It really hurt to hear you put me off . . ."

"Well, that's what I'm paying this guy for," Harold said. "I gotta keep my mouth shut."

"Even if it's your own son?"

"Yup."

"Well, I understand where you're coming from, but I'm really hurt you can't even talk to your own son."

Harold wavered.

"I will call you and talk," he said. "There will be a time when I call you and talk to you. Right now I can't say anything."

Robert directed words of farewell to his mother: "Probably the best thing now, Mom, is that we don't talk at all. You guys can't talk to me, so we probably shouldn't talk at all until this thing is cleared up."

"No," Lois said. "I still want to talk to you."

That same night at 9:45 P.M., Robert placed a collect call to Greg Kindle at the White Bear police station.

Greg turned on his tape recorder.

"You got a call, huh?" Greg said.

"Yeah . . ." Robert said. "It's probably the most that we will ever hear from Lois Jurgens as to what happened. I've got her recollection as to what happened. I've got her defense to everything . . . I've got the exact detail of the day in question . . ."

"Holy cow!" Greg said.

"It was really, boy, I tell you, I've interviewed a few people and it's never been a homicide . . . Felony thefts, rape, stuff like that . . . But I tell you, any skills I had, I really had to put to the test tonight . . . You know, it took a little digging, and the wife was looking at me like, you lying son of a bitch. You know, because it was tough for me. I had to play her buddy and I don't like her."

"Holy cow! I can imagine," Greg said.

"What happened was, Mother . . . this Renee deal was gettin' to Ma . . . Renee on TV . . . Mama must've started getting pretty lonely. She must've really been down and out because she called me when Dad wasn't home . . . I've got everything written down as to what was said . . ."

Reviewing his notes as he spoke, intoxicated with the insights he'd gleaned, Robert walked through the highlights of his conversation with Lois. He felt he finally understood his mother.

"Then she kind of went into her childhood . . . And . . . now I can see a pattern of her being abused as a child . . . And I can now see some of the reason as to how this got carried over . . . Her reason or, you know, her ability to do this to Dennis is because it happened to her . . . This was what she was accustomed to . . . And this was how she was gonna reprimand Dennis . . . I mean, that's . . . that's one good thing that came out of this. I know why he was beaten . . . You can kind of see a pattern as to how she got this into her . . . When she lost her temper, the only thing she could revert to is the way . . . she was treated and the way she was reprimanded when she was a kid . . ."

"Yeah," Greg said. "What goes around comes around."

Robert also felt he understood now why he had lived and Dennis had died.

"Had I been like Dennis, been a little hyper, or went through that stage when you don't wanna eat food . . . He did everything wrong, I did everything right . . . I must have toed the mark half-assed decent . . . And then she was accustomed to that and when Dennis came in, she probably assumed that gee, we're gonna get another kid. He's gonna be just like Robert. And he was just the opposite . . . As a result, he paid the price . . . Usually, if I would do something, Dennis would take the pain for him and me. This little guy . . . I could have screwed up something awful but she'd come over and lay into Dennis because Dennis was the hyper one and didn't want to eat and he threw his shit on the wall . . . And ah, I feel bad about that. I feel bad that's the way it had to be, but boy . . . God . . . I was Mr. Perfect . . . Even if I did something wrong, Dennis took the receiving end . . . poor Dennis . . ."

Greg turned the conversation to more immediate matters. The Jurgenses had hired one of St. Paul's most prominent criminal defense attorneys, Douglas Thomson, and the police wondered what he was up to.

"We heard . . . Ron heard it from someone . . . that this attorney has hired a former policeman or something who is purporting to be a White Bear Lake cop. And this guy is calling people within the family to see if they're gonna talk or not."

"Well," Robert said, "I heard the same thing tonight from a reporter, from Bonner from the *St. Paul Dispatch*. He said that Mrs. Puckett [Sherwood] and others are scared to death . . . and they're really getting nervous and they're really paranoid because there's rumors that the defense right now is getting family members together and getting compatible reports from each and every one so that everything coincides when this thing hits the fan . . ."

"Uh-huh," Greg said.

"And you know, it's the big . . . ah . . . that Jerome's involved. But . . . ah . . . you were right. Jerome has been in contact with her . . ."

"So he has—she said that she talked to Jerome?" Greg asked.

"Yup, yup."

Robert turned back to his conversation with Brian Bonner.

"Mrs. Puckett now is really getting nervous and you know, they're thinking this is gonna come to trial and they're wondering what the police are really doing . . ."

"Now who said this? Your mom?"

"No, this was that Brian Bonner from the *St. Paul Dispatch* . . . He's very close to Puckett. I guess he said he talks to her like two times a day."

"Sherwood." Greg finally corrected him. "Sherwood is her name."

"Yeah, Sherwood," Robert said. "He says she is just outraged. She's really upset. She's afraid of what will happen . . . And she's gonna try everything that she can to make sure that they keep working. And I just told him, I said, someone should sit down with her and explain to her this is not like watching 'Miami Vice' or things of that nature. These things take time, you know . . . And the longer it's being worked on, I said, you'd think that would be a good sign . . ."

"This is Bonner you were talking to?" Greg was not pleased.

"Yeah, everything was off the record. I didn't talk to him for a real long period of time . . . I'm keeping friendly with him so they don't bug me or harass me . . . If you wanna check with me once a week . . . you can do that, I says . . . but I'm not gonna sit down and talk with you . . . so you can get my story on because it's gonna be prime time when this comes . . ."

Greg felt relieved.

"Yeah, no police officer in his right mind would do that . . ." he said. "I mean, you know, you can't trust the press . . . I mean, anybody that goes to bat with the press is nuts and we know that . . . You know, that's good thinking. I'm proud of you, kid."

Robert did not want to hang up yet. He still didn't understand just how Dennis had died.

"And the night in question . . . something's wrong there. I remember Dennis being okay. My recollection of it being at night may be off. Maybe this did happen in the morning . . . But he was okay at one point. At what point did she beat him to death?"

"Probably over a period of time," Greg said.

Robert still couldn't let it go. Peritonitis was painful and protracted and incapacitating. How could Dennis have been okay just before he died?

"They've got the cause of death, a rupture, but was it a delayed type process?" he asked. "Was it something where he sat on the toilet . . . and then he was placed back in his bed and died? But he was talking. I heard him talking . . . My dad was talking to him . . . my dad was the last one to see him alive. My dad and I were the last ones to hear him alive . . . And he was fine."

"Uh-huh," Greg said. "Yeah, I don't know."

"What process internally happened to kill him between that time . . .?"

"Yeah . . . I don't know."

"That's what's bugging me now. Did she go in there and thrash on him? And Harold may have heard this? I think this is where Harold comes in playing the cover part . . . That's about as close as my imagination can tie it . . ."

"I don't know anything different myself," Greg said. "That's where Mike McGee comes in and all the rest of that business . . ."

"Those screams . . . There were screams. He wasn't screaming in the bathroom when Harold took him in there."

"It's a long time ago," Greg said. "The sequence of events might not be quite right, but sooner or later the pieces will fit together and maybe all that business will be clarified somehow. I don't know at this point exactly how, but you know, the kid was definitely abused and died because of that abuse. There's no question about that. We'll just have to see how it shakes down."

Robert was finding it difficult to hang up.

"The spooky part about it is when she said he was laying there staring at the ceiling . . . Ah, what a deal. Well, I know you got a night ahead of you yet, but I figured I'd better talk to you . . . To me this was important . . . It answered some questions for me and I know her reasons, which I've never known before . . ."

"Well, listen," Greg said, "keep us posted if you hear anything else and thanks for giving us this information and, you know, just take life easy and relax and we'll see what we can do on this end . . ."

"Okay, will do," Robert said. "Thanks for listening."

CHAPTER 33

Very Nice People

The night Robert called to report his conversation with Lois, Greg Kindle had been working late at the station, trying to catch up with the news media and the business in Georgia. "Anybody who goes to bat with the press is nuts," Greg told Robert, but all the same, the enterprising journalists had altered the detectives' plans.

Before Dennis Cassano's article and Frank Mann's broadcast, Ron and Greg were mainly thinking of a journey to Arizona, to the homes of Lloyd and Donna Zerwas and Richard Norton, three people who'd signed written statements in 1965. The Kentucky kids would be helpful in reconstructing Lois's patterns, but they weren't the top priority— that is, they weren't until the headlines and broadcasts made them so.

The problem went beyond the public impression of authorities moving too slowly. Greg and Ron had learned that the three Howton kids in Georgia had provided reporter Dennis Cassano with signed releases that would allow him to read their sealed juvenile files. Such critical information spread across the *Star and Tribune* front page, the detectives feared, could taint the prosecution.

At 5:00 P.M. on November 6, even as Robert was talking to Lois on the phone, Greg reached Renee at a number in Carrollton, Georgia.

"We were well aware of your involvement in this case," he explained. "Out of necessity, we took care of some other matters first, but now we want to interview you and your brothers."

Renee understood, and was willing to talk. She had much to tell, she said. But she didn't know about her brothers. It might be hard to get hold of them.

Greg felt annoyed.

"I don't want to come off like a chafed rectum in this thing, but you tell your two brothers that when we get down there if they're not present, we'll have the Georgia state police pick them up."

Greg actually had no idea if the Georgia troopers would do such a thing, but he figured the notion would make a real nice impression on those two guys.

Next, Greg brought up the matter of the releases.

The television and newspaper interviews, he said, had caused their investigation "some setbacks." He would appreciate it if she'd not do any more interviews. He'd also appreciate it if they would rescind those releases they'd signed for the newspaper. "The releases could be catastrophic," he said.

Okay, they hadn't understood, Renee said. She'd rescind her release and talk to her brothers about doing the same.

"We'll be down there in four days," Greg said. "See you then."

Good, he thought. She understands the program.

It was snowing on the morning of November 10, when Ron and Greg's plane lifted off the runway, bound for Atlanta. Three hours later, they were driving through Georgia's rolling green meadows, under a bright, warm sun, headed toward Carrollton, some forty miles southwest of Atlanta.

Just beautiful, Meehan thought. Ron was rather odd for someone who'd lived fifty-two years in Minnesota—he liked warm weather.

Pulling into Carrollton, they couldn't help but notice a fair number of pickup trucks, many occupied by the sort of fellows who wore Beechnut baseball caps and favored rifles mounted on brackets in their rear windows. Thirty-caliber deer rifles, reminiscent to Ron of the M-1 he'd carried in Korea, seemed particularly popular. The detectives met Renee at the town's new Ramada Inn, where they'd rented a room. The motor hotel looked as if it had risen from the ground just for their purpose, for it was nearly empty and still unfinished—the construction workers hadn't even installed the Ramada Inn sign yet.

Renee reminded Greg of a hillbilly country and western singer. She had light brown hair, a long jaw and big, vibrant blue eyes. She seemed at once vulnerable and tough. She struck him as the type of woman who, at the right time and in the right place, you could talk into just about anything. Her neediness was that palpable—but so was a certain hardness. If you did her wrong, Greg thought, you wouldn't want to fall asleep next to her.

Her story sounded all too familiar. Renee, fifteen when she fled the Jurgenses' eleven years before, had later tried living with her former foster mother in Kentucky but never could make it feel right. In the eleventh grade she'd moved in with a boyfriend she thought she was going to marry. She'd borne a son, Michael, now four. In time, she'd drifted south, in search of her natural mother.

Greg began the interview at 6:30 P.M., sitting in their hotel room, Ron present but off to one side. Renee spoke freely into the tape recorder for a good hour. She remembered everything, and she hated Lois. The detectives mainly listened, not needing to prod her with many questions.

Lois was "a damned ravin' maniac." The abuse "was an everyday thing with her." She'd "always throw up in our faces that she was made to do this as a child." Renee didn't know what Harold's problem was—he tried to stop Lois, but not in a real forceful way. "He's not much of a man at all. And I blame him just as much as I do her . . . Harold just took all this stuff. I hate to say it but he was like a whooped pup. He bowed when Lois said bow, you know. It was like he was afraid of her himself . . ."

Just past 7:30 P.M., Renee's two brothers, Mike and Ricky, sauntered into the room. They were both about five feet ten inches and 180 pounds, and with their Beechnut baseball caps they fit right into the Carrollton scene.

The young men appeared to have felt the need for some form of relaxant before arriving at the Ramada. The threat about the Georgia troopers had apparently worked, Greg thought, but you couldn't exactly say they were entirely here. Where Renee burned with memories and anger, her brothers seemed blunted and fogged. It was a long time ago and they had moved on.

But their stories, too, were familiar. After the court removed them from the Jurgenses', Mike and Ricky, at ages thirteen and eleven, had returned to Cherie Riley's foster home in Kentucky, and like their sister, they'd found it hard to adjust. In time, they'd drifted south, in search of their natural father. Mike was now twenty-three, Ricky twenty-one.

The detectives didn't want to lose them—if we tell them to come back in a half hour, they reasoned, they might not return at all—so Ron decided he would interview one down at the hotel bar while Greg questioned the other in the room.

Ron ushered Mike into a quiet side booth at the lounge, ordered him a beer, and looked around. The Ramada bar was a classy place with plenty of wood and carpeting, but Ron still saw a fair share of those Beechnut caps, mostly on the heads of men in their twenties, a good number just then turned their way. Not the ideal spot for an interview, Ron reasoned, but it would have to do.

Presently, one of Mike's friends sauntered over. He was about five feet eight inches and 220 pounds.

"Hey, how ya doing?" the friend grunted.

The friend sounded to Ron like a meathead.

"This is the cop from Minnesota investigating the homicide," Mike replied, by way of introduction. Ron winced and shook his head at Mike.

Meathead wanted to shake the Minnesota cop's hand. Ron obliged, and though his own right hand resembled a small ham, he could tell Meathead was trying to outsqueeze him.

"Hey, just kind of cool those introductions right now," Ron told Mike after his friend walked away.

A real background setting for an interview, Ron thought. A real treat.

Later that night, Ron and Greg, full of the day's stories, decided they were in need of a nightcap. When they walked into the hotel bar, the baseball caps again turned their way and conversations trailed off. The detectives took seats at a round table in the middle of the floor. Greg lit a cigarette, his first in four years, and they both ordered gin and tonics. They drained their glasses and ordered a second round.

The interviews had gone well—all three youngsters had rescinded the releases they'd given the Minneapolis paper—but the detectives felt overwhelmed both by their strange surroundings and the three kids they'd just interviewed. The Howtons seemed so lost, and haunted.

"You know, I'm really glad we're on the second floor," Ron said after they returned to their room. "Because from the looks on some of those faces down there, I'd think they'd drive straight into our motel room if they could and park right here, just to see what the Minnesota detectives really look like."

Ron was lying on his back in his shorts, talking, when he fell asleep in midsentence. Soon he was snoring.

"Ron," Greg called, standing at the foot of his bed.

Just as Ron opened his eyes, Greg dived headfirst on top of him. At first unsure what was going on, Ron didn't know whether to throw a punch or laugh. Given his partner's reputation for a crushing left jab, Greg decided the indecision was perilous. Then Ron began chuckling.

What the hell, Greg thought. We needed a change of pace.

On November 20, nine days later, Ron and Greg drove the twenty minutes east through the Minnesota countryside to the rural region near Stillwater and Lake Elmo. The skies were cloudy now, the temperature just over thirty degrees. Where Nolan Avenue narrowed and grew more thickly wooded, the detectives slowed. Harold and Lois Jurgens lived a half mile down the road, but that was not their destination. Off to their right, Greg finally spotted what he was looking for—a redwood sign with jagged borders hung from two vertical poles and a cross beam. The white letters curved in a slight arch: *Stone Hill.*

When Greg had called and explained their business, June Bol had sounded warm and welcoming. "Fine, come on out," she'd said.

Now her dogs were nipping at the detectives' heels as they knocked at her front door. June ushered the two men to the kitchen table, crowded as usual with a portable phone, a radio, memo pads and a pile of mail. She settled at this center of her universe and delivered steaming cups of coffee to her visitors. A picture window opened before them to the rolling valley, and a muted winter sun filled the kitchen.

June, though pleasant, acted nervous. In truth, she was a reluctant witness. When she had first heard that the Jurgens case was being reopened, she'd felt conflicted. For one thing, her husband Richard's aged mother, a sister to Lois's father, was living in their home. Family was involved.

"All that time," her husband's brother had said one night over dinner. "Lois isn't going to hurt anybody anymore. Why don't they let it go?"

Part of June had agreed, but still, she took issue with her brother-in-law. "Do you mean that if someone gets by with something for twenty years, then they should be set free?" she'd asked.

Moreover, even after all these years, June was afraid of Lois, and that reason alone made her hesitant. Lois had called her just one week ago, urging her not to talk to anyone. June knew she had to speak to these detectives, but she didn't want to contribute more than absolutely necessary.

She relaxed as she talked, though, for she was quite impressed with her visitors. She took a particular liking to Greg Kindle. Greg had once raised quarter horses, so he could talk to her about the Tennessee walkers they had out back. With his experience handling juvenile cases, he could also talk to her about the problems she'd experienced over the past eleven years with Grant. She'd raised the Howton boy ever since he fled to them in 1975, and it hadn't been easy. June told the detectives about incidents of stealing money and sassy rebellion. Greg asked about her philosophy on raising the boy, and about her husband's. Her way was much softer, she explained.

"I think, based on my experience, you had better agree more with your husband and less with Grant," Greg said. "Because Grant's out to lunch and your husband's got the program figured out . . . You moms are all soft and sometimes you need to toughen up a little."

June took Greg's advice well. Maybe he was right, but she had trouble being tough. The three laughed and joked over that for a while.

Robert was being wonderful, the detectives told her. He was helping with the investigation, and had remembered so much. He even remembered episodes involving Dennis's death—a fall down some stairs, a dunking in a laundry tub of water.

June looked at Ron and Greg. She hadn't meant to talk this much, but she had to.

"He told me that story, too," she said. "'He really didn't cry, Aunt June.' That's what he told me."

June talked about Lois and Harold. Over the years, she said, Lois has been a sick person, often under the influence of tranquilizers. She usually stays in her bedroom now, even when relatives come calling, and rarely leaves her house. June hadn't seen her in person for quite some time. June once thought Harold a fine man, but she'd

grown disenchanted with him over his failure to stand up and protect the children. Imagine being so afraid of your wife you have to tell
the kids to holler and pretend you're hitting them down in the basement. When she heard that, she said, "I really started going downhill
on caring for Harold."

Later, as Greg and Ron were preparing to leave, June studied
them. By now she felt they were almost her friends. They were really
top-quality people. June wavered. There'd been a conversation years
ago, one she knew she should tell these detectives about, for it would
be vital to their case. But she'd be betraying Harold, and a lot of
people had told her this investigation wasn't helping Dennis anyway.
Still, Ron and Greg were so nice.

"I wasn't going to tell you this . . ." June began.

Ron thought she looked relieved. Greg thought she looked
troubled.

One afternoon several years after Dennis's death, June continued,
Harold asked her to baby-sit his four children from Kentucky while
he was at work. It was August of 1973 and Lois was away at a hospital. When Harold came to get the kids, June was making supper, and
her husband was off at a meeting, so she asked Harold to stay. They
all ate together, Harold and June and their combined total of nine
children. Afterward, the kids all ran off to play, and Harold sat with
her at the kitchen table over coffee. June thought him a pleasant man,
and enjoyed visiting.

"I wasn't home when Dennis died."

Harold had started speaking casually, just out of the blue.

Closing her eyes now, retelling the story, June could still remember his words. She recited them to Greg and Ron without hesitation.

I wasn't home when Dennis died. I was doing some electrical work for some friends in Wisconsin when Lois called.
She called and said, "Dennis and I have been at it again,"
and I knew what that meant. So I put my things together
and went right home, and when I got there I put Dennis in
bed with me. In the middle of the night Dennis had to go
potty and I took him in the bathroom and he said he was
done and I looked in the pot and nothing was there. Then
I took him back to bed with me and in the morning he was
dead.

As he told this story, June said, Harold sounded almost gentle. June sensed he trusted her, felt close to her. She found his words startling, and didn't know how to respond. He's kind of saying Lois did it, she thought. At least it proves she was really mean to Dennis, really terrible. June had felt frightened. She'd said nothing to Harold, and the moment had passed. Later that night, as soon as he came home, June had told her husband of the conversation, then put the matter aside.

When June finished her story, Ron and Greg looked at each other. Here was Harold telling it like it was, apparently for the only time. Most important, here was proof that put Lois alone with Dennis the weekend he died.

The detectives felt this way even though a central detail in Harold's story seemed inexplicable. Peritonitis involved extended, agonizing pain, so how could Dennis be talking normally on the toilet shortly before he died? This was not a new puzzle for the detectives, of course, for Robert, his memory matching Harold's, had asked the same question just days before, as had VanderWyst and Korolchuk in their final analysis in 1965. But it was not a question Ron and Greg felt compelled to answer. Their job, after all, was to collect whatever evidence was needed to put Lois behind bars. Perhaps the medical examiner could sort out exactly what had happened to Dennis during that Palm Sunday weekend. It was an interesting issue, but it wasn't that relevant to their task.

One other point did trouble Ron and Greg. What had Harold meant when he said, "I wasn't home when Dennis died"? Didn't he mean he wasn't home in the two days just before he died?

June shrugged when the detectives raised this point. "That's the way he said it. That's exactly how he said it."

The question passed.

"This is important," Greg told June. "Thank you very much for sharing this with us."

June already was wondering whether she should have told this story. She hadn't thought through the implications—now she'd have to testify. She would rather not say anything if she knew they'd get their conviction without her. There still was no proof, really. Harold's statement proved Lois was mean to Dennis, but what else?

"I can't imagine anyone killing a kid," June said to the detectives.

Greg pulled the coroner's photos of Dennis's body from his briefcase and slapped them on the table. "You can imagine it if you look at these," he said.

June demurred. She didn't want to look.

"You better look," Greg said. "You'll get tough. It'll toughen you up."

After she looked, June agreed. The photos did make her tougher.

At eleven o'clock the next morning, Greg Kindle met the fourth of the Kentucky youngsters, Grant, at Mac's Diner on Seventh Avenue in North St. Paul. Grant had never been formally adopted by the Bols, but he'd taken their last name.

Grant Bol was twenty-five now and full of edgy nerves. He fidgeted and squirmed and jerked his head about, as if he were trying to catch someone tailing him. All the same, there was something gentle and sensitive about him. He spoke quietly, thoughtfully, almost with a sense of wonder.

Minutes after Greg met him at Mac's Diner, Grant wanted to leave, because he thought he saw June Bol's father, the former North St. Paul chief of police, sitting at the counter over coffee. So they walked down the street to a Dairy Queen, but that was closed, so they returned to Mac's. Surveying the place again, Grant decided that June's father wasn't there after all. They settled at as isolated a table as they could find, but this didn't afford them much privacy, for the diner was packed, people all around them, children crying and waitresses calling to one another. Grant swallowed cup after cup of coffee as his eyes darted about, never at ease. He patted at the hairbrush in his back pocket, reassuring himself it was still there.

Grant talked to Greg about life with Lois, then also spoke freely of his problems since fleeing the Jurgenses. He'd been seeing a psychiatrist to help deal with his experience, he said, for he'd spent years trying to block everything from his mind. He'd given the Bols trouble, stealing money and drinking and staying out all night. Later he'd married and his wife had borne him a child, but then they'd divorced. She was a heck of a gal, but it didn't work out. Now he was trying to find work as a nurse's aide in a hospital.

"It's all going to work out," Grant said.

Greg drove back to White Bear Lake feeling jangled. Grant made him nervous.

At 4:20 P.M. that day, Ron Meehan escorted prosecutors Mindy Elledge and Jeanne Schleh to Dr. Roy Peterson's office on Fourth Street in White Bear Lake. Peterson, silver-haired but still energetic at sixty-eight, was nearing retirement after maintaining a practice for more than thirty-five years. Soon he and his second wife could turn without distraction to the pleasures of their redwood ranch house at the edge of the lake in Mahtomedi, on the site of the old Wildwood Amusement Park.

The doctor and his three visitors pulled chairs into a circle in his small office. Peterson had never altered the decor—the shag carpet and wood veneer paneling now seemed a period piece. The doctor acted gentlemanly but nervous, chain-smoking and shifting about in his chair. Lawyers made people act like that, Mindy and Jeanne had learned. That was why Ron had come. Peterson knew him.

Jeanne—days away from being replaced by Clayton Robinson— conducted the interview. At the start, she kept the case records in her briefcase, for the plan was first to test his memory, then feed him the police and medical reports for review.

Peterson said he didn't recall too much about the Jurgens family or treating Dennis. He did remember one incident clearly—Dennis's genitals getting burned by scalding hot water. This had struck him as unusual, he said. Why hadn't Lois's own hands been burned? Dennis was the talk of the Mounds Park Hospital nurses while he was there, both for the horrible strange burns and the bruises all over his body.

"There was no child abuse reporting system in place in those days," Peterson explained. The remark slipped from the doctor's mouth casually, a tossed-off line more than a defense, and be it from ignorance or tactics or generosity, his interrogators let the misstatement pass unchallenged. Then the doctor pushed it a step further: "I called the welfare department back then, but nothing ever came of that." Meehan and Schleh took notes, still saying nothing.

Peterson continued. He thought it was the coroner who had called him to the scene of Dennis's death. When he arrived, Dennis was dead. He couldn't recall whether the child was stiff or cold. He examined only the chest and face, enough to pronounce death. It was not his job to determine the cause of death. Upon finding the child dead, the coroner was called. He didn't recall any statements or explanations given by the parents about Dennis's death. He didn't recall giving much thought to the cause of death.

Mindy, Jeanne and Ron didn't know what Peterson had said at the 1965 custody hearing, or even that he'd testified, since they didn't have a transcript of that proceeding. What they did have were the original police reports by Korolchuk and VanderWyst, the pathologist's autopsy report, the Mounds Park Hospital burn records and the welfare department's adoption file. Now Jeanne pulled these documents from her briefcase. She'd spent two weeks studying them, and with her newly acquired knowledge, she intended to refresh the doctor's hazy memory.

This she did with speed and ferocity. Leaning forward, looking him in the eye, she pumped question after question, barely waiting for the answers. Had he maybe seen more than he was saying? Jeanne asked. The records show it wasn't the coroner who called you there, so who did? Wouldn't peritonitis involve an extended period of pain and disability? If Dennis died of peritonitis, what specifically would cause that? A punch to the stomach? Falling down the steps? The heel of a woman's shoe?

Jeanne placed report after report before the doctor. Would this refresh your memory? Would this? This?

Peterson struggled to answer, but he grew tangled in his words and thoughts. The doctor was known for examining patients with alacrity, but now talked at half speed. Listening and watching, Ron started feeling sorry for Peterson. The doc, after all, had taken care of Ron's own family for some twenty-five years, at a discount. Jeanne was popping the questions so fast, even if Peterson did know, there's no way he could answer. She was giving him a mental block. *Doctor, isn't it kind of strange . . . Doctor, isn't it a fact that you could have . . .* Ron feared Peterson was going to drop over with a heart attack any minute. Jeanne could say fifty words before he could say five. The doc was still thinking about her first question when she was asking the third one.

Dr. Woodburn's autopsy report, handed over by Jeanne, appeared to be a revelation to Peterson. Only a severe blow to the abdomen could have caused a bowel rupture of this nature, he said. Yes, there would be severe pain and later possibly symptoms of shock and unconsciousness. No, he did not recall ever talking to the pathologist, Dr. Woodburn, about this. Yes, the abdominal adhesions suggested the infection had been going on for some time. No, he didn't recall anything more about the morning of Dennis's death. No, he didn't recall talking to Jerome Zerwas or to the Jurgenses.

Near the end of the interview, Jeanne reached once more into her briefcase.

"Dr. Peterson, I have some photos here of Dennis Jurgens's body," she said. "I'd like you to see them."

Peterson's face seemed to collapse as he studied the photos. He looked shocked and sad.

"My God," he said. "This is awful."

He stared at the photos.

There was no question this was child abuse, he said. There was no doubt this was a battered child. Peterson repeated his earlier thought: "Only a severe blow could have ruptured the bowel."

Jeanne peppered him with more questions, and he tried to keep up.

No, the blood-red nose did not appear to be caused by a cold. Yes, the scars on the abdomen did seem to be caused by a belt or stick. Yes, the marks on the back of the ears were consistent with fingernails. Yes, the picture did seem to indicate malnutrition.

Peterson's eyes traveled between the autopsy report and the photos. He felt the need to repeat himself once more. "The only thing that could cause such a severe injury was a severe blow . . . a deliberate blow."

"Is this the body you saw at the Jurgens home when you went there that Sunday?" Jeanne asked.

Peterson lit another cigarette.

The body was covered with a blanket, he said. He didn't see all these marks. It was not his job to determine the cause of death. His job was only to pronounce him dead.

Could he give them any insight into Mr. and Mrs. Jurgens?

Peterson looked about at his visitors. He appeared lost.

"They seemed like very nice people to me," the doctor said.

CHAPTER 34

Arizona

On November 24, three days after the visit with Dr. Peterson, Ron and Greg finally left for Arizona. The detectives' destination, Bullhead City, perches on the Colorado River directly across the water from Nevada and just north of the California border, with the closest big jet airport in Las Vegas.

When their plane landed there, Ron joined a long, winding line of some seventy-five travelers at the Alamo car rental desk. Greg used the time to remind his partner of a particularly dubious four-cylinder Chevy subcompact they'd rented earlier in their journeys.

"We can't get over the mountains in a little four-banger," was how Greg put the matter.

After an hour's wait in line, Ron finally reached the counter, only to be told that his car—another Chevy subcompact—wouldn't be ready for half an hour, after cleaning and servicing.

"What's your special today?" Ron asked.

Alamo had a Buick Riviera available for $24 a day, just $3 more than the Chevy.

"Sign us up."

The Buick was maroon and new and quite unlike anything Ron and Greg had seen in White Bear Lake. When Greg turned the ignition on, the radio was blaring, and he couldn't figure out how to turn it off, for a blinking dashboard computer seemed to control everything. The detectives finally summoned an Alamo attendant for a lesson. Soon they were rolling south on Highway 95, following the course of the Colorado River through an empty high desert of spare sagebrush, Greg at the wheel monitoring the outside temperature, the inside temperature, the engine temperature, the radio volume, the miles per gallon. He couldn't take his eye off the dashboard.

"Greatest damn car I've ever been in," he said. "A piece of work."

They stopped for lunch at a steak house in Searchlight, Nevada, that advertised sirloins for $3.99 in blinking neon lights. Waiting for their food, Ron wandered to the slot machine with half a dozen quarters. On the sixth pull, bells rang and red lights flashed. Ron returned to the table just as the steaks arrived, $25 in hand.

Past Searchlight, the windblown sagebrush thinned until the two-lane Highway 95 stretched into a brown void, empty of all vegetation. Few cars came this way, for Interstate 15, some thirty miles to the west, traversed the same north-south route out of Las Vegas. Ron and Greg passed an abandoned gas station, then a lopsided cabin with broken windows and no door, the only signs of life for miles. In time, Ron spotted a sign—*Needles, 5 miles*. Ron frowned as he studied the Alamo map. Needles was over the border in California, well south of their goal.

"Greg, there's something wrong here," he said. "That last road, ten miles back, must be the one we've got to cross."

Greg pulled the Riviera into a sweeping U-turn, and soon they were heading east on Highway 163, a road even more desolate than 95. No one, and nothing, lived here. Now they were climbing and turning through the appropriately named Dead Mountains, headed for Pyramid Canyon, grateful for the Buick's strong engine. "Purring like a kitty cat," Ron grunted. The detectives felt as if they were traveling to the ends of the earth.

By now, Meehan and Kindle had found plenty of relatives willing, even eager, to talk—the initial resistance they'd experienced with the Kopp family hadn't proved to be widespread. This was 1987, after all, not 1965, and besides, now there was a new generation of less guarded Zerwases available—the nieces and nephews who'd played with Dennis as children. The detectives hadn't even needed to track them all down—family members were calling the police station regularly. We have stories to tell you, they'd say. It got to the point after a while where Greg didn't want to hear any more. Black eyes and torn ears and force-feeding—the same descriptions told over and over lost their horrific feel and instead took on a numbing quality. And always, the relatives' stories came with a common theme and question for the detectives: *Lois should never have been allowed to have children. How could she ever have been allowed to adopt children?*

Most of these accounts, though, were once removed or fuzzily recalled. That was why this Arizona trip now was so critical. Meehan and Kindle were journeying to the homes of those in the Zerwas clan who'd witnessed Dennis's abuse most frequently and directly. Moreover, Lloyd and Donna Zerwas and Richard Norton were the only family members who'd defied whatever authority had silenced the rest of the Zerwas clan in 1965. Only through them could Meehan and Kindle learn what the missing statements contained.

When they got there, Bullhead City did not make much of an impression on Greg.

The town was named for Bullhead Rock, a local promontory that had all but disappeared with the construction of Davis Dam in 1941 and the formation of Lake Mohave. With the dam, the town's steamship ports—Isabel, Callville, Aubrey and Alexandra—either fell into disuse or, like the rock itself, disappeared beneath the raised waters of the Colorado. Bullhead City, though, struggled on.

Greg could see nothing but blowing sand, punctuated here and there by a few tired storefronts and houses. That was all—wind and sand and sagebrush and cactus and one scraggly main drag. Without glasses—goggles would be better—he'd have to scoop sand out of his eyes with a shovel. The wind wouldn't stop blowing. Greg was sure some parts of Arizona were beautiful, but this reach of the southern Colorado River basin, he firmly believed, was not.

Directly across the river from Bullhead City, on the Nevada side, a very different town towered bizarrely over its sister. The community of Laughlin, Nevada, in fact, seemed to rise out of an entirely different world. Here at the foot of Lake Mohave and Davis Dam, a developer named Don Laughlin had built a booming bargain-basement alternative to Las Vegas. Multistoried hotels and casinos rose on the waterfront—one in the shape of a monstrous steamship—flaunting their neon lights in Bullhead City's face. Don Laughlin had built a bridge connecting the two towns, but the match did not seem to take. Instead, the faded and the garish stood opposite each other in the stark, windy desert.

"This is the armpit of the world," Greg said.

Ron, though, felt more content. Here at the end of November, he could walk outdoors in a short-sleeved shirt. It was warm in Bullhead City.

They checked into the only motel that promised some comfort, a two-story affair with a Spanish motif called the Silver Creek Inn. Once settled, they began making phone calls, setting up their appointments for the following day.

At half past nine the next morning, Ron and Greg drove the short distance to Mohave Valley. Mohave, Greg decided, was worse than Bullhead City. Some fifty trailers sat in a flat bare plain, the wind gusting to fifty miles per hour, sand everywhere. The trailers, surrounded by junked cars, rusting pickups and flat tires, looked defeated by the sand and the wind.

Richard Norton greeted them outside the door to his trailer. He was sixty now, and with his leathered face, jeans and boots, he had the look of an Arizona cowboy.

"Good to see you, Dick," Ron said. He knew Norton from his White Bear Lake days. Norton had moved to Arizona in 1980, and his first wife, Donna, Lois's sister, had died some three years later, in March of 1984.

Norton glanced up and down the road leading to his trailer, then quickly ushered his visitors inside, saying he didn't want to stand outside talking. Greg thought he was acting like a man hiding out from the Mafia—it was as if someone was coming to blow his brains out any minute.

That, as it happened, was precisely what Norton thought. There's a hit man out there looking for me, he explained. They've been after me for years.

After some conversation, it became clear that Norton had a tendency for inflated self-dramatization. Ron and Greg heard him out, waiting until everyone felt comfortable. This took some time, for Norton liked to talk. He spoke with animation and great volume, on occasion turning to address his new wife, a Latina some twenty-five years his junior, and his wife's sister.

"These guys are the police," he kept telling the women in Spanish, knowing they were fearful of the law. Their agitated reactions seemed to give him some delight.

When the conversation finally turned to the detectives' reason for being there, though, Norton changed. He had a precise memory, and much to say about the Jurgenses and the Zerwas clan. This guy, Greg thought, knows what he's talking about. Not a crazy bone in his body.

Norton was sitting on a couch, Ron and Greg in chairs facing him. The trailer looked better from the inside, clean and decently furnished, with photos of daughters and grandchildren hanging from the walls.

Norton wanted to talk about Jerome Zerwas, a man he did not care for at all, but Ron and Greg listened without asking questions. That's not why we're here, they reminded themselves. Jerome's activities had no more to do with putting Lois behind bars than did questions about peritonitis.

A lot of things would be nice to know if we could pursue them, Greg reasoned. But they wouldn't prove a homicide. What Jerry Zerwas did or didn't do twenty-one years ago was interesting, but in and of itself wouldn't make or break the case. If they could prove that Jerry influenced Dr. Peterson or dipped into those files, so what? They'd end up with an interesting story about a policeman who decided to protect his sister, but in 1986 that's no crime anymore. Statute of limitations is long gone on that stuff. And it would have diddly squat bearing on the homicide case.

Greg and Ron had been around too long not to understand the system that was guiding their every move. Yes, they'd started out intending to find out just what had happened in 1965, and they'd told Robert they'd find out. But with so much pressure from the press and Jerry Sherwood to produce a tangible, visible result, they knew their chief and the prosecutors weren't going to let them spend a lot of time and money on side trips that didn't provide something directly helpful to their homicide prosecution. Greg and Ron had to account for each step they took, and file overtime slips for every hour spent on the case beyond their normal shifts. Convicting Lois for killing Dennis was the purpose of their endeavor—and when it came down to it, the true limit of the legal system's reach.

In time, Norton finished talking about Jerome and turned to memories of Dennis. Now, for the first time, Ron and Greg heard the story of Thanksgiving Day 1963, when Lois force-fed Dennis his own vomit. Now, for the first time, they caught a sense of what the missing statements had revealed in 1965.

"Dennis very seldom cried," Norton said. "He would just quiver. His lips would quiver, a tear would run down his face. He just didn't do anything . . . Everybody knew she was abusing Dennis and no one was surprised when Dennis died . . . My wife didn't understand why nothing was done with Lois. We discussed it many times, why something wasn't done about the little boy's death."

By the time they finished the interview, Norton felt comfortable enough to venture into the outside world. Come on, he told the detectives. I'll give you a tour.

Ron and Greg ended up downriver at Lake Havasu City, gazing with perplexity at the famous London Bridge.

That evening, the detectives found Lloyd and Donna Zerwas at their home on Honeysuckle Road. At fifty-six, Lloyd still looked a good deal like his older brother Jerome—big and strong and handsome in a Roy Rogers sort of way. Lloyd also still shared Jerome's cocky charm, sense of humor and flirtatious way with women. Ron thought he was lots of fun.

His wife Donna was also a lot of fun, and being a Norton, quite a talker. When she gets going, Ron thought, she could talk your left arm, your right arm and your feet off. She adored Lloyd, thought the sun rose and set on his head, but she was the one who had packed her bags and headed for Arizona when she'd had enough of the Zerwas clan. Lloyd had followed, and found work at the phone company. He always seemed to be laughing at Donna, but in a playful, appreciative sort of way. They'd been married for thirty-five years.

They were clearly happy to see Ron. They guided the visitors around their home, and Meehan was impressed. The house appeared well-constructed, with a yard, an in-ground pool, fancy rock landscaping and nice furniture. Lloyd had built most of it himself—he'd worked all his life, and still spent long days in the hot sun atop towering telephone poles. You work for as long as you can, was his philosophy. At least then you get a regular paycheck.

Buoyed by the White Bear police department expense account, whose meager limits nicely matched the Bullhead City culinary offerings, the detectives took the whole Arizona gang out to dinner that evening at a Mexican restaurant—Lloyd, Donna, their seventeen-year-old son Jake, Richard Norton and his wife. It was past ten o'clock when they returned to the house on Honeysuckle Road.

Even though the evening had gone well, Lloyd and Donna still weren't all that sure they wanted to talk into a tape recorder. They'd given statements twenty-one years before, to no end other than harassment and threats from Lois. They feared going again to court, they felt scared of Lois, and they doubted the investigation would lead to anything.

Ron worked to reassure them, explaining the various ways things could go. Their statements tonight might be enough, he said. Possibly there'd be a grand jury. There might be a complaint and Lois might plead guilty to manslaughter, which meant no trial.

"Who knows," he said. "I don't know . . . But we're for real. We're going to nail that lady and book her in jail . . . We're going to go all the way with this thing."

Lloyd and Donna hesitated, looking at each other. Their conversation drifted, still uncommitted.

They'd been foster parents to nine children over the years, they said. They loved kids. They'd baby-sat Dennis on several occasions. In fact, Dennis had stayed with them once for a full week in the summer of 1964, when the Jurgenses went on vacation.

"Oh, yeah?" Ron said.

Yes, Donna said. Lois brought over jars of junior baby food, even though Dennis had a full set of teeth. Don't feed him the family's food, Lois said, because he doesn't know how to chew. And don't give him water after six o'clock, because he'll wet his bed. But we never gave Dennis that baby food. He sat with our children, at home and in a restaurant, eating steak, hamburger, french fries, whatever we were having. He drank water at night. He never gagged or wet his bed. He was a happy-go-lucky, affectionate, laughing little boy. He played with our children, he played with our dogs, he got dirty. The only thing wrong with Dennis was bruises—he had black-and-blue marks on his arms, his legs, his back. When Harold came to pick him up, Dennis was happy to see his dad, but a little bit reluctant to leave. In fact, the boy wet all over the front seat of Harold's truck.

"Dammit," Donna snorted, "Dennis was a normal little boy."

By now, Ron had turned on the tape recorder. It was eleven o'clock at night.

Lloyd and Donna could remember when they had first heard of Dennis's death. They and their daughter Nancy had been getting ready for church that Palm Sunday morning when the phone rang, Donna said. So it must have been about half past seven.

How could it have been half past seven? Ron thought. The call to the police came at ten o'clock. Donna was talking now, though, and he didn't want to interrupt. The moment, and the question, passed.

A relative was calling to say Dennis was dead, Donna continued. She thought they were talking about another nephew, Dennis Donald, who was a teenager, and she figured it was a bicycle or car accident. No, the relative had said, it's Lois's Dennis. Donna had walked into the bathroom to tell Lloyd. "My God," he'd said, turning from the mirror and his shaving. "She finally killed him."

Lloyd and Donna were alternating now, each jogging the other's memory. They'd told it all to Korolchuk and VanderWyst, then again at the juvenile custody hearing, so this was their third go-around.

"I told her many times to give Dennis back," Donna said. "Please give Dennis back wherever you got him from before it's too late. Give him back. And she, and exactly what she said was, 'I can't do that because that would affect Robert because Robert wouldn't know why I got rid of him . . . and I would never, ever be able to adopt another child.' That's exactly what she told me."

Once they'd dropped by the Jurgens home in the middle of the day, Donna said. Lois had taken them in to see Dennis's beautiful bedroom. It was a lovely room, full of nice furniture and neat rows of stuffed toys—a setting which made even stranger the sight of Dennis lying spread-eagled in his crib, his hands and feet tied to the posts. When he's untied he gets up and touches everything in the bedroom, Lois had explained. He plays with the toys. I have to keep him tied.

That Thanksgiving in 1963 when Lois force-fed Dennis, Lloyd recalled, he'd thought of saying something, but just didn't want to stick his nose in. What he wanted was to get the hell out of there. Over the years, he'd often considered that day, and others.

The memory of his failure stopped Lloyd, drained the sparkle from his eyes. He frowned and hung his head and studied the backs of his tanned, calloused hands.

"I blame myself . . . I should have intervened. If I had it to do over, I would do something. I did testify, and I did try to get her to give Dennis back, but I don't know why I didn't do something before he died. It's a good question. I've thought about that often over the years."

Returning to the Silver Creek Inn near four in the morning, Greg and Ron sat in silence on the edges of their beds in the darkened motel room. In a way, their interview with Lloyd and Donna had bothered them more than anything else they'd experienced during their investigation. Greg could relate to Lloyd and Donna more than most of those they'd talked with, but that made understanding their behavior all the more difficult.

Of course, he didn't have to understand their behavior to put Lois in jail. He didn't have to understand lots of things. But he couldn't let go just yet.

"What's wrong with those people?" Greg asked Ron. He was whispering. "Why didn't they do something for that kid? I can't understand how they could watch someone treat a child like that and not get up and punch someone's brains out. God bless them for telling the truth, but goddamn. Lloyd is a big, strong man, without a cowardly bone in his body. I can't understand."

Greg stopped himself. No use going down this road.

"Trying to figure out why people do things and what makes them tick, you can drive yourself crazy," he said. "You start thinking about that stuff, you're in big trouble."

Ron only grunted. His mind was following another avenue. What he'd heard here told him there was one hell of a patrol out there, controlling people in the Zerwas family like Lloyd.

What the hell, he figured. His job was to reconstruct, piece by piece. The two-week investigation was now two months old, though, and he had no idea when they'd be done. Ron crawled into bed, pulling the blankets about him.

A phone call woke the detectives two hours later, at six in the morning. Karlene Hilsgen, one of Richard Norton's daughters who lived nearby, wanted to be interviewed.

They'd have to talk to her by phone later, Ron said, because they were leaving that morning. They had a plane to catch in Vegas at one o'clock.

That was one of the mistakes of their whole operation, Ron thought. He made a note to tell the chief they should have more input into scheduling their flights. They needed an extra day, it seemed, on every trip.

The return journey turned out to be fun. Reaching Las Vegas with time to spare, Ron conducted a tour of the casinos. After Greg lost five dollars at Caesar's Palace, he stopped betting. "Imagine," Ron said, "a farm boy from North Dakota, losing the egg money under crystal chandeliers."

At the airport, they bumped into Ron's old White Bear Lake neighbor, now working as a Budweiser salesman in Las Vegas. Jeff Nash was a former bouncer at a Maplewood bar, on his way back to White Bear for the Thanksgiving holiday and delighted to have company. On the plane, he bought two or three rounds, and the detectives felt obliged to reciprocate. Greg focused his attention on Tanqueray gin martinis, Ron on Jack Daniel's and water, and soon they and Nash had a party going. Their stewardess was wonderful—the type they could bounce lines off and get some in return. Somewhere over the country's midsection, she announced the pilot was her husband, and distributed Northwest flight pins. By the time the aircraft landed in the Twin Cities, Ron and Greg had decided they were going to lead Jeff off the plane in handcuffs, just to kid his waiting mother and brother. Mrs. Nash couldn't be fooled, though. As they walked down the concourse toward her, Jeff's hands cuffed behind his back, she started laughing.

"I know you two guys," she called out to the detectives. "I know this is a setup."

Ron and Greg suddenly realized they'd better settle down, for they were drawing a lot of attention to themselves.

Oh, well, Greg thought. At least we haven't talked about the case since we hit Vegas.

Ron Meehan, though, hadn't let go of the conversation Greg started at the Silver Creek Inn. There was someone, he decided, he needed to see.

Days after returning from Arizona, Ron sat in his office, looking across his desk at Jerome Zerwas. Their meeting was not that unusual, for over the years since he'd left the force on disability, Jerome regularly called Ron or dropped by for a beer, and in recent weeks he'd taken to visiting the station often, checking on the progress of the investigation. Ron still considered him a good friend—he figured he knew Jerome real well, as well if not better than any of the guys on the force. He felt he could talk to him.

"God, Jerry, the things we've seen . . ." he said. "Why the hell didn't you do something?"

"I didn't see that stuff," Jerome answered.

"Jerry, there's information from Pete and Bob that you did tell them you were going to do everything in your power to stop a successful investigation of the case."

Jerome leaned forward, his hands on Ron's desk.

"That's a dirty lie, mister," he said. His voice was rising with every word. "I'll tell them that to their faces. I'll take a polygraph . . . That's a dirty lie, mister."

He always says that when he gets mad, Ron recalled. He calls you *mister*. Meehan lit a Winston and studied his old friend.

Yet another pointless side trip, Ron told himself. Greg was right about all that. Keep your eye on the case in chief—that was the advice Mindy Elledge and Clayton Robinson had given them. In lawyers' jargon, *case in chief* meant all the prosecution's affirmative evidence to support the murder charge. How events precisely unfolded in 1965, and why Dennis's death was not then prosecuted, were questions beyond the pale of the case in chief. What a doctor or a neighbor or a policeman did or did not do in 1965 was intriguing, but they weren't out to prove a conspiracy or a theft of police files or a failure of moral courage—such acts, committed twenty years ago, either were no longer crimes or never had been. They were out to put Dennis's killer in jail.

Acts committed twenty years ago—the thought tugged at Ron. He couldn't remember telling his wife in 1965 that Lois had killed her kid—he'd been so busy then with two jobs and all, he'd only had time for his own business. But if Liz said so, he knew it was true.

Under Ron's gaze, Jerome shifted about in his seat, fidgeting. Meehan sensed he had more to say, thought the conversation was going to open up, but then the moment passed, and Ron didn't press further.

If Jerry's going to talk to me, he reasoned, he'll talk. Maybe someday down the road.

Ron didn't know what else to think.

Everybody's got their problems, he figured. Everybody makes mistakes in their life.

CHAPTER 35

Christmas 1986

During the Christmas season of 1986, Gerane Wharton-Park, a Napa, California, psychotherapist, was staying with her brother David at his home in Flint, Michigan. On the morning of December 20, she left her brother's house and drove across the Canadian border to Toronto for a visit. When she returned late that afternoon, David's wife Heidi ran out to the garage to greet her.

"Gerane, Gerane," she said. "You had a call from the White Bear Lake police."

Gerane first thought one of her California clients, in Minnesota for Christmas, had gone belly up. Or perhaps this was something about an escaped Napa State Hospital patient. Turning the matter over in her mind, Gerane suddenly had another idea. The memory was twenty-one years old, but insistent. Could this call, Gerane wondered, be about the Jurgens case?

Gerane Rekdahl had left her job as a Ramsey County caseworker in May of 1964, moving with her husband to Berkeley. There she raised her own children, then went to work in the Solano County, California, adoptions unit, losing her job in February of 1968 when the availability of abortions sharply reduced the volume of adoptions. A divorce followed—accompanied by a name change to Gerane Wharton-Park—then a master of social work degree from Cal State Sacramento, a clinical license and a private practice. Gerane had not thought of the Jurgens case for years.

Mindy Elledge and Ron Meehan had spent hours tracing her present whereabouts.

She returned Greg Kindle's call late that day.

"I guess you wonder why I called," the policeman began.

"Yes, I do."

"Do you remember the Jurgens case?"

Gerane felt queasy. "Yes, I do."

"Did you know that the boy died at home in 1965?"

"Oh, my God . . . no."

"Do you remember the name of the child?"

Remember his name? She could see the baby's smiling, impish face even now. "Dennis Puckett."

"How could you remember that from so long ago?" Greg asked.

Gerane knew immediately this was a case of child abuse, and she felt dismayed. She felt sorry they'd fallen the wrong way on this one. She felt sorry she hadn't followed her gut feelings. For the moment, she also felt guilty.

"It was a difficult case," Gerane answered.

Days later, Ramsey County flew her to St. Paul, where Mindy Elledge and Clayton Robinson showed Gerane her old case log and the photos of Dennis's body, then took her deposition. Gerane was appalled and never stopped feeling bad, but in time, she shed her sense of guilt.

"When I think where I was then," she explained, "and where the country was, I can't slay myself. You can't live beyond your time or beyond what you know. We work in a dark field. In our field, you're going to work with successes and failures, right and wrong choices. One hates to think you were involved in something like this . . . You just hope you have had more successes than failures."

Ron and Greg's interviews during December often went like that. Their arrival at a person's home or office regularly dredged up painful memories and regrets, but also reasons and explanations.

Greg, for example, traced the former Kentucky caseworker Peter Crego to upstate New York, where he'd become a minister, and called him there on December 15. When they began talking, Crego barely remembered the Howton children's adoption, but his memory improved, if selectively, as the conversation continued.

Someone, an attorney, had contacted him often on that case, Crego recalled. A Mr. Fink had tried to persuade them to approve the adoption. Crego, though, had trouble remembering anything about a boy who'd died under the Jurgenses' care.

"This is where my mind goes blank . . . My mind is blank on this . . . Evidently we had to have asked questions. I still don't know to this day how much we knew about the death of that child . . . We evidently *did* ask questions . . . That I *do* know. I remember that much . . . Does that answer what you're saying?"

"Yeah," Greg muttered.

"I guess we had reason to believe that it was a calculated risk . . . in favor of the children . . ." Crego continued. "We knew something wasn't right, but I don't know how much we knew. Obviously, if there had been something horribly wrong the couple themselves would have been charged and we wouldn't have been, you know, in the process of—of working an adoption for them. There obviously had been no legal action taken against the Jurgenses at that point . . . Right from the beginning when the Jurgenses' application came in it was like this was a heaven-sent situation . . . If there had been one red flag I can't imagine that we would have pursued it any further. Everybody seemed to be very positive about the Jurgenses. And the vague fact that she [Lois] had received some [psychiatric] care or something like that . . . and again, the whole question of whether she was responsible for the death of the child . . . Obviously, if she had been . . . she would have been charged . . ."

Minutes later, Kindle had heard enough.

"Well, it's been nice talking to you Peter," he said. "Bye-bye."

The next day, Ron and Greg, accompanied by Mindy and Clayton, visited Ruth Weidell in her office in St. Paul's Centennial Building, headquarters for the state department of public welfare. Weidell's office consisted of a desk and a file cabinet, divided by partitions from rows of other desks in a vast open room. She was a small, dark-haired woman with a crippled arm—Greg thought it came from polio or a birth defect.

She'd been suspicious about the death in the Jurgens home, Weidell said, so initially wouldn't give permission for the adoption. Over a period of months, though, Bob Lageson at Lutheran Social Service had satisfied all her department's questions. The Jurgenses had even gotten a letter of recommendation from their pastor.

"All the information we had was on the fence," Weidell said. "What do you do? It was only an accusation . . ."

It was funny, she added. The postplacement reports all indicated the adoption was running smoothly.

"After they were placed I saw newspaper clips about them as a musical group . . . I read in the paper they'd formed a musical group . . . I saw a photo in the paper of the group. I thought maybe we'd done a good job . . ."

Later that afternoon, the prosecutors and detectives met Bob Lageson in a conference room at the Ramsey County attorney's office. He was a mild-mannered man who seemed to Clayton and Greg sluggish and embarrassed. He hung his head during much of the interview.

Lageson could tell them little. "I've really had a hard time with this," he said softly. "To think you had a part in something like this."

The former caseworker had a question. He too had seen newspaper accounts and photos of the kids in a music group. "There were good days in that home, weren't there?" he asked. "They weren't all bad, were they?"

Learning that Wayne Armstrong had passed through White Bear Lake a month earlier without phoning, Ron called the former police chief in Colorado.

"Hey, Wayne, sorry I missed you when you came through White Bear," Ron began.

Armstrong apologized. He was only there for a short time, he explained, before a change of plans forced him to leave.

Meehan had called Armstrong once before, back in October, but the former chief then had sounded unhelpfully vague. Ask him a question, he'd ask the same one back, dragging out his words in a slow drawl, lapsing into silences until Ron spoke up. Soon they'd lost the thread entirely. Ron had left it that Armstrong would call if he ever got back to Minnesota. Ron would buy him lunch, they'd go over things.

Now, in December, Wayne had been spotted over at Chester's Restaurant on White Bear Avenue but hadn't contacted Ron.

"Since we last spoke," Meehan said on the phone, "Greg and I have interviewed a lot of people and recovered lots of documents . . . There are lots of written statements and photos missing from the case file, Wayne. Do you know anything about that?"

He'd never taken an original copy of any police report from the station, Armstrong said. That would be a crime and he would never consider such a thing. A lot of cases back in those days weren't charged that should have been. The way he looked at it, if the officer conducted the investigation to the best of his ability, it wasn't for the officer to worry if they weren't charged. That was the way he looked at it.

"If I had any knowledge of any records being tampered with," Armstrong said, "I would have dealt with it for sure at the time . . . That was one thing I did not tolerate."

One night that December, Greg was working late at his desk, preparing reports, when the phone rang.

"This is Jerry Sherwood," a woman's voice said. She sounded distraught.

Greg had never talked to or met the woman before.

"People have told me Lois Jurgens is threatening witnesses and that they're not going to testify," she said.

"Well, who's telling you that?" Greg asked.

"I'm not going to tell you," Sherwood said.

Even in the best of moods Greg was not inclined to deal with this type of approach, and after a fourteen-hour workday, his tolerance threshold was lower than normal.

"I'm not going to listen to your baloney," he snapped.

When Jerry Sherwood suggested Greg was not doing his job, Kindle offered the thought that he was indeed, and what's more, didn't need her assistance.

"You start in on me, I start in back," he warned.

Just then, Ron, overhearing the exchange, entered Greg's office, shaking his head. "Let me talk to her," he said.

Within minutes, Meehan had assured Jerry the investigation was going just fine. They hung up, the situation defused.

Fine, Greg thought. But I was getting ready to tell her to get bent.

Jerome Zerwas called Ron several times during the month of December.

Once, he had a complaint. His granddaughter had come home from her fourth-grade class saying she'd talked to someone whose dad was a White Bear cop. This cop, it seems, had been talking all about the Jurgens case, only he wasn't using the name Jurgens. He was using the name Zerwas. Jerome was greatly upset about this.

Another day, Jerome called to say he'd heard from Harold that his name was mentioned in the records connected with Robert's adoption. Jerome wanted to explain what that was about. Back in 1960, he said, he'd been out one night with a Ramsey County sheriff's deputy who told him a gal working at the truck stop over by Landfall Village was pregnant and planning to give the baby up for adoption. Jerome said he'd passed the information on to his sister, but had never met the woman at the truck stop. He had only seen her from a distance. She was a cute blond lady. That was all he knew about that.

During yet another phone conversation, Jerome reported that although the Jurgenses' lawyer wouldn't let them talk, they wanted Ron to know that a lot of things said about them were lies.

"Lois said that to me in a calm manner," Jerome pointed out.

"Well, due to the fact that she is so calm about the whole situation," Ron replied, "maybe you should try again and see if she might change her mind and talk to me about the case."

In early December, an assistant Ramsey County attorney bumped into a stranger, an animated young woman, on Cedar Street in downtown St. Paul.

"Do you know where the *Pioneer Press Dispatch* offices are?" she asked. The attorney pointed the way toward the newspaper.

"I'm the adopted daughter of the Jurgenses," the young woman then said. "Maybe you've seen me on TV . . . Gould you recommend a lawyer?"

Renee had come up from Georgia, and somehow had ended up staying at Jerry Sherwood's apartment. When he found this out, an outraged Clayton Robinson called Sherwood and insisted on coming to her home that very night.

"You will fuck things up," he told her, "if Doug Thomson finds out a witness is staying in your house . . . And if you fuck up this case, I am going to tell who did it."

So Renee ended up switching to the home of Pam Docken, who was Lois Jurgens's niece, Richard Norton's daughter, and, as it happens, a friend of St. Paul reporter Brian Bonner. It did not take Bonner long to befriend Renee.

◆   ◆   ◆

On December 17, Greg received a call from Richard Norton in Arizona. A St. Paul reporter, Brian Bonner, was working on a story that would show the extent of the cover-up in the Jurgens case back in 1965, Norton announced. Kindle relayed this news to Mindy Elledge, who told Jim Konen, who told Tom Foley. The county attorney decided he had to respond—he'd try to temper whatever was coming by announcing that the case was going to the grand jury in January. They just had to move now.

That same day, Foley also decided to let Paul Lindholm talk to Bonner about his reasons for not prosecuting the case twenty-one years ago. At 2:45 P.M. Mindy was summoned to a meeting in Foley's office. Present were Lindholm, Konen and the office's press liaison, John Wodele. Mindy later summarized the conference in her log:

"Konen said Brian Bonner wanted to interview Paul about why case wasn't charged in 1965. I said I didn't think it was a good idea. Paul may be a witness. Foley thought Paul should have opportunity to 'absolve' himself and the office. Konen thought so, too . . . Clayton was in, but was not asked to the meeting . . . I told Clayton of meeting. He couldn't believe it. He and I went to Konen. Clayton said, 'Paul may be a witness.' Didn't change anything. At about 4:00 P.M., Brian Bonner interviewed Paul Lindholm, with Konen present."

Bonner's article, cowritten with staff writer Linda Kohl, appeared across the top of the front page of the St. Paul Pioneer Press Dispatch on Sunday, December 21. "Child's fatal abuse was known but ignored," the banner headline read.

Bonner had managed to talk to several Zerwas family members, including Pam Docken. He'd also talked to former Washington County caseworker Carol Felix, the former coroner, Tom Votel, and the current medical examiner, Michael McGee. The heart of the story, though, came from the Howton children's sealed Washington County juvenile records—the very records the prosecutors had kept from the Minneapolis Star and Tribune a month before.

Bonner hadn't gotten a release. Instead, he'd convinced Renee to visit the Washington County courthouse and dictate portions of her juvenile record into a small tape recorder he provided—she could do this, since they were her files. What Renee read into the tape recorder happened to include Carol Felix's impassioned seven-page summary of all the facts surrounding both Dennis's death and the Kentucky adoptions. More than eleven years after her angry efforts had failed to rekindle interest in either a small boy's death or the later Kentucky debacle, Carol Felix's report now had provided the crux of Bonner and Kohl's revealing story.

"They all dropped the ball," the reporters quoted Felix as saying. "There wasn't a single person there who wanted to do anything other than drop the ball. They didn't want to admit even to themselves that this baby boy had been murdered. So they denied it."

In an accompanying sidebar, Bonner and Kohl presented interviews with Renee and Grant, and made reference to Robert, but only by his first name. Since they hadn't been charged, the Jurgenses still weren't identified in the newspaper. Nor was Dennis.

Once again, the news media provoked a response from Lois. At five o'clock that Sunday afternoon, the phone rang in Robert Jurgens's home.

Had Robert seen the newspaper article on the kids? Harold and Lois wondered. Had he noticed that his name was mentioned as well?

They both sound so nonchalant, Robert thought. He tried to guide the talk toward Dennis, and the old days. This was not hard to do, for the topic by now seemed to have crowded out all others. The conversation waxed almost nostalgic.

Do you remember the sunglasses we used to wear? Robert asked.

Yeah, you guys really liked the sunglasses, Lois said. Do you remember the tap dancing class I took you guys to?

Robert had forgotten, but now a memory returned. He recalled skipping about the room with those cleats on.

I remember our little white sailor suits, Robert said. I remember how Dennis liked to drink out of a bottle and throw his food around.

Yes, Lois said, he always did like to nurse the bottle.

Robert decided to push.

"I remember you, Mom, coming in to Dennis and picking him up and seeing him limp . . . I remember Dr. Peterson coming with a brown bag . . . For some reason, I thought Uncle Jerome was there, too . . ."

No, Harold and Lois said quickly. Of course not. Jerome wasn't there.

"I don't know why I thought that," Robert said.

No, no, Jerome was never there, they said. Pete Korolchuk was there. Pete had been a very, very good friend of the Zerwas family. In fact, he'd stayed with Grandma and Grandpa . . . Pete should never have been on that case because they were such good friends.

Harold, more talkative now, felt inclined to relive with Robert the night Dennis died. Once again he told of taking Dennis to the bathroom, of looking in the empty toilet, of the broken watch, of putting him to bed and of finding him dead in the morning.

Was he blue at the time? Robert asked.

No, he was perfectly normal, Harold said. And they hadn't heard anything out of him prior to his death.

"That's something that's always bothered me," Harold said. "He never screamed like he was in pain . . . He never screamed like he was in pain."

The conversation turned back to the day's newspaper article. Lois read out some passages from the story—the quotes from Renee and Grant about abuse—and as she did so, she grew emotional.

"I can't believe that these kids say these things. Those kids don't know how well they had it . . . They don't know how well they had it."

When she read Renee's quote about being forced to hide and burn her sanitary napkins, Lois began to cry.

"That's the way my mother had her kids do it. That's the way we had to do it when we were younger . . ."

They'd been talking for more than two hours now. Robert decided he'd better tell them what was to come.

"I hate to lay some bad news on you, but I've been subpoenaed to testify before a grand jury on the twenty-eighth of January at nine o'clock in the morning in Ramsey County."

Lois and Harold grew quiet. They were expecting that, they said. They just hadn't known when the date was.

Were they aware of anyone else who'd been subpoenaed? Robert asked.

No, they said. Robert was the first. This was news to them.

"I'm going to go to the grand jury and I'm going to tell the truth and that's all there is to it," Robert said.

"That's the only thing you can do," Harold said. "That's what you have to do. Tell the truth."

CHAPTER 36

In Search of the Past

On his fifty-second birthday, October 8, Ron Meehan had missed his weekly bowling night, along with the big cake-and-beer party his bowling pals had planned, because a police meeting lasted until ten o'clock. He didn't want to miss the group's Christmas bash as well, so despite the investigation, Ron went bowling on Monday night, December 22, 1986. Afterward, he and his pals sat around over beers, "just discussing everything," Ron would say later, "and trying to analyze the whole world."

When he returned home at one in the morning, he found a note on his pillow. "Greg will pick you up at two o'clock," his wife had written.

Ron called Greg. It turned out Mindy Elledge and Clayton Robinson had concocted a plan the previous afternoon that would require the policemen to serve subpoenas before dawn.

"Geez, I just got home," Ron said. "I'm not going to get any sleep, and we got things to do later today."

"Hey, stay in bed," Greg said. "No big deal."

"Okay," Ron said. "But make sure you take a uniform with you. It'll still be dark."

Greg called the Washington County sheriff's office and arranged to meet a uniformed deputy at five in the morning on a certain stretch of Nolan Avenue in the rural edge of Stillwater. They were going to visit Harold and Lois Jurgens.

◆   ◆   ◆

For weeks, the prosecutors had been searching for a document that they'd come to regard as crucial to their case—the transcript of Robert Jurgens's 1965 custody hearing. From the Ramsey County welfare department files, they knew such a hearing had taken place one month after Dennis's death, but they didn't know who testified, or what they'd said, or even if there was a transcript. They could only surmise.

A transcript might answer so many questions. The dead could speak from the grave, the memories of older witnesses could be refreshed, Lois and Harold's own words could be recovered. They'd have convincing corroboration for the statements Greg and Ron were now collecting. What people had said then, just weeks after Dennis died, promised a precision and accuracy unlike anything the prosecutors could glean from witnesses today. Mindy and Clayton, however, had thrown out mountains of search warrants over four states, to no avail—Ramsey County didn't have a transcript, nor Washington County, nor the Jurgenses' former attorney Ed Donohue.

Maybe, the prosecutors now reasoned in late December, either the Jurgenses or their new attorney, Doug Thomson, had a copy. To find out, they devised a strategy that required precise timing. Greg was to serve the Jurgenses with grand jury subpoenas and court orders demanding photos of Dennis and any documents they might have relating to the 1965 juvenile proceedings, then rush to downtown St. Paul and serve the same papers on Thomson.

What Harold will try to do, Clayton had explained, is get the paperwork to his attorney right away. You've got to get to Thomson first, as soon as you serve Harold, because otherwise Thomson will be warned, and can put the transcript in someone else's office. When you arrive with his court order, Doug legally could say it's not here, even though it could be right across the hallway.

Of course, Clayton could have asked a Ramsey County deputy sheriff to deliver the papers to Thomson while Greg was handing Harold his subpoena, but by now the prosecutor was reluctant to use an unknown officer in this way. He'd come to trust Greg and Ron implicitly, and wanted to work only with them.

In the early morning dark, Greg drove twenty-two miles south to the White Bear police station to pick up the papers left by Mindy the night before, then headed east toward Stillwater. At five o'clock he met Deputy John O'Hearn on the road beside the Jurgens home. There was no address marker, only numbers scratched on a nearby cable box. Washington County, Greg noted with some satisfaction, had sent him a large moose of a man.

They were supposed to wait until Harold left his house and climbed into his car for the drive to work, then hit him there on the driveway with the court papers and take him back inside to get what they were seeking.

Greg gripped the steering wheel of his Pontiac 6000. This car, he figured, should beat anything Harold's got.

An hour passed, then a second one, without Harold leaving his house. The officers' cars, once concealed in the dark, were now visible in the early dawn's light on a narrow, empty country road. Greg radioed the White Bear police dispatcher, who patched the call through to Clayton at his home.

"It doesn't look like Harold's going to work," Greg said. "Should I go to the door?"

"Yes, yes," Clayton said. "Go to the door."

At 7:10 A.M., Greg and Deputy O'Hearn began climbing the steep driveway. At the top, to the left of the house, two aged pickup trucks, a camper and a rusting school bus formed a tableau that looked much like an abandoned junkyard. Circling around, the officers rang the bell at the back door. No one answered. Greg pushed the button a second time, then noticed someone watching them from a window. One minute later, Harold opened the door, dressed in his pajamas, his hair uncombed. He looked back and forth at the two men standing before him.

"I'm Detective Greg Kindle with the White Bear Lake Police Department. I have grand jury subpoenas and court orders for both you and your wife."

After the detective read the information contained in both documents, Harold shook his head.

He couldn't possibly find photos of Dennis right then, he said. His attorney had advised him to cooperate, and he would, but his wife didn't want them in the house. He needed twenty-four to forty-eight hours to produce the pictures.

How do you feel about it yourself? Do you want me in there? Greg asked silently, biting his lip. Without Ron to signal restraint, he'd have to be his own control.

"The court order states these photos should be turned over immediately," Greg said.

Harold turned sideways then and pointed to the inside of his home. "Officer, look at this," he said. "There is no way I can find the pictures while you stand here and wait."

Greg, peering past Harold into what seemed a large family room, saw what he had to admit was a bizarre, ungainly mess. Towering piles of bric-a-brac and figurines rose everywhere, to within three feet of the ceiling, leaving little room even to walk. There were prints and curios and miniature statues—of little boys and girls, of farmers with pitchforks—the sort of shelf and wall items most commonly described in the Midwest as "home interiors" and often sold at household gatherings, much like Tupperware. It looked as if Lois had bought a warehouse full of home interiors. Whether she was collecting them or selling them at women's parties Greg did not know.

Kindle, noticing a shade move at a window, saw Lois looking out at them.

"Do you have any transcripts of the 1965 juvenile proceeding pertaining to Robert?" Greg asked Harold.

No, he didn't, Harold said. He'd never seen them, and never had anything to do with them, and knew nothing about that.

Clayton had said not to waste time if they don't have what we want. Hit them with the paperwork and get back to Doug Thomson in St. Paul.

"Okay," Greg said. "I'll give you until two o'clock this afternoon to deliver the photos to the White Bear police station."

When Harold said he could comply with that deadline, Greg handed him the subpoenas and court orders and turned toward the driveway. It was 7:20 A.M. They'd been standing at the doorway for ten minutes.

Greg pushed the Pontiac to 75 MPH between Stillwater and St. Paul, first on empty country roads snaking through prairie farmland, then on the interstates. Parking his car in a downtown lot, he sprinted the half block to the county attorney's office on St. Peter Street and caught the elevator to the fourth floor. There Clayton and Mindy, while peppering him with questions, handed over the papers to serve on the Jurgenses' attorney. Greg turned and bolted from their office.

Doug Thomson's quarters were in the Amhoist Building directly across St. Peter to the west—but for the shaded windows, the prosecutors would have been able to see Doug as he worked at his desk. Sprinting across St. Peter and entering the Amhoist Building's lobby, Greg spotted an elevator door about to close.

"Hold the door," he called out.

A man's hand popped out from inside the elevator.

"Thanks," Greg said, walking through the open door.

"What floor?" the man said.

"Third."

Greg, looking to his right as the elevator started its ascent, realized the man standing next to him was Harold Jurgens. Harold now was wearing slacks and a sports jacket and his hair was combed, but it looked to Greg as though he was still wearing the top to his pajamas. In his right arm he held the paperwork Greg had handed him just a half hour before.

"Nice day," Greg said.

"Yes, the weather is fine," Harold said.

Greg realized Harold didn't recognize him. The light had been dim on the Jurgenses' back porch, and besides, as he stood in the elevator, the White Bear detective didn't look much like a policeman. He was wearing a waist-length leather coat and a brimmed hat, the sort Bing Crosby used to wear. As it happened, Greg called his hat Bing and wore it often during the winter.

"After you," Harold said when the elevator doors opened on the third floor.

"No sir, after you."

Greg followed Harold—still unaware—straight into Doug Thomson's suite. A short, jumpy man in a three-piece suit darted from an inner office and grabbed the paperwork from Harold's arm.

"Is this it?" Doug Thomson asked. He had thinning gray hair and thick spectacles.

Squinting, holding the documents close to his eyes, Doug started scanning through the paragraphs. Halfway through, he suddenly looked up and stared at Greg.

"Who are you?" the attorney asked.

"I'm Detective Greg Kindle, White Bear Lake police, and I've got the same papers for you, Mr. Thomson."

Doug looked at his client, then back at Greg, trying to understand how they came to be standing together in his office.

"Do you have an answer for me, Mr. Thomson?" Greg asked.

"You can tell the county attorney we'll answer this at the time of the grand jury," Thomson snorted.

"Very good," Greg said, choosing not to push. "By the way, do you have a telephone I could use? I'd like to give them that message right now."

On the phone, Mindy told Greg to come on back across the street. There was nothing more to do. From Thomson's words, Mindy knew he didn't have the transcript.

CHAPTER 37

A Cry from the Ground

The brief autopsy report written by Dr. Robert Woodburn on Palm Sunday, 1965, was by current standards a cursory, inadequate document. What is more, Woodburn, a private pathologist without forensic training, was not held in high esteem in some Ramsey County legal-medical quarters. These matters increasingly worried Mindy and Clayton in early January of 1987 as they prepared for their grand jury date at month's end. Expecting that Doug Thomson would catch on and challenge the autopsy, they felt the need to substantiate Dennis Jurgens's cause of death, as well as the estimated time range of forty-eight hours between the fatal blow and his demise. There was only one way to do that, of course. They would have to dig up Dennis's body.

Near the end of the first week in January, Mindy called the county medical examiner.

"I think we ought to get the body exhumed," she told Michael McGee. "We need to do another autopsy."

McGee considered. He had once exhumed a body ten years in the ground. The Jurgens body was almost twenty-two years old.

"You're not going to find anything but soup," McGee said. "It's been too long."

"What do you say I have the funeral director from back then call you?" Mindy asked.

◆   ◆   ◆

Ron and Greg had found Jim Honsa just where he'd been in 1965, and just where Jerry Sherwood had found him—at the Lake Mortuary across from St. Mary's Church, one block from the White Bear police station.

When the two plainclothes detectives walked in one late-December afternoon, Honsa offered them coffee and wondered what he'd done wrong. We're here to investigate the Jurgens case, Ron explained. Oh, shit, Honsa thought. Here we go again.

The police pumped him for details that day. How was Dennis buried? What would his body look like now? What would be left?

"People don't rot," Honsa told them. "If you kill the bacteria, and there's no oxygen, there will be no decomposition. The body should be in good shape."

What about the entrails and organs? they asked.

"They're in a bag at the foot of the casket," Honsa said. "Children that age, you don't put the organs back inside. They'd look pregnant."

"Do you know for sure?"

"Just like I did it yesterday."

He'd had to use an inordinate amount of cosmetics on the face to cover the bruises and the fingernail marks behind the ears, Honsa explained. He'd thought the markings looked suspicious, but it was not his place to point them out to the police. Besides, he thought the police knew.

Why's that? Ron asked.

Because Lieutenant Jerry Zerwas came to the funeral home before the viewing, Honsa said. He remembered it clearly, he said. Jerry Zerwas examined the condition of the body, including the marks behind Dennis's ears.

Now, a month after this chat with the detectives, Honsa called McGee at Mindy's request.

"They want to get this baby back," the medical examiner said.

"It will be in good shape," Honsa promised. "I embalmed him good."

"Where are the organs?"

"In a separate bag."

"Muslin?" McGee asked. Cloth would leak.

"No, plastic. And I added a strong solution."

It was as if the funeral director had foreseen a day when someone would come looking.

Mindy called Honsa to make the arrangements. She wanted to exhume at night, to avoid the news media. Honsa disagreed.

"If you do it at night," he said, "there'll be lights and trucks attracting special attention. Let's just do it normal. It'll look like a regular funeral."

Honsa was right. Anyone walking by the small St. Mary's Cemetery at ten in the morning on Friday, January 9, would have believed he was seeing a funeral underway. A dozen or so people stood around an open grave, heads bowed under cloudy skies and bare oak trees, heavy coats and mufflers pulled tight against a temperature just reaching twenty-four degrees. Yes, one or two in the group seemed to be stomping about impatiently on the frozen winter ground, but that was not so odd, given the brisk morning chill.

The vault company's truck, as it happened, just then was having trouble pulling the crypt from the hard earth, due to stubbornly heavy mud suction. When the workers finally yanked the bulky container from the grave and popped its seal, the cemetery visitors—including McGee, Mindy and Honsa—found inside a four-foot-by-three-and-a-half-foot yellow metal casket sitting in an inch of moisture. Honsa guided his men as they slid the casket, unopened, onto a plastic sheet in the rear of his hearse. Minutes later, he pulled through the cemetery's low gates and headed toward the medical examiner's office in downtown St. Paul.

McGee, Mindy and Jim Essling met Honsa on the driveway that leads through a garage into the medical examiner's basement autopsy room.

"Okay, Jim," McGee said. "Thank you."

"No, wait," Honsa said. "Can I stick around?"

McGee shrugged.

Two morgue attendants carried the small yellow casket to a steel table in the center of the autopsy room. The room had changed little since the building rose in 1964 under the guidance of coroner Tom Votel—here, still, was the dirty white tile floor, the wall of stainless steel crypts, the double bank of fluorescent lights hanging from a low ceiling above the center table. Twenty-one years and nine months after his death, Dennis Jurgens's body had returned to the precise spot where it had lain at midday on Palm Sunday 1965.

The fluorescent lights cast a pale glare on the rusted gold and bronze metal of the casket's surface. Lifting up the first cover,

McGee noted a name plaque bearing two lines on the far right inside corner:

DENNIS JURGENS
1961–1965

When the attendants opened the casket itself, even those in the room most experienced with such matters felt nonplussed. There, lying supine on a gold and brown velvetlike material, the head supported by a pillow of the same material, was the figure of a small child in perfect if weathered shape, like an ancient man preserved in time. The body was mummified, with the brown, leathery, wrinkled skin preferred by movie directors when imagining creatures from outer space, but it was remarkably intact. Dennis was dressed in turquoise shorts with a matching vest over a long-sleeved white dress shirt and bow tie. Knee-high tan stockings enclosed each foot. Blond hair, one to two inches long, still covered the top of the head, as did a crown of withered flowers. Just where I put it, Honsa thought. Beside the body lay a white Styrofoam heart bordered by lace, assorted dried flowers and plants, and a banner with the words "God Son." At the foot of the casket on the right side was a tied, heavy white plastic bag containing the perfectly preserved organs.

None of this, however, was what first claimed McGee's eyes. Standing over the open casket, he couldn't help but contemplate the boy's face. There, on the forehead, nose and cheeks, McGee could clearly see dark round markings, some bluish-black, some brownish-black, some reddish, some greenish. Dennis's bruises were still visible on his now leathery brown skin.

McGee spent Friday afternoon and Saturday performing the new autopsy. In time, he observed and noted bruises across most of Dennis's body, as well as a gaping tear in the skin and tissue at the base of the penis, but he was seeking something else—he needed a cause of death. Alone in the autopsy room late on Saturday night, he inspected the gastrointestinal system, his eyes probing inch by inch from the lower esophagus to the colon. The entrails, he thought, were in marvelous condition. At half past two on Sunday morning, January 11, he found what he was seeking. There, in the midportion of the small bowel, in the ileum, set amid a brown-black hemorrhage, he could see a small oval hole, three-eighths by one-eighth of an inch in size. Here was the killer, still visible after almost twenty-two years. Through this rent in the bowel, infectious fecal material had flowed to Dennis's abdomen, causing death. McGee took a magnified photograph of what he'd found.

The medical examiner's thoughts just then turned not to the wonders of science, but of religion. He felt he understood why Dennis Jurgens's death was now so improbably coming to their attention, and why the boy's body had remained so surprisingly intact, as if awaiting their inspection, as if frozen in time until the right moment. McGee thought about the book of Genesis.

Where is your brother? God asked Cain in Genesis. I am not my brother's keeper, Cain answered. Abel's blood cries out from the ground, God replied.

That was the reason for this case, McGee believed. Any other explanation was bullshit. Dennis's blood had cried out from the ground.

"I've been doing this job for too long not to know there are lots of dead babies in the ground who were killed," McGee told others later. "This just didn't happen here, with this one boy . . . The difference in this case is that Dennis's blood cried out from the ground."

Later that Sunday, McGee called Honsa to say they were ready for reburial. Honsa arranged for a new vault and presided as Dennis's body once again was lowered into the hard earth at St. Mary's Cemetery.

CHAPTER 38

Grand Jury

Two weeks into the new year, preparing for a January 28 date in court, the Ramsey County attorney's office spread grand jury subpoenas to some dozen witnesses in the Twin Cities area, including Jerome Zerwas. As a result, at 2:30 P.M. on January 21, Jerome called Ron Meehan with a question: "Why am I being subpoenaed, since I had nothing to do with the case?"

"At the time of Dennis's death," Ron explained, "you were the number-two man in the police department. Through the course of the present investigation, we've discovered that a number of written statements and photos were missing from the file. That's one reason you're being subpoenaed."

"I never read those reports or had anything to do with that," Jerome said. "I know nothing about them being missing."

Days later, Jerome called Ron again. Now he was greatly upset with several items he'd read in the newspapers that suggested he had covered up the case in 1965. "Contact Wayne Armstrong," Jerome urged. "He'll verify that I didn't cover up anything."

On the evening of January 25, three days before the grand jury was to hear the Jurgens case, Robert received a call from Harold and Lois.

Would they be able to talk to him when he was down from Crookston at the courthouse? they wondered.

No, he said. He would just be slipping in to testify and then would leave, as he had to get back to work.

"What will happen if we're indicted?" Lois asked.

Turn yourselves in to the Ramsey County jail for processing, Robert said.

In truth, Robert was not planning to be in the courthouse at all during the grand jury proceedings on January 28 and January 29, for he'd already testified. Mindy and Clayton had decided to sneak him in two weeks early—in private, on January 14—for several reasons. Grand jury proceedings are closed to the public and press, but the prosecutors worried that reporters and cameras hovering outside the courtroom might upset Robert. They also wanted in general to avoid excessive news media coverage, fearing that the doggedness of reporters such as Brian Bonner might provoke a change of venue, and thus a loss of the sophisticated urban jury the prosecutors desired. Finally, they simply didn't want to try the case in the press—they wanted a clean case.

Three of the grand jurors had wept as they listened to Robert, and afterward, the entire jury wanted to vote right then on an indictment. Mindy had to calm them down by explaining there was quite a bit more evidence to hear in the coming days from some fifteen other witnesses.

The main portion of the grand jury proceedings began on Wednesday morning, January 28. The grand jury is the prosecutors' domain alone—no judge presides, and no defense attorney is present to raise objections or cross-examine witnesses. Mindy and Clayton's task, through the witnesses' testimony, would be to convince the jurors there was enough evidence to go to trial.

Bob VanderWyst, ravaged by bone cancer, hobbled to the stand as the first witness. Responding to Mindy's questions, he recounted his memories of Palm Sunday and the three-week investigation that followed.

"It was around April 30 that we were told that it was the end of the investigation," he said after finishing his account.

"Who told you that the investigation would stop there?" Mindy asked.

"The chief of police . . . Wayne Armstrong."

Q: During your investigation in 1965, where were the records of your investigation kept?

A: There was a separate file set up and all our reports went on the chief's desk.

Q: Was this usual procedure for police officers in White Bear Lake?

A: No, it wasn't . . . We had received some interference and so they set up a special file in the chief's room and he kept the records.

Q: Who was interfering with your investigation?

A: Well, Lieutenant Zerwas.

Q: Who had access to the chief's office at that time?

A: Well, Lieutenant Zerwas had a key to the chief's office . . . and the chief had a key.

Q: Did Jerome Zerwas ever make any statement to you about the investigation?

A: Yes, he did . . . He said that 'I will do everything in my power to keep my sister clear' . . .

Q: Did you record this statement in a police report?

A: We made a report on this, yes.

Q: Have you looked through the police reports that we have on this case from your 1965 investigation?

A: Yes, I have.

Q: Is that particular report contained within the investigative reports that we have?

A: No. That is not in the reports . . .

Q: Have you looked through the police reports that we have from your 1965 investigations and determined whether anything else is missing?

A: Yes, there are other reports missing . . . It seems like all the statements that were taken are missing.

Pete Korolchuk, following his former colleague to the stand, corroborated VanderWyst's testimony.

Q: During your investigation into the death of Dennis Craig Jurgens, where were the records that you made kept?

A: All of the records that were made were submitted to the chief of police, Wayne Armstrong, because he wanted to keep those records out of normal channels, where everybody could see these reports as they were being processed . . .

Q: In 1965, who had access to the chief of police's office?

A: The chief of police and Lieutenant Zerwas.

Q: During your investigation, did you ever have any conversation with Jerome Zerwas about the investigation . . .?

A: Well, Lieutenant Zerwas had mentioned at that time that he was going to do everything that he could to help his sister.

Q: Did Jerome Zerwas ever say anything to you that would indicate that he was familiar with the reports that you were making in investigating the death of Dennis Jurgens?

A: There was one incident that did come up that would lead me to believe that, yes, he was familiar with the reports that we had . . . The chief of police approached both Officer VanderWyst and myself and said that the statement that we had made accusing Jerome . . . was untrue.

Q: Who did he say said that it was untrue?

A: He said that Jerome said it was untrue.

Q: Is there any doubt in your mind that Jerome Zerwas ever made that statement to you?

A: There is no doubt in my mind. I was there and other people were there.

Later in the day, Jerome Zerwas took the stand.

"I'd like you to describe, if you will, for the grand jury, your relationship with Lois, other than that of being a sister," Clayton began.

"Our relationship is not close," Jerome said. "While I lived in White Bear Lake, I would dare say I wasn't over at their house over five times in all the years they lived there."

He had never seen Lois abuse Dennis, he said, and had never seen signs of abuse on the boy's body. He had no contact with Lois at all on the day of Dennis's death. He did not, he insisted twice, view the dead boy's body prior to the funeral, and he saw no bruises on Dennis at the funeral.

Clayton pressed. "Is it your testimony that you never went to the mortuary to view the body of Dennis Jurgens other than at his wake? Is that correct?"

Jerome revised. "No. I was over there just prior to the wake—a few hours before the wake."

Jerome denied ever making any sort of threat to VanderWyst and Korolchuk about protecting his sister. He denied removing any documents from any file. He denied now having any documents in his possession.

"I didn't even see none of the reports or any of that stuff," he said. "I don't have no idea what they did . . . I went directly to the chief of police on Tuesday when I returned back to work and went into the office and told him that I didn't want any part of the case. I didn't want any part of the case at all. It's a conflict of interest . . . I said, I didn't want anything to do with it. I advised him to get a hold of Ramsey County authorities and have them handle the case."

The prosecutors saved their most critical witness almost for last. With some trepidation, only after first offering the testimony of Lloyd and Donna Zerwas, Richard Norton and assorted other relatives, Clayton finally called Harold Jurgens to the stand.

Harold represented a gamble on Mindy and Clayton's part. His role in the whole Jurgens affair, quite apart from legal issues, intrigued and puzzled many people. He was by all accounts a warm, caring person, but apparently he'd also allowed Lois to abuse a number of children over the years, children he had seemed to adore. How to explain him was beyond the prosecutors' reach. Lois's former psychiatrist, Dr. James Garvey, had talked of the "secondary gain" passive people derived by expressing their repressed anger through their mates, but this was not the sort of theorizing that just now occupied Mindy and Clayton. They had to decide what to do with Harold.

Whatever responsibility he bore for Dennis's death, Minnesota law didn't recognize "accessories after the fact" to a homicide, and the statute of limitations precluded any charge other than murder. Did Harold's passivity and failure to intervene make him so accountable for Dennis's death that he could be prosecuted for murder? The prosecutors, although offended by Harold's role, did not think so.

One of their key trial strategies, instead, was to keep Harold out of the picture, to keep him from clouding the case against his wife. They needed to place Lois alone in the home with Dennis during the forty-eight-hour period in which the doctors said he suffered his fatal injury. Mindy and Clayton worried that Harold, under a lawyer's tutelage, could raise reasonable doubt on this point. He would, they feared, try to muddy the precise cause of death by saying he was there and had struck Dennis. In their parlance, he would "try to take Lois out."

To protect against this, Mindy and Clayton wanted to call Harold before the grand jury so they could pin him to a story now, and in that way at least put a box around his testimony before the trial. When they subpoenaed him, though, he'd demanded full immunity. Clayton had resisted at first. Since we can prove he wasn't there in the home when Dennis died, the prosecutor argued to Ramsey County District Judge David Marsden, Harold is not going to be indicted and thusly has no need for immunity. Judge Marsden wasn't satisfied with that reasoning, though, so Mindy and Clayton had decided to roll the dice. They'd give Harold his immunity in exchange for hearing his story.

It was against this backdrop that Harold reluctantly stepped to the witness stand late in the afternoon on January 29, forced to that spot by the threat of being cited for contempt of court. He was now sixty-five, two months away from retirement at Muska Electric, and he looked almost venerable with his dark suit, tinted eyeglasses and receding silver hair.

The day before, he'd visited his priest, Father Thomas Mroczka, and the two men had gone to lunch together. Over the years, Harold had often confided his troubles to priests, but in more recent times, he'd been seeking his solace in a decidedly less conventional segment of the Catholic Church. The St. Processus & Martinian Catholic Church on Menomin Street in St. Paul was part of a small breakaway group called the Society of St. Pius V, a faction that rejected modern church sacraments in favor of the pre-Vatican II Latin Tridentine mass. Harold's church shared some common ground with the excommunicated French Archbishop Marcel Lefebvre—Father Mroczka so doubted John Paul as pope that he believed the seat of Peter was vacant—but the Society of St. Pius V had broken with Lefebvre in 1983 and gone its own way. At lunch, Harold hadn't talked to Father Mroczka at all of Dennis's death, but the topic could not be so easily avoided on the witness stand.

Clayton Robinson led Harold once more through his familiar account of the night Dennis died, and questioned him about reported incidents of abuse. Harold denied most of what Clayton suggested in his questions, and professed a faulty memory to the rest.

"I cannot say yes and I cannot say no," he responded to query after query, repeating the same words so often that Clayton finally felt impelled to ask if anyone had instructed him to use that precise language.

Mindy was disgusted. Harold's acting as if he's the smoothest guy in the world, she thought. He believes he's schmoozing with the jury.

Not until Harold's turn on the witness stand approached its end did Clayton move to the heart of the matter.

"I'd like you to start with the day, that Friday [before Dennis's death], and tell me what your events were, what you did during that day," he said.

"I went to work Friday. It was a normal day for me . . . Normal day."

Mindy and Clayton glanced at each other. So here it was. According to the 1965 police reports and June Bol's memory, Harold had left for Wisconsin that Friday morning, but now, on the stand, he was placing himself in the Jurgens home.

"When did you leave to go to wherever it was you went?" Clayton asked.

"Saturday morning."

"Where did you go?"

"Hawthorne, Wisconsin."

He was taking himself out of the picture a day late, making his departure only twenty-four hours before Dennis died. The doctors said Dennis's fatal blow had occurred within forty-eight hours of his death.

Clayton would have to show part of his own hand now. Did Harold have a conversation once with June Bol while Lois was away, hospitalized? he asked.

"I could have, yes."

"During that conversation, did you tell June Bol that your wife had called you in Hawthorne, Wisconsin, on April 10, 1965, and said that she had been at it again with Dennis?"

"I cannot guarantee that one, yes or no," Harold said.

"Why can't you answer that question, sir?"

"I don't recall. I'll have to go to the negative point on that, then . . ."

"Did Lois Jurgens ever tell you that she had been at it with Dennis Jurgens sometime on April 10, 1965?"

"The way you put it, I cannot say yes or no."

Clayton invited Harold to tell in his own words about the phone conversation.

"There was something about a mess . . ." he said. "There was a mess that had been made. Not just Dennis, but Dennis and Robert . . . and . . . the basement being flooded . . ."

Clayton now decided to force the question. He'd rather hear it now, he reasoned, than at the trial.

"Did you strike Dennis Jurgens on April ninth, which would have been Friday?"

"No," Harold said, "not Friday."

"Did you strike Dennis Jurgens on April tenth at any point in time?"

"Yes," Harold said, "I did."

Just as they had thought—Harold was trying to take Lois out.

"Where did you strike him?"

"I believe it would be above the hip joint in the abdomen area."

"Why did you strike him?"

"Dennis did something that morning before I left, I don't know what it was, I gave him a good hard swat and he was turning and I hit him by the—but I shouldn't have hit him. It wasn't intended there . . . I was going to give him a darn good swat and he turned and I hit him with the side of my hand. I admit when my hand hit him it was harder than it was anticipated . . . When he started to turn the swat didn't land where it was supposed to land. It turned out to be the side of my hand . . . I felt bad about it. I'm being honest with you on that."

"What time was it that you hit Dennis Jurgens?" Clayton asked.

"I said it was in the Saturday morning before I went to Hawthorne, Wisconsin . . . five, six in the morning, like I said before."

Clayton knew Harold had not told this story to the police in 1965. But what had he said at the juvenile court custody proceeding a month after Dennis died? Would his words then contradict what he now was saying?

"Were you as candid as you possibly could have been about the death of Dennis Jurgens during that [1965 juvenile] hearing?" he asked.

"I don't believe Dennis's death was brought up at that hearing," Harold said.

"You don't believe there was any discussion whatsoever about Dennis's death?"

Harold looked downright smug. "No, not that I know of."

Clayton longed for a look at that 1965 proceeding. Where, oh where was that transcript? Did it even exist?

"Have you ever had a transcript of the juvenile court proceeding concerning Robert Jurgens?" he asked.

"I, myself, haven't."

"Who to your knowledge has had possession of that document?"

"My attorney . . . Edward T. Donohue."

Clayton considered. Why would Donohue ever have gone to the bother and expense of ordering a transcript for a juvenile custody hearing, particularly when Robert was eventually returned? You normally ordered a transcript if you were appealing a court's ruling. They got Robert back, so what was appealed? And when? And where?

"Why was that document obtained by Mr. Donohue?" he asked.

"I don't know," Harold said. "He wanted it and I paid for it. That's all I know, sir."

After three hours on the stand, Harold stepped down.

The grand jurors, before retreating to deliberate, had a question for the prosecutors: Could they indict others in this case besides Lois Jurgens?

Mindy thought she knew just which people the jurors had in mind, and the notion appealed to her, but she didn't feel she could be encouraging. She explained to the jurors about the statute of limitations. They couldn't now file obstruction of justice or accessory after the fact charges for something done twenty-two years ago, she explained. They could charge a person for perjuring himself before the grand jury in the past forty-eight hours, but Mindy didn't see how they could prove such a case, even if they believed beyond doubt that someone had lied.

With that, the jurors retreated to a conference room. When they soon after returned from their deliberations, Ron Meehan, waiting in the empty courtroom with Mindy, looked at his watch with some surprise. Only six minutes had elapsed.

At 4:45 P.M. on Thursday, January 29, the grand jury delivered its sealed report, and minutes later, Doug Thomson received a call from a court clerk, asking that he have his client in the courthouse at 9:30 the next morning. Although the clerk would provide no further information, Thomson knew this meant Lois had been indicted. Had the grand jury decided not to issue an indictment, the "no bill" would have been made public immediately and no court appearance would be needed. Judge Marsden had before him a "true bill," even if he would not say so.

The detectives and prosecutors had prevailed. When Ron and Mindy left the courthouse together early that evening, they found before them streets full of half-frozen slush—some three-and-a-half inches of snow had fallen that day, and the temperature had dipped to twenty-eight degrees—but Ron for once hardly noticed Minnesota's sloppy January chill. He and Mindy walked up Fifth Street toward their cars, passing through Rice Park, which was filled with ice sculptures, adornments for St. Paul's annual winter carnival. Pausing for a time in the winter night, talking over the case, Ron eventually looked down at his feet and realized he was standing in frozen slop up to his ankles.

"I didn't even feel it I was so ecstatic," he told Greg later, "and I hadn't had a drop to drink . . . I was just thrilled to death. I was walking nineteen feet off the ground . . . A brand new pair of shoes just shriveled up, though. Had to throw them away."

When he arrived home in White Bear Lake fifteen minutes later, Ron reached into the refrigerator and popped the top off a Blatz.

"Liz, I've got to get going right away," he told his wife. "I've got to get to the station and call Greg long distance, and all the witnesses."

He drove his unmarked police squad car north on White Bear Avenue, following the road as it curved along the south shore of the lake. Lost in his private celebration, about to swing from White Bear Avenue to the northbound lanes of Highway 61, Ron didn't at first realize he was still sipping from his Blatz. The notion of such an unseemly violation horrified him, so he quickly placed the open can on the floor of the squad car.

Minutes later, at the station, he called Greg, who was sitting in a motel in Brainerd, 110 miles north of the Twin Cities, attending the Minnesota State Juvenile Officers Association's annual convention.

"We did it, baby," Ron said.

Greg prepared himself a martini from the fixings he'd thought to bring, just in case, when he had packed for his trip north.

Later that night, Ron called Robert Jurgens, Lloyd Zerwas and all the other witnesses. He'd promised them they were going to prosecute the case this time, and he wanted them to know his word was good.

Aware that an indictment was imminent, radio and television newscasts that night finally identified Harold and Lois Jurgens by name for the first time since the case was reopened in early October.

Local viewers of the evening news saw Harold looking distraught, even bereaved, dressed improbably in a rust-colored polyester suit. "I'm not allowed to say nothing," he told journalists who
stuck microphones before his face.

"It's like a bad dream for the Jurgenses," Thomson told reporters
and camera crews who visited his office. "It's kind of hard to come to
grips with, to understand why it's happening after twenty-one years.
They are both bewildered."

"I honestly believe if I hadn't tried to find my son this wouldn't
be here today. We wouldn't have an indictment," Jerry Sherwood said
tearfully. She was going to set up a fund to help other abused children, she reported. "Dennis was here for a purpose. He was not here
to die."

The next morning in Ramsey County's courthouse, the wood-
paneled fourteenth-floor corridor leading from the elevators to
Judge Marsden's courtroom filled with reporters, photographers
and no less than six television camera crews. Each time the elevator doors slid open, the cameras' lights flooded the hallway with
their overwhelming glare and the technicians asked each other, "Is
it her?"

Lois finally appeared with Harold and Doug Thomson, wearing a black tweed coat and a white pillbox hat adorned with a black
veil, feathers and ribbon. "Aunt Peacock," some of the nieces had
called her in past years, bemused by her preference in hats. Now Lois
walked down the swarming, illuminated corridor with deliberation,
her hands clasped together at her waist, her face blank.

Once in courtroom 1415, unsure of where to go, the couple
took seats near the rear. Lois, so severe and unpliant, so oddly stiff-
necked, was giving many people the willies now—she fulfilled their
imagined notion of a child abuser. Waiting, she folded her hands on
her lap and held herself immobile. A moment later, her eyes, but not
her head, moved slowly to the left. Seated four rows toward the front,
amid friends and her daughters, was Jerry Sherwood.

"Ma, here she is," one of Jerry's daughters said.

Sherwood's lawyer, Ray Harp, fearing she might leap from her
seat, stretched out a leg to block his client. Jerry, though, only turned
and looked at Lois. For a moment, their eyes met.

"There was hatred in both our looks, I must admit," Jerry told
people later. "Although the reasons for the hatred were different."

When the proceeding began at 9:30 A.M., Lois rose and approached Judge Marsden's bench. Her attorney, Doug Thomson, stood to her left, Mindy and Clayton and Tom Foley to her right.

The only question now involved the charges. The statute of limitations had expired for manslaughter, and first-degree premeditated murder seemed unlikely.

The clerk of the court read the indictment.

Lois stood accused of murdering Dennis "on or about April 10/11, 1965." She was charged with one count of second-degree murder and two counts of third-degree murder, as those offenses were described under 1965 statutes.

Listening from the back of the courtroom, Ron Meehan felt surprised and pleased. He had assumed they'd only get a third-degree charge. In Minnesota, second-degree murder meant killing someone with intent but without premeditation. Third-degree murder meant killing someone without either intent or premeditation, during the course of committing a felony assault or while using a dangerous weapon.

As each charge was read to her, Lois voiced her plea.

"State of Minnesota versus Lois Germaine Jurgens," Clerk Michelle Danielson began. "The above defendant is hereby accused and charged by the grand jury of the above-named county in the state of Minnesota by this indictment of the offense of count one, murder in the second degree. How do you plead?"

"Not guilty." Lois spoke sharply and clearly.

"Count two, murder in the third degree. How do you plead?"

"Not guilty." Lois sounded irritated at being required to answer a second time.

"Count three, murder in the third degree. How do you plead?"

"Not guilty."

Near the front of the spectator seating, Jerry Sherwood began to sob.

The proceeding lasted twenty-five minutes in all. After Judge Marsden imposed the $25,000 bail requested by Clayton, a bailiff handcuffed Lois and led her away for booking and fingerprinting. "My purse," Lois blurted, more in surprise than anger, when the bailiff took it from her in the small anteroom.

Spectators filed from the courtroom, but a small group lingered. They were well-wishers, gathered about Jerry Sherwood, hugging her and offering congratulations. White Bear Lake Police Lieutenant

Buzz Harvey approached and shook her hand. Trust us, we are on
the same side, he'd told her four months before, on the morning of
September 18. Now he had a question:

"Has your faith in the system been restored?"

"Somewhat," Sherwood replied.

In time, Sherwood and her coterie turned and plunged into the
sea of cameras and microphones that filled the corridor.

"I'm grateful it's all happened," she told reporters, wiping away
the tears that had washed her face for most of the proceeding. "But
this is just the beginning. There is still the trial . . . I feel some of the
weight has been lifted . . . It's put me through hell. I don't think I'll
ever forget it the rest of my life."

In another corner of the hallway, White Bear Lake Police Chief
Philip Major and Ramsey County Attorney Tom Foley stood before
a second bank of microphones.

"Was there a coverup in 1965?" Phil Major was asked.

This was a difficult question for a police chief who felt both protective of his department and suspicious of what had transpired there
years before. Major came from the new, more educated and professional breed of police officers who'd supplanted the colorful and
rough-edged small-town cops of a previous era. When he'd first read
the 1965 police file, after Jerry Sherwood had appeared at the station in
September of 1986, Major couldn't understand why the police hadn't
been at the county attorney's office, jumping up and down, demanding a prosecution. Then he'd learned of VanderWyst and Korolchuk's
stories about pressure and interference, but that still hadn't provided
an entirely suitable explanation. All the talk he'd heard in recent weeks
about how society wasn't sensitive to child abuse twenty-two years ago
hadn't helped much either. Major remembered 1965, and to him, those
weren't insensitive times at all. That, he recalled, was the year of the
big flood and the civil rights demonstrations—black and white hands
clasping, volunteers piling sandbags on the banks of the Mississippi.
Major found it hard to believe that everyone had been so uncaring and
uninvolved then. It didn't seem to him there was that much time difference. It wasn't that long ago.

The police chief surveyed the noisy scene before him.

No, there wasn't a coverup in 1965, Major told the reporters. The
police reports, he said, suggested "no administrative involvement
either positive or negative."

"I think the entire system failed," Tom Foley agreed. "I think you have to look at what took place back there. There was not the recognition of the child abuse problems today. We're much more sensitive . . . and much more aware of the child abuse problem."

The homicide charges, Foley said, "would be the only charges brought in this case." Any prosecution of other criminal activity is "barred by the statute of limitations . . . The only thing the grand jury can do is look at murder charges."

Of course, Foley added, "any other illegal activity surrounding the [homicide] not barred by the statute of limitations that comes out through the course of this investigation and trial will be pursued."

Apart from one journalist and two artists finishing their sketches of Lois, only a solitary figure now remained in the courtroom as the press conferences unfolded in the noisy corridor. Harold Jurgens sat alone in the back of the chamber, puzzling over just what he should do. Doug Thomson was answering a television reporter's questions in the hallway—"Memories fail, trying to go back over a quarter of a century"—and Lois was in custody, in the small room behind the judge's bench. Harold leaned forward and peered through the open door.

"I can see her back there. I just want to sit here and see her," he said.

Then the feathers and ribbons he could see atop her hat disappeared from view. Guided by two hefty matrons, Lois was being led to the Ramsey County Adult Detention Center across the street.

"Do you suppose she's still back there?" Harold asked the journalist, Doug Grow of the *Minneapolis Star and Tribune*. "They just walked off and left me. What do I do now? Guess I'll go back and see if I can find her. They can't do more than kick me out, can they?"

Harold rose and walked from the courtroom into the rear chamber. A moment later, he returned.

"She's gone," he said.

With that, he turned and walked through the double doorway of the courtroom, into the corridor and the torrent of reporters and lights.

CHAPTER 39

If's Going to Be a Fight

Standing against a wall of bookshelves in his law office on St. Peter Street in the weeks before Lois Jurgens's trial, Douglas Thomson asked a question of a visitor:

"Gee, if they make a movie out of this, do you think they'd let me play myself?"

Like most in his field, Thomson, a diminutive man of fifty-seven, was not the least shy about seeking or basking in publicity. Well before the Jurgenses approached him with their problem, Thomson had established himself as one of Minnesota's most prominent and colorful criminal defense attorneys. He'd represented a killer who claimed God, Jesus Christ, the Holy Ghost and the Virgin Mary as inspiration, and another who'd smothered his mother-in-law with a pillow in pursuit of a vast inheritance. These and other cases had put Thomson regularly in the local newspaper headlines.

In the courtroom, he had displayed a penchant for impassioned oratory that included recitations from the likes of William Penn and Abraham Lincoln. Rather than present his own elaborate defense, he preferred to attack the prosecution's case. He had a reputation as a fierce cross-examiner who didn't hesitate to destroy a witness.

Thomson also had a reputation as one who enjoyed the pleasures of the bottle, the racetrack and whatever there was of nightlife in St. Paul. Those who frequented the city's downtown bars could not help but bump into him on occasion, sometimes as he orated beside a bar stool, his left hand tucked inside the vest of his three-piece suit and his right index finger splitting the air for emphasis. By the spring of 1987, however, he was telling people that he'd settled down.

"Those nights of the lights flickering on my shoulder in a bar at one o'clock for last call are over," he informed Paul McEnroe of the *Minneapolis Star and Tribune* not long before Lois's trial.

Some in town also thought his days as a main-ring defense attorney were over. He'd handled his share of murders and drug cases in recent years, but there'd been nothing in a decade to equal the fireworks that earlier had made him such a storied figure in town. Thomson sometimes objected when journalists cast him as a habitué of bars and racetracks—"you wrote bullshit about me"—but in truth he appreciated their need for colorful characters. What really rankled was their occasional suggestion that he was over the hill.

"I've had good cases. It's just that presswise, there hasn't been anything this big for any lawyer in five years and I happen to have it, so everybody notices again," he explained to one reporter.

Thomson was clearly enjoying the renewed attention, as well as the complexity the coming murder trial presented. In his comments, he sounded like a connoisseur of murder—despite his client's plight, he just couldn't hide his excitement.

"This case probably involves more challenging issues than any I've ever had . . ." he told Paul McEnroe. "You've got everything involved from forensic pathology to psychiatry to dim memories—just a myriad of courtroom issues compared to most cases . . . It doesn't have the pizzazz of an allegation of murder with a woman involved and it doesn't have the element of murder for hire. But it's got the tragic circumstances of a young child that died and a woman whose tranquil life has been wrecked after twenty-two years. It's going to be a fight, but there's no reason for it to get nasty. But if it does, I'll be ready."

When the Jurgenses had first contacted him in the wake of Brian Bonner's initial newspaper article, Thomson hadn't known exactly what to think. Harold was garrulous and devoted to his wife, and Lois spoke angrily, going on and on about "the Nortons," seeming unable or unwilling to keep to a point or provide helpful information. They both mentioned a 1965 juvenile hearing, but all in all, the lawyer didn't take their concerns seriously.

"There's nothing to do," Thomson told the Jurgenses. "Because of the age of the case, I don't think anything will come of it."

Then the grand jury letters had arrived, saying the Jurgenses were the target of an investigation and inviting them to come in for questioning. But Thomson still didn't think much would happen. Twenty-one years was a long way to reach back into the past.

When the county impaneled the grand jury and subpoenaed Harold, revealing he wasn't a target, Thomson did feel surprised—he'd assumed both wife and husband were under investigation. He fought the subpoena, arguing that Harold could not be compelled to testify against his spouse under 1965 laws, but Judge Marsden chose instead to apply the current law, which permits spousal testimony in cases involving injuries to children. That meant Harold needed his own attorney, since his legal interests now might be at odds with Lois's, so Thomson had enlisted his former partner, Joe Friedberg.

Then they all sat and waited, empty-handed. Until there's an indictment, the defense cannot see the files being accumulated by the prosecutors and police, and has no way to gauge what the other side intends. Thomson tried to imagine what type of indictment the county would seek from a grand jury, and he wondered if he could get it dismissed. He hoped the indictment, if it came, would include manslaughter as an underlying felony, for that offense was excluded by the statute of limitations. He began to rehearse his orations about the fallibility of quarter-century-old memories.

When the indictment arrived and Thomson finally saw the prosecutors' files, though, much of his strategy collapsed. The reports and statements were obviously a problem, but they weren't what so unsettled Thomson. It was the photos of Dennis's body that destroyed his defense. The pictures were devastating, Thomson thought—bad beyond belief. He imagined them blown up to poster size, sitting on an easel before a stunned jury.

Thomson took to rising before dawn each day to walk five miles along the Mississippi River, thinking out a new strategy. He would file motions to challenge the indictment. He'd try to waive the statute of limitations on manslaughter and get the charge limited to that lesser offense: If conviction seemed imminent, he would pursue a mental illness defense. Above all, though, he would admit in court from the start that Lois physically and mentally abused her son—the facts were so vividly overwhelming, it would be useless to contest them. He would admit the abuse, but take issue with the notion that this abuse caused the boy's death. Where, after all, was the proof for that inference? Where was the evidence that linked a precise action by Lois to the ruptured bowel that caused Dennis's death?

In time, Thomson would fail to find a single pathologist who could provide alternative explanations for the boy's ruptured bowel—he tried five—but by then the lawyer's course was set. He would not so much dispute the prosecution's case as he would assault its meaning. All the ear-yanking and smacking and yelling in the world, Thomson figured, does not cause a hole in a small boy's ileum. An abused child could still accidentally fall down a flight of stairs.

Doug Thomson's reasoning, of course, had a familiar ring, an echo from the past. Thomson's analysis of Lois Jurgens's case in 1987 was not all that different from Dr. Thomas Votel's and Paul Lindholm's in 1965. During the intervening twenty-two years, the coroner's and prosecutor's thinking had become the defense attorney's.

On February 6, Mindy recorded the following entry in her log:

"We were reprimanded for contacting Doug Thomson. We are making disclosures in this case pursuant to Rule 9.06. In other words, we are filing descriptive rather than filing the case documents. This has upset the press. Foley told us he had heard that Doug Thomson was going to release his copies to the press. Clayton contacted Doug Thomson and explained that we were not filing the documents to assure that his client gets a fair trial. He agreed. We sent a confirming letter. Foley and Wodele got very angry. Foley even called Clayton at home to yell at him. Jim Konen backed us. They want us to let them decide what's best for the press. We told them we had no idea that talking to or communicating with another lawyer constituted "press contact.""

Three days later, Mindy reported another exchange:

"Tom Foley took an even greater 'hands-on' approach today. Clayton was working on a motion to bring Thomson in 2 wks. before the 3/23/87 trial date on all his motions and disclosures. Foley vetoed the motion. He wants us to set a 'realistic' trial date during the last 3 wks. of April because he has vacation plans May 17 and wants to sit with us throughout the trial. He said to call Thomson and arrange this. Thomson wants May 11 because he can't try it in April. Foley said to give him time to decide on a date."

Certain kinds of press contact apparently were more acceptable than others, though. Twin Cities viewers turning on their television sets one day soon after the indictment found Tom Foley and Doug Thomson side by side in chairs, talking on a local news show about their preparation for the trial.

"Thank you for joining us," host David Nimmer began, and the two lawyers nodded ever so slightly, as if lost in thought on other matters. They both looked serious and without expression, but their differences were more pronounced than their similarities. Tom Foley, tall and pleasant-looking, possessed the hallmarks of a modern television-age politician—he was composed and polished, but also colorless and cautious. By contrast, Doug Thomson, a good half-foot shorter and twenty years older than the prosecutor, bedecked in a dark three-piece suit with an outsized white handkerchief billowing from his breast pocket, half-bald and squinting through thick glasses, seemed a character out of Dickens or Lewis Carroll. The two men wouldn't look at each other, although they sat inches apart. Foley, in fact, gave the appearance of being bored, or perhaps preoccupied. He talked at length about "my duty and responsibility . . . to see that justice is done" while Thomson muttered about "intriguing legal issues." Only when Nimmer asked if this case might set precedent in other courtrooms did Foley seem to brighten. He gathered himself for an extended answer.

"Certainly, if there are cases around the country . . . I think those prosecutors have to take a good close look at what the facts of their particular case show and determine whether to charge or not charge someone with a crime . . ."

A month later, the March 7, 1987, edition of *People* arrived on the newsstands featuring a story that the Ramsey County prosecutors could not help but notice. "A Tale of Two Minnesota Mothers: One Seeks the Truth behind Their Son's Death, the Other Stands Accused," read the three-line headline on a story that occupied three full pages of the magazine.

The report largely involved an account of Jerry Sherwood's life and effort to get the Dennis Jurgens case reopened. "In my heart, I had been afraid that there would never be a chance for justice to be done," she said, as she posed for a photo with her four children and a grandson.

In its final paragraphs, the article tried to address the question of why this case hadn't been prosecuted twenty-two years ago.

"The assistant police chief in White Bear Lake in 1965 was Jerome Zerwas, who is Lois Jurgens's brother and is now fifty-nine and retired from the force. The current police chief, Phil Major, doubts that Zerwas had the authority to block an investigation and believes he removed himself from the case. Zerwas confirms that he bowed out immediately because of the family connections. 'It wasn't right for me to get involved,' he says. 'No police officer would have.'

"More than twenty years later it is hard to determine why the apparent murder of a little boy was ignored. 'The system was not as sensitive then to child abuse,' suggests Prosecutor Foley. 'People were much more willing to accept a rationale for an incident, other than it being a criminal act . . .'"

Several elements of this story irritated the prosecutors, not the least the suggestion that justice wouldn't be realized without Jerry Sherwood's continued prodding. What truly enraged Mindy and Clayton, however, was not a distortion or embellishment, but a hard, gleaming fact, one buried in a solitary paragraph in the middle of the article. It quoted Jerry Sherwood as she talked about a phone call she'd placed to Lois Jurgens in 1980:

"'I asked her what kind of little boy he was, and she said he had been a good, happy little boy. She didn't say much else except that when he was found he had black blotches all over his body, and they didn't know where the wounds had come from . . .'"

Jerry Sherwood, as it happened, had never told this story to the prosecutors. Until they read the *People* article, Mindy and Clayton didn't know that Jerry had even talked to Lois. The business about the disappearing black blotches was what made this phone conversation so critical to them—here was the defendant talking directly about Dennis's death, admitting the presence of bruises on the body before it left her house.

As a result of the *People* article, a meeting convened in the Ramsey County attorney's office midday on Wednesday, March 11, involving Mindy, Clayton, Greg Kindle, Ron Meehan, Jim Konen, Jerry Sherwood and her attorney, Ray Harp. The prosecutors and police had resolved to restrain their anger—this required considerable effort by both Mindy and Greg—and let Clayton do all their talking. Their efforts turned out to be pointless, for it was not their wrath that dominated the meeting, but Jerry Sherwood's. When Mindy explained that she would have to testify about this phone conversation, Jerry erupted. If she were a witness, she couldn't attend the trial, for witnesses can only be in the courtroom when they are testifying. Jerry Sherwood definitely wanted to be in that courtroom.

She flew around the conference table as the others remained seated, sobbing and delivering a stream of invective at the prosecutors. Bitterly, she relived her first meeting with Mindy and railed at the way the case had been handled.

"God damn you . . . This will stop me from attending the trial . . . The reason you're doing this is you want me out of the courtroom."

Mindy tried to sound gracious: "Jerry, you never told us about the Lois phone call."

"God damn you," Sherwood responded, "you never asked the right questions."

Keep your mouth shut, pal, Greg told himself.

Sherwood's attorney had a question: "Can we ask the judge not to sequester Jerry?" Yes, Mindy and Clayton agreed, they'd cooperate with that request. Only then did the meeting turn to its true purpose. At 12:40 P.M., with a tape recorder running, Ron Meehan began his interview with Jerry Sherwood.

"Jerry, we'd like to talk about the statement you made in an interview with *People*," he said. "Could you tell us about your conversation with Lois Jurgens?"

CHAPTER 40

Lois

In the early afternoon on Tuesday, March 17, the phone rang on June Bol's cluttered kitchen table. "Hello, June, how is Aunt Esther doing?" a woman's voice asked.

Lois Jurgens was calling to ask about June's mother-in-law, who lived in the Bol residence. Lois regularly inquired after her father's elderly sister, but just now she was violating a court order, for Judge Marsden had instructed her not to communicate with potential witnesses in the upcoming trial.

All the same, June did not protest or resist Lois's approach, mainly because she didn't find the phone call intimidating. It seemed to her that Lois simply had the need to call somebody. On the phone, Lois sounded more upset than angry, particularly about certain aspects of the recent news coverage.

There was, for example, the reporters' recurring references to what they called the "odd, vintage forties-style" hat she wore at the arraignment. That hat, Lois informed June, was new. Harold had bought it for her in January, and her attorney had told her it looked very nice. Lois also didn't like the papers referring to her as arrogant and detached and cold.

June searched for the right words in response. "I thought you looked like you were scared, and were trying to be brave," she finally offered.

No, Lois said, she was not scared. She held her head high because she had nothing to be ashamed of. She had done nothing wrong and had no reason to be afraid.

June thought she understood Lois's attitude. The woman strongly believed she was innocent. She felt this was her cross to bear. She felt that God was giving her a lot of crosses to bear.

The conversation turned to other topics. Lois asked where "the kids" were now living. Where's Renee? she wondered. Where is Grant? June didn't feel wary—Lois basically knew where they were anyway, so she wasn't divulging secrets. Ricky and Mike are in Georgia, she said. Renee is in Kentucky. Grant is in the Twin Cities area.

"I don't know what to expect in the days to come," Lois said.

"I think Harold can advise you on that," June replied.

The conversation drifted then to general pleasantries. June mentioned that she'd just celebrated her sixtieth birthday twelve days before, and Lois offered her best wishes. Then June explained that Aunt Esther was away, visiting at another relative's home.

"I'll have her call you when she gets back."

No, that won't work, Lois said, sounding sad. Her phone had been changed and was now unlisted. Upon her lawyer's advice, Lois explained, she couldn't give anyone the new number.

By the time June hung up, she felt almost sorry for Lois. She couldn't forgive the woman for killing Dennis, but she thought Lois was a sick person, and in her own way had tried very hard. She wanted and loved those children, June believed. She wanted them to have things. She wanted them to play musical instruments. She wanted to be a good mother, but she wasn't emotionally capable of that role. She'd wanted to become more than she was, to dress beautifully, to rise above her origins and to have a good family. How sad, June thought, and what a waste.

Few shared June's sympathetic attitude about Lois, but no one following the Jurgens case lacked an opinion of some sort about the stiff-necked defendant. As the days went on and Lois's stern, unflinching visage appeared time and again on the television screen and news pages, both those involved in the trial and those watching from afar grew increasingly mesmerized. What was Lois's story? they wondered. How could she have done all that to her kids?

The fabric of Lois's life, after all, was more mundane than monstrous. She was unlikable, but really not all that different from other overbearing, intrusive people. Perhaps she was a little angrier and more forceful, but still, she was a familiar type. Lots of people had a hungry need to shape and control their environment. Despite what the experts said, many following the Jurgens story just couldn't believe a sane person was capable of brutalizing a little boy simply because he disrupted her need for order. If mental illness didn't explain Lois's behavior, what could?

Lois's niece, Nancy Baker, daughter of Lloyd and Donna Zerwas, was one who struggled with such questions.

"Did it snap something in her head when she was told that they would never have any kids?" Nancy asked Greg Kindle one day on the phone. "And then when she did get these she still couldn't accept the fact that they weren't her flesh and blood . . . I don't know . . . It was like, you know, she was striking out at somebody and . . . and it didn't really need to be striking out at these children, but that's who got it because they couldn't defend themselves . . . Funny thing is, she was very good to my boys when she seen 'em. She'd hug 'em and kiss 'em and tell 'em who she was. You know . . . In front of me, or in front of any other children's parents, she was always good to 'em. She loved kids. She really did. That's why I don't understand it . . . She always showed love for them other than to her own that she brutalized . . . I have to admit I think she's mentally disturbed somewhere deep down inside . . . I cannot hardly believe that she did what she did just because she was a mean person."

A good number of others, though, believed Lois indeed was evil incarnate. At the arraignment, Jerry Sherwood's son Dennis Craig, shaken and teary, had found it necessary to leave the courtroom after staring across an aisle at Lois. Doug Thomson, although accustomed to defending all sorts of unadmirable characters, sensed he was being regarded as the agent of a malignancy. Ron Meehan longed to see Lois behind bars. "I think she is evil," Mindy Elledge said flatly, biting off the words with a bitter finality.

Drs. Kempe and Steele's by-now-familiar notion that abusers were usually not devils or maniacs but themselves victims of abuse was a theme faintly acknowledged but not warmly embraced. If you haven't had love you can't give love, a few of the more delicate souls would point out, but for the most part the horrible and unspeakable details of Dennis's tortured existence tended to overpower such thoughts. Besides, the precise nature of Lois's childhood remained a matter of some dispute.

Only a few social workers and doctors, after all, were privy to her medical records, and over the years, Lois's own accounts had varied widely. At times she painted a beatific portrait of a rural life amid farm animals, fun-loving siblings and strong, caring, disciplining parents. At other times, she modified the picture, allowing that she'd endured an impoverished and deprived childhood and a father who was iron-handed if not downright tyrannical. Once in a while, she went further, and talked of specific examples of physical abuse involving razor strops and beatings in the shed.

A hint of this darker version can be found in comments one of Lois's brothers, Donald, made to his wife Mary before they divorced. "Donald's own mother was abused by a cruel stepmother, so that's all Donald's mother knew," Mary Zerwas recalled. "Donald said his mother spanked them all with an ash shovel, the one-year-olds on up. John Zerwas, too—he kicked, hit. Above all, the kids were left to shift for themselves. Donald was ignored."

A more direct and much darker hint can be found in a conversation Lois had one day in 1987 with a distant, long-ago school chum.

A district manager for a Minnesota school district, a reticent gray-haired widow by the name of Irene Balzart, wrote and then called Lois after seeing her discussed in the newspapers. They'd once been close companions at Smith Elementary School in White Bear Lake, but their ways had parted forever when they were fourteen. Irene remembered Lois as a lovely, fragile girl, and couldn't imagine how she'd changed so much.

She later recounted their phone conversation:

"Lois's elderly mother had come to visit her that day. It seems another sister had just told their mother that Lois was raped by their father. Lois was upset because her mother had been told. She didn't want to hurt her. Lois said to me: 'Oh, I was so upset . . . Why bring that up now? The damage has been done. Why bring that up now?'"

Irene was inclined to believe this report, not the least because her late husband Bill had dated Lois when they were teenagers, and had talked about her on his deathbed. "I think Bill knew something, I think Lois told him something. There was some trauma," Irene said. "And he'd just cut her off after that. He'd hurt her. When he was dying, he wanted to contact her, to apologize, to make peace."

It must be said that most of Lois's siblings fiercely dispute these darker memories. They are adamant and certain and insistent: the family was abysmally poor, but never abused. "And I fly without wings," Lloyd Zerwas snapped when asked about Lois's tales of abuse, drawing an imaginary X in the air as if he were crossing that item off a list. "I never heard the man swear," Lois's eldest sister, Eloise, said of her father. "He was never one to sit and drink. I have no memory of any battling . . . Lois imagines that she was made to work and raise everyone. That's not true. She's describing how our mother lived, not herself."

In the days preceding the Jurgens trial, the question of Lois's childhood and its influence on her character evolved from a matter of mere curiosity to one of legal import, for Doug Thomson suddenly announced he was planning to invoke a mental illness defense in addition to a not guilty defense. Under Minnesota rules of criminal procedure adopted in 1983, that meant Lois's trial would involve two separate but continuous phases—one to hear and decide the not guilty defense, and then if that failed, a second to judge the mental illness defense.

Mindy and Clayton were dismayed, for now they had to scramble to ready a response, but they weren't entirely surprised. In preparation for this possibility they'd already subpoenaed and briefly reviewed the records concerning Lois's mental health treatment. Now they focused their full attention on these documents.

Here were ten years of treatment and commentary by Dr. Garvey. Here were the repeated hospitalizations. And here were the first accounts of Lois's troubles as a young woman back in the years just after the war—the records from her visit to the Mayo Clinic in 1951.

Leafing through the documents one morning, Mindy and Clayton came upon one that was almost impossible to read. It was eight pages long, the handwriting cramped, the scribbled words squeezed together, the lines piled atop each other and spilling beyond the margins. Puzzling out the signature at the bottom, the prosecutors finally realized they were holding the original report written by Dr. Norman Goldstein, the psychiatrist who had evaluated Lois at the Mayo Clinic so many years before.

What Lois had said in later years, out of expediency to social workers, out of anger at her kids, out of her own needs, could now be compared to what she'd said just a handful of years past her own adolescence, well before she first tried to adopt a child. It took Mindy and Clayton only moments to see that Lois as she turned twenty-six had provided Dr. Goldstein an unflinchingly grim portrait of her background—*Father alcoholic and brutal toward mother and children . . . Patient left home at age fifteen years because father was drunk and beating mother . . .* Turning the pages, Mindy and Clayton reached Dr. Goldstein's diagnosis, prognosis and recommendations: *A twenty-six-year-old married woman with a longstanding psycho-neurosis of the mixed type . . . she may go on to a paranoid schizo-phrenia . . .*

Attached to the end of the Mayo report, Mindy and Clayton found a series of brief letters. Here was a "To Whom It May Concern" letter prepared by the Mayo Clinic in April of 1952, summarizing Lois's condition, requested by the Jurgenses for consideration by other doctors. Here was a similar letter in December of 1954, from the Mayo Clinic to the Hamm Memorial Psychiatric Clinic in St. Paul, where Lois then was a patient. Here was a third letter, in June of 1955, the one where the Mayo Clinic had informed the Bureau of Catholic Charities of Dr. Goldstein's unambiguous conclusion: *It was fortunate that the patient was unable to carry through pregnancy at this time . . . She would be a poor candidate for adopting a child at this time.*

Clayton tossed the documents on his desk. So they knew back then, he thought. They knew.

With a mental illness defense pending, both the defense and the prosecution now hired doctors to interview and evaluate Lois once more.

Lois's contact with the defense psychiatrist began on an uncertain note. Visiting Doug Thomson's choice, Dr. James Stephans, she failed to make any mention at all of her past psychiatric treatment. They talked on March 16 for an hour and a half without the subject arising, and afterward, Dr. Stephans told Thomson he didn't think there was anything wrong with his client. When the lawyer informed the psychiatrist of Lois's history, Dr. Stephans expressed surprise, and suggested they send the patient back for another visit.

So Lois saw Stephans three times more, on April 18, April 23 and May 11, and in these sessions the doctor eventually managed to turn the conversation to the topic of Dennis's abuse.

"I don't know what they call abusive," Lois said.

What was her idea of abuse? Stephans asked.

"If you don't feed a child, if you don't bathe it, if you don't show love, that's abusive," Lois said.

Did she think beating a child was abusive?

"I don't believe in it," Lois said.

Stephans confronted Lois with specific facts from assorted court records, including the police records. Did she ever force-feed Dennis some horseradish? Did she ever force him to eat his own feces? Did she ever put a clothespin on Dennis's penis?

Lois either denied most such episodes—"a bunch of lies. How can people dream that up?"—or said she couldn't recall.

Did she pick Dennis up by the ears?

"If I did, I can't remember," Lois said. "The only thing I remember is that with both of the boys . . . we'd cuff our hands over their ears and lift them off the ground. They'd love it. To us it was a game . . ."

With that, as she often did during these examinations, Lois strayed from the topic and began talking about how her parents had treated her.

"I had strict parents," she said. "I was an abused child. It was my obligation to take care of all those other little kids . . . Took them up on a barn floor once, there were no walls, my little sister fell out, was knocked out for a while. My mom came out with a broom. She beat me all the way back to the house. I had carbuncles on my back. The beating burst them, and she broke the broom handle on my back. I had no dinner that night. I had malnutrition and rickets. That's what I call abuse. My father beat us with a razor strop."

On Wednesday, April 30, Lois visited the adult psychiatric unit at St. Paul–Ramsey Hospital for a ninety-minute session with Terry Zuehlke, a licensed consulting psychologist retained by the prosecutors. The meeting included an interview and the completion by Lois of the Millon Multiaxial Personality Inventory.

Zuehlke asked Lois why she believed she was charged with murder.

"Because twenty-two years ago my son was found dead in bed," Lois replied. "The biological mother, in 1980, made up her mind to locate her firstborn child. I feel this woman is trying to compensate what she is doing because of the guilt she is carrying in her mind for giving up her child."

Lois was upset with the law for allowing the biological mother to pursue a child she'd given away. Lois didn't think it was right. In the past, she said, such records were sealed away forever.

"All I was, was a person that loved children and wanted children very badly . . ."

Dennis, she said, ". . . got lots of loving even though they say he didn't. We didn't buy any different presents for Robert than we did for Dennis . . . There was no loving one child more than the other."

Their home life, she said, "was wonderful . . . I came from a big family. There were lots of people coming and going from my parents' house all the time. When I got married I wanted my husband, my home and my children; that's all I wanted out of my life."

The psychologist asked Lois about her mental health history.

"Everybody has some mental problems," she said. "I was a workaholic . . . My yard was like a park. I never had those things when I was a child."

She was depressed at the time Dennis died, she allowed, but she didn't think she had any significant emotional problems.

"I didn't do anything crazy," she said.

The next day at 5:45 P.M., Lois returned to the psychiatric unit of St. Paul–Ramsey Medical Center for a longer session with the prosecution's psychiatrist, Dr. Dennis Philander. It was Thursday, April 30, just four days before the start of the trial, and Lois seemed irritated.

When Dr. Philander asked about her visit to the hospital the previous week for testing, she said: "We had a two-hour notice to get our rear ends in here . . . I don't know what the deal is. I was supposed to come into the hospital because the county attorney had requested it."

Lois digressed to complain of gaseous distension and belching. "I ate too much tonight. When I eat too fast this happens."

Philander asked Lois to talk about when they first got Dennis.

We picked him up one day in Shakopee, Lois said—the day after his first birthday.

"Did not know where he was living. What the caseworker told me was this lady . . . [was] taking in any children, retarded children, blind children, and that she had a large room with half a dozen kids there . . . I suppose she throws the bottles in there, with toys and cats . . . Poor Dennis also in there, hyperactive, seemed very unhappy. They had cats in there, toys. Maybe they all fought about the toys. The day I picked him up the child was dirty, his clothes were dirty. He had on a corduroy jacket with a light flannel lining . . . with a cap to match with a visor and ear flaps and a tie cloth underneath the chin, a buckle on the right side, on one side or the other; I don't know where boys have the buckle . . . He did not have a pair of mittens; he did not have a snowsuit in the dead of winter; all he had on was rags. The diapers in the bag looked like they were thrown in mud water and then dried out. When I got home I burned them . . ."

When Philander tried to discuss Lois's interaction with Dennis, she instead began talking about her own childhood. She was the baby-sitter for all the younger children, she said. "I had everyone else . . ."

Again Philander tried to turn the conversation to Dennis, but Lois continued talking about her own background.

Her mother was always pregnant. Jerome and Lyle and Lloyd and Donald . . . She had to wait nine years before she had another sister. "You think [my mother] was trying to populate the earth . . . All these other children were underneath me. They were like dolls to me—I took care of them, fed them and changed them. I pampered them; I took care of all the children from Donald on downward. I carried them, even Lloyd, around on my hips."

When Philander finally did manage to direct Lois's attention to the weekend of Dennis's death, she spoke freely and at length. The essence of the story had not changed, but now the details seemed richer, more vivid, and in some way more revealing than in any account ever offered before.

Late 1964 and early 1965 had been a heavy snow winter, Lois said, and the basement started to flood that weekend.

"I had to push the water out with a garage broom, and took Dennis downstairs, sat him on the toilet and had gone back to my chores. Then he came out. I said to be careful, because there was water on the floor. He ran and fell . . . As far as I know he was healthy and strong. I fed him good food and the same food as Robert. All the time he ate good food. All of us ate off the table. If we had fish, they had fish; if we had meat, they had meat; if we had potatoes, they had potatoes . . ."

Lois recalled her last conversation with Dennis. He had been put to sleep, but the thunder and lightning must have wakened him, she thought.

"It is so sad. It all occurred so fast. What is worse, I said 'God is moving the furniture around up there' when he asked me to explain the thunder and the lightning. I did not want him to be afraid of lightning and thunder because I was deadly afraid of stuff like that when I was small."

When she was coming through the living room the next morning, on the way to the kitchen to make coffee, she checked Dennis's room.

"I opened the door. I thought it was quiet, then I thought he was praying . . . He was laying there looking up at the ceiling. He did not say nothing; he did not say nothing. Then I put my hand to see if he would follow my hand's movement. I thought he had gone blind. I called to my husband that he can't see; then my husband came in. My husband picked Dennis up, shook him in his arms to see if he did not know what happened. He was still warm. Then I tried to breathe into his mouth . . . I could not get him to breathe. Then his face started to show psychedelic spots—blue, green, yellow—like when you put glitter dots on his face. Then I told my husband, and he called Dr. Peterson."

Lois said she held Dennis for a while, hoping and praying. "I thought he was just going blind. He was fine the night before." Then Dr. Peterson came and said Dennis had expired.

When Lois finished her story, Philander began to review with her the various 1965 police reports, asking that she comment or explain as they went along. Soon Lois's hallmarks, anger and denial, reappeared—along with a few signs of a possibly muddled mind.

Mr. Jurgens stated that he had checked Dennis several times during the night of April 10, 1965 and April 11, 1965:

"I was so tired when I went to bed. I checked right out. My husband is an only child; his mind is a light sleeper; his mind is not having brothers and sisters. To have children—it fulfilled his fatherhood; but also as a pal, he liked them. Why he checked them, you have to ask him. I went to bed and went to sleep. I had been pushing a wet broom for three days in the basement; my furnace would have rusted and fallen to pieces."

Dennis was gasping for breath or gurgling at 9:30 A.M. on April 11, 1965:

"That is a lie; a bunch of B.S., as far as I'm concerned . . . I got married to have a husband, a house and children. I was not made to be a stenographer; I don't want that job for anything."

The crib was by the north wall with the head of the bed on the west side.

"I was trying to tell you; like if you took an ink pen, little spots all on his face; fluorescent colors."

Cheryl Bartholmy (daughter-in-law of Lois's sister Eloise) reports Lois picked Dennis up, put her hand over his mouth and nose so he couldn't cry, until Dennis turned red.

"She is not even a blood relative. She is married to a nephew. She was only in my house on one occasion . . . She is as crazy as a bedbug; just moralized."

At the base of the penis there was an open break:

"I don't let my kids play with their penis. He could have gotten stuck with something . . . but not play with his penis."

Possible condition of malnutrition present in the body:

"I had rickets as a child and malnutrition . . . I came from a big family; sometimes I did not know if food would be on the table or not. At our [Jurgens] house we had vegetables and fruit and milk, meat, fish, cheese, vitamins and everything . . ."

Regarding Ivan DeMars (neighbor on Gardenette):

"The idiots who lived next door; had limited activity, two big dogs that crapped in their yard; kids pick up the dogs; the poor wife, she never had a decent life; when the kids do something wrong they would take them in the basement."

Re: Clarence Bartholmy (her sister Eloise's husband):

"A soak of an alcoholic . . . He has not been dry since 1940."

Re: Sharon Kopp (her sister):

Lois had no comment.

Lois put a clamp-type clothespin on the end of Dennis's penis while he knelt on a broomstick reciting the rosary:

"No, why would I do something like that? People do have wild imaginations."

Lois pulled Dennis's ears so hard the blood was running out:

"Who said this and who has seen this?"

Lois hit Dennis with a drumstick:

"All fabrication. I don't have drumsticks."

Dennis was lying in his crib with nylon stockings tied around his wrists and ankles:

"Are these people having nightmares? I . . . never did anything like this. It's all a lie . . ."

The session ended at 10:00 P.M., after four hours and fifteen minutes.

As will regularly happen when two sides in a courtroom each hire experts, the doctors who examined Lois for the defense and the prosecution provided those who paid them with differing opinions.

For the defense, Dr. Stephans concluded that Lois was psychotic in 1965, suffering from paranoid schizophrenia and delusions. Her illness, he said, began a year or two before the year 1951.

For the prosecution, Dr. Philander concluded that Lois suffered not from any psychosis, but from a personality disorder. More precisely, he thought the testing suggested a mixed personality disorder with prominent passive-aggressive, compulsive and histrionic traits.

Philander's judgment bore a marked resemblance to those reached by other psychiatrists throughout the years, including Dr. Teeter and Dr. Garvey. The consensus had not changed in thirty years: Lois Jurgens was neurotic, inflexible, repressed, angry and full of denial—but not crazy. Those seeking to explain or understand Lois's actions would have to look within the realm of normal behavior, just as they had to in Judge Gingold's courtroom twenty-two years before.

"The profile gives no indication of any emotional problems of psychotic proportions. . . ." the prosecution's psychologist, Terry Zuehlke, wrote. "I see in this woman . . . fantasies of an ideal family life and marked feelings of denial and anger regarding the charges she is facing."

CHAPTER 41

The Past Recovered

In anticipation of the coming trial, the Sunday, May 3 edition of the *St. Paul Pioneer Press Dispatch* featured a banner headline across the top of its front page, alongside a photo of a smiling Dennis Jurgens before his death. "Time Lapse a Major Element in Jurgens Trial," the headline read. The article beneath it was written by Brian Bonner.

> The murder trial of Lois Jurgens opens Monday in St. Paul amid a legal, medical and social environment that has changed dramatically in the 22 years since her adopted son died.
>
> The time lapse could be a valuable ally to Ramsey County Attorney Tom Foley . . . or it could work to the advantage of defense attorney Douglas Thomson . . . The jury will hear testimony from forensic medical experts who are better able to identify child-abuse injuries than they were two decades ago. That, combined with society's heightened awareness of child-abuse issues, could favor the prosecution. But the time warp may also aid the defense. Prosecution witnesses may have fuzzy and unreliable memories, leaving jurors unconvinced. Original police files are missing. And few of the authorities and experts who will testify had any firsthand knowledge of the original investigation.
>
> "It's a two-edged sword," Foley said. "Time will hinder the case in a lot of respects. It will help it in others . . ."

Thomson said it will be difficult for a jury to determine how the boy died.

"When you clear all the smoke here, what happened is that Dennis Jurgens died of a specific type of ailment or injury . . ." he said. "The issue is: How did this occur? That's the only issue in this case. How far can they go? . . . They don't know how the bowel ruptured . . . I haven't seen any evidence that anybody witnessed whatever caused the death."

Reading this article only underscored what Mindy and Clayton already knew—along with a beneficial evolution in attitudes, the passage of twenty-two years also brought all manner of problems involving murky memories and indirect evidence. Above all, the prosecutors still worried about Harold—would he testify and would he muddy the waters by trying to take Lois out? Apart from establishing the medical evidence, the heart of their trial strategy involved keeping Harold off the stand and proving that he was out of the house the weekend of Dennis's death. As they began the process of selecting a jury on Monday, May 4, the prosecutors still longed for the direct, immediate evidence they felt they needed to realize their goals. They had never stopped looking for the 1965 juvenile transcript, but their flurry of subpoenas and court orders had yielded nothing—the document seemed to have vanished. Now they were running out of days.

Questioning the jurors during voir dire, Thomson shrewdly made a point of portraying Lois as an unlikable mother whose behavior was despicable and abusive toward Dennis. He wanted to weed out jurors who seemed repelled by such disclosures—which would emerge at trial anyway—and keep those willing to set aside Lois's odious nature. The prosecutors in turn focused on the basics—by their count, the twelve jurors finally assembled had among them twenty-one children.

After lunch on Friday, May 8, just as the lawyers were questioning the final juror, Tom Foley appeared in the courtroom with a message for Mindy and Clayton.

"Got a call from the Washington County attorney's office," he said. "I think they have something you want, some documents."

Unsure what Foley could be talking about, Mindy and Clayton continued questioning the prospective juror. An hour passed. Then in the late afternoon, a messenger appeared, bearing a written message from Foley. When Clayton unfolded the single sheet of paper he saw two short sentences scrawled in Foley's hand: "Dick Arney has the transcript. He'll wait for you."

Dick Arney was the Washington County attorney. A Washington County assistant clerk, it turned out, had chosen that day to empty a long-forgotten evidence cabinet. There, amid piles of dusty, yellowing documents, she'd come across a bulky file labeled *State ex rel Jurgens v. Bol.* Inside she'd found assorted court papers related to a habeas corpus petition filed in 1968, in which an attorney by the name of Donohue, on behalf of a couple named Jurgens, was seeking to regain custody of a child then living in the home of Richard and June Bol. Accompanying the petition was a supporting exhibit, a hefty document totaling some 780 pages. Ed Donohue had attached to his habeas corpus motion the entire transcript of Robert's juvenile court custody proceeding.

In all the subpoenas they'd prepared in the past four months, Mindy and Clayton had always requested a juvenile court transcript classified under the name of Robert Jurgens. It could not have occurred to them to ask for a file under the name Bol. Even if they had, the inquiry most likely would have proven fruitless, for the habeas corpus petition made *State ex rel Jurgens v. Bol* a civil, not a juvenile file. Moreover, its index card was missing from the Washington County court catalog. Mindy and Clayton were the beneficiaries of a not-so-simple twist of fate—in fact, two twists of fate.

Without the fortuitous cabinet-cleaning project, the transcript certainly would not have been discovered on the eve of Lois Jurgens's trial, but even before then providence played a critical role. The courtroom animosity sparked twenty-two years before by Judge Archie Gingold's stubbornness and Ed Donohue's doggedness had driven the Jurgenses' attorney to appeal the custody matter in another court. Only because of that appeal was a transcript of the juvenile proceeding prepared. In a sense, then, the Jurgenses themselves had taken the steps that now placed the transcript in the hands of the prosecutors.

Bolting from the Ramsey County courthouse late that Friday afternoon, Mindy and Clayton headed for the Washington County courthouse in Stillwater. The moderately heavy end-of-week traffic was crawling near the I-694 beltway because of road construction, and Clayton began to fume. His eagerness was mixing with anxiety.

What might they find in the transcript? What if it showed major discrepancies with what his witnesses were now saying? Would this discovery force a delay in the trial? If so, what about all the complicated logistics of witnesses now flying in from all over the country?

They reached the Washington County courthouse past the 5:30 P.M. closing time, and found the building locked for the weekend. They'd been told to go to a particular door, but it was now unclear which one. Banging windows and rattling knobs at random, they finally happened to knock on the Washington County attorney's window.

Dick Arney opened a side door and escorted his guests to the county clerk's office, explaining as they walked how his people had happened to find the transcript. A moment later, they were in the clerk's room, the bulky document before them. Arney retreated to his office, leaving Mindy and Clayton to examine their booty. They fell on the pages, thumbing through them hurriedly, reading just enough to confirm they indeed had what they'd so long been seeking. They were most interested just then in an index that would tell them who had testified. There it was—and yes, here were listings for Harold and Lois Jurgens.

Mindy and Clayton immediately flipped to Harold's testimony and started reading. On page 612 of the transcript, assistant county attorney Bertrand Poritsky had asked Harold the critical question.

Q: Mr. Jurgens, were you out of town on the evening of April the ninth? That would be a Friday night.

A: If it was preceding Dennis's death.

Q: And, were you out of town on Saturday, the following day?

A: Part of the day.

Clayton and Mindy flipped ahead, to page 616.

Q: During the time when you were away from home, where did you go?

A: Hawthorne, Wisconsin.

Q: And, is it fair to say that you left on the morning of the ninth to go to Hawthorne?

A: If we are still talking about the same Friday morning.

Q: I said, the ninth.

A: Yes.

Q: What time did you leave?

A: Six-thirty, quarter to seven.

Q: Is it fair to say then that from six-thirty on the ninth until nine to nine-thirty on the tenth you were away from home?

A: Yes.

Harold had told the grand jury he'd left home on Saturday, not Friday, and his whole attempt to "take Lois out" hinged on that claim. The 1965 transcript destroyed the man's credibility. In that late Friday moment in Stillwater, staring at the critical passages, Mindy and Clayton knew Harold Jurgens could never take the stand at the coming trial. Not only could he not testify, he was in trouble—Mindy and Clayton began to feel the urge to prosecute him for perjury committed before the grand jury. No statute of limitations for such a recent act of lying, Mindy observed.

Outside in the parking lot, the two prosecutors did a dance together, arm in arm. "Time for a pizza party," Clayton said.

Heading west on Highway 36, they stopped at Carboneri's and lugged their bulky package inside with them. While Clayton ordered the pizza, Mindy called her husband to report they'd be having a guest for dinner. Waiting for their take-out order, the two settled at a table and began to read.

Here were Bob VanderWyst and Pete Korolchuk talking, and the neighbors, and Lloyd and Donna Zerwas—all saying precisely what they'd told Greg and Ron twenty-two years later. Virtually everything matched. Here were dead people talking—Lois's sister Donna and the coroner's deputy Saveiro Pitera. Here were doctors testifying from fresh memories and from now-missing notes and files. Here were the specific dates and precise chronology that memories had obscured over the years. And here, too, was Jerome Zerwas.

It was like reading history, Clayton thought, like opening a door to history. He could visualize the juvenile courtroom. The words put him right there at the 1965 hearing.

To say that Mindy and Clayton were delighted diminishes the sense of amazement they felt.

"Mindy and I thought this was divine providence," Clayton told friends later. "I am not a believer in that stuff, but this made me a believer. There is no explicable reason why this would happen. A dusty cabinet, that particular day . . . Someone was helping us."

Later, though, after the first excited looks, it turned out that the transcript was not without problems. Reading the volume more carefully over the weekend, Clayton found precisely what he'd feared. Just as the 1965 hearing revealed discrepancies in Harold's testimony, so too did it suggest falsehood in one of the prosecution's most critical witnesses.

Over time, the detectives and prosecutors had found all sorts of relatives willing to testify against Lois, but most were either peripherally connected figures or members of the Norton wing of the family. It would surely help, they'd reasoned, to have at least one main witness without that association.

So after lunch one afternoon in early January of 1987, Ron Meehan had toyed with the notion of calling Lois's unmarried sister Beverly, then living in Lemon Grove, California, a small town ten miles east of San Diego. He'd hesitated, with good reason.

Ron knew Bev from way back as a tough, strong gal who could probably whip about half her brothers—not at all the sort likely to cooperate with the police against a relative. He figured the odds were nine to one she wouldn't even talk to him on the phone for more than a few minutes, let alone agree to a formal interview. All the same, he had felt on a high that day, full of piss and vinegar. He reached for the phone as he composed an opening line.

"This is ol' Ron Meehan from the city of White Bear Lake, a tower of power from the frozen tundra," he began.

Bev laughed. Ron took that as an encouraging sign.

"I'd like to get together with you and talk over the Dennis Jurgens case in 1965," he said. "As you know, we're investigating it and we'd really like to talk to you, since you were on the list of witnesses in 1965."

"Well, when do you want to do it?" Bev replied. Just like that, simple and direct.

Ron hadn't set eyes on Bev for twenty years when he met her in a Bob's Big Boy in Lemon Grove on the morning of January 12, but he could have spotted her anywhere. All the Zerwas gals had the same look—Bev was stocky and wore polyester slacks and seemed a bit rough around the edges. But once they drove to the San Diego courthouse and sat down with Clayton, she sounded strong and direct and self-assured. "I spoke to my mother," Bev explained, "and she told me to tell the truth." Her memory was sharp, her manner calm, and she talked freely for two hours. Most important, Bev's stories—black eyes covered by sunglasses, torn ears, Dennis tied spread-eagled to

his crib—had confirmed all the statements from the Norton wing of
the family. No, she allowed, she'd never asked Lois about the bruises
because she figured it was none of her business, and she wasn't a nosy
person by nature, but when subpoenaed a month after the funeral to
testify at a juvenile court hearing, she'd told the truth. Clayton, scrib-
bling notes on a lined yellow legal pad, had celebrated silently.

Now, leafing through her testimony in 1965, Clayton found that
Bev had in fact served much more as a witness for the Jurgenses than
for the county. Reading the exchanges, he could see Poritsky laboring
largely in vain to draw from her damaging testimony about her sister.
Talking about a day when she had found Dennis tied spread-eagled
in his crib, she'd waffled.

Q: Did you notice anything unusual about the arrangements
concerning Dennis?

A: Nothing unusual.

Q: All right. What did you observe about Dennis?

A: Ah, just that Mrs. Jurgens said that she had a problem keeping
him in bed because he had fallen out a few times. . . . She tied his leg
to the crib so he wouldn't fall out.

Q: Do you have an opinion from having observed Dennis in his
crib whether he was made a prisoner . . .?

A: I would say it was for his own protection.

Q: Was it ever shocking to you?

A: No.

Q: Did you ever feel that the child was being mistreated as a
result of this?

A: No.

Q: Do you have an opinion as to whether or not Lois Jurgens was
a good mother to both of these children?

A: I would say she was a good mother.

Q: And do you have an opinion as to whether or not both Mr.
and Mrs. Jurgens are suitable persons to have the custody of Robert?

A: I think they are.

Q: Was there ever anything, based on your observation, to indicate to you that the treatment of either one of these boys, as far as
Lois was concerned, was abnormal in any respect?

A: No.

Clayton grew incensed as he read these passages. She lied to us,
he thought. She'd seemed so ideal, but she'd snookered us, and even

now she was sitting in St. Paul waiting to testify. Clayton didn't doubt that Doug Thomson would find this discrepancy—he was a master at just that. Now Doug would have an opportunity where before there'd been none.

On Monday morning, May 11, one day before the start of the trial, Clayton summoned Bev to a small conference room in the county attorney's office. He placed on the table before her two documents—a copy of her 1965 testimony and a copy of what she'd said to them in San Diego.

"I'm going to leave you in here," he said. "Study them. I'll come back in a little while."

Clayton returned after giving her enough time to compare her words, past and present.

"There's a difference," he said. "These two are not the same. Which is true?"

Bev looked the prosecutor in the eye. Her mouth had dropped open when she'd first met Clayton in San Diego—Bev did not come from the type of background that included many young black prosecutors in three-piece suits—but he'd disarmed her, as he usually did in such situations, by plunging right in with a friendly, outgoing greeting. They'd connected.

"What I told you," she said now.

"Why the difference?"

"Well, Mr. Robinson, you have to realize what kind of family we're in. My father told us to stick together. I lied then to protect my sister."

"That's going to be used against you," Clayton warned.

Bev shrugged but kept her eyes fixed on Clayton's.

"I'd still be willing to take the stand if you want."

Clayton considered. This woman was not here under subpoena and did not have to testify. She could pack up and leave.

"Okay," Clayton said. "Let's do it."

CHAPTER 42

The Trial

The Ramsey County courthouse was built in the 1930s, and at the time of Lois Jurgens's trial it still featured ponderous, manually operated elevators and a subdued upper Midwest version of Art Deco design. Judge Marsden had ordered renovation of the largest courtroom he could find for the trial, the one on the eighth floor numbered 801. The two banks of cylindrical glass and brass Art Deco light fixtures were polished to a gleam, and the old painted-over windows that made the chamber seem so dark were torn out and replaced with new, clear glass.

For all that, the courtroom retained a hint of dowdy age. It was compact and rather narrow, only twenty-five feet in width, with seats for just 150 in twelve rows. Because it lacked air-conditioning and the temperatures in mid-May were reaching into the seventies, Marsden kept the windows open, sacrificing quiet to comfort. The sounds of cars and buses on Kellogg Boulevard, and the sonorous horns from barge traffic on the nearby Mississippi, filled the room whenever the talking stopped.

The entire proceeding carried an air of antiquity. At sixty-three, Marsden himself suggested a figure from the past, with his full head of wavy white hair, abundant mustache and habitual bow ties. Doug Thomson, best known for cases tried ten to twenty years before, found it necessary to hold transcripts and reports an inch or so from his face to compensate for his eyesight. Lois appeared each morning in crocheted shawls and old-fashioned hats that left onlookers hard put to decide just what era they came from.

After a conference among the lawyers in Marsden's chambers at 1:00 P.M. on Tuesday, May 12, the proceedings officially began.

The defense and prosecution teams sat facing each other at a single table placed perpendicular to Judge Marsden's bench, with Mindy, Clayton and Foley to the judge's left. Lois, sitting next to Doug Thomson's associate Deborah Ellis and directly across from Foley, wore a black crocheted shawl, a black chiffon scarf and a brimmed hat with a black ribbon and bow.

It is common to think of trials as suspenseful journeys to climactic revelation, but that would not be an accurate description of what unfolded in Ramsey County courtroom 801 in May of 1987. For one thing, it is possible that the trial of Lois Jurgens was decided in the dramatic beginning moments, when Mindy Elledge offered her opening arguments. What she said was not as conclusive as were the three enlarged photos she showed the jury. The first was of Dennis at the time he was placed with the Jurgenses, smiling and fat-cheeked and round-faced, his eyes bright and full of sparkle. The second, taken soon after, was of Dennis in knee pants sitting next to Robert, animated and happy, clutching a round ball larger than his own smiling face. The third was a photo of Dennis's body lying on the coroner's table on Palm Sunday 1965, emaciated and battered, the fists clenched and the arms raised, the face distorted in pain.

"You will hear testimony that at the time of his death, Dennis Jurgens looked like this," Mindy said.

Doug Thomson did the best he could in response.

Lois was a bad and unlikable person, he said in his opening statement. She had battered Dennis severely, but the abuse Dennis suffered at her hands did not cause his death.

"Lois Jurgens should never have been allowed to adopt a child . . ." he argued. "That is not a defense to murder, but it doesn't prove murder."

Returning to his chair, Thomson glanced at his client, fearing her anger at the unflattering words he'd spoken about her. What he saw provided him both relief and wonder. Lois wasn't even looking at him. She showed no reaction at all.

In time, as the hours and then days passed, everyone in the courtroom grew mesmerized as they watched Lois. She emerged each morning from the elevator with head raised, her manner imperious, her hands clasped together before her at waist level, proceeding like a queen toward the courtroom door. One day, discomfited by a camera thrust into her face, she swung her purse at the offending photographer. The hats changed daily—one was wide-brimmed with sequins, another a sort of bowler, a third a white pillbox. Spectators found her fascinating and unfathomable. During light moments, they wondered what hat she would appear in the next day. During darker moments, they wondered whether she would ever allow any expression to cross her impassive face. Barbara Peterson, the court reporter, was seated so that she looked into Lois's face, and after the trial she swore she hadn't seen the defendant blink but once. Speaking live from the courthouse steps, TV reporters offered pop psychological diagnoses—"having children was important to Lois because she grew up in a family of sixteen children"—and fielded questions from increasingly incredulous anchors in the newsrooms. Did Lois show any response? the anchors would ask each evening, as if that were the goal of the whole endeavor. No, the reporters would say solemnly. None at all.

Doug Thomson labored uphill all the way, flaying away at the prosecution's string of witnesses. Even Beverly Zerwas proved an unhelpful target. During his direct examination, Clayton, not waiting for Doug to raise the issue, gingerly led Bev to acknowledge her lies at the 1965 hearing.

"No, I wasn't truthful . . ." she said, "probably because I felt the family should try to stick together."

On his cross-examination, Doug thought to pillory her. "And you admit here in open court that you committed perjury?" he thundered.

Bev didn't flinch. "That's exactly what I am doing," she said.

Watching from his seat, Clayton rejoiced. No one admits perjury, and she just had. No juror would disbelieve her. His gamble had worked.

A string of other relatives—Lloyd and Donna Zerwas, Nancy Baker, Richard Norton, his daughter Karlene Hilsgen and his sister Darlene Gary—repeated Bev's stories, together painting a portrait of unremitting torture. When Lloyd Zerwas's wife Donna took the stand, the spectators finally got what they were yearning for—a reaction from Lois.

Q: And what did she tell you her actions were in regard to Dennis's ability to go to the bathroom?

A: That she helped him go to the bathroom by sticking her finger into his rectum and taking and pulling his stool out.

Q: Now, do you recall Lois Jurgens's fingernails at that time?

A: Yes, I do . . . They were long, very nice-looking nails, long.

As Donna Zerwas spoke those words, Lois pursed her lips in objection, then impatiently thrust her hand into Debby Ellis's face, spreading her fingers to display her short, stubby nails.

Clayton's interrogation of Donna Zerwas continued.

Q: Has your memory faded at all concerning these events?

A: No . . . Because of the way that the children were treated, and I love children . . . I have five grandchildren . . . We have never seen anything like we had seen with Dennis. It was unreal then, it is unreal today.

Q: Mrs. Zerwas, can you tell the jury why even though you saw these acts of Lois Jurgens done to Dennis, why you did not report that to the welfare authorities or police agencies or some agency such as that?

Donna swallowed hard and studied the courtroom floor.

A: I wish I could truly answer that question. I can't. I had foster children of my own and my daughter . . . I really did not have a reason. I don't know.

When Donna's testimony ended, a friend entered the well of the court and threw her arms around the distraught witness. Donna had to be helped off the stand.

Barbara Venne testified under a shadow of a vague threat, for the night before the trial began, a Zerwas nephew had pulled his car alongside her husband and daughter, waving what later proved to be a toy gun at them. Venne reported the incident to the police but told Clayton, "I will testify no matter what."

Now, on the stand, the childhood friend of Lois's niece appeared vulnerable and fragile.

"Do you recall Dennis Jurgens's funeral?" Clayton asked.

"He had a crown of roses placed on his head, and Dennis was very blond and very fair-skinned, and through the roses you could see bruises on his head, and it appeared as if the roses were placed on his head to cover up."

Clayton handed Barbara one of the coroner's photographs of Dennis's body.

"Who is this a photograph of?" he asked.

Barbara could barely talk.

"Dennis," she whispered.

"You have to speak louder," Clayton said.

Barbara drew a breath.

"Dennis."

As the hours and days passed, one figure after another from the past appeared and settled into the witness stand—Dr. Peterson, Dr. Votel, Gerane Wharton-Park, Father Reiser, Jim Honsa. They came as valuable informants to testify for the prosecution against Lois Jurgens, so were asked by the lawyers for information, not an explanation of their own actions years ago. Father Reiser remembered "nothing in particular" about Barbara Zerwas's funeral in January of 1965, but thought "it would be extremely difficult" for a three-and-a-half-year-old to recite a rosary. Dr. Peterson could "recall seeing some [bruises] but it's not very clear." The county welfare department "finally had no exact reason why we could turn this family down," Gerane said.

Cross-examining these witnesses, Doug Thomson attacked whenever he could, and his efforts on a few occasions managed to convert Mindy Elledge's relentless intensity into a display of temper.

"I know she is going to lead the witness," he said at one point when the judge suggested his objection had been premature. Mindy rose to the bait.

"I object to Mr. Thomson making statements. He knows how to make objections, Your Honor. He went to law school."

Marsden had to intervene: "Now come on, counsel, calm down . . ."

On another occasion, arguing a point to the judge at the bench, beyond the jury's earshot, Doug agitated Mindy by talking too loud—she feared his voice was rising to the jurors' ears.

"Keep your voice down, please," she said. He kept talking. "Could you keep your voice down?" she said again. He continued. "Will you keep your voice down?" she insisted. By the time Doug was finished talking, the prosecutor was fuming.

"Your Honor, first of all, I would ask that if Mr. Thomson is going to make a record at the bench, that he be directed to keep his voice down so that the jury can't hear it."

"I don't think that the jury heard that," Marsden replied.

Despite the brutal revelations being offered by witness after witness, few in courtroom 801 escaped the temptation to watch and gossip about this type of interplay. To many, Mindy's zealous manner seemed effective and sharp-minded, if somewhat grim, while Clayton's approach appeared poised and well-prepared, if a bit inflated—"maybe I could enlighten the court" being the sort of thought lawyers usually keep to themselves when talking to judges. Tom Foley sat by them day in and day out with an empty yellow legal pad on the table before him—an unusual appearance for a county attorney with little trial experience, but not for an elected official with a natural appreciation for the spotlight. Over time, Doug Thomson and his associate Deborah Ellis appeared to retreat into a defensive, protective shell. Debby later said she even avoided the coffee breaks back near the judge's chambers because Mindy glowered at her. They came to feel like interlopers, she explained, obstructing a chamber full of people on a grand mission. There was little possibility here for Thomson's celebrated oratory.

On the morning of Wednesday, May 20, one week into the trial, Bob VanderWyst took the stand. The advancing bone cancer now left him almost incapacitated, but Pete Korolchuk had suffered a massive heart attack on May 3 and VanderWyst was needed.

Mindy tried her best to get VanderWyst's story about Jerome's threat into the record, but the rules of evidence against hearsay proved a stumbling block. VanderWyst couldn't testify about what precisely Jerome had said to him—a witness can only recount the defendant's words and Jerome wasn't the person on trial. What he'd described under oath at the 1965 juvenile hearing and before a grand jury, VanderWyst couldn't repeat at a criminal trial, and the transcripts of those two earlier proceedings were not public documents. VanderWyst could only allude in general terms to what he felt was Jerome's threat. An extended period of questioning, interrupted five times by Doug Thomson's successful objections, yielded the following minimal exchange after the lawyers' arguments were stripped away:

Q: Did you ever, during the investigation that you conducted, feel that you got any interference from Jerome Zerwas, the defendant's brother?

A: Yes, we did.

Q: Did you have some concerns about further conduct of your investigation after this conversation?

A: Yes.

Q: And what were they?

A: We went to see the chief of police and also the assistant county attorney.

Q: About this conversation you had with Lieutenant Zerwas?

A: Yes.

That was all. Mindy, laboring to eke out even this much, never asked VanderWyst why he stopped his investigation after just three weeks. Nor did she pursue the matter of the missing police reports. The jury and spectators were left to infer what VanderWyst's oblique references were all about.

Some of the reporters covering the case noticed these loose ends and approached VanderWyst after the day's session concluded, to no avail. The retired officer wouldn't elaborate on his testimony—Judge Marsden had imposed a gag order barring witnesses from talking with reporters, and VanderWyst always respected the rules.

Jerome, however, proved less reluctant. When *Minneapolis Star and Tribune* Reporter Dan Oberdorfer tracked him down later that day in Elk River, the former lieutenant spoke freely. It was inappropriate for Pete Korolchuk to handle the investigation in 1965 because he'd lived in the Zerwas home, Jerome said. Back then, VanderWyst had told him only that the child had fallen down steps and had a bruise on his forehead the size of a dime. If he had known Dennis actually had numerous bruises, he would have suspended Vander-Wyst for lying.

Oberdorfer's interview with Jerome appeared in the next morning's newspaper. "Yesterday's developments raise new questions about why [Lois] Jurgens . . . was not prosecuted in 1965 . . ." Oberdorfer concluded.

Robert Jurgens wore a blue pin-striped suit with a yellow tie when he followed VanderWyst to the stand, but with his short, curly blond hair and soft mustache, he still looked boyish—not at all like a policeman. It was late on Wednesday, May 20, one month and two days shy of his twenty-seventh birthday. Talking of events that had happened when he was not yet five years old, Robert spoke softly, occasionally glancing at Lois sitting thirty feet away. At times in his testimony, he referred to Lois as "my mom" or "my mother." Mindy Elledge asked the questions, and Robert's responses echoed, in more polished fashion, what he'd told Meehan and Kindle a half year before.

Q: Do you have any recollection of what it was like before Dennis was placed in your house?

A: I recall it just being a very quiet home. I was lonely and afraid.

Q: Do you remember Dennis?

A: Yes.

Q: What do you remember about what Dennis was like?

A: I remember being real happy when he came into the house because I had someone to play with and he was full of energy and we had a good time.

Q: What is the first thing you recall preceding Dennis Jurgens's death?

A: I recall the time when I was riding on this redwood trike in the basement, and I recall Dennis being down there and we were playing and my mom was always in the basement . . . I then recall her grabbing him by the ears and submerging his head several times in the water that was in the tub . . . She would grab him by the ears and put his head under the water, bring it up, put it under, bring it up, put it under . . . Dennis would gasp for air and he was crying at first—the first time—and then he was just overcome by trying to breathe, so he would just gasp for air.

Q: What did you feel like?

A: I was terrified. I was afraid—I—I didn't know what to do. I—it was a terrible sight.

Q: Do you have another recollection of anything happening shortly before Dennis's death?

A: Yes.

Q: What is that?

A: I was riding my trike again in this area and I heard a loud thud or several thuds and rode my trike over to the—near the base of the stairs—and Dennis landed after rolling fast, he landed at the base of those stairs . . . I saw the last part of his fall, and he landed on the base of the stairs on his stomach . . . very hard . . . He, you know, like he almost flew down the stairs.

Q: What part of his body did you say landed at the bottom of the stairs then?

A: I recall him landing on his stomach.

Q: After you saw Dennis on the floor in front of the stairs, what do you recall happening?

A: I recall my mother running—or coming down the stairs . . . Like she was running down the stairs . . . She then began to holler at Dennis and then picked Dennis up and started to hit Dennis and shake Dennis . . . shaking him and hollering at him and calling out his name . . .

Q: How did you feel at that time?

A: I was terrified, what do you do, you know?

Q: What did Dennis do?

A: He cried . . . he was hurting, he was crying.

Q: Now, after the laundry tub incident and the stair incident, what is the next thing you remember in connection with Dennis Jurgens's death?

A: I remember a night, in fact to the best of my recollection, that night it was storming out, it was thundering and lightning and I remember being afraid to go to bed . . . Something must have awoken me . . . There was a light on in the hallway . . . It was dark, the shades in my bedroom were pulled and to the best of my knowledge it was at night or early before the sun would come out . . . I then recall, well, just hearing my dad and Dennis talking and it had something to do with a watch, and any more of the conversation I don't know. I just remember something about a watch . . . They were in the bathroom.

Q: What is the next thing you remember?

A: The next thing that I recall is hearing some screams and hollers, and I got out of my bed, and I went into Dennis's room because this is where the scream and hollers were coming from . . . I believe at that point it was light in the living room and it was light out at the time . . . I recall my mother—I walked in just as she was picking him up out of the crib, and she again was very upset and Dennis's body was just kind of draped, and his arm was just hung and he wasn't normal . . . he wasn't moving or nothing, he was just limp.

Q: What did she do then?

A: She began to violently shake Dennis and holler his name, and there was no response, and then she continued to do this and slap Dennis and was hitting Dennis pretty hard on the back, and this is what she just continued to do, and then she hollered for my dad, and she said, "Harold, you better come in here," or something to that effect or, "Harold, get in here," or—

Q: What do you recall happening next?

A: Well, before Dad got in the room she had laid him back down into his crib, and he was laying on his back I believe when she put him down, and then I was told to go to the living room, and I did so and sat on a chair in the living room . . . I remember a man with a black bag, a medical bag, and I remember there were some police officers or two there . . .

The courtroom by now had settled into a breathless silence, punctuated only by an occasional gasp and by the sound of automobiles passing on Kellogg Boulevard, eight flights below.

At the lawyers' table, Doug Thomson, looking beyond the witness's emotional impact, believed he was hearing something helpful to Lois's case. Robert's memories, after all, perfectly matched the Jurgenses' story. Dennis had fallen down the stairs. Dennis had been alive and talking normally just before his death. Thomson made a note to raise these issues in his closing argument.

Minutes later, when Mindy showed Robert a series of recent photographs of his old White Bear Lake home, taken on the Sunday before the start of the trial, the witness's voice began to quaver.

Q: Mr. Jurgens, were you present at the house at 2148 Gardenette in White Bear recently when some people from the crime bureau made these photographs?

A: Yes.

Q: Was this the first time that you were back in the house since you were removed after Dennis's death?

A: Yes.

Q: How did you feel being back in the house?

A: It was a very eerie feeling.

Q: When you were at the house when these photographs were taken, did it make you recall anything concerning Dennis's life?

A: Yeah, and my life.

Q: What do you recall?

A: Well, when I first walked into the room, I—it was just as I had remembered it. In walking through the house and in particular walking into Dennis's bedroom, it was very tough, I—

Robert stopped talking, then tried to say something, but could not continue. Looking down from the bench, the judge realized he was crying, and quickly banged his gavel.

"We'll take a ten-minute recess," he said. In truth, Marsden just then was losing his own composure.

Later, Mindy asked Robert to describe how Dennis's reactions to his mother changed over time.

A: Dennis, from what I recall, he used to cry, you know, like I did, and when he'd get a spanking he'd kind of try and get away, or when he was going to get his ears or hair pulled he'd try to get away, and later on Dennis didn't do as much crying and he didn't do any running away. I would recall that he more or less submitted and would just kind of whimper and not get into that heavy crying.

Q: Was there any difference between your relationship with your mother and Dennis's relationship with your mother that you remember?

A: I—I don't know exactly the reason why, but I—I cherished my mother. I was afraid of her, but she was number one in my book because I had to be, I looked up to her, I did anything she said, I ate my food, I picked up my toys, I kept neat, and Dennis didn't and as a result Dennis received more traumatic reprimands.

Mindy handed Robert one of the coroner's photos of Dennis's body taken in the morgue on the day of his death.

Q: Have you ever seen Dennis with injuries like that?

A: Yes.

Q: How often would you say that you would see Dennis with injuries like that?

A: Most of the time.

Q: Mr. Jurgens, why is it that you have come forward at this time and told about these things?

A: I have always wondered and never had any answers, and after he passed away I didn't have a brother anymore, and I just think I kind of owe it to him.

"I have no further questions," Mindy said.

Doug Thomson thought Robert was a snitch, and he saw no way to attack him other than to develop that notion. So on cross-examination, he walked Robert through the series of phone conversations and interviews he'd had since October with the White Bear Lake police, showing as best he could how Robert had pumped his parents for information, then passed the results to the investigators.

Q: On November 6, 1986, that was a conversation that you had had that day with your mother, is that correct?

A: Yes.

Q: And one of the purposes in that conversation that you had with her was to try to get as much information out of her as you could so you could report it to the White Bear police, isn't that correct?

A: Yes.

Q: And so—and you did do that, isn't that correct?

A: Yes, I did.

Q: And did you tell Kindle and Meehan that in order to do this you had to play her buddy and you don't even like her?

A: Yes, I did.

Watching her son, Lois remained without expression.

Later, though, she did show a response to Robert's testimony.

"How tall is your mother?" Thomson asked Robert.

"I believe she is five foot two . . . or five foot four."

As Robert offered the initial, shorter estimate, Lois pursed her lips and shook her head.

Near the end of his cross-examination, Doug Thomson asked Robert a question the prosecutors would have loved to raise but by the rules of the law, could not.

"You think your mother caused Dennis's death, don't you?" he said.

Silence filled the courtroom for a moment as Robert hesitated.

"Yes," he said softly.

Thomson, regarding Robert's testimony as helpful to Lois, wanted the jury to understand that Robert wasn't on Lois's side. But up on the bench, Judge Marsden thought: Old Dougie just made one bad mistake.

Although the emotional tenor of the trial was dominated by Robert's testimony, the legal core centered squarely on Michael McGee. For the prosecutors, the medical examiner's testimony was critical.

By establishing the window of time in which Dennis suffered his fatal injury, McGee would keep Lois alone in the house as the only logical perpetrator. By explaining the nature of Dennis's injury, McGee would eliminate accidental causes such as a fall on the floor. By explaining the battered-child syndrome, McGee would lead the jury to infer what had happened in the Jurgens home on Palm Sunday weekend in 1965.

Responding to Clayton's questions, McGee proved to be a masterfully self-possessed witness, precise and authoritative.

Q: Is it possible for you, to a reasonable medical certainty, to state when the injury was inflicted which caused Dennis Jurgens's death?

A: Yes . . . To a reasonable medical certainty . . . If . . . the time of death [is given] as 9:30 in the morning, it is my impression that the subject received a blow to the abdomen with resulting peritonitis that at the outside was forty-eight hours preceding this time of death on 4/11/65.

Q: So the outside of forty-eight hours counting backwards from 9:30 A.M. on 4/11 would have been 9:30 A.M. on 4/9, is that correct?

A: Correct.

Q: And that is an outside figure?

A: That is my outside figure . . . I can only give you ranges . . . The range for me is eight to forty-eight hours.

Q: Do you have an opinion as to whether or not a child slipping and falling on a flat basement floor is capable of rupturing his small bowel?

A: I don't believe so . . . I believe some instrument was used in applying or delivering the injury to the abdomen . . . The internal injuries present in the body are not consistent with falling down the stairs.

Q: Before anyone would succumb to peritonitis . . . they would be in excruciating pain?

A: Yes.

Q: It would be your opinion that they would probably be in a morbid state, in a state of shock, an hour and a half before they died?

A: Yes, I believe that is true.

Q: And in your opinion, the evidence of Dennis Jurgens being in the bathroom shortly before that, it was your opinion that he did not do that?

A: I don't believe that it would be possible . . . His state had gone to the point where he was almost in a cardiovascular collapse . . . and may have been in the process of losing consciousness . . .

It is fair to say that by the time Clayton completed his direct examination, McGee had handed the prosecutors all they needed. It is also fair to say that he had avoided handing them what they didn't need. McGee's comments were incomplete.

In posing and answering questions, Clayton and McGee had accepted the official time of death, 9:30 Sunday morning, for that quite nicely meant the critical forty-eight-hour box extended back to Friday morning at 9:30, some three hours after Harold had left the house for Wisconsin. Although McGee went along with Clayton's presumption, the medical examiner did not at all believe that Dennis had truly died at 9:30 A.M.

McGee had said as much before the grand jury. The medical examiner's testimony then had been unequivocal: When the photos of Dennis were taken on the coroner's table between noon and 2:00 P.M. on Palm Sunday, the extent both of rigor and livor—settling of the blood in the corpse—suggested the child had been dead for approximately eight hours.

If Officer VanderWyst found the body's arms so stiff at 11:30 A.M. that he was afraid he'd break them, what did that tell about the time of death? Clayton had asked McGee before the grand jury.

"It tells me that at the time he examined the child at 11:30 . . . the child has been dead for some time . . ." McGee had responded. "I believe that you could state that the subject has been dead a minimum of six hours and possibly longer, anywhere from eight to maybe twelve hours . . ."

If McGee were right, that meant that at the latest, Dennis had died at 5:30 A.M. He could have died at 3:30 A.M., or even 11:30 P.M. the night before. Now at the trial, however, Clayton was not inclined to open that troublesome box. Inside, after all, were unanswerable questions that could only muddy the picture. During McGee's full day on the witness stand, Clayton never once asked the medical examiner when he thought Dennis had actually died.

Doug Thomson was not equally inclined to let the matter pass, for his entire defense hinged on pointing out discrepancies in the various witnesses's statements. Since the use of rigor mortis and livor mortis is an imprecise craft when judging time of death—particularly when it involves young children with infections—Thomson saw a chance to undermine McGee's credibility.

Q: Now I believe when you testified at the grand jury, you put the time of death around midnight, the midnight before, didn't you?

A: I don't remember making that statement.

Q: Doctor, do you know of any authority whatever that says that the state of rigidity for rigor mortis is a reliable method of trying to ascertain the time of death?

A: By reliable, [if] you mean the exact time of death, no.

Q: But you attempted to do that in your grand jury testimony, did you not?

A: I was attempting to give an estimation . . . No exact time was offered . . .

Talking in his office some time after the trial, the medical examiner was not nearly as elusive.

"No one can tell the time of death from rigor alone," he said, "but 9:30 A.M. to 11:00 A.M. is not enough time for rigor. I've never seen that before. I can't tell you when Dennis died. But was it 9:30 A.M.? NO. Can I tell you when? No. Can I say how far off the official time is? Hours. Can I say for sure? No. But I don't believe 9:30 A.M., and neither do you."

Why didn't he say this at the trial?

"I would have, but Clayton didn't ask. No one asked."

It was not that Clayton and Mindy weren't aware of the puzzling, unanswered questions in the Jurgens case. They realized Robert's memories contradicted Michael McGee's judgment of when Dennis died. They knew Robert's description of the bathroom scene didn't fit with the notion that Dennis suffered excruciating pain from peritonitis for hours before his death. They understood that the Jurgenses couldn't have found Dennis dead in his crib, for they'd listened to McGee explain privately that Dennis's raised, stiff arms meant the body had been moved after death.

The prosecutors, however, had not focused on such questions while preparing for trial, or even discussed them. The answers, after all, wouldn't prove whether Lois actually inflicted the fatal injury. Mindy and Clayton couldn't see how knowing the precise time and nature of Dennis's death would help convict or exonerate Lois. Such information related only to whether Lois was lying about the details. What is more, they and McGee knew from experience that jurors' attention tended to wander after an hour of listening to medical examiners' testimony. They needed to streamline McGee's presentation, hone it to the essentials.

"I can't say we developed any particular theory about those questions," Clayton recalled later. "Whatever Robert's memories, the medical evidence was clear enough it couldn't be disputed."

In passing moments, of course, Clayton and Mindy couldn't avoid wondering. When did Dennis die, and where, and in what position? Why were the body's arms raised? When was Dr. Peterson really summoned? Had Jerome been called first? Could Dennis have been saved? Who, besides the Jurgenses, was culpable?

However intriguing these questions were, though, the nature of the legal system gave the prosecutors no reason to seek their answers, and no avenue either. Despite the goals voiced by authorities upon first reopening the Jurgens case, they now were pursuing a verdict, not ventilating the past. On the eve of the trial, talking to reporters about what happened in 1965, Tom Foley said: "I'm not comfortable with some of the answers I've heard. But we left that and had to proceed. There's really nothing we can do about what happened back then anyway."

The legacy of *State v. Loss* was abundantly apparent in the prosecutors' basic courtroom strategy. In 1987, Mindy and Clayton didn't need to prove what caused Dennis's ruptured bowel. In 1987, they didn't need an eyewitness or a confession or a clear understanding of how Dennis died. Jurors now were more than willing to infer what they once would not have believed. At Lois's trial, it just did not matter precisely what had happened in the Jurgens home on Palm Sunday weekend in 1965.

One other dimension of the Jurgens saga never was explored in courtroom 801—the prosecutors never called the four Kentucky children to the stand, and never made any dimension of their experiences a part of the trial. In chambers, Judge Marsden had ruled the Kentucky matter to be character evidence only, not usable to demonstrate Lois's propensity for abuse. If Thomson called family and neighbors to endorse Lois's temperament, the prosecutors could counter with the Kentucky children, but that was all. The White Bear detectives' scramble to Georgia the previous November, in response to the news media's clamorous attention, had been for naught.

Early on Wednesday afternoon, May 27, June Bol became the prosecution's final witness. Once more, she faced Lois from a witness stand and felt her hard eyes from thirty feet away. June told her story about Harold—*I wasn't there when Dennis died*—and retreated as quickly as she could.

After three weeks, Mindy and Clayton were finished. They'd presented all there was of their case in chief. In the end, despite Robert's affecting testimony, the prosecution comprised little more than what had been known in 1965—even Michael McGee's testimony had simply echoed, with greater sophistication, Dr. Woodburn's before Judge Gingold twenty-two years before. At three in the afternoon on Wednesday, May 27, the state rested its case.

With it now his turn, Doug Thomson faced a dilemma. There was no point in calling a string of relatives and neighbors to support Lois, as Ed Donohue had done in 1965, because he'd already acknowledged that Lois was an abhorrent child abuser. The defense attorney's only hope rested with Harold Jurgens. If Lois's husband took the blame for hitting Dennis, a reasonable doubt might be planted in jurors' minds about a precise cause of death.

But would Harold testify? If Doug called him, would he claim his Fifth Amendment right against self-incrimination?

Asked this question by the prosecutors before and during the trial, Doug Thomson had always insisted he didn't know—Harold, after all, no longer was his client. Mindy and Clayton didn't find this a satisfactory answer. If Harold were called to the stand and there invoked the Fifth, he'd be implying to the jurors that he had in fact done something bad to Dennis. By the rules of law, for just this reason, a lawyer can't call a witness to the stand if he knows he'll claim the Fifth, and that is why Doug Thomson's professed ignorance of Harold's intentions so irritated the prosecutors.

Mindy and Clayton had tried to force the issue in chambers just before the trial by filing a motion to compel Harold to indicate his intentions, but the judge hadn't ruled. Now, on Thursday, May 28, the morning after the state rested, the judge convened a hearing in his chambers that included Harold and his attorney Joe Friedberg, the prosecutors and Doug Thomson.

The Court: I think it would be appropriate . . . to make a record with respect to Mr. Jurgens's desires.

Mr. Friedberg: I have counseled Mr. Jurgens . . . I have advised him that in my opinion he should not testify, that he is in jeopardy of the state using his answers in an attempt to incriminate him . . . He has told me that he will follow my advice.

The Court: Do you wish to interrogate him?

Mr. Friedberg: Mr. Jurgens, have I advised you that I believe it is in your best interest not to testify?

Mr. Jurgens: That you did, sir.

Mr. Friedberg: And are you going to follow my advice?

Mr. Jurgens: I sure am.

Anticipating this decision, over the previous weekend Thomson had filed a motion and brief seeking to have Harold simply read his grand jury testimony to the jury. Marsden, however, was not inclined to allow something so dubious to enter the record unchallenged.

"Well, I have considered both . . . [Harold's] 1965 testimony . . . and the January testimony before the grand jury . . ." the judge told the lawyers. "I am obliged to sustain the position of the state and deny the request of the defendant to call Harold Jurgens for purposes of reciting his grand jury testimony. There is a total lack of independent corroborating evidence . . . indicating the trustworthiness of the statement . . . That is all I have to say."

Clayton and Mindy had been right—the 1965 transcript was now blocking Harold's path to the witness stand and any chance he had to save his wife.

Moments later, a communal gasp rose in the crowded courtroom when Doug Thomson announced the defense was resting its case without calling a witness. The prosecutors were less surprised. He can't call Harold and he can't call the Zerwas family, Clayton reasoned. We have him in a box.

All that was left were the final arguments.

Clayton Robinson went first, rising to face the jury shortly after 9:00 A.M. on Friday, May 29. He reviewed the evidence step by step, describing once again each injury inflicted on Dennis. He expressed regret that social workers and doctors had failed to "see through Lois Jurgens's subterfuge," and that neighbors and relatives had not come forward sooner to report what they'd witnessed. Then he turned to the dimension of his case that a prosecutor could not have offered successfully in 1965. He asked the jury to infer from circumstantial evidence what the state had not proven directly—that Lois had delivered a blow that ruptured Dennis's bowel.

"I submit to you that battered children are typically not the type of individuals that you would see out on the street struck in their lower abdomen with a blunt object," he said. "That is a crime that occurs at home. It is consistent with a private crime, the private punishment that Lois Jurgens inflicted . . . You jurors are selected partially because of your common sense, and as jurors you are not asked to abandon your common sense . . . The state must prove that the defendant caused the death of Dennis Jurgens [but] the law does not prefer one form of evidence over another . . . It is fair for you to believe that Lois Jurgens caused that fatal injury to Dennis . . ."

When Clayton finished, Judge Marsden called a ten-minute recess. Then it was Doug Thomson's turn. His only hope was to challenge directly the prosecution's contention.

"This is not a homicide case, this is a case of abuse," he began. "On the one hand, the abuse of Dennis Jurgens, and on the other hand, the abuse of reason and the abuse of common sense. The only reason at this moment that you and I are face-to-face is not because of any team effort, it's because of a whim and the caprice of one individual, Dr. Michael McGee.

"On October seventh of last year he changed a death certificate on his own to homicide. Dr. Votel, who testified here, who was the coroner in 1965, stated . . . 'it was my feeling that a battered child could be a battered child, but death could be caused by some other factor, such as a fall or an accident, and I was willing to wait until the information was obtained . . .'

"On October seventh of last year nothing, nothing changed. There was no piece of evidence whatsoever that Dr. McGee relied on in changing the designation to homicide. There have not been any medical or scientific advancements that could have been employed by Dr. McGee to in any way jump to the conclusion he did on his own back on October seventh. It may be true that the battered-child syndrome has been studied over the last twenty-two years, so that some of the niceties and studies can now be recognized as giving rise to the syndrome, but there is nothing about the advancement in the recognition of the battered-child syndrome that in any way came into play when Dr. McGee changed that death certificate . . . There is not one shred of evidence in this case that Lois Jurgens caused the death . . .

"Now Robert Jurgens was a very important witness in this case . . . There isn't any question about his bias . . . He thinks that his mother killed Dennis . . . But in spite of that, most of his testimony here was candid. His description of Dennis falling down the stairs . . . Dennis landed on his stomach. He landed very hard . . . And he also testified in detail about the morning in the bathroom, the morning that Dennis died . . . He . . . related the following. 'I remember hearing Dennis talking to Dad in the bathroom and he seemed fine. He wasn't in any pain . . . How could he just be so fine and die all of a sudden?' That was very critical and important testimony. That was eyewitness testimony . . . There was no evidence as far as Robert Jurgens testified to or that any other witness testified to that Lois Jurgens ever kicked anyone. There is not testimony of that kind . . .

"What caused the external trauma? The only evidence in this case of any external trauma that would have caused the ruptured bowel is the fall down the steps . . . There is no duty or obligation whatsoever upon us, the defense, to establish how Dennis Jurgens died. The burden is upon the prosecution to prove the cause of death . . . The burden is on them to prove beyond a reasonable doubt that she caused the death . . ."

As the noon hour approached, the packed courtroom grew hot and stuffy and two jurors seemed on the verge of closing their eyes. "Well . . . I have gone much further than I had anticipated," Thomson said hurriedly, realizing he was losing his audience. "I am going to close . . . Thank you."

After a discussion among the lawyers in chambers, Judge Marsden recited his instructions to the jury.

"You are not to speculate as to possible answers to questions which I did not require to be answered . . ." he said. "A fact may be proved by either direct or circumstantial evidence, or by both. The law does not prefer one form of evidence over the other . . . Circumstantial evidence is indirect proof by proving one fact from which an inference of the existence of another fact may reasonably be drawn . . ."

Marsden then explained the charges, and what needed to be proved if the jurors were to convict Lois. The statutes as they existed in 1965, the judge had decided, would rule deliberations in this trial.

In 1965, Marsden said, the statutes of Minnesota provided that whoever causes the death of a human being with intent to cause the death of that person but without premeditation is guilty of murder in the second degree. In order to find the defendant had an intent to kill, you must find that the defendant acted with the purpose of causing death.

In 1965, the statutes of Minnesota provided that whoever caused the death of a human being without the intent to cause the death, while committing or attempting to commit a felony offense, was guilty of murder in the third degree.

The felony offense indicated in Lois Jurgens's indictment was aggravated assault. Whoever intentionally inflicted great bodily harm upon another was guilty of aggravated assault.

Great bodily harm meant bodily harm that creates a high probability of death, or causes serious permanent disfigurement, or causes a permanent or protracted loss or impairment of function of any bodily member or organ.

When he completed this explanation, Judge Marsden added one other instruction. By 1987, it was a commonplace directive for this type of trial, and involved only two uncomplicated sentences.

"The term battered-child syndrome has been used in this case, and is a recognized legal, as well as medical, concept," Judge Marsden said. "Simply put, it is a condition by which children are injured other than by accident."

Talking privately during the course of the trial, Judge Marsden had marveled at how Robert had survived his childhood and emerged a productive citizen. Now, as the jury retreated to its deliberations at half past two on Friday afternoon, Marsden invited Robert to his chambers.

"I felt so emotional," the judge explained later. "I wanted to commend him."

The jurors were emotionally agitated too, but not undecided, when they began their deliberations after a quick, late lunch.

"I'd like a show of hands," said the foreman, John W. Johnson. "Who thinks Lois Jurgens is not guilty?"

No one raised a hand.

The jurors had found Robert's testimony personally moving, but it was the expert medical testimony alone, coupled with the morgue photos, that they found overwhelmingly convincing. They held little regard for Harold, and some wished they could pass judgment on him as well. Several jurors expressed compassion for Lois, because of her troubled childhood and because they felt she was now a harmless older woman. Some jurors wanted to know more about why Dennis's death was overlooked for so long.

Their only significant division came not over the question of whether Lois killed Dennis, but whether she intended to do so. Intent meant second degree murder, lack of intent meant third degree murder. The jurors' differences on this issue did not run deep, though, for all told, their deliberations required only three hours.

Courtroom 801 was nearly empty when the jury appeared at half past five on Friday to deliver its verdict, for it was past courthouse business hours, and the quick decision was unexpected. Jerry Sherwood was there, though, hard to ignore in a white dress decorated with giant black polka dots the size of grapefruits. Surrounded by her four children, she occupied the front bench of the spectator section, the judge having allowed her to remain after her testimony. Two rows back, Harold sat by himself in the same burnished rust suit he'd worn to his wife's arraignment. Lois settled at the lawyers' table a moment later, a white crocheted shawl over a black skirt and print blouse, a small black pillbox hat on her head.

Sherwood's daughter Misty grasped her mother's hand as they rocked back and forth nervously.

"Members of the jury, have you returned a verdict?" Court Clerk Michelle Danielson asked.

The clerk received the verdict forms from the jury, showed them to the judge, then continued.

"Members of the jury, hearken unto your verdict as it will be recorded upon the records of this court. State of Minnesota, County of Ramsey, District Court, Second Judicial District. File Number 44463. State of Minnesota versus Lois Germaine Jurgens. We the jury find the defendant not guilty of the charge of murder in the second degree—"

Here Jerry Sherwood, misunderstanding, started to moan with dismay.

". . . but guilty of the charge of murder in the third degree."

Jerry Sherwood's moans turned more to a shriek, as commotion filled the courtroom. Her family and friends gathered about her, cheering and hugging one another, whooping and shouting and leaping into the air, as she collapsed, sobbing, into her daughter's arms.

"Please, please, restrain yourselves," Judge Marsden exclaimed. "No further demonstrations in the courtroom."

Lois looked behind her at Sherwood's group, then turned away without expression. Despite the guilty verdict, no bailiffs came to lead her away, for the trial was not over. Doug Thomson still had a mental illness defense to offer the court.

"Members of the jury," Judge Marsden continued. "We are going to recess at this time until Monday at two o'clock. At that time you will resume with phase two of this trial, dealing with the issue of mental illness . . . The defendant will remain free on bail."

Minutes later, in the corridor outside the courtroom, Sherwood appeared both jubilant and tearful as she faced the by-now-familiar sea of television cameras. Her hand covered her mouth in wonder.

"We did it," she said. "My kids told me God's going to do what's right, and He did. Justice was finally served after twenty-two years. Denny can rest in peace now."

In a corner near the elevators, Robert Jurgens stood alone, crying.

Lois waited in the courtroom for several minutes with her husband and attorneys, then rose to leave. Harold and Debby Ellis linked arms and led the way as Lois followed, hiding her face and head underneath her white shawl. Thomson trailed behind, chiding the shoving throng of shouting reporters for what he called the "carnival atmosphere" surrounding the case. On the warm, muggy sidewalk outside the courthouse, still running a gauntlet of cameras and microphones, Lois finally provided an audible response to all that was transpiring.

"I've never seen so many monsters in all my life," she snapped at the journalists. "Sickos!"

During all of the next week in courtroom 801, various psychiatrists and psychologists debated whether Lois was a paranoid schizophrenic or just a repressed, angry woman. The roles were reversed from 1965—now it was the state that insisted Lois was sane, the defense that she was psychotic.

"Lois Jurgens has been and is a stainless steel paranoid schizophrenic . . ." Doug Thomson argued. "Dennis Jurgens was dealt a bad hand by fate, but Lois Jurgens also suffered from the vagaries of fate. She didn't go out and purposely acquire this disease."

"She didn't think she was punching a pineapple . . ." Mindy Elledge countered. "She is, plainly and simply, an evil woman. You don't need a psychiatrist to tell you this. You can rely on your own experience and your own common sense."

The jurors spent more time deliberating Lois's sanity than her guilt—five and a half hours in all.

"It was quite difficult because we were most concerned about this woman and we all totally just racked our feelings and our brains . . ." one juror later told television station WCCO-TV.

Waiting, Mindy grew increasingly nervous as Clayton patted her on the back and told her not to worry. Outside in a hallway, Jerry Sherwood was talking about what she'd do if Lois were found not guilty. If Lois so much as looked cross-eyed at her, Jerry said, she was going after her with both fists.

The courtroom was packed when the jury finally returned at midday on Friday, June 5. Moving through the eighth floor corridor, Harold clearing a path, Lois again walked with her white shawl hiding her face and head. Entering the courtroom, she settled in her seat, draping the shawl over her chair. She was wearing a lavender dress trimmed in white eyelet lace, and her hat was also lavender, with a satin ribbon and bow.

The court clerk read the verdict: "We the jury find the defendant guilty of murder in the third degree."

The clerk turned to the jury. "And this is your true verdict, so say you all?"

In unison, the jurors replied: "Yes."

At the lawyers' table, Mindy and Clayton embraced, and were soon joined there by Meehan and Kindle, Greg hovering over them like a guard, worrying about the Zerwas clan, urging them to move to a protected corner of the room. Ron blinked back tears. Jerry Sherwood sagged in her chair, weeping. Lois displayed no reaction.

After the jury left the courtroom, Doug Thomson and his client approached the bench, where Judge Marsden pronounced his sentence, an indeterminate period ranging up to twenty-five years, the penalty specified under the 1965 law. It would be up to the state commissioner of corrections to decide precisely how long Lois served, Marsden said, but if he were sentencing her under present law, he would have made it at least fifteen years because of the barbaric cruelty reflected in the evidence.

Did the defendant have anything to tell the court? the judge asked.

Lois leaned forward and talked softly. She had not brought any clothes, she said. There were many things she would like to say, but it would take hours.

The spectators began filing from the courtroom as Lois returned with Thomson to the lawyers' table. Those still in the room watched in fascination as Lois crooked her finger at Harold, summoning him. As he headed toward her, Lois pointed at her purse, lying under the table, but Harold couldn't immediately reach his wife through the crowd.

"Harold," Lois snapped impatiently. "Harold, come here."

When he did manage to reach her side and grab the purse, the couple kissed, and a moment later Harold walked from the courtroom into the tumultuous corridor. Then a heavyset matron led Lois through a back door, the first leg of the journey to the Women's Correctional Facility in Shakopee. An odd circle had been joined. Lois was returning to reside behind bars in the small town where Gerane Rekdahl and Scott County officials, at their fateful meeting a quarter century before, first decided to deliver one-year-old Dennis to the Jurgens home.

Cacophony filled the eighth floor hallway, jammed full of reporters, spectators, thick power cords, bright lights and bulky broadcast equipment. Before a bank of cameras and microphones, Tom Foley elbowed aside a tearful Mindy.

"This verdict is a tremendous victory for the system," the county attorney said. "I am very pleased that the system that failed Dennis Jurgens twenty-two years ago was able to reexamine its failure and successfully prosecute the perpetrator for murder, even though it's twenty-two years late . . . Dennis Jurgens has finally seen justice done in Ramsey County."

No, Foley added in response to a question. The prosecutors are not considering a murder charge against Harold. They will examine his grand jury testimony to determine if he committed perjury, but it is doubtful they will bring charges.

A reporter thrust a microphone at Mindy. Why, he asked, did it take so long for the case to come to trial?

"In 1965," Mindy said, "people didn't think white, middle-class families on a nice tree-lined street in White Bear Lake would murder their children. That's the bottom line."

"Beautiful," Lloyd Zerwas told reporters. "It's my sister. I love her dearly. But I don't give a damn who it is. She did wrong . . . Each and every one of us in the family was aware of some type of abuse. It bothers me that more of them didn't talk."

"I think it's fantastic," Sherwood told a sea of microphones. "It's unbelievable. I don't feel anything for Lois. I really don't. I hope someday she finds her own peace, because I've had to search for a long time for mine . . . It's the greatest day of my life."

Soon Sherwood was racing down the stairs to a television interview awaiting her on the sidewalk below. As she descended, she chanted, over and over: "Twenty-five years, twenty-five years . . . Dennis would have been twenty-five years old in December, and she got twenty-five years. I'm so happy."

CHAPTER 43

Celebration

On Tuesday, September 1, three months after the jury delivered its final verdict, Robert Jurgens journeyed the four hours from his Crookston home to White Bear Lake. There, in a quiet courtroom in the town's municipal building, he presented his own appreciation plaque to the four people he described as his "best friends"—Ron Meehan, Greg Kindle, Mindy Elledge and Clayton Robinson.

These are people he would "trust with my life," Robert said during a brief ceremony. They had "filled in the gaps" of his memory. "They know more about me than I do . . . The four suffered great consequences but they carried on, reached from deep inside and went forward . . . It was the small things they did for me that meant so much. They took me out to dinner and opened their homes . . . They went out of their way to make me feel comfortable . . . In this business we seldom get awards, so we do it among ourselves. When one comes, it's a nice feeling. I want them to know that feeling because I don't know how to repay them."

Robert struggled with his words only when it came time to recite the inscription on the plaque.

"I know the Lord had Dennis by my side as I prepared this inscription," he said, swallowing hard.

Signed by Robert and engraved with the names of the two detectives and two prosecutors, the plaque read:

IN LOVING MEMORY
OF
DENNIS CRAIG JURGENS
We met you in a picture and loved you from the start.
Our special dedication was you within our hearts
The final curtain closed now and we know you're standing tall
Rest in peace now, Dennis, your memory's with us all.

When Robert finished reading the words, Ron Meehan gathered him in a bounteous bear hug.

"I have no family now," Robert murmured.

Congratulatory scenes like this played themselves out on a number of stages in Minnesota, with a variety of characters, for all sorts of people derived considerable satisfaction from the outcome of the Lois Jurgens trial. Those who pursued, unraveled and prosecuted the case felt understandable pride. Others took pleasure in the notion that justice had finally been realized. Spirited and sometimes strained discussions attempted to identify the chief heroes—the police? the prosecutors? Robert Jurgens? Jerry Sherwood? Many saw in the case vivid evidence of a country's increased awareness about child abuse. That, above all, was often cited as the chief theme of the story.

The congratulatory mood continued for months, as did the attention to those involved in the case.

Ron and Greg received honorable mention awards in Minnesota's annual Police Officer of the Year competition. National correspondents traveled through the Twin Cities area to poke through court documents, round up assorted witnesses and compose retrospectives on the case for big city newspapers and magazines. In February of 1988, the monthly *Twin Cities* magazine appeared on newsstands featuring a cover photo of Jerry Sherwood and a nine-page story inside bearing the title, "The Wrong Side of the System— Dennis Jurgens's Natural Mother Tells the Harrowing Story of her Life." In the summer of 1988, a producer and camera crew from the CBS television show "60 Minutes" appeared in town, followed weeks later by Diane Sawyer, who, equipped with the results of her team's voluminous reportage, one morning pursued and finally confronted Harold as he left the Shakopee prison.

"Mr. Jurgens, I'm Diane Sawyer from '60 Minutes.' We'd like to talk with you about Dennis," the newswoman began.

"I know you'd love to do that, wouldn't you?" Harold said as he continued walking.

"Why don't you tell us about Dennis? Did you see him being injured? Were you there? Did you see it? Did you try to protect him? Did your wife hurt him?"

"No."

"What kind of woman is your wife?"

"Beautiful woman, a very nice woman."

By mid-1988, a year after the trial ended, most of the legal issues raised by the Jurgens case had been resolved.

The medical examiner's effort to identify other undeclared Ramsey County child murders, launched just as the Jurgens case was reopening, had yielded nothing that supported further prosecutions. Jim Essling handed Michael McGee dozens of dubious files, but they remained just that, unknowable at such a distance of time and murkiness of detail.

In early May of 1988, a divided Minnesota court of appeals upheld Lois Jurgens's conviction by a two-to-one vote, making multiple references to *State v. Loss*. The two prevailing judges allowed that the evidence didn't establish how the fatal trauma was inflicted, but said, "in a case where the 'battered-child syndrome' is established, the state need not show the specific circumstances of the injury causing death . . . the prosecution unquestionably benefited from the Supreme Court's recognition of the 'battered-child syndrome' in *State v. Loss*."

Two months later, on July 6, the Minnesota Supreme Court declined to review the case. Soon thereafter, the state corrections department decided that under her indeterminate sentence, Lois should serve a minimum of eight years in prison. That meant she would be at least seventy when released.

In the Ramsey County attorney's office, Mindy and Clayton discussed with Tom Foley the possibility of additional prosecutions related to the Jurgens case, to no avail. The statute of limitations and lack of evidence prevented everything but a charge of perjury against Harold, and a conviction there wouldn't even yield a prison term. Foley just did not want to take that action.

"We don't want to look like grandpa bashers," he told Mindy.

◆   ◆   ◆

In truth, now that Lois was confined behind bars, most of those involved in the Jurgens case were far more eager to identify heroes than they were to recognize villains. Reflecting on why the Jurgens tragedy happened, few were inclined to point fingers or fix blame or make judgments.

The "system" hadn't worked, the prosecutors and detectives and judge readily acknowledged to those who asked. But people didn't have any idea what child abuse was. People saw clean, ordered houses, that's what people saw, or wanted to see. It was easy to fool people. Some, like the coroner and caseworker and neighbors, just lost track or were overwhelmed or were afraid.

"I don't want to be in a position of judging basically decent people who failed to do something or chose not to," Greg Kindle said soon after the case was over. "Moralizing, pointing fingers at others, is just not the point."

"I don't believe there were any villains in 1965," Judge Marsden told a visitor to his chambers in the winter of 1987. "There is much more advanced forensics and awareness now . . . This happened years before the battered-child syndrome was recognized. In hindsight, they were negligent, but not consciously wrongdoers. We must resist hindsight. I can't call any of them a bad guy, but I can say they didn't do their jobs very well."

If these observations in some ways conflicted with the unflinching facts of the Jurgens case and the actual timing of Henry Kempe's revolution, they all the same reflected accurately how a good number of people felt. There were understandable reasons for such sentiments. Some of those disinclined to pass judgment, after all, had come to see in the Jurgens affair the uncomfortable shadow of their own actions in other times and places. Others, examining in fine, unrelenting detail how all sorts of people behaved at a critical moment in their lives, had simply found the experience discomfiting. They'd ended up feeling vulnerable.

"It makes you wonder," said Ann Hyland in the prosecutor's office, "just how our decisions now will be looked at twenty-five years in the future."

CHAPTER 44

Jerome

In late July of 1987, Jerome Zerwas happened to be driving north on Bald Eagle Avenue in White Bear Lake when he spotted an old friend, Bill Butters, walking at the side of the road. Jerome pulled over and braked.

"Hey, Bill, how are you?" he called out.

When Jerome's father died in 1980, Butters had thrown his arms around him, right in front of half a dozen people over at the Big Ben's on Highway 61, and Jerome had always valued that sign of support and friendship. Now, though, standing at the side of Bald Eagle Avenue, Butters seemed uncomfortable. He looked away, then said he had to go, and Jerome could tell the man didn't want to talk to him.

Butters wasn't the only one who gave Jerome a cold shoulder in the aftermath of Lois's trial. The chilliness from his old White Bear cop buddies was the worst.

"I feel real bad about it," Jerome told people. "Because Ron Meehan used to call me every couple of months and we'd meet with a lieutenant in North St. Paul and go out and have lunch, okay . . . And if something happened, Ron would call me and report it to me . . . that so and so was sick or whatever . . . But since our December conversation there in 1986 Ron Meehan has never talked to me since. We used to be invited to all the police Christmas parties and we've never been invited to a Christmas party since 1986."

In truth, Jerome had become the topic of considerable speculation. Suspicious talk about him had reached as high as the chambers of the Minnesota Court of Appeals—"there was evidence of
interference in the 1965 investigation of Dennis's death by Jurgens's
brother, White Bear Lake police lieutenant Jerome Zerwas," the justices wrote in their opinion rejecting Lois's appeal—but nowhere
was the conjecture greater than in White Bear Lake. Although
Lois's conviction had satisfied the needs of the public officials and
exhausted the reach of the judicial system, a good many townsfolk
still nursed opinions about the former lieutenant's role in the Jurgens affair.

Many truly liked and admired Jerome. The retired banker Dick
Long, the retired grocer Bill LeVasseur, the retired high school principal Roy Wahlberg, and Bob Brass at the Ben Franklin five-and-
dime all warmly endorsed him and dismissed suggestions that he'd
interfered in the case. "He was always a good cop, he always got the
facts and acted on them," Wahlberg told those who asked. "He came
when we called and took the troublemakers down to the station. He
had class. He talked with a tone of voice that made them listen. I
respected him . . . I can't believe he covered up."

Others saw it differently. Those who judged Jerome to be an
operator more or less assumed he'd been up to something, if only
because he always played by his own rules. Even some of those with
a subtler understanding of Jerome, and an appreciation for him, harbored a certain wonder.

"I think well of Jerome," said his eldest sister, Eloise. "He's my
favorite brother. He's sensitive to people, a good person, one who
supported the family a lot . . . Dennis's death would have put him
in an awful spot. He had pride in his name. Being a police lieutenant was something . . . To get anywhere from where we began . . . It
doesn't make sense for anyone to say 'Father told us to lie to protect
the family.' Father didn't care about that . . . Maybe Jerome . . ."

Then there were those who supported Jerome even if they
thought he had in fact tried to obstruct the investigation. The Jurgens affair didn't happen because of Jerome, they pointed out—back
then, thousands of other babies were put in the ground in the same
fashion. And despite Jerome, Korolchuk and VanderWyst still managed to puncture the Jurgenses' story in their seven-page final analysis. The prosecutors in 1965 turned down the case for reasons other

than the missing and withheld statements. "So the investigation went through whatever Jerome did," Judge Bill Fleming observed with some satisfaction, after learning of these matters. "He didn't stop it or cover it up."

Talking about Jerome made other people plain nervous, for the lieutenant had a litigious bent. In June of 1988, a year after the trial, he filed a $50,000 personal injury lawsuit against Robert Vander-Wyst and the city of White Bear Lake, claiming that VanderWyst's public statements about him were "false" and made with "malice" and "malign[ed]" his "character, reputation and integrity." This lawsuit reduced VanderWyst—then three months from death, racked with pain and penniless—to making countless sobbing phone calls to friends and city officials, but Jerome would not back down.

Pride drove the former police lieutenant to such action even more than did money. Simply avoiding prosecution hadn't satisfied him—he cared as much for the good opinion of his fellows as he did for the respect of the law. The prospect of a tarnished image left him openly troubled.

Many months after the trial's end, Jerome was still urgently disavowing knowledge of Dennis's death and imploring everyone—friends, relatives and more distant visitors—to believe him. He solicited a notarized affidavit from his old chief, Wayne Armstrong—"I received no indication from the assigned officers or any other sources that Lt. Zerwas interfered . . ."—and began distributing copies widely. He showed others a comment Bob VanderWyst apparently made to a *Minneapolis Star and Tribune* reporter in December of 1986—"It was a good investigation . . . [Jerome] didn't have anything to do with the investigation"—even though these passing words were at odds with everything VanderWyst had said under oath before or since.

He knew nothing of the case, Jerome told people. He worked every Sunday for many years, so he didn't hang out at his parents' house and never saw or heard about any of the abuse. He had no idea why some family members backed down from talking to Korolchuk and Vander-Wyst. He hadn't the slightest idea what had happened to the missing statements. He never visited the mortuary to look behind Dennis's ears for fingernail marks. He never talked to Norma Potter. He never threatened VanderWyst and Korolchuk. Vander-Wyst violated all the rules by never telling him about the bruises on

Dennis. "I think they bungled the case so bad that they had to have a scapegoat and they figured I was a good one," he said.

In this vein, Jerome one day midway through the summer of 1987 phoned White Bear Lake Police Chief Philip Major. He wanted to describe the encounter with Bill Butters and once again proclaim his innocence.

"I just had to call," Jerome began, sounding agitated, "to convince you all this wasn't true—"

Major started to cut him off, but Jerome kept talking.

"I didn't know nothing," Jerome was saying. "I was busy working in those days. I never spent time at family things. I never saw or heard nothing. I didn't know."

Major reflected on that notion for a moment. The two men were not contemporaries—Major, thirty-nine, had joined the force as a patrolman in 1973, not long before Jerome left, and had replaced Korolchuk as chief in 1984—but they knew each other fairly well. Major thought Jerome a strong cop in the old sense, a protector, a man who would marshal forces around a family member just as readily as he would safeguard his town's citizens.

"Okay," Major told Jerome. "If you want to talk about this, let's talk. Let's pull our reports. Let's look at VanderWyst's very first report. Now, how can you say Bob came to you at two o'clock that Sunday and reported that the boy had just a dime-size mark on his forehead?"

"I don't know why," Jerome said. "That's just what he said."

"Were those kids abused?" Major asked.

"We saw those kids. We had them over. We watched them change clothes. We never saw. There were no bruises."

"Come on," Major said. "It doesn't make sense. All the relatives saw."

"I never saw any of that. Honestly, Phil."

"Jerome, I've known you for years. I want to believe you. Why don't you come down to the station? We'll go over the reports and sort this out."

The chief waited for days, the file of reports on his desk, but Jerome never appeared.

More than a year later, in October of 1988, Jerome still felt compelled to defend himself. This time he was sitting in his lawyer's office, talking to a visitor who'd arrived bearing a copy of the 1965 transcript. Mindy Elledge and Clayton Robinson, mining that document for what they needed to make their case in chief, had by necessity ignored certain peripheral passages that were nonetheless of considerable interest. In these passages, the words from 1965 sounded so different from those in 1988.

Bertrand Poritsky, for example, questioning Donna Zerwas in 1965:

Q: Have you discussed this [the abuse] with anybody before you came into court here?

A: Matter of fact, we discussed it with the whole family.

Q: Did you ever say anything to anybody about [Thanksgiving Day]?

A: Yes, we told a few people about it . . . It's a large family and there are quite a few that we told . . . Gerhard and Jerome and Rosie . . .

Q: You told Jerome?

A: That's right.

Q: When did you tell Jerome?

A: Shortly after it happened.

And Poritsky questioning Lois's sister, Donna Norton:

Q: Did you ever talk to anybody about this or tell anybody about this situation?

A: Yes . . . practically the whole family.

Q: Tell me who you told about [Thanksgiving Day]?

A: My mother and father . . . My brother, Jerome Zerwas, and his wife, Rosie, heard about it.

Q: You never mentioned this to any of the public authorities at all?

A: No. In our family you don't dare say much.

And Jerome himself, describing his close contact with Lois and Dennis:

Q: How often would you say that you would be in the Jurgenses' home during the past five years?

A: In the summer months, quite often, approximately three times a week. Alone patrolling, I'd see my sister in the yard with the children and stop and chat for a few minutes.

Q: Lieutenant Zerwas, prior to April 11, when is the last time that you saw Dennis?

A: It would have been the Sunday before [his death] . . . My sister [Lois] came over to our home with both of the boys . . .

Q: And where was Dennis?

A: He was at our home . . . I was in the house with the children, all the children.

Q: Did you notice any bruises on his skin?

A: No.

Q: Before then, Lieutenant Zerwas, do you recall when you saw him? And under what circumstances?

A: Well, I saw him at least twice a week regular.

Most interesting of all, though, were the multiple references in the 1965 transcript to the police station meeting at 6:30 P.M. on Palm Sunday, where Korolchuk grilled Harold about the inconsistencies in the Jurgenses' story.

"I wasn't there on Sunday. I stayed home on Sunday," Jerome had insisted about that critical day. But under oath on the witness stand at Robert's custody hearing, both Pete and Bob had described Jerome's presence that Sunday night with unhesitating precision. And so, as it happened, had Jerome Zerwas.

Ed Donohue, the Jurgenses' attorney, had asked the questions of Jerome:

Q: Did you have occasion to go to the police department that day?

A: Yes.

Q: Or that evening?

A: Yes, yes.

Q: And, how did you happen to go down there? What was your reason?

A: I was called down by Sergeant Korolchuk.

Q: At about what time?

A: About, at about 6:30 P.M.

Q: And who was present when you arrived?

A: Ah, Chief Armstrong, Officer VanderWyst, Sergeant Korol-chuk . . . We were in the chief's office . . . And at that time they called Mr. Jurgens to the police station.

Q: And, do you know what the purpose was in calling him down there?

A: Yes, they wanted to ask him some questions in regard to the bump on the forehead.

Q: And, were these questions asked in your presence?
A: Yes.
Q: How long did Mr. Jurgens remain at the police station?
A: I'd say a good half hour.
Q: Had you called Mr. Jurgens down to the police station that day?
A: Yes, sir. I did.

Jerome frowned when this passage was read to him by his visitor. A moment before, he'd been talking assuredly, his eyes sparkling with jaunty humor. Now he leaned forward, still challenging and confident, but his eyes had darkened.

"That was on a Monday," he said. "That wasn't on no Sunday. I did not go down to that police station on Sunday . . . I was not present when Harold Jurgens was questioned . . . They didn't have a meeting at six o'clock . . . They said that I was present at that meeting, which I wasn't . . . I never left the house on Sunday."

At this point in the exchange, Jerome's lawyer, David Singer, thought it wise to enter the discussion. He tried to explain to his client that this transcript recorded Jerome's own words, not what other people said about him. The lawyer and client started talking to each other.

Singer: That's what you said. Not what they said.

Jerome: I can't help it that somebody put it in there because I didn't. I didn't do none of that stuff.

Singer: What I'm talking about is what he is reading is what you said.

Jerome: Yeah. I know that. I didn't say that . . . I didn't go to the police station on Sunday.

Singer: Are you saying the transcript is wrong?

Jerome: I'm saying it's wrong. One hundred percent wrong . . .

Singer next tried his best to fine-tune his client's response.

Singer: Think you misunderstood what you were being asked at the time of that hearing?

Jerome: No . . . It never happened.

Singer: No, no, no. Do you think you misunderstood the questioning? When somebody asked you the question and you answered yes . . .

Jerome: No, no. I don't think so.

◆   ◆   ◆

The day after this meeting, Jerome's wife Rose called the visitor to offer an explanation for the confusion.

"That testimony you read yesterday sounds like VanderWyst talking," she said. "I think they got the people on the witness stand mixed up."

That didn't seem likely, it was pointed out. Certified court transcripts don't usually involve such errors. Besides, in the transcript, the lawyers kept addressing the witness as Lieutenant Zerwas, and the witness described himself as a White Bear police lieutenant who lived on Park Street and had a sister named Lois Jurgens.

"Well," Rose Zerwas said, "it still sounds like Bob VanderWyst."

Jerome's wife had another thought.

"I wish you had asked about the good times, the good things," she said. "Like the time Jerome saved a little girl having an asthma attack . . . You should see our family photo albums . . . Why don't you come up to Elk River and see them sometime?"

CHAPTER 45

Memories, Still

Tom Axelrod graduated from Johnson High School in east St. Paul in 1941, then spent six years fighting with the Seventieth Division's K Company, arriving in Europe—he volunteers this proudly—"just when the mess was starting." Back home from battle, he found work at the telephone company and settled in White Bear Lake, drawn there by the abundance of water and dearth of people. He'd reached the level of dispatcher-tester by the time he retired in 1985. After that, with free time on his hands, he turned with considerable satisfaction to the task of editing the Company K newsletter, called "Good Company," a chatty eight-page affair that keeps enthusiastic track of the aging veterans, now scattered around the country, who fought together decades before.

On the bottom of the second page of the April 1988 edition of "Good Company," Axelrod wrote the following item:

> I don't know how many of you have seen the article about the Jurgens' baby from White Bear Lake, who was murdered by his mother, but they are now running it as a featured story in the *Los Angeles Times*. It's truly one of those it could never happen to me deals. When the Jurgens lived in White Bear Lake, they lived kiddie-corner from us in what we consider the greatest neighborhood in the world. Everybody in this neighborhood loves everyone else. We're truly as one big

family. We always had block parties when we were younger and even now we just walk into each other's homes. We were always family except for one family—the Jurgens. We were all living our lives and here this child was being tortured to death. Her family and her social worker were guests of her home and they never said a thing. None of us neighbors ever entered her home, or even talked to her, but there is still a feeling of guilt amongst us. They were very distant and didn't mix at all, but still couldn't one of us have saved this child's life? Not really—no one even knew of the child's existence. Yup, one of those it could never happen here deals.

Sitting in his living room in the summer of 1988, Axelrod repeated that last thought. "I wish we had done something," he said, "but what?"

Memories can play tricks, of course. Another neighbor remembers the Axelrods, at the time of Dennis's death, saying they'd always believed something was wrong in the Jurgens home, but didn't want to get involved. It is known that Alice Axelrod went bowling weekly with Dorothy Engfer, who talked often about Dennis's abuse, so perhaps time had simply dimmed or refined the Axelrods' powers of recall. The floods and the rampaging Mississippi and the wind in their faces while iceboating, after all, were sharper in their minds than the All-America City award or the civil rights marches. "Dorothy was gentle and sweet and had no children of her own," Alice Axelrod pointed out. "So if she said something to us, we would just think she was exaggerating."

The legal system had imprisoned Lois Jurgens for Dennis's death, the town's gossip mill had directed blame toward Jerome Zerwas, and the journalists had peopled the story with unambiguous villains and heroes according to their needs, but others in the community unavoidably saw matters from a different, more uncertain and intimate angle. The abstract "system" so often invoked during the Jurgens prosecution was for them something more particular, inhabited by individuals they knew. Watching the Jurgens prosecution from afar, the community of people who had lived and worked alongside Harold and Lois in White Bear Lake so long ago couldn't help but feel they were watching a replaying of their own past. They were on the whole satisfied with that past—they'd fashioned lives not unlike those they'd imagined in the first years after the war—but all the same, few felt like celebrating.

The dominant feelings were puzzlement and a sad wonder. In the aftermath of Lois's trial, people in White Bear Lake not infrequently gathered in coffee shops and living rooms and school auditoriums to talk among themselves and to visitors about the Jurgens affair. Unlike the public officials—constrained within their prescribed roles—they had an urge to explore the matter, to ventilate, to understand. For the most part they felt neither defensive nor guilty, just troubled. The Jurgens case, after all, had revealed an image of a community and of human nature that was not the one many believed they knew.

More than a few said the whole affair "was a black eye" for their town, and more than a few felt compelled to relive the past by unearthing mementos from the spring of 1965. One morning, Bud Korfhage, the town's department of parks and recreation director, sat at his desk in a long-shuttered junior high school now converted to administrative offices, leafing through the *White Bear Press*'s All-America City souvenir edition, published three days before Dennis died. Another morning, the retired banker Dick Carlson turned the pages of the Lions Club scrapbooks until he found the photos and program for the 1965 vaudeville show. The retired grocer Bill LeVasseur spent days plunging into storage chests until he came up with the speeches he made as chamber of commerce president in response to the All-America City award. You just don't think these kinds of things happened in White Bear Lake, they volunteered. You just don't imagine.

"White Bear Lake has an image of a good place to live," said Milt Knoll, the town's mayor back in the mid-1960s. "This is not wrong, not false. It's true. We were active, involved. But this did happen. We didn't know about child abuse then. People were coming out of World War II, determined to build something, create families, get on with it, create utopia. Who wanted to look at stuff like child abuse?"

Others, more closely connected to the Jurgens case, felt compelled to explain themselves.

In the aftermath of Lois's trial, the former coroner Dr. Thomas Votel composed letters and organized "talking points" and provided everyone who inquired with detailed written summaries of his actions, both in the matter of Dennis's death and throughout his tenure as coroner. He did so more with stoic sadness than defensiveness or aggression. "I was excited the day Michael McGee called to say he was reopening this case," he told people, looking perplexed. "I didn't expect to get blamed . . . I always looked back at the coroner's tenure as a pretty successful part of my life. We got a new building. A plaque with my name is at the front door. We made changes and improvements. I had fun and enjoyed the work . . ."

Judge Archie Gingold, at eighty still fiercely alert, appeared in his Ramsey County courthouse office one morning lugging a heavy leather briefcase full of all his files on the topic of child abuse—journal articles he'd read, speeches he'd given, newspaper interviews describing his campaign for a child abuse team, editorials supporting that campaign. File by file, he pulled out the materials, rereading some of them, summarizing others, tossing them one by one onto a conference table until he'd emptied his briefcase. Only then did he settle into a chair. "I never forgot that case," Gingold added after a moment of reflection. "I never forgot that case."

Father Reiser's unceasing sanguinity seemed at least temporarily dampened by the revelations of the Jurgens prosecution. Despite his presence at the 1965 hearing, the priest told one visitor who came calling at the Church of the Epiphany that he never knew there was any suspicion concerning the death of Dennis Jurgens. If he'd had suspicions at all, he certainly would not have written a letter of recommendation for the Kentucky adoptions. "I didn't steer people correctly, but it wasn't on purpose," he said. "When I hear that things like this happened, it's just unreal. This alerted me that the real nice, perfect family might not be so."

If Dr. Roy Peterson was more hesitant than most—"He wouldn't be available. How did you get our number? I'm asking you a simple question. How did you get our number?" his wife said to one caller— in the end, the doctor also felt the need to explain, even if he had to labor. "You see, when I said the burns and the death weren't unusual, I was thinking of it medically," he said one morning in his living room overlooking the lake and Manitou Island. "I wasn't thinking of the cause, of how they occurred. No one asked me if I believed the Jurgenses. I would have said no."

Not everyone denied responsibility, however. More than a few were troubled by their own roles back then. The Jurgenses' former neighbor, Donna Neely, berated herself for not doing anything: "I wish we had said something, I wish we had been smarter. All I know is something happened and we didn't do anything and we were aware." The former mayor, Milt Knoll, blamed himself for wanting only positive thinking in town: "Maybe I should have gotten involved in the police department. Wayne was not a strong guy. I knew Jerome dominated it, but I didn't think good or bad about that. I just didn't deal with it."

None, though, felt more haunted than the Jurgenses' former next-door neighbor Ivan DeMars, whose wife Gladys had provided Gerane Rekdahl with a glowing recommendation of Harold and Lois. In 1965, he'd testified only that he had heard Lois call Dennis stupid, and in 1987 he'd testified not at all, having told the prosecutors he remembered nothing. But in the summer of 1988, a full year after Lois's trial, he sat in a wicker chair in an enclosed patio on the side of his house talking as if Dennis had died that day. It was dusk, the room dim, but DeMars made no move to turn on the overhead light. He was sixty-seven, and years before had placed his wife, debilitated by Huntington's chorea, in a North Dakota nursing home. Following his mind's eye, he began to act out what he'd truly seen. His thick arm swept down in a low arc, knee-level, fast and hard. He winced and shook his head.

"My wife and I got angry at the abuse," he said. "My wife saw more than I did. It was so very upsetting. I love little kids. I just couldn't believe it . . . It never occurred to me to intervene. If I had it to do over, if I saw it now, I couldn't stand and watch. I'd do something. Dennis was a nice little kid. I could see nothing wrong with him. I should have stepped forward and said what I thought. I feel that way. I regret that. I would have done different now. I wish I had then . . . But that was the way of the neighborhood. You just minded your own business. We were brought up that way. And yet it's difficult to know that I let it all go on . . . His intestines busted, his penis half off, all those bruises . . ."

The room now was almost dark, DeMars all but lost in the shadows. He continued talking without reaching for the light switch. The retired steelworker was weeping.

"We told the police and the people at the hearing only what we actually knew. We'd decided that. We didn't stretch or go further . . . What more could we do? My wife and I were certain she'd beaten him to death, and were very upset . . . In the neighborhood, after his death, it was the talk for some time . . . Then over the years we didn't think of it much. I had it pretty well filed away until I saw it in the paper. I couldn't believe it. I thought, this sure is a long time . . ."

DeMars rubbed the back of his hand across his eyes. "It's sad. The good Lord must have had it mapped out that way, I guess. Dennis didn't have to face everything else we all face . . ." Appearing to derive some comfort from that thought, he rose to usher his visitor out, shuffling through the dark toward the door.

"There are things a person doesn't have control of," DeMars said, now speaking mainly to himself. "The good Lord . . . He's got the thing set up before you start."

Not even June Bol could find complete absolution when she looked inward. No one had thought to propose her as a hero in the Jurgens tale, but she did not resent this omission. She felt no inclination toward self-congratulation.

"I should have believed them, what people told me about the abuse back then," June told a visitor in the summer of 1988. "I should have gone over to Lois. I should have said, 'Don't you want this little boy?' Why didn't I call her sisters? Why didn't I do this? Maybe I could have done something to save that little boy . . ."

On the Bols' rolling front lawn the forest of poplars and maples was in full leaf, and the abundant green valley stretched forever from the front window. As always, June was sitting at her kitchen table, but she now seemed less at ease than usual.

". . . and Robert, he recently asked me, 'June, why did you send me home? Why did you let me go home? I wanted to ask you that all these years . . . Why did you let me go home?' In my heart I wasn't secure with that, but there wasn't anything to do. I wasn't really knowledgeable. My husband, either. I didn't see . . . I didn't have the guts to stand up . . ."

Her rescue of the Kentucky kids, and the home she provided for the second eldest, Grant, left June feeling no more satisfied than her efforts with Dennis and Robert. Grant, after all, had been a trial. He could do what he wanted in the Bol home, he could make choices, June didn't try to control him, and in time he'd started to take advantage of that freedom.

He'd always be coming home late, calling from the bowling alley, and June, always accepting his story, would go out with a coat over her pajamas at two in the morning to get him. If Grant can only have one person he can depend on, he'll be okay, she kept thinking. But then he'd steal money and June would have to ask, "Did you borrow ten dollars?"—let it be called that instead of stealing, she figured. Whenever he misbehaved, she thought of his rough background. Once, when he was in the eleventh grade, arriving home at two in the morning drunk on a school night, he stood sassing June until she angrily pushed on his shoulder and he fell backwards into the dog's water bowl. Sitting there furious and embarrassed, he glared at her, battling himself not to swing back. "Don't you ever hit me," he snarled. They both knew June hadn't been hitting him, but she didn't argue the point. "I won't," she said softly. "I won't."

Only years later did June realize that Grant's troubled adolescence had taken its toll in her home, had taken attention away from her own children, especially the youngest, Carolee. Now soft and unfocused at twenty-two, Carolee claimed she always had to be good to compensate for Grant.

And for all that, June hadn't managed to save him. As she sat in her kitchen, Grant, twenty-seven, was residing forty-five miles to the north, a patient at Hazelden—the same drug and alcohol rehabilitation center Harold had driven Lois to thirteen years before. The Hazelden business puzzled and troubled June almost to distraction. The people there had told her that by supporting Grant and allowing him his ways, she was part of the drinking problem.

"They called me a . . ."—June frowned, reaching for the word—"an 'enabler.'"

She turned and looked out her picture window. Her eyes filled with tears and she bit her lip. The thing was, she'd always liked Lois. She'd never wanted to be her enemy. It seemed to her there was a good side of the bad people she knew and a bad side of the good people.

June blinked back the tears and forced a smile.

"Come on," she suggested to her visitor, her eyes full of mischief now as she scrambled toward the front door. "Let's go down the road and look at Harold's house."

In the end, the conversations always turned to Harold. During the months of self-examination in White Bear Lake, during all the discussions of how and why Dennis had died, of what could have been done, one question always remained a greater enigma than the others. What about Harold? people would ask, then shake their heads in silence.

Harold had told June Bol that he'd taken Dennis into bed with him that last, final night. Had Dennis died in Harold's arms? Could that explain the corpse's odd position?

In the aftermath of Lois's trial Harold Jurgens more than once appeared in the White Bear Lake area, going about his errands amid townsfolk who, for the most part, didn't recognize him. Everyone knew the Zerwases, particularly Jerome, but few had ever met the Jurgenses. Harold regularly took breakfast alone at the Embers Coffee Shop at Highway 94 and White Bear Avenue, and often visited Father Mroczka, sometimes helping out around the Sts. Processus & Martinian Church. He drove to Shakopee to visit Lois for every hour of every day allowed by prison policy. He enthusiastically followed the Minnesota baseball and hockey teams. Once, Harold's nephew Dennis Donald saw him at a hardware store, buying electrical supplies. Standing near the store's front counter, they talked briefly.

"I guess I've lost Robert, too," Harold said sadly.

"Well, a person can love and hate someone at the same time," his nephew offered by way of comfort.

For a while, a group of workers laboring at a local construction site would sit around at lunch talking regularly about the Jurgens trial. One quiet, silver-haired electrician among them would listen, eat, say nothing, then get up and resume his tasks. Only later, studying their newspapers and TV screens, did the construction workers realize he was Lois's husband.

On Memorial Day of 1988, Harold appeared alone at St. Mary's Cemetery and stood at Dennis's grave. One row over and a couple of headstones down the line, Jerome Zerwas and his family happened to be contemplating the grave of the Zerwas family's patriarch, Lois's father John, who'd died in 1980. When Jerome spotted Harold, he walked to his side and greeted him warmly with a handshake. They stood together talking quietly for a moment under a hot, steamy afternoon sky, their eyes on Dennis's grave.

"How are you, Harold?" Jerome asked. "How's things going?"

"Well, I just got through having open heart surgery," Harold replied. He lifted his leg and pulled at his trouser cuff, showing where the doctors had taken a vein for his triple bypass operation. Then he unbuttoned his shirt to display his scarred chest.

"Was it painful when they put your chest back together?" Jerome asked.

"Well, really, there was no pain to it," Harold said. "What hurt me the worst was the leg. That might sound crazy, but the leg hurt and the chest didn't."

Then one day Harold called Walter Moore, his former supervisor at Muska Electric. Moore was not happy to hear from the man. Harold had retired from Muska Electric in March of 1987, just before Lois's trial started. In the shop, he'd never said anything about the case, except for the one time he told Moore, "I'm going to stick by my wife." At the retirement dinner, Moore, feeling disinclined himself, had enlisted someone else to give the customary farewell speech. He just didn't like Harold.

He'd been suspicious ever since Harold called him that Palm Sunday morning to say he wouldn't be at work the next day because his son died. "Shut up, I'm talking to Walt," Harold had snapped at his wife while on the phone. That had seemed so strange. Then Moore had seen the bruised body in the casket at the funeral, and felt certain the boy had been murdered.

God damn Harold, why'd he tolerate it? Moore thought. If that had been my wife, she would have been a dead wife. "Weird Harold," the guys at work called him. He could talk your ear off, always complaining about his sex life, how his wife turned him down. Moore didn't want to hear about those things. God damn Harold. He'll be judged.

Now, on the phone, Harold was telling a long-winded story. The gist of it was that he had some tools that belonged to Muska. He wanted to square it with the Lord.

"What the hell," Moore told him. "Forget about it, Harold."

"No, no," Harold said. "I need to make it right with the Creator."

First thing the next morning, he brought the tools into the shop.

AUTHOR'S NOTE

This book is intended to be a chronicle of certain events that did, in fact, happen. It is based on interviews, police reports, county welfare department logs, records of court proceedings, private journals and assorted other documents. More than one hundred people were interviewed in person, dozens of others on the telephone. I lived in White Bear Lake for three months during the summer of 1988 and visited the town on several other occasions, during which I was fortunate to be welcomed and befriended by a number of local residents. I was also fortunate to find that many of the people who played roles in White Bear Lake and in the Jurgens story a quarter-century ago were still alive, residing in Minnesota, and quite willing to reminisce. Accordingly, the great majority (but not all) of the chief characters depicted in this book were interviewed by me. When I describe what they thought or said, it comes either from what they told me or, in some cases, what they told others, often in recorded conversations. Except for a handful of minor characters who appear on a single page in the book, then disappear, all names are real, as are all places.

The documents—a great wealth of them—provided the book's critical background. Through these records I often was able to compare what one person said on different occasions spread over twenty-two years. I could see whether events remembered now, years later, were also reported or described back when they actually happened, either in writing or conversation. Above all, I could build a unified chronology from disparate sources.

Assembling a chronicle such as this requires the cooperation of a great many people, to whom I am forever indebted.

Most particularly, my gratitude to White Bear Lake Police Detectives Ron Meehan and Greg Kindle, and to assistant Ramsey County Attorneys Clayton Robinson and Melinda Elledge, is boundless. Day after day for weeks on end, they shared with me their memories and insights. Without their gracious, patient cooperation, my task would have been impossible.

A good number of the other characters who populate these pages also provided invaluable assistance. There are too many to mention here, but I must register my especially strong appreciation for Robert VanderWyst, who spent countless hours with me during the last painful months of his life, and for June Bol, who opened her home and her life to me with compassionate generosity.

For the account of White Bear Lake's early history, I am particularly indebted to "The White Bear Lake Story" by Nancy L. Woolworth, a booklet published in 1968 under the auspices of the White Bear Lake area chamber of commerce, and to "Mahtomedi Memories" by Alice R. Smith, Sharon F. Wright and Judy Kaiser, published in 1976 by its authors. In assembling the story of White Bear Lake in more recent decades, I was fortunate to have unlimited access to the *White Bear Press*'s wonderfully preserved bound collection of past editions. The Minnesota Historical Society provided a wealth of information about both the distant and near past, including complete microfilmed editions of all local newspapers published a quarter century ago. The White Bear Lake chamber of commerce's scrapbooks about the All-America Cities competition were invaluable.

For my descriptions of Lois Jurgens's arraignment and trial, I was assisted by videotapes of local television stations' newscasts on those days, as well as news stories appearing in the *St. Paul Pioneer Press Dispatch* and the *Minneapolis Star Tribune*—particularly articles written by Brian Bonner, Linda Kohl, Dennis Cassano, Doug Grow, Dan Oberdorfer and Joe Soucheray.

The account of Henry Kempe and the revolution in awareness of child abuse was aided immeasurably by an extended interview with Dr. Brandt Steele in Denver, as well as the untiring efforts of my researcher, Nina Green. The stories of the Loss case and the trip to Colorado benefited happily by the fact that John Tuohy and Dr. Homer Venters do not throw away old files.

A special thanks to Robert A. Jones, Tawny Crail, and Marti Devore for helpful advice with an unpolished manuscript, to Kathy Morris for illuminating Minnesota, and to Jan Williams, who transcribed hours of taped interviews with uncommon skill and good spirit.

The editors at the *Los Angeles Times* provided the imaginative environment in which I first wrote about the Jurgens story, and later, the time in which to complete this book. Among others, I am indebted to Tim Rutten, Mike Miller, Shelby Coffey III, and, particularly, Bill Thomas.

At Bantam Books, Ann Harris provided elegant and meticulous editing, and Stephen Rubin made the project possible with his unceasing faith and support.

I have no words to express properly my regard and appreciation for Kathy Robbins, who is my agent, friend, mentor, cheerleader and scold. Suffice it to say this book would not exist but for her.

IMAGE GALLERY

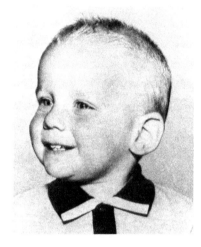

Dennis Jurgens.

Dennis's death certificate, signed by coroner Thomas Votel on May 11, 1965, a month after his death. The cause of death, in box 18, is given as peritonitis; in box 20a, under the heading "Accident, Suicide or Homicide (specify)", Votel wrote "Deferred."

Dennis and Robert.

Dennis's grave in St. Mary's cemetery.

The Zerwases in 1949, when Lois was twenty-four years old. Top row, from left: Lyle, Joe, Elenora, Lois, Donald, Jerome, Lloyd, Donna, Eloise, Gerhard, and John, Jr. Bottom row, from left: Frank, Gayle, Gloria, parents Lois and John Zerwas, Sr., Sharon, and Beverly.

Twenty-seven years later, in 1976, the Zerwas clan assembles to celebrate the seventy-fifth birthday of their mother. On the lower level, from left: Gerhard, Elenora, Jerome, the parents Lois and John Zerwas, Sr., Gloria, and Gayle. On the second story, from left: Donna Norton, Frank, Lois Jurgens, Eloise, Beverly, and Sharon. On the steps, from the top: Joe, Donald, John, Jr., Lyle, and Lloyd. (Photo by Webb White, The Photographers Guild)

Jerome (right) stands with city manager Ed Bayuk and police chief Louis Kieffer in front of the White Bear Lake Police Department in 1956. (Ginnie Weiss Long. Courtesy of Ed Bayuk)

March 4, 1965: The letter from George Gallup announcing White Bear Lake's All-America City Award.

A Citizens' Organization for Better Government
Founded 1894   Incorporated 1923

NATIONAL MUNICIPAL LEAGUE

CARL H. PFORZHEIMER BUILDING
47 East 68th Street • New York, N.Y. 10021
Telephone LEhigh 5-5700

March 4, 1965

Mrs. Georgia M. Hillman, Secretary-Treasurer
Chamber of Commerce of White Bear Lake
Manitou Building
310 Washington Avenue
White Bear Lake, Minnesota 55110

Dear Mrs Hillman:

Congratulations!

It gives me great pleasure to notify you, on a confidential basis, that White Bear Lake has been named an All-America City for 1964 by the National Municipal League and Look Magazine.

This decision was reached by the All-America Cities Award Jury, of which I was foreman, at San Francisco, California, last November following the presentations. Subsequent investigations confirmed our judgment.

I salute the citizens of White Bear Lake whose effective action has won this award and sincerely hope they will view this honor as a further incentive to play a positive role in the affairs of their community.

Once again may I extend my most sincere congratulations.

Sincerely yours,

George H. Gallup
Chairman of the Council

The house at 2148 South Gardenette Drive, White Bear Lake, where the Jurgenses lived from 1957 to 1967. (Patti Wahlqusit, *White Bear Press*)

Judge Archie Gingold, who presided over Robert Jurgens's custody hearings and for five years wrestled over what to do. (*St. Paul Pioneer Dispatch*)

Jerry Sherwood with her son, Dennis Craig McIntyre, 18, at Dennis Jurgens's grave in St. Mary's Cemetery. This photograph accompanied Brian Bonner's October 12, 1986, article that first reported Jerry's search and the revised death certificate. (Joe Rossi, *St. Paul Pioneer Dispatch*)

Social worker Carol Felix, called in when Renee and Grant fled the Jurgens home, read the file on Dennis's death and was convinced he had been murdered. (*St. Paul Pioneer Dispatch*)

Detective Ron Meehan (seated) and Greg Kindle in the White Bear Lake police department. (Patti Wahlqusit, *White Bear Press*)

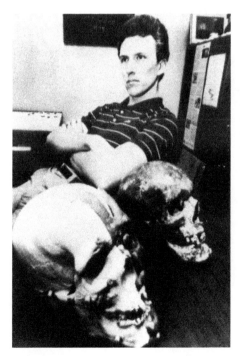

Ramsey County medical examiner Michael McGee changed Dennis's death certificate to homicide twenty-one years later. (*St. Paul Pioneer Dispatch*)

Lois walks past the TV cameras on her way to the courtroom on January 30, 1987, to plead not guilty to three counts of murder. Her attorney Doug Thomson (left) follows, and Harold Jurgens is behind him. (Richard Marshall, *St. Paul Pioneer Dispatch*)

After conviction in phase 1 of the trial on May 30, 1987, Lois hides her face in a shawl as she leaves court with Harold and defense attorney Deborah Ellis. (John Doman, *St. Paul Pioneer Dispatch*)

Lois enters the courtroom with Harold on June 5, minutes before the jury delivered its phase 2 verdict. (John Doman, *St. Paul Pioneer Dispatch*)

Jerry Sherwood hears the guilty verdict. (John Doman, *St. Paul Pioneer Dispatch*)

Robert Jurgens embraces Ron Meehan on September 1, 1987, after presenting an appreciation plaque to the detectives and prosecutors who brought his mother to trial. (Duane Bradley, *Minneapolis Star Tribune*)

INDEX

ABOUT THE AUTHOR

Barry Siegel is a Pulitzer Prize–winning journalist and the author of seven books. Born in St. Louis and raised in Los Angeles, he joined the *Los Angeles Times* in 1976 as a staff writer and became a roving national correspondent in 1980. His articles have garnered dozens of honors, including the Pulitzer Prize for Feature Writing, two PEN Center USA West Literary Awards in Journalism, the Livingston Award for Young Journalists, and the American Bar Association Silver Gavel Award. In 2003, Siegel left the *Los Angeles Times* to become founding director of the literary journalism program at the University of California, Irvine. His books include the Chumash County trilogy of legal thrillers; the Edgar Award finalist *A Death in White Bear Lake: The True Chronicle of an All-American Town* (1990); and, most recently, *Manifest Injustice: The True Story of a Convicted Murderer and the Lawyers Who Fought for His Freedom* (2013).

OPEN ROAD

INTEGRATED MEDIA